BRITISH FURTHER EDUCATION

A critical textbook

BY

A. J. PETERS

PERGAMON PRESS

OXFORD · LONDON · EDINBURGH · NEW YORK

TORONTO · SYDNEY · PARIS · BRAUNSCHWEIG

Pergamon Press Ltd., Headington Hill Hall, Oxford
4 & 5 Fitzroy Square, London W.1

Pergamon Press (Scotland) Ltd., 2 & 3 Teviot Place, Edinburgh 1

Pergamon Press Inc., 44–01 21st Street, Long Island City, New York 11101

Pergamon of Canada, Ltd., 6 Adelaide Street East, Toronto, Ontario

Pergamon Press (Aust.) Pty. Ltd., 20–22 Margaret Street, Sydney, N.S.W.

Pergamon Press S.A.R.L., 24 rue des Écoles, Paris 5°

Vieweg & Sohn GmbH, Burgplatz 1, Braunschweig

First edition 1967

Library of Congress Catalog Card No. 66–29959

Printed in Great Britain by A. Wheaton & Co., Ltd., Exeter
2856/67

BRITISH FURTHER EDUCATION

To the guinea-pigs
of Merseyside

"Further education will, we believe, be the next great battleground of English education" (Crowther Report, 1959)

CONTENTS

LIST OF TABLES

PREFACE

IT IS generally agreed that the expansion of further education in this country must be continued. Both the national need for trained manpower and the duty which a civilized community owes its citizens demand this. Therefore more and more people will become involved in further education in one way or another, and will need some understanding of its complex, varied and quickly changing pattern. In other countries, too, people are experiencing similar changes, and many will look with interest at what is happening here. Overseas students, particularly from the Commonwealth, are wanting to come to Britain in increasing numbers. But sources of information about British education are scattered and confusing.

This book is an attempt to give a coherent account of the whole of what may be statutorily defined as the system of Further Education in Great Britain. Roughly this means public provision for the education of persons who have left school, other than at universities, colleges of education or establishments run by the armed services. A large amount of material from England, Wales and Scotland has been brought together, to form (it is hoped) an intelligible pattern. Most aspects have been examined, though the supply, training and conditions of teachers have only been touched on in places, and the curriculum as such has not been considered. The last chapter contains critical comments against a political background.

I must express my thanks to the following colleagues and friends who have helped me by reading chapters and appendices during their preparation: Michael Argles, Olive Banks, J. N. Briscoe, J. Burr, F. J. Callaghan, J. D. Carsley, D. A. R. Clark, W. H. Cooper, C. V. Vinten Fenton, Joyce Harland, J. K. Lamberton, N. F. Newbury, L. S. Newton, W. J. Norman, D. G. Pritchard, K. J. Rowlands, S. Rubinstein, John Vaughan, Norman Wilson and H. R. B. Wood. I should also like to thank the many people, too numerous to name, who have kindly sent me information by post.

I must thank, too, the following for permission to reproduce certain material: Borough Polytechnic and National College for Heating, Ventilating, Refrigeration and Fan Engineering (Table 21); British Aircraft Corporation (Table 15); City and Guilds of London Institute (Tables 10 and 11); the Controller of Her Majesty's Stationery Office (Tables 22, 25 and 26); and the Middlesbrough Education Authority (Table 17).

None of these is responsible, of course, for expressions of opinion, nor for the omissions, repetitions, ephemeralities and errors to which a book of this kind is peculiarly liable.

School of Education
University of Liverpool
October 1966

NOTES

"BRITAIN" or "British", as used in this book, refer to Great Britain, that is England, Wales and Scotland only. Because of its separate Parliament, much smaller size and rather different educational tradition, Northern Ireland has been omitted. Also omitted are the Isle of Man and the Channel Islands which are Crown dependencies and not part of Great Britain.

"The main Acts" or "the Acts" usually means the Education Act, 1944, and Education (Scotland) Act, 1946 or 1962.

"Board" means Board of Education for England and Wales.

"Minister" and "Ministry" mean Minister and Ministry of Education for England and Wales.

"Ministers" means Minister of Education *and* Secretary of State for Scotland (before 1st April 1964).

"Ministries" means Ministry of Education *and* Scottish Education Department (before 1st April 1964).

"Secretary of State" means Secretary of State for Education and Science (1st April 1964 onwards) *or* Secretary of State for Scotland, according to context.

"Secretaries of State" means Secretary of State for Education and Science *and* Secretary of State for Scotland.

"Department" means Department of Education and Science (DES) (1st April 1964 onwards) *or* Scottish Education Department (SED), according to context.

"Departments" means DES *and* SED.

"Authority", unless clearly to the contrary, means a local education authority in England and Wales or an education authority in Scotland.

"College", unqualified, means a grant-aided establishment for Further Education in England, Wales or Scotland.

A year in brackets following a title or author's name is the date of publication. "N.d." means that no date is marked on the work. Full bibliographical details can be found in Appendix 2.

An expression such as 1963–4 means the period of the academic year from September 1963 to July 1964.

Circulars and Administrative Memoranda mentioned are those of the Minister or Secretary of State for Education and Science. Those of the Secretary of State for Scotland are called "Scottish Circular" or "Scottish Memorandum". After 1st April 1959 in England and Wales a number following a stroke indicates the year of issue : thus Circular 1/59 means Circular 1 (1959).

"Scheme" spelt with a capital initial means *Scheme of Further Education and Plan for County Colleges* submitted by an authority to the Minister under Sections 42 and 43 of the Education Act, 1944, or its Scottish equivalent under Section 7 of the Education (Scotland) Act, 1962. "Plan" alone, spelt with a capital initial, means the Plan for County Colleges alone.

In naming different types of establishment, capital initials can very easily get out of control. Therefore they are reduced to a few, being used only in cases where there might otherwise be a risk of confusion between the precise meaning of a term and possible looser meanings. This risk is thought to be present only with the following : Central Institution, National College, Regional College, Area College and Local College. All other types of establishment are therefore spelt with small initials. On the usage of capital initials for the terms Further Education, Adult Education and Youth Service see p. 3.

Titles of journals, where shortened, have been printed in accord with rules recommended in *World List of Scientific Periodicals*, fourth edition (1963 onwards); for the full titles see Appendix 3.

Statements written in the present tense were believed to be true on 22nd October 1966.

CHAPTER 1

THE MEANING OF "FURTHER EDUCATION"

The definition adopted in this book

The post-war pattern of British education

Like many terms, "further education" can be used either in loose, general senses, or in a precise, narrower one. In a wider sense it might mean any education undergone by someone who had left school, whether in a definite institution or organized course, by self-directed study, or merely through life itself. This book, however, is concerned with it in an exact, contemporary, statutory meaning. To understand how this is arrived at, the general pattern of education must first be sketched.

Great Britain has two separate but related educational systems—one for England and Wales and one for Scotland. Both have their recent origin in the White Paper *Educational Reconstruction* which was placed before Parliament in 1943. A foundation stone was the Education Act of 1944 which came into force in England and Wales on 1st April 1945. It established the office of Minister of Education, whose duty was to promote, direct and enforce a national educational policy. This was very different from the Board of Education of the previous system, which, under the Acts of 1899, 1918 and 1921, had merely been "charged with the superintendence of matters relating to education". Similar new duties and powers were given to the Secretary of State for Scotland by the Education (Scotland) Act, 1945, consolidated in new Acts in 1946 and 1962.

To most of the then local education authorities, too, the post-war Acts gave new duties. Under the previous system, dating from 1902, *all* authorities had had the *duty* to provide or aid elementary education, and *some* had had also the *power* to provide or aid education beyond elementary (then called "higher" education). Only in Scotland, since 1908, had there been a statutory *duty* (on school boards) to provide evening classes in industrial crafts. But under the new system *all* authorities had the *duty*; and it was a duty to "secure the provision" of education at all its stages, adequate to the entire needs of the community. At the same time the

1

number of authorities responsible for education was reduced so as to include only county and county borough councils and certain "joint" bodies. There were then 146 such authorities in England and Wales and 35 in Scotland; but the London Government Act of 1963 and other changes have added another 16 in England, making 197 altogether.

The authorities could not carry out these wide duties just as they wished, however. They had to perform them only in accord with the policy determined by the Minister or Secretary of State, and in a manner which he or she considered adequate. To make this possible they had to draw up Schemes and Plans to show how they intended to do it, and to submit these to their Minister for approval. They could always change their Schemes, but any new proposal had to be similarly approved, and an authority was not allowed to provide anything not included in its approved Scheme. Thus the authorities had to have their Minister's permission for what they were to do. The Ministers could also carry out measures themselves. The result has been a partnership with the central government in control.

Further Education within the post-war pattern

Educational facilities, said the Acts, were to be organized in three unified stages, to be known as primary, secondary and further. Further education was thus seen as the third of a continuous series of naturally progressing phases. It was defined in Section 41 of the 1944 Act as follows:

(a) full-time and part-time education for persons over compulsory school age; and
(b) leisure-time occupation, in such organized cultural training and recreative activities as are suited to their requirements, for any persons over compulsory school age who are able and willing to profit. . . .

The Scottish Acts of 1945, 1946 and 1962 contained a threefold definition:

(a) compulsory part-time and in exceptional cases full-time courses . . . to young persons . . .;
(b) voluntary part-time and full-time courses of instruction for persons over school age; and
(c) voluntary leisure-time occupation, in such organized cultural training and recreative activities as are suited to their requirements, for persons over school age.

The teaching of Gaelic in Gaelic-speaking areas was added in the 1962 Act.

Obviously these definitions cover all sorts of activities for persons *over compulsory school age*, and this was clearly what was generally intended. In Section 8 (b) of the 1944 Act, however, provision for school pupils *below* this age was also regarded as "further" if it was in pursuance of a Scheme of Further Education. Conversely, provision for pupils above this age was "secondary" if provided in a Plan for Secondary Education. And, of course, pupils still at school were not to be debarred from using facilities for further education if these were considered suitable. Therefore, what made any given provision "further education" was its inclusion in the appropriate Scheme, rather than the age of the students catered for, or whether or not they had left school.

These Schemes are now being put into effect as required by the Acts. However, an Order in Council transferred the functions of the Minister of Education to a new office, the Secretary of State for Education and Science, from 1st April 1964. Before this, further education in its statutory sense could have been defined as a part of the provision secured by the Minister of Education or Secretary of State for Scotland. But now, since the Secretary of State for Education and Science has much wider functions than the Minister of Education had, a sharp statutory definition is more difficult. Nevertheless, the earlier definition will still continue to be useful.

In this book, therefore, further education is defined as : EDUCATION PRIMARILY INTENDED FOR PERSONS WHO HAVE LEFT SCHOOL, THROUGH PROVISION SECURED EITHER BY THE MINISTER OF EDUCATION, BY THE SECRETARY OF STATE FOR EDUCATION AND SCIENCE ACTING IN THE CAPACITY OF THE FORMER MINISTER OF EDUCATION, BY THE SECRETARY OF STATE FOR SCOTLAND, OR BY LOCAL EDUCATION AUTHORITIES IN ACCORDANCE WITH APPROPRIATE SCHEMES OR PLANS APPROVED BY EITHER OF THESE MINISTERS OR SECRETARIES OF STATE.

When used in this specific sense it is spelt henceforth in this book with capital initial letters. This distinguishes it from "further" or "tertiary" education used to mean the *entire* field of provision for school leaves. Adult Education and Youth Service are similarly treated.

The kinds of education included

To discover exactly what is meant by this definition we must examine more closely : first, the documents laid before Parliament; second, the publications and practice of the Ministers; and third, the approved Schemes of authorities.

The chief Parliamentary documents have been mentioned : namely, the White Paper of 1943 and the 1944 and 1946 Acts. In the White Paper, "Further Education" was a chapter heading, but was not defined. Legislation was therein proposed to introduce "compulsory part-time education" in working hours for young people under the age of eighteen, to expand "technical, commercial and art education", and to encourage the growth of "adult education". Under a different chapter heading, administrative action was urged to develop the Youth Service, which was intended to become an integral part of the education system. Thus four broad kinds or sectors of education after school were thought of here : COMPULSORY PART-TIME; TECHNICAL, COMMERCIAL AND ART; ADULT; and THE SERVICE OF YOUTH.

The 1944 Act's definition is not quite as easy to interpret. It is twofold; but "(a) full-time and part-time education" could include any kind, and "(b) leisure-time occupation for persons willing to profit" could mean any kind conducted during leisure time and voluntarily. At first sight, therefore, the division might appear to be between the whole and the part, namely, between education conducted either voluntarily or compulsorily at any time, and that conducted voluntarily during leisure time only. But (b) is further described as "organized cultural training and recreative activities", which are clearly non-vocational; therefore (b) means education which is not only *conducted during leisure time*, but is also *orientated to leisure-time pursuits*; and is voluntary. By implication, (a) must be the rest : either *conducted during working time* or *orientated to work* or *both*; and either voluntary or compulsory. Thus the distinction really separates education or training during work or for work or both, from activities or preparation for activities which are both conducted during leisure time and intended for the enrichment of leisure time. Roughly this means (a) vocational *versus* (b) non-vocational. Therefore the first two of the White Paper's four broad kinds of education would come under (a) and the second two under (b). The Scottish Acts followed the White Paper even more closely by separating (a) into compulsory and voluntary.

Secondly, the thinking in the Minister's Pamphlets Nos. 2 (*A Guide to the Educational System of England and Wales*) and 8 (*Further Education*) followed this pattern too. And so did the Ministers' practice : for they have maintained certain establishments providing "full-time and part-time education"; and they have aided bodies promoting "organized cultural training" and "recreative activities".

Thirdly, we come to the Schemes of authorities. In England and Wales there are three of these, but with one, the "development plan" for primary and secondary education (required in Section 11 (1) of the 1944 Act), we are not here concerned. The other two are a "plan" for the provision of what were to be called "county colleges" (Section 43 (2)), and a "scheme" for developing Further Education otherwise than at county colleges (Section 42 (1)). This split occurred because it was intended that compulsion would soon be introduced, as proposed in the White Paper. The new type of college was to cope with this compulsory provision; but, in addition, the existing facilities had to be developed immediately. The Act therefore called for the two parts in separate sections. Similarly, the Minister's views thereon were published separately in two Pamphlets, Nos. 3 and 8; and her Further Education Grant Regulations, 1946, excluded county colleges.

However, it was obvious that county colleges could be properly planned only in close relation with the whole. In her Pamphlets and in Circulars 133 and 139, therefore, the Minister asked authorities to combine the "schemes" and the "plans". In accord with the addendum contained in Circular 133 the authorities grouped their proposals under the following headings :

Full-time and part-time education
    General provision
        Liberal education
                } (full-time, part-time day and evening)
        Vocational training
        County college attendance
        Agricultural and horticultural education (full-time, part-time day and evening)
        Correspondence courses
    Social and recreational provision for leisure time
        Facilities for persons under eighteen years
        Facilities for adults
    General arrangements and Relations with other authorities and bodies
        Provision of courses for teachers, youth leaders and wardens, other than in training colleges
        Organizing staff needed
        Service to persons living outside the area
        Use of institutions in other areas (including awards to students)
        Fees to be charged (including arrangements with other authorities)
        Constitution of Governing Bodies of institutions
        Consultation and co-operation with other authorities and bodies
    Programme for the first five years
        Sites and buildings
        Capital expenditure
        Annual maintenance cost

By the end of 1949 the Minister had received 119 of these combined Schemes and Plans, and they were reviewed in his report for that year. Here, too, appeared the same four broad groups as in the White Paper.

Thus all the sources share the same two basic lines of division : the one separating that which is either vocationally orientated or conducted during working time or both, from that which is neither; and the other separating the compulsory from the voluntary. In the 1944 Act and the Schemes "full-time and part-time education" meant the first kind and included the compulsory provision.

There was some variation, however, in the place of what was called "liberal education". The White Paper, the two Acts and Pamphlet No. 8 included the "more serious and solid" non-vocational studies as "leisure-time occupation", but Circular 133 put them under "full-time and part-time education". The Schemes did both, for there was an overlap : drama groups, for example, might appear under either or both headings; but activities under "full-time and part-time education" tended to be the more rigorous ones. Obviously there is administrative convenience in this, and it prevents the drawing of too hard-and-fast theoretical dividing lines.

Thus, except for this small discrepancy, a consistent pattern of thought can be extracted from the official language of the basic documents of the post-war era.

Some kinds of education excluded

Not all the education and training of people over the compulsory school age can be included in our definition.

As mentioned, that in secondary schools is ruled out by the main Acts. Teacher training is also out, as it is not contained in authorities' Schemes of Further Education; and this includes that in colleges of education (technical) and art training departments.[1]

Universities and university colleges and some English colleges of music and drama are excluded because they have never been under the Minister of Education or Secretary of State for Scotland. Only because they have so recently passed out of the ambit of these Ministers have the Royal College of Art, the College of Aeronautics and the colleges of advanced technology been included, and reference made to the Scottish College of Commerce and Heriot-Watt College.

Also excluded are institutions aided or managed under the ægis of ministers other than the Secretary of State for Education and Science or Secretary of State for Scotland : such as the two forester training schools in England and Wales under the Minister of Land and Natural Resources and Secretary of State for Wales respectively; nursing schools under the Ministry of Health; the College of Air Training partly under the Board of Trade; establishments such as the Royal Naval College maintained by Service departments; special facilities provided for Crown employees and their dependants; the Council of Industrial Design under the Board of Trade; the Arts Council, British Broadcasting Corporation and other bodies which have received grant from the Treasury; or training or rehabilitation centres

---

[1] However, the training of teachers was included in the chapter called "Further Education" in the Secretary of State's *Education in 1964* and *Education in 1965*. Does this foreshadow a change in the concept?

aided or maintained by the Minister of Labour or industrial training boards; though some of these are mentioned where relevant. Similarly excluded are the Youth Employment and Disablement Resettlement Services, for which the Minister of Labour bears the main responsibility.

Excluded also are provisions by local authorities other than education authorities, such as community centres under housing committees, training centres under health committees, playing fields under parks committees, or museums, libraries and art galleries under library authorities (though the latter were brought under the Secretary of State for Education and Science by the Public Libraries and Museums Act, 1964).

Provision for people undergoing full-time national service, if any, is also ruled out since it is not a responsibility of local education authorities; but such people may, of course, use facilities ordinarily provided, and special arrangements can be made between education and Service authorities.

Also ruled out are unaided private establishments such as independent correspondence colleges, schools for the handicapped, theological colleges, industrial research bodies, private colleges of commerce, works schools, flying schools run by airlines, adult retraining centres or social clubs. However, independent establishments may, if their proprietors wish, be inspected and recognized by the Secretary of State as "efficient"; ninety-one were so recognized in England and Wales in 1964–5.

A distinction must also be drawn between *further education* and *industrial* or *works training*. The latter is specific occupational training, provided usually by an employer at the place of work, or at a training centre under the Ministry of Labour or industrial training board. Nationally it comes under the purview of the Minister of Labour. However, each of these activities reinforces the other, and there is no clear boundary between them. Indeed, Section 16 of the Industrial Training Act, 1964, deems further education to include industrial training.

Its relations with other fields

Consultation and co-operation, which authorities and Secretaries of State must develop with other bodies where appropriate, bring all sorts of interests into direct relationship with Further Education. For example, youth and community-centre services link it with important groups of voluntary organization; student grants and the charging of fees bring other authorities and universities into an authority's purview; and interests outside education altogether, such as industrial firms, the Prison Commissioners or the Services, develop connections with it. Such relations are fostered by national, regional and local advisory councils. Doubtless relations between authorities, industry and other agencies will also be fostered by industrial training boards, and in the field of physical recreation by national and regional sports committees. The impact of educational co-operation within the Commonwealth is also growing.

Reference to excluded sectors is therefore made where desirable, and particularly in Chapters 14, 16 and 19 where the field of further or tertiary education has to be considered as a whole.

Notes on further study

The basic documents have been mentioned. These are : the White Paper *Educational Reconstruction* (1943); the Education Act, 1944, and Education (Scotland) Acts, 1945, 1946 and 1962; the Minister's Pamphlets, *A Guide to the Educational System of England and Wales* (No. 2, 1945), *Youth's Opportunity: Further Education in County Colleges* (No. 3, 1945), *Further Education* (No. 8, 1947) and *Citizens Growing Up* (No. 16, 1949); Circulars 133 (with two Addenda) and 139 (1947); and the authorities' Schemes of Further Education and Plans for County Colleges (1948 onwards). The 119 Schemes received by the Minister by the end of 1949 were reviewed in his *Education in 1949*, pp. 27–29. For Scotland see the Fyfe (1946) and McClelland (1952) Reports.

The McClelland Report and Pamphlet No. 8 are the only known published studies of the whole field of Further Education in their respective countries. Hitherto there has been no published study of the post-war system in Great Britain as a whole.

The development of the system can be traced separately in the annual reports of the Ministers, Secretaries of State and authorities, and, for England and Wales from 1961 onwards, the annual *Statistics of Education* (especially Part 2). *Education in Scotland in 1952* contained a historical section *Technical Education in Scotland* which was issued separately as a pamphlet (1953). See also Scottish Circulars 405 (1959) and 514 (1962).

However, there have been several useful short introductions and summaries of the system and of its parts. The most concise is perhaps that in the Central Office of Information's annual *Britain, an Official Handbook*; see also its five pamphlets : *Vocational Education and Training in Britain* (available on loan, 1955), *Education in Britain* (1955, 1960), *Technological Education in Britain* (1957, 1960), *Technical Education in Britain* (1962) and *Youth Services in Britain* (1963), all of which contained reference lists of publications. Venables's *British Technical Education* (1959) was also very short, and shorter still was Chapter 29 of the Crowther Report (1959). There were also the Ministry's booklet *Britain's Future and Technical Education* (1958) and the DES's pamphlet *Further Education for School Leavers* (1966) and broadsheet *The Educational System of England and*

Wales (1964). See also Pedley : *The Educational System in England and Wales* (1964). For Scotland see the SED's *Public Education in Scotland* (1963), Chapter VI. West's *Technical Education in Scotland* (an address at the summer meeting of the Association of Technical Institutions, 1959) pointed out some differences between the Scottish and English systems.

Hogg's *ABC Guides to the Education Acts 1944 and 1946* and Dawson's *Education Acts 1944, 1946 and 1948: a Detailed Index* were useful short reference books for England and Wales.

For a fuller treatment of technical education see Venables and others : *Technical Education, its Aims, Organisation and Future Development* (1955); and Payne : *Britain's Scientific and Technological Manpower* (1960); though these, of course, are now out of date in many respects.

The public-libraries and museums system after the 1964 Act was described in Circular 4/65.

Published sources for the study of British Further Education in 1964 were reviewed by the present author in *Brit. J. educ. Stud.*, vol. 13 (1964–5). Two other bibliographical publications were Argles and Vaughan : *British Government Publications concerning Education* (1966); and the present author : *A Guide to the Study of British Further Education* (NFER, 1966).

See also the DES's quarterly journals *Trends in Education* and *On Course*.

CHAPTER 2

THE AIMS OF THE NATIONAL SYSTEM OF FURTHER EDUCATION

General and specific aims

THE Government's purpose in introducing the new system, in the words of the White Paper *Educational Reconstruction* (1943), was

> to provide means for all of developing the various talents with which they are endowed and so enriching the inheritance of the country whose citizens they are.

Education, said Parliament in the 1944 Act, must "contribute towards the spiritual, moral, mental and physical development of the community" by providing facilities for activities suited to the pupils. And colleges for young persons were to provide such

> physical, practical and vocational training as will enable them to develop their various aptitudes and capacities and will prepare them for the responsibilities of citizenship.

These words accepted by Parliament define what may be called the general purpose, "orientation" or "immediate orientation" of the system.

Authorities, administrators and practitioners, however, require rather more detailed guidance than this. Therefore it has fallen to the Ministers, charged with the duty of promoting education and securing the execution of the national policy thereof, to formulate its immediate aims or "objectives" in more specific terms.

The orientation of an educational system is to serve certain needs. To convert it into objectives one must consider what the *particular* needs are at the given place and time. In the quoted passages two sets of needs were stated: those of a society, and those of the individual students who are both a part and a product of that society. Particular aims of a curriculum, therefore, should be derived from an assessment of such needs, both as they actually are and as they are expected to become, followed by a process of mediation between them. This is what the Ministers, with the aid of whatever surveys, studies and advice were available, have tried to do.

Under the British system, the decisions on what is taught and how it is taught, so as to attain these aims, are then left to the teachers concerned.

The needs of Britain

Economic growth

The expected economic needs of this country in the post-war world, especially INVESTMENT, PRODUCTIVITY and EXPORTS, were much in the thoughts of the President of the Board of Education in 1943. In his White Paper he wrote :

> The initial and natural advantages that gave this country, almost for the asking, its place of pre-eminence in world manufacture and world markets have long been fading. More and more in the future will it be necessary to rely on the capacity, adaptability and the quality of our industrial and commercial personnel.

Thus it was recognized that *people* were the country's greatest natural resource, and *trained people* its greatest need. Similarly the Minister tended to stress the contribution of education to productivity and exports, as, for example, in Circular 4 (1944) on art education; and no less than seventeen working parties appointed by the President of the Board of Trade between 1945 and 1947 to inquire into ways of improving methods of production and distribution in particular industries recommended the better education and training of workers as one of the ways.

Therefore it is not surprising that in 1943 the Board wanted to see part-time day release given by employers taking the place of the traditional reliance on evening classes :

> The country cannot afford to rest content with a system under which the technical education of its potential skilled workers, industrial leaders, or commercial executives is left so largely to the initiative of the young employees themselves. . . . From the point of view of the country's manufacturing industry, agriculture and commerce, the training afforded by a system of part-time education in conjunction with employment is long overdue. . . . Much closer collaboration between industry and commerce and the education service is essential if the country is to develop a national system and to secure a personnel with a training and knowledge adequate to the needs of the future.

However, a scientific revolution was developing even more quickly than had been thought. By 1945 the Percy Committee was urging the development of full-time and sandwich release. The country's future, said the Ministers somewhat tardily in their White Paper *Technical Education* (1956),

> will turn largely on our ability to secure a steady increase in industrial output, in productive investment, and in exports of goods and services of the highest quality at competitive prices. One industry after another is being compelled to follow its competitor, supplier or customer in modernising its techniques, knowing that unless new materials are discovered and new methods applied, British industry may fall behind in the race. The pace of change is quickening, and with it both the need and the demand for technical education.

Commercial education, too, would become more important than ever. Full-time and sandwich courses were to be encouraged.

The need also to promote DEVELOPMENT IN UNDERDEVELOPED TERRITORIES OVERSEAS began to be stated in later publications such as those of the Central Office of Information.

The Percy Committee's concept of educational expansion as an aspect of a planned national recruitment programme led to another important post-war development: studies of MANPOWER. In 1952 the UNESCO report *Education in a Technological Society* recommended regular estimates and forecasts of manpower needs, and soon afterwards OEEC set up a manpower committee. Besides the Registrars' Generals' departments which conduct censuses there are now several bodies in UK concerned with manpower matters. The chief one is the Committee on Manpower Resources for Science and Technology. This was formed in 1964 from what was then the Committee on Scientific Manpower, a committee of the Advisory Council on Scientific Policy. It is responsible jointly to the Minister of Technology and Secretary of State for Education and Science. The Advisory Council on Scientific Policy was reconstituted as the Council for Scientific Policy. Until 1960 there was also a Technical Personnel Committee of the Ministry of Labour, which watched over short-term aspects of the supply of scientists and engineers. The Minister of Labour has a National Joint Advisory Council, through which he can consult with both sides of industry; and a National Youth Employment Council. Following the Industrial Training Act of 1964 there is also an interdepartmental Committee on Training for Skill which advises appropriate ministers, and a Central Training Council (with Welsh and Scottish committees) under the Minister of Labour (see also Chapters 5 and 6). The Ministry of Labour set up a Manpower Research Unit in 1963. All these bodies have influenced educational policy in one way or another.

Three important aspects of a country's manpower structure are the kinds of work performed, the number of people engaged in each, and the balance or pattern of the whole.

Kinds of work, of which the 1951 censuses distinguished over 40,000, have been classified both "vertically" according to their particular industry, and "horizontally" according to the level of skill, knowledge or experience required. To take an example of the use of the first division, the censuses recognized twenty-seven "orders" of occupation corresponding broadly with groups of industries. Agriculture, fisheries and mining have been grouped by some writers as "primary", the manufacturing and constructional industries as "secondary", and commerce, administration and personal service as "tertiary". Charges in the relative magnitude of these groups have been studied. Kähler and Hamburger, for instance, showed that in the USA between 1840 and 1940 the percentage of workers employed in agriculture, forestry and fishing ("primary") fell from 78 to 18, but in manufacturing and mechanical industries ("secondary") it rose from 11 to 24, and in trade, transport and communications ("tertiary") from 4 to 23. These trends have continued, and the developing broad pattern of further education has reflected them.

"Horizontally", grades or levels of work have been divided into unskilled manual, semiskilled manual, skilled manual, intermediate, professional, higher administrative and so on. Over the country as a whole the 1951 censuses recognized five such divisions; Glass (1954) used seven; and so did a Cambridge survey (see BACIE, 1963). Trained employees of the British engineering industry were divided by the Percy Committee into : (1) senior administrators, (2) engineer scientists and development engineers, (3) engineer managers (design, manufacture, operation and sales), (4) technical assistants and designer draughtsmen and (5) draughtsmen, foremen and craftsmen. The White Paper of 1956 recognized three categories for which the majority of students passing through technical colleges into manufacturing industry were being trained. The "technologist" had studied the fundamental principles of his subject and should be able to initiate practical developments, accept a high degree of responsibility and in many cases push forward the boundaries of knowledge in his field. The "technician" was a specialist practical assistant to a technologist, needing not only practical aptitude but also a good knowledge of relevant mathematics and science. The "craftsman" was a manual worker able to carry out skilled practical tasks. Examples were—technologist : the university graduate in engineering; technician : the assistant designer, instrument artificer or skilled laboratory worker; craftsman : the engineering fitter or maintenance electrician. To these three grades the Crowther Report added that of "operative"—one who carried out specific operations using machinery or plant which did not need traditional craft skills ("semiskilled"). The category "pure scientist" could also be added. All may be subdivided.

Surprisingly little is known of the composition of the British working population in terms of these categories. There are only the censuses to go on, which on this point are of doubtful reliability. The Urwick Committee drew attention to this deficiency as long ago as 1947. It is thought that about one-fifth of the male working population are in "skilled" occupations (craftsmen) for which apprenticeship is the normal training, and that about half are semiskilled or unskilled. In 1956 craftsmen made up more than one-third of the manpower of manufacturing industry; they were most numerous in engineering and building, but operatives were commoner in the chemical and petroleum industries. About 41 per cent of boys and 6 per cent of girls leaving school entered apprenticeships or learnerships in skilled occupations in 1965 (Table 9). Over 50 per cent of boys and many more girls became semiskilled and unskilled, but of these, 8 per cent of boys and

c

4 per cent of girls received some form of systematic training lasting for at least one year for semiskilled jobs. The Percy Committee thought that the greatest scarcity was in the category of the organizing scientist and technologist able to apply research to development (in its groups 1–3).

The second post-war manpower study in Britain was the Barlow Report on the supply of scientists (1946). This led to the creation in 1947 of the permanent Advisory Council on Scientific Policy which soon afterwards set up a Committee on Scientific Manpower. The latter published a series of reports, the most elaborate of which was the joint survey usually called the Zuckerman Report (1956). By asking employers the Technical Personnel Committee estimated the country's "stock" of qualified scientists and engineers to be about 135,000 in 1956. ("Qualified" meant either holding a university degree or its equivalent, or being eligible for corporate or graduate membership of a professional institution of scientists or engineers.) By assuming (a) that there was a 1 : 1 relation between the rate of increase of industrial production and the number of qualified scientists and engineers employed by industry, and (b) that this rate would continue at least at the 1955 figure of 4 per cent per year, the Committee on Scientific Manpower then calculated that something around 220,000 would be needed in 1966. To get this rate of increase, the output would have to be about doubled in fifteen years, from 10,300 in 1955 to 16,900 in 1966 and nearly 20,000 in 1970. This recommendation, too, was accepted by the Government, and these target figures inspired the programme of technical education launched with the White Paper of 1956. The Committee slightly revised them in 1959 and again in 1962. The main shortages at the time of writing are of chemists, chemical engineers, physicists, metallurgists and mechanical engineers.

The question of the proper balance between pure scientists and technologists has received some attention. It is now generally thought that in the past the proportion of technologists trained in Britain has been too low. Certainly we have made far more discoveries than we have been able to use, and the initiative in production has passed in many cases to other countries.

The problem of producing a balanced manpower becomes even more urgent when technicians and craftsmen are taken into account, as they must be. Hitherto scientists and technologists have been the only categories given substantial quantitative study.

By contrast, neither the present "stock" nor future demand for technicians and craftsmen is known; and the supply has been at the mercy of an apprenticeship system which until 1964 had not been subject to government control since 1819. The White Paper of 1956 wanted the number of young workers given day release to be doubled in five years, but did not say *why* this was the rate proposed. The Carr Committee (1958) made no estimates. The Industrial Training Act of 1964, as explained later, was a first step towards more active government measures in this field. But there is no coherent manpower policy for technicians or craftsmen as yet; and for commercial personnel it has hardly even been thought about. Thus *The National Plan* (1965) could not be based upon any but very simple overall manpower considerations.

As a step towards such overall concepts, rough estimates of the expected *ratio* of technicians to others have been made, but they vary widely. In the USA the President's Commission on Higher Education (1947) thought that there should be from three to five semi-professional assistants to every professional engineer. In the Soviet Union, according to Barker (1955), the ratio was to be raised to between two and four. Lord Weeks said "at least two" per graduate.[1] The White Paper (1956) suggested five or six technicians for one technologist. *The National Plan* said four. In an inquiry, the Ministry of Labour (1960) found 1·6 in the chemicals and allied industries but 7·6 in motor-vehicle and aircraft manufacture. However, it is difficult to define the work of a technician, and there is likely to be much variation from one industry to another. It is probable, nevertheless, that technicians will be found to be the most scarce of all the groups, particularly as the supply of scientists and technologists expands. Their management responsibilities, too, are growing, and this increases the demand for the higher education of technicians.

Manpower policy must, of course, take account of changes in the POPULATION which is its source. Obviously a *healthy* people is a need of any society. The Education Acts extended the School Medical Service (before it was absorbed into the National Health Service) to cover students aged under nineteen, and made it a duty of authorities to include facilities for physical training and recreation in their Further Education provision.

The size and age composition of a population must also be known. For some time its size was relatively static in Britain owing to the reduction in both birth and death rates. In 1949 the Royal Commission on Population thought that the birth rate, which was then falling from its 1947 peak, would continue to decline for another fifteen years, resulting in a drop in the proportion of young people. Actually it fell only until 1955 and then rose steadily till 1964. This means that the number of sixteen-year-olds, which reached a peak in 1963–4, will fall to a trough in 1969–72 and then begin to rise again. Between 1956 and 1962 the number of school leavers grew from just over half a million to nearly three-quarters of a million, but fell in 1963. The need to expand the intake of apprentices, learners and students of all kinds to make full use of this "bulge" has impressed all educational advisers. The Crowther Council's proposed programme, too, was timed to the temporary fall in the population of fifteen-year-olds. As a

[1] In the House of Lords, 21st November 1956.

source for industry the bulge has been reinforced by the "trend" to longer staying at school and the "swing" to increased popularity of science subjects.

The geographical distribution of population and of the extent and type of employment, said the Minister in Pamphlet No. 8 and Circular 133, must be taken into account too; and it is the responsibility of authorities and regional advisory councils to assess local needs. Nevertheless, there is still little known about the local distribution of apprentices, for example.

Effects of occupational pattern, social mobility and family form within the population have also been considered by advisory committees, notably the Central Advisory Councils and the Robbins Committee. The term "social class", by the way, is generally used as synonymous with "horizontal" occupational grade, when "working class" means the three manual grades (see p. 13). Although this usage involves an erroneous concept of social class it has proved useful as far as *manual* workers and their children were concerned. It has been shown, for example, that although the proportion of children of manual workers coming forward for higher education increased over this century, it is still very much lower than in the population as a whole, and has probably not increased since before the war. So there is much wastage of ability in this group, particularly among children of semi-skilled and unskilled workers, and especially among girls. The trends towards earlier marriage, smaller and more compact families and greater expectation of life, though unsettling to adolescent girls, have increased the reserve of middle-aged married women. The 1956 White Paper stressed the growing opportunities for girls in technical education, while the Minister has tried to get trained married women to return to teaching and has encouraged authorities to train mature people as teachers.

Technological advance

Essential to all policy is some assessment of changes likely to be associated with the advance of technology. It is important to distinguish *technological* trends (namely those arising from the application of scientific knowledge to production, distribution and exchange) from *sociological* (those connected with economic and social relations of people and groups of people within society); although, of course, these interact with one another, and their effects are intimately connected.

One such change is the altered balance of industries, already mentioned, with the decline of some and rise of others. Another is the expansion of scientific activity, which, some writers have suggested, seems to be doubling itself every ten to fifteen years. A third is the rise in the proportion of people engaged at technician, technologist and managerial levels. Others are the breakdown of traditional boundaries of knowledge, the spread of large collective enterprises and the development of ever higher levels of integration and interrelatedness within society. It is possible, for example, that the present trend towards the specialization of occupations may be arrested or even reversed. There are also important implications for æsthetics, consumption and leisure. These changes are likely to call for an increase in general education, scientific knowledge, æsthetic awareness, occupational flexibility and qualities of teamwork in the population.

The nature of many jobs is changing now, particularly as *mechanization* (the *doing of jobs* by machines) spreads. In commerce, for example, the skills of shorthand and book-keeping are already obsolescent and so is much arithmetic; whilst according to the De La Warr Report there is no longer a place for the unskilled worker in agriculture. In industry, work performed by traditional craftsmen tends to be done by semiskilled so that the distinction between craftsmen and operatives becomes more blurred. *Automation* (the *control of machines* by machines) intensifies these changes and brings new ones of its own. It affects perhaps most the ordinary operative, whose work of controlling a machine or plant comes to be done by a regulating device.

It used to be thought that the growth of industry must depress the level of skill and initiative required from the ordinary worker. It certainly did so during the earlier phases of the industrial revolution when whole industries were built with the forced labour of pauper children operating machines. Mechanization was then advancing rapidly. Adam Ferguson, Adam Smith's teacher, observed (1783) :

> Many mechanical arts . . . succeed best under a total suppression of sentiment and reason. Manufactures, accordingly, prosper most where the mind is least consulted.

The Hammonds have recounted how a Lancashire millowner agreed with a London parish to take one idiot with every twenty sound children supplied. The rise of industries built on such labour economically destroyed the skilled handicrafts which had preceded them. Proudhon (1846) thought that as the efficiency of the machine increased the intelligence of the worker declined. Henry Ford's production line from 1914 converted the paleotechnic machine minder into the neotechnic conveyor-belt nut tightener cartooned by Chaplin and Clair in the 1930s. One end-point of this expectation was the "epsilon-minus semi-moron" of Aldous Huxley's *Brave New World* (1932), amiably blaspheming "Oh Ford!" when the lift he was operating accidentally stuck in its shaft. "Man's final conquest," wrote C. S. Lewis (1943), "has proved to be the abolition of man". The Minister showed traces of this thinking in her Pamphlet No. 1 (1945).

Other writers, however, notably Owen and Marx, thought differently. "Modern industry", wrote Marx (1887), "compels society to replace the detail-worker of today by the fully-developed individual, fit for a variety of labours, ready to face any change of production." More recent thought and experience support this view. In the present phase of industrialization, with the coming of automatic control of machines, it seems to be agreed that the level of work required from many operatives is rising. At present there are two chief kinds of worker most closely affected by automation : machine minders in the engineering and similar manufacturing industries, and process watchers in chemicals and petroleum. To either of these the introduction of automatic control means that instead of regulating one process manually a worker supervises several processes with the aid of instruments. To do this he or she has to know much more about the plant, equipment and what the instrument readings mean. Thus there is a trend towards supervision rather than manipulation, a stress on conceptual elements in work rather than motor elements, and a need for knowledge of processes rather than manual dexterity. All this should make such work not less but more intelligent and responsible, and probably more interesting. In some cases, however, the need for subjective judgement by experienced operators is reduced, or the degree of personal contact with the material decreases, or there may be a lot of watching and waiting with little else to do.

The picture emerging is that instead of a growing majority of workers performing increasingly humdrum tasks, separated by an ever widening gap from a small highly trained technocracy, as was once expected, we may rather find that we need a growing majority of increasingly *skilled* and *adaptable* workers and managers. The Cambridge survey mentioned earlier has estimated that this country will need a net increase of 155,000 craftsmen and 50,000 technicians, and a net decrease of 45,000 clerical and 151,000 unskilled workers, during *each year* between 1961 and 1970. In general, the level of knowledge and skill demanded from the population as a whole may be expected to rise.

Obviously this conclusion poses formidable problems of training, retraining and continuous education of workers of all ages.

Political and social progress

Britain's need for enlightened citizens and parents, making a population willing and able to advance her society and her culture, has been stressed as much, but studied far less, than her need for workers.

Our need is twofold, said Pamphlet No. 8 : to produce not only skill, but also "social leadership".

> There is a palpable need for fully-trained citizens. . . . The need is implicit in the responsibilities of a democratic society. . . . If a great extension of technical education is essential to the well-being of our economic life, so equally

is a wide development of general adult education necessary if we are – as individuals or as a nation – to deal competently and democratically with the complex political questions of our time.

There must be equality of educational opportunity, said the White Paper of 1943, and also diversity of provision, which was "just as important".

> But such diversity must not impair the social unity within the educational system which will open the way to a more closely knit society and give us strength to face the tasks ahead.

Pamphlet No. 8 opened with an eloquent plea for planning, certainly of education, but also, almost by implication, of society as a whole : "we must plan for a balanced community".

There was no attempt here, however, to suggest more clearly what the political tasks might be. Certainly no radical change in the structure of society was envisaged in these documents. The need for people who could bring about changes which would certainly not be wanted by other people was implicit; but British society was thought of as being more or less homogeneous, the needs of all being the same. There was no hint that people from different social classes or other subcultures might be unable to agree about the "right" solutions, or indeed might have quite different, even opposed needs. The deeper political implications of technological advance were not considered either. Nor were the dangers of the international situation, which were not then as obvious as they have since become. "Social leadership" in a "democratic society" would somehow carry us through. The official body which seemed nearest to suspecting that such broad political questions might have specific educational implications was the English Central Advisory Council in *School and Life* (1947.) But the need for a general theory of social change, however rough, able to give some inkling of the sort of changes likely during the lifetime of the students, does not seem to have been widely felt, nor the need for a pattern of social aims.

Anyway, official practice is to leave such matters to political parties; but these are noticeably rich in social-class bias and noticeably poor in social theory. Consequently, grave and fundamental errors have been made; as when the post-war Government, defenceless against the middle-class prejudices of the Norwood Report, retained secondary education in the restrictive pattern from which it is only now beginning to break out (see Chapter 19).

Aesthetic vigour

A function of art education, said the Minister in Pamphlet No. 6, is to raise the level of public taste and appreciation. A high level of civilization, said Pamphlet No. 8, requires that as many people as possible should share in the appreciation of cultural achievements. Elsewhere in Pamphlet No. 6, however, art education seemed to be regarded as either an *economic* (especially for exports) or a purely *individual* need. There was little more than a hint of a concept of a *national* need for *educated consumers.* The Council for the Encouragement of Music and the Arts (Arts Council), the organization which embodies the realization that æsthetic activities are a communal need in their own right, does not now come under the Secretaries of State, while the Council of Industrial Design has always been under the Board of Trade. Perhaps the value of an economic pressure within the UK in the direction of higher standards of design, efficiency, quality and variety in production has only recently begun to be recognized. Yet technological advance has brought a widening range of products, including the greatest works of art, to within reach of all, whilst also providing leisure to pursue their appreciation. However, a new spirit seemed to pervade the White Paper *A Policy for the Arts* (1965).

Educational planning

The Minister's hint at a need for the planning of society has been mentioned. The need for *educational* planning was stated quite explicitly, and indeed, as has been seen, was fundamental to the Acts. And although it was intended to cater for the country's output of workers primarily through technical, commercial and art education, and for its citizens, parents and consumers through county colleges, Youth Service and Adult Education, such functions were not to be confined to these sectors. "There are no frontiers to education", the Minister wrote; provision should be based on "an assessment of the educational needs of the community as a whole."

There was no sign of recognition of the economic, social-class and ideological roots, old and deep, of the cleavage between "education" and "industrial training".

The needs of students

Categories of student

Broadly there are eight major categories of person attending college, centre or club : adolescents attending full-time courses; adolescents training by part-time day or evening-only courses for skilled or semiskilled occupations, many being apprentices or sponsored trainees of some kind; adolescents in unskilled employment attending during their working time; adolescents enjoying recreational activities; adults, mostly young, taking full-time or sandwich courses, mostly advanced; adults training in occupational skills or improving their vocational qualifications mainly by evening study; adults attending non-vocational courses; and adults enjoying recreational activities.

Adolescent growth

All young people, said the White Paper of 1943, need the *continuation* of supervision and help during these critical early years after leaving school. Without this, their education would suffer from "under-exposure, under-development and insufficient fixing". To ensure such help for those most in need, compulsory further education was regarded as necessary.

The general features of school leavers have been well studied and taken into account in publications of the Ministers and their advisory bodies. Pamphlet No. 3, for example, discussed well-known adolescent characteristics such as the rapid growth of intellectual, manual, athletic, appreciative, creative and critical powers; the breaking away from dependence on family and adults; the disposition to form and join groups and to conform to their behaviour; and the struggle for adaptation to an adult role in the world. Needs which arise from these characteristics include : experience of a satisfying yet ambivalent relationship with adults; experience of participation in community life; opportunities for purposeful activities to develop personal powers; and a feeling of recognition, prestige and reward.

Vocational needs are more specific, varying among all the four categories of adolescent student. They are usually quite explicit among those receiving part-time training for skilled and semiskilled occupations, and among full-time students too; but they may be neglected or unknown among the unskilled or irrelevant in recreational activities.

Adult interests

Many adolescent needs continue into adulthood, and adults have needs of their own; but the adult student has not been as well studied as the younger colleague, and little is known of his or her psychology.

The four adult categories differ from one another somewhat. A student attending a vocational course may well be a young man trying to further his career. He may have been recently married or have young children; perhaps be without a house of his own, saddled with hire-purchase payments and not very high in the salary scale; perhaps too, having to travel a long way to attend the course, receiving little or no encouragement from his employer, or attending entirely during his evenings. The vocational needs of such a student would obviously be paramount.

Non-vocational adult students may have quite different needs. They are likely to be older and to have more leisure. They include a high proportion of middle-aged married women whose families no longer require all their attention. Their needs are various : to develop personal interests or skills, pursue leisure-time studies to a deeper level, improve standards of recreational activity, extend the range of æsthetic appreciation, prepare for holidays, escape from children or dull surroundings, meet new friends or talk with old ones. Providing facilities for leisure-time occupation, said Pamphlet No. 8,

is the opportunity for a wide extension of the educational and social resources making for individual happiness.

Specific aims in Further Education

By mediating between these two sets of needs, a list of objectives can be derived.

Promotion of health, hygiene and bodily growth was stressed in the 1943 White Paper. However, the Acts did not make physical education compulsory in Further Education as they did in schools.

Other essential purposes, said the White Paper, were :

training in clarity of expression and in the understanding of the written and the spoken word, together with some education in the broad meaning of citizenship – to give some understanding of the working of government and the responsibilities of citizens and some interest in the affairs of the world around them.

These objectives were elaborated in Pamphlets Nos. 3, 8 and 16. In Pamphlet No. 3, in particular, it was hoped that young people, by the time they were eighteen, would understand how to live a healthy life, be able to work hard, learn to use their leisure well, be ready to have their imagination stirred, improve their power of language, appreciate the place and responsibilities of the family in a healthy community, be well acquainted with conditions in this country and want to improve them, be interested in the people of other countries, know something of the leadership and co-operative service necessary in a democratic community, and be honourable, tolerant, kindly and independent. It was thought that there would probably be a daily assembly with an act of religious worship in county colleges, but this was not to be compulsory. The corporate life in the colleges, said Pamphlet No. 8, should foster self-governing student societies "to extend the students' range of interests and their social powers".

Aims such as these were to be attained primarily through county colleges, which at that time were intended for all young people who were not already receiving full-time education. But the Youth Service, too, was to play an important part, having as its purpose the physical and social training of young people for the responsibilities of citizenship. And to complete the social aims, in the words of the White Paper, it would be

> within the wider sphere of adult education that an ultimate training in democratic citizenship must be sought.

Vocational aims were dealt with in Pamphlet No. 8. Workers who enjoyed their work, it said, made better workers; but they should acquire an understanding of human relationships as well as technical knowledge. For the more responsible posts in industry and commerce a high standard of general education would be necessary. For those doing repetitive work, on the other hand, there should be more emphasis on leisure-time pursuits. The need for adaptability was stressed in the White Papers of 1956 and 1961.

The education of young workers, said the Crowther Report, should be woven of four strands : finding a way about the world as workers, consumers and citizens; forming standards and values; developing physical and æsthetic skills; and continuing basic education, with vocational bias where appropriate. The London authority, in its report *On From School*, and the Minister's Committee on General Studies have accepted these as a basis for their suggestions. The former derived four groups of objective from them : vocation, leisure time, training for citizenship and preparation for marriage.

The aims of higher education, put forward in the Robbins Report and accepted by the Government, included instruction in vocational skills, the endowment of people with all-round culture, the advancement of learning by creative work and research, and the transmission of common standards and habits of citizenship on which a healthy society depends. Thus vocational skills were here recognized as offering a worthy educational aim.

The aims of non-vocational education for adults contained a rather different emphasis, being concerned more with enriching the present than with preparing for the future. The Minister stressed the importance of homecraft courses for women in Circular 117 (1946). General adult education, said Pamphlet No. 8, should "develop those interests and activities which go to the making of a full and satisfying life".

These, then, were the aims of the system as formulated or accepted by different Ministers, mainly during the formative period between 1943 and 1947. Whether they have been attained, however, or even pursued, is quite another matter. But this is a question better left until the final chapter, after the system as it has naturally evolved has been examined and described.

Notes on Further Study

The general orientation of the system was laid down in the White Paper of 1943 and the main Acts.

The specific objectives of Further Education have been stated by the Ministers, mainly in Pamphlets Nos. 3 (1945), 6 (1946) and 8 (1947), and more recently in the White Papers of 1951, 1956 and 1961. Paragraph 105 of Pamphlet No. 3 (for county colleges) is the most explicit list. The aims of the Youth Service were given in the Board's Circular 1516 (1940). All these inspired the authorities' Schemes of Further Education and Plans for County Colleges (1948 onwards). For the recommendations of committees see the McClelland (especially Chapter IV), Crowther (especially Chapter 17), first Albemarle (especially Chapter 3), Newsom (especially Chapter 4) and Robbins (especially Chapter II) Reports.

There is a considerable literature on curriculum theory, educational sociology, educational economics, technological change, the psychology and sociology of adolescence, and so on, which there is not space to list here. UNESCO bibliographies and abstracts contain useful summaries : see, for example, Choynowski : *The Psychology of Adolescence* (1963). Useful also were Beryl Board's bibliography on the effect of technological progress on education (1959), Floud and Halsey's on the sociology of education (1958) and Blaug's on the economics of education (1964).

On manpower see the Registrars' Generals' censuses of 1931, 1951 and 1961; the Percy (1945) and Barlow (1946) Reports; reports of the Parliamentary and Scientific Committee (1946, 1947, 1950, 1954); annual reports of the Advisory Council on Scientific Policy (1948–1964) and Ministry of Labour's Manpower Research Unit (No. 1, 1964); UNESCO's *Education in a Technological Society* (1952); OEEC's *Shortages and Surpluses of Highly Qualified Scientists and Engineers in Western Europe* (1955) and *Forecasting Manpower Needs for the Age of Science* (1960); OECD's *Resources of Scientific and Technical Personnel in the OECD Area* (1963); the Committee on Scientific Manpower's *Report on the Recruitment of Scientists and Engineers by the Engineering Industry* (1955), *Scientific and Engineering Manpower in Great Britain* (1956), *Scientific and Engineering Manpower in Great Britain 1959* (1959), *The Long-term Demand for Scientific Manpower* (1961) and *Scientific and Technological Manpower in Great Britain 1962* (1963); *The National Plan* (1965); and the Committee on Manpower Resources for Science and Technology's interim report *A Review of the Scope and Problems of Scientific and Technological Manpower Policy* (1965). More general were Kähler and Hamburger : *Education for an Industrial Age* (1948); Jaffe and Stewart : *Manpower Resources and Utilization* (1951); McCrensky : *Scientific Manpower in Europe* (1958);

Carter and Williams : *Science in Industry* (1959); Payne : *Britain's Scientific and Technological Manpower* (1960); Vaizey : *The Economics of Education* (1962); OECD : *Science, Economic Growth and Government Policy* (1963) and *Economic Aspects of Higher Education* (1964); BACIE : *Economic Growth and Manpower* (1963); and Harbison and Myers : *Education, Manpower and Economic Growth* (1964). Much of this more general work is American; for comparison see Nozhko : *Methods . . . within the USSR* (UNESCO, 1964). See also UNESCO : *Economic and Social Aspects of Educational Planning* (1964).

Prandy's *Professional Employees* (1965) was a sociological study of scientists and engineers. Touraine's *Workers' Attitudes to Technical Change* (1965) was a survey of research.

The Ministry of Labour's survey of technicians in the chemicals and engineering industries was reported in *Ministry of Labour Gazette*, December 1960. Proportions of skilled workers in the whole working population were discussed in the ITC's *Training Boys in Industry* (1960).

On the impact of automation see Congress of the USA : *Report on Automation and Technological Change* (1955); Institution of Production Engineers : *The Automatic Factory: What does it Mean?* (1955); and DSIR : *Automation* (1956). A short summary of expected technological trends of importance to education appeared in the second Brunton Report (1963), Chapter XII. See also the Crowther (1959), third Oldfield-Davies (1961) and Newsom (1963) Reports.

On the needs of youth and young workers see the Minister's Pamphlet No. 3; Stanley's *The Education of Young Citizens* (1945); the reports of Oxford University Department of Education's conferences on *The Young Worker* (especially the *Sixth*, 1956); the Crowther and first Albemarle Reports; Appendices II and III of the first Bessey Report (1962); and the LCC's *On From School* (1962). The British Council of Churches has commented in *Over 15* (1961) and *The Church and Technological Education* (1966). See also Dorothy Silberston : *Youth in a Technical Age* (1959); Musgrove : *Youth and the Social Order* (1964); and Mary Morse : *The Unattached* (1965). For Commonwealth students in UK see Chapter 16 and *Notes*.

CHAPTER 3

HOW FURTHER EDUCATION
IS PROVIDED

The three pillars of the system

As mentioned in Chapter 1, the Acts gave to both central and local government the duty of ensuring that efficient education is provided. They could do this either by helping others to provide it, or by providing it themselves.

The ways of "securing the provision" are therefore very varied, depending on the balance in which these two methods are combined. They can be thought of as falling into three stages: assisting other organizations to establish and/or maintain facilities; maintaining facilities already established by others; and establishing and maintaining facilities. Examples of the first stage are: paying all or part of the expenses of maintaining a building; giving grants for travel, research, conferences, special events, salaries, expenses or training; awarding scholarships and other benefits; lending equipment; allowing free tenancy of rooms or halls with heating, lighting and caretaking; offering advice; providing the services of specialist officers such as youth organizers; helping to draw up programmes; assisting with publicity; providing play space and other facilities; and making capital grants or interest-free loans. Thus "securing the provision" can range from stimulating small voluntary activities to building and maintaining huge institutions. Authorities use all three of these stages, but the central government uses mainly the first two.

Thus there are three pillars of the system: the Secretaries of State, the authorities, and the voluntary and other non-government bodies concerned. The three are by no means equal, however: for most of the *volume* of provision is by authorities; much of the *drive* comes from voluntary effort; and the basic *responsibility* is with the Secretaries of State, who must promote the system as a whole, so as to secure the execution of national policy. The Secretaries' control is exercised mainly in the fields of standards, organization, finance and distribution of facilities. But the three operate as a partnership, with initiative coming from any one of them.

26

How the central government secures provision

Ministers and departments

As mentioned, education in Great Britain is under the surveillance of two Secretaries of State: the SECRETARY OF STATE FOR EDUCATION AND SCIENCE and SECRETARY OF STATE FOR SCOTLAND. Both are chosen by the PRIME MINISTER and appointed by the Queen. They are Members of Parliament, to which they are individually responsible. They are also members of the Cabinet, at the Prime Minister's invitation, and therefore share in the decisions of the government. They are also, of course, leading members of the political party in power.

The Secretary for Education and Science is helped by two MINISTERS OF STATE FOR EDUCATION AND SCIENCE, and the Secretary for Scotland is helped in his educational responsibilities by a MINISTER OF STATE. Each of these three Ministers has a parliamentary secretary who is also an MP. Since October 1964 the Secretary of State for Education and Science has also had two parliamentary under-secretaries: one in charge of physical recreation (popularly called "Minister for Sport") and the other for the arts and leisure ("Minister for Culture").

As also mentioned in Chapter 1, the responsible head of the government's education department for England and Wales between 1st April 1944 and 1st April 1964 was the MINISTER OF EDUCATION. He presided over his office or MINISTRY in London, which carried out his decisions. It was divided under a permanent secretary into several branches each dealing with a particular aspect such as schools, Further Education, research and intelligence, architects and building, external relations and legal matters. There was a separate department for Wales and Monmouthshire under its own permanent secretary. Special study groups were set up as desired.

Another department, the DEPARTMENT OF SCIENTIFIC AND INDUSTRIAL RESEARCH (DSIR), under the MINISTER FOR SCIENCE, made grants in aid of research in its own and other establishments.

Universities in England, Wales and Scotland were under the TREASURY, "buffered" by the University Grants Committee (UGC) which was the body actually dealing with them. The Treasury also aided the arts through the Arts Council, BBC and other bodies; and it aided certain colleges.

Following the Robbins and Trend Reports, however, the Ministry of Education, Ministry for Science, those functions of the Lord President of the Council dealing with agriculture, and those functions of the Treasury relating to universities were merged into a new DEPARTMENT OF EDUCATION AND SCIENCE (DES). The duties of the Minister of Education and Minister for Science were transferred to the Secretary of State appointed to take charge of this new Department. At present, one of the two Ministers of State assisting him is continuing the work of the former Minister of Education, and the other is looking after higher education and science for the whole UK. Each presides over an administrative unit run by a permanent secretary. One of these units is nearly the same as the former Ministry of Education for England and Wales, which therefore continues the activities described above. The Treasury's responsibilities for sponsoring the arts are also to be transferred to the DES. The DSIR was dissolved in 1965.

The Secretary of State for Scotland, who was unaffected by these changes, presides in like manner over the SCOTTISH EDUCATION DEPARTMENT (SED) in Edinburgh, which is similar in structure to the former Ministry of Education, though smaller. He also controls the DEPARTMENT OF AGRICULTURE AND FISHERIES FOR SCOTLAND (DAFS), which has administrative oversight of the three colleges of agriculture (see p. 59) and the SCOTTISH DEVELOPMENT DEPARTMENT (SDD) which pays "block grant" to authorities.

Each Secretary of State is helped by councils and committees of various kinds (Table 2), by the officers of his department and by an independent staff of Her Majesty's Inspectors (HMIs) who report on whether efficient education is being provided and give him a link with authorities, organizations and teaching staffs. Each Secretary of State must make an annual report to Parliament, which is published.

Government departments marginally concerned with Further Education include LABOUR, HEALTH, AGRICULTURE FISHERIES AND FOOD, HOUSING AND LOCAL GOVERNMENT, PUBLIC BUILDING AND WORKS, and, since October 1964, TECHNOLOGY, LAND AND NATURAL RESOURCES and ECONOMIC AFFAIRS. The Ministry of Technology has taken over some of the duties of the DSIR.

The SECRETARY OF STATE FOR WALES has no executive responsibility for education but has oversight of all Welsh matters. Therefore he consults his education colleague when necessary.

In matters to do with the Commonwealth, with which they have become increasingly involved, particularly since 1959, the Secretaries of State co-operate with their colleagues of other government departments, such as the COLONIAL OFFICE, COMMONWEALTH RELATIONS OFFICE and MINISTRY OF OVERSEAS DEVELOPMENT (ODM; formerly DEPARTMENT OF TECHNICAL CO-OPERATION), and with other bodies including the state-aided British Council.

The Forestry Commission is supervised in Scotland by the Secretary of State, in England by the Minister of Land and Natural Resources and in Wales by the Secretary of State for Wales. Its educational activities in Scotland, therefore, come within our scope but not those in England or Wales.

The Development Commission, Medical Research Council (MRC), Agricultural Research Council (ARC) and Nature Conservancy, although not government departments, have functions similar to those of the DSIR. Between 1959 and 1964 there was also an Overseas Research Council to assist and co-ordinate research within the Commonwealth, but it did not dispense money. Since 1965 there has been a Science Research Council (SRC) and a Natural Environment Research Council (NERC), both under the Secretary of State for Education and Science, the NERC having absorbed the Nature Conservancy in England and Wales. The SRC and NERC now pay research and postgraduate–student grants instead of the DSIR and ARC respectively. Also formed in 1965 was a Social Science Research Council (SSRC) with an education division; this has taken over postgraduate awards in this field from the Secretary of State (see Table 1).

The GENERAL REGISTER OFFICE, London, and GENERAL REGISTRY OFFICE, Edinburgh, each under a REGISTRAR GENERAL, are responsible for regulating the registration of births, marriages and deaths, planning and carrying out censuses and compiling and analysing statistics thereof. The various committees concerned with manpower questions are mentioned in Chapter 2.

The Council of Industrial Design (CoID), which is under the BOARD OF TRADE, fosters appreciation of design in manufactures. It has an education section. There is a Scottish committee.

The CENTRAL OFFICE OF INFORMATION (COI) and SCOTTISH INFORMATION OFFICE (SIO) produce informative pamphlets and other material. The COI has a research unit – the Social Survey.

Stimulation of bodies other than authorities

The Secretaries of State do not tender, nor employ direct labour, for the erection of educational buildings, in the way, for example, that an authority does. Only in certain museums are teachers employed as civil servants. In all other cases the central government works by stimulating, aiding and perhaps also directing the work of others.

Each Secretary of State does this through the use of four chief methods: controlling financial aid; making orders and regulations as empowered by Acts of Parliament; sending representatives to participate in the work of governing, advisory, examining and other bodies; and giving suggestions and advice.

In England and Wales there are seven categories of organization in the field of Further Education receiving FINANCIAL AID from the Secretary of State (Tables 1 and 3). These are: the governing bodies of certain colleges; the so-called "responsible bodies" which provide liberal education for adults; certain national voluntary associations also promoting this kind of activity; national and local bodies promoting social and physical training and

D

TABLE 1

FURTHER EDUCATION (ENGLAND AND WALES): CATEGORIES OF ORGANIZATION
AND INDIVIDUAL DIRECTLY AIDED BY THE SECRETARY OF STATE FOR EDUCATION
AND SCIENCE, 1964–5

A. *Organizations*

1. *Governing bodies of direct-grant establishments*

   35 establishments providing technical, commercial, art and agricultural education and residential adult education. Aided by capital and maintenance grants under Further Education (Grant) Regulations, 1959, Section 18. Listed in Table 6.

2. *Responsible bodies*

   Providing liberal education for adults. Teaching costs aided under Further Education (Grant) Regulations, 1959, Sections 19–20. Listed in NIAE: *Adult Education in 1964* (1965).

   (a) *Extra-mural departments of universities and university colleges*
       23.

   (b) *Voluntary associations*
       17 districts of the WEA, plus the Welsh National Council of YMCAs.

   (c) *Joint bodies*
       2, containing representatives of 2(a), 2(b) and authorities.

3. *National voluntary associations*

   8 associations promoting liberal education for adults. General expenditure aided triennially under Further Education (Grant) Regulations, 1959, Section 21. Listed in Secretary of State for Education and Science; *Education in 1964*, Appendix C (1965).

4. *Bodies promoting social and physical training and recreation intended primarily for adults*

   Aided under Physical Training and Recreation Act, 1937, Section 3 (as later amended).

   (a) *National headquarters grants*
       43 organizations listed in *op. cit.*, Appendix B.

   (b) *National coaching and administration grants*
       5 organizations listed in *op. cit.*, Appendix B.

   (c) *Local capital grants*
       42 local voluntary associations providing community centres, 292 local voluntary associations providing village halls, 370 local voluntary associations providing playing fields, etc. (*Op. cit.*, Table 16.) No lists published.

5. *Voluntary youth organizations*

   Promoting social and physical training and recreation intended primarily for persons aged under eighteen. Aided under Social and Physical Training Grant Regulations, 1939.

   (a) *Headquarters grants*
       40 organizations listed in *op. cit.*, Appendix A.

   (b) *Special grants*
       11 organizations listed in *op. cit.*, Appendix A.

   (c) *Local capital grants*
       514 projects aided in respect of capital costs of providing youth clubs, etc. No list published.

6. *Voluntary associations providing facilities for disabled and handicapped persons*

   Aided under Special Schools and Establishments (Grant) Regulations, 1959. No list published.

7. *Bodies carrying on research and other services*

   Aided under Educational Services and Research Grant Regulations, 1946. 12 organizations listed in *op. cit.*, Appendix E.

TABLE 1 (*continued*)

B. *Individuals*

1. *State students*
    Undergoing certain full-time postgraduate courses in arts or social studies.[1] Aided under State Awards Regulations, 1963. No list published, nor the number given.

2. *Mature state scholars*
    Persons aged at least 25 undergoing full-time first-degree courses in arts or social studies. Aided under State Awards Regulations, 1963. Up to 30 awarded each year, but no list published.

3. *Research and other workers*
    Aided under Educational Services and Research Grant Regulations, 1946. 3 persons named in *op. cit.*, Appendix I.

   Sources: as named.

recreation among adults; national and local voluntary youth organizations; voluntary associations providing for the disabled and handicapped; and bodies carrying on research and other services.

These bodies are aided under five ACTS or CODES OF REGULATIONS, which prescribe the conditions they must fulfil in order to receive grant. College governing bodies, responsible bodies and national associations promoting liberal education are aided under one code. They must satisfy the Secretary of State regarding their constitution, general standing and financial circumstances, the character and cost of their facilities, and the efficiency of their teaching and organization. They must not exclude anyone from using the facilities on "other than reasonable grounds", nor may the grant be used to promote denominational religious instruction. Their premises must conform to the Secretary of State's standards, and alterations to them may not be made without his approval. They must supply him with any information he may ask for, and keep the establishments open to HMIs. The Secretary of State may also require that courses may not be given without his permission, and may impose further requirements. He may pay a grant towards capital and maintenance costs, usually to the headquarters in the case of an organization, and towards the salaries of teachers. Establishments aided in this way are called "direct-grant".

Grant-aided organizations promoting social and physical training and recreation are aided under two other instruments. They must be non-profit-making. The Secretary of State must be satisfied that the property and facilities in question are adequately secured, fully used, properly maintained, free from religious conditions limiting their use, and open to HMIs. Such organizations include : national associations providing primarily for people aged eighteen and over; local associations putting up community centres, playing fields and the like; the headquarters of national voluntary youth organizations which because of the non-local character do not attract

[1] Social studies were taken over by the SSRC in 1966

grant from authorities; and local youth groups needing capital to obtain premises.

The other two codes of regulations are for organizations looking after the disabled and handicapped, and for those conducting research and other services.

The Secretary of State in England and Wales also makes awards directly to individuals, but in four categories only (Table 1) : mature state scholars, educational researchers, students at university departments of education and graduates taking certain postgraduate courses in arts subjects. The last-named awards are called "state studentships", if for one year, and "major state studentships", if for two or three years. Until 1966 they were also given in social studies, but, as mentioned, this field has now been taken over by the SSRC.

In Scotland, since 1961, student awards for *all* full-time courses of university and comparable level are made by the Secretary of State.

For the sciences, grants from the research councils (DSIR, MRC, ARC, SRC, NERC and SSRC) have been mentioned. Those of the DSIR (now SRC) are of three types : "advanced course studentships" to enable graduates to take courses; "research studentships" for training in research; and "research fellowships" to established research workers.

Postgraduate awards outside the fields mentioned are left to authorities.

REPRESENTATIVES of the Secretaries of State have for many years partici-pated in certain examination schemes, notably the National Certificates and Diplomas, and have served on subject advisory committees of the City and Guilds of London Institute. The Departments have actually conducted some examinations—the Ministry, for example, part of the National Diploma in Design, and the SED the Scottish Certificate of Education—but these responsibilities are being shed. In such ways the Secretaries of State can influence the content of curricula.

The Secretaries of State are also responsible for the Victoria and Albert, Science and Royal Scottish Museums, the National Museum of Antiquities, the National Galleries of Scotland and the National Library of Scotland. These are the only educational establishments under their direct administra-tion (though the Royal College of Art was until 1948). They also aid certain local museums.

POLICY, SUGGESTIONS AND ADVICE are issued in the brief publications of the Secretaries of State : "White Papers" include statements of general government policy; Pamphlets contain guidance to authorities and teachers; Building Bulletins provide news and advice to authorities; and Circulars and Administrative Memoranda, only some of which are on sale to the public, disseminate decisions and opinions on a wide variety of topics. Through the Inspectorate, also, the Secretaries of State are able to spread their influence. HMIs write pamphlets and arrange courses for teachers by which new ideas are spread through the profession. Of course the Secretaries of State are themselves influenced, too, by authorities, teachers, inspectors, voluntary bodies and so on, with whom there may have been considerable consultation before the issue of a Circular. As mentioned, they also appoint members of statutory and other national advisory councils.

Control of authorities

The Secretaries of State have three normal ways of controlling authorities. These are similar to those already described.

First, as has been mentioned, authorities' Schemes of Further Education (and Plans for Primary and Secondary Schools, too) must, according to the Acts, be APPROVED by him.

In England and Wales the Schemes have never been approved in one piece, but only bit by bit. What actually happened was that surveys of the areas were made and Schemes drawn up; but it was impossible at that time to carry them out, and undesirable to crystallize future intentions too early and for too long ahead in a period of rapid change. So they were examined at the Ministry, modifications were suggested and agreed, and finally individual items were approved in order of importance. Some authorities expressed considerable disagreement with the Minister. After further discussion the approved items were divided into instalments and put into annual building programmes. The latter are now what the Secretary of State actually approves. New proposals, not in a Scheme at all, or departures from it, can be made at any time, but must be approved before they can be carried out.

In Scotland the Schemes are now submitted under Section 7 of the Education (Scotland) Act, 1962. Amending Schemes are submitted annually. There is no prescribed time limit on the period for which approval is given. The Schemes are more detailed than in England and Wales. They cover courses, and not only all advanced evening courses held in day centres but also all daytime courses including non-advanced. Thus control is tighter and more centralized, though a great deal of consultation and discussion, both formal and informal, goes on.

With this power the Secretaries of State can control the system closely, steering its progress in the direction they choose. For example, they can decide whether the main effort in a given year is to be in the sphere of nursery schools, infant schools or technical colleges. In practice, following the tradition of partnership with authorities, they usually exercise it only at certain key points, notably the control of capital investment, the designation of colleges, and the prevention of "extravagent" building by limiting its cost per square foot of approved accommodation (or per average nightly attendance in the case of youth clubs).

Because of the widespread need for new buildings in the presence of a chronic scarcity of building resources, the control of capital investment is the most important of these. Therefore this control has to be fitted more closely into the government's overall policies than the others. The nation's building needs are far greater than the capacity of the building industries to satisfy them. The government cannot regulate, except within narrow limits, the *overall size* of the public share of building, as opposed to that of private customers, without reimposing building controls. It can only decide what would be reasonable public expenditure in the light of the need to avoid a too inflationary competition with private investors for the available resources. But it can closely regulate the *distribution* of this share among the different sectors of public expenditure, according to its scale of priorities within public investment. Therefore the Treasury annually allots to each Secretary of State a portion of the public share by telling him the total amount of capital expenditure he may approve. The Secretaries of State then allocate this sum among their own and the authorities' projected capital expenditure.

In February 1965, capital projects in authorities' building programmes (including built-in but not movable furniture and equipment) were of three kinds according to their expected cost :

(1) under £2,000 ("miniminor projects"), which did not require the Secretary of State's approval and need not be charged to the authority's allocation, but must be reported to him;

(2) between £2,000 and £20,000 ("minor projects"), for which the Secretary of State approved an overall sum ("minor works allocation") which the authority might not exceed but was free to distribute as it liked among such projects; and

(3) over £20,000 ("major projects") which must be individually approved by the Secretary of State and charged to a separate individual allocation. For Youth Service building, projects costing over £2,000 needed separate approval.

It was then announced, however, that the "miniminor" category was to be abolished and its projects treated as "minor". On 1st April 1965 the limit for Youth Service building was raised to £2,500.

Separate pieces of equipment costing over £500 also need approval.

In this way the parameters or dimensions of education are regulated by the Treasury in accord with the general policies of the government.

Second, the Acts also empower the Secretaries of State to make certain ORDERS IN COUNCIL and REGULATIONS which are binding on authorities. Through these the Minister in England and Wales has controlled such things as the salaries and conditions of employment of teachers, medical and dental inspection and treatment of younger students, purchase of expensive equipment, composition of governing bodies, distribution of advanced courses, awards to students and pooling arrangements for certain costs. He also approves the plans for new building and alterations to buildings, though a wide field of freedom is left to authorities and architects in matters of design. Unlike those for schools, standards of Further Education premises are only loosely supervised. The distribution of advanced courses, however, is under tight control (see pp. 138–9). Most of these regulations date from 1959 or later and belong to the "block-grant" system which came in with the Local Government Act of 1958; and at some points the Minister had relaxed his control in comparison with what it had been under the earlier "percentage-grant" system.

Third, the Secretaries of State issue SUGGESTIONS AND ADVICE in the ways already mentioned. Most of their Circulars and Administrative Memoranda are addressed primarily to authorities.

The Secretaries of State also have certain "big stick" RESERVE POWERS. In England and Wales, if he believes, for example, that the standards of provision laid down in his regulations are not being observed, the Secretary of State can ask the Minister of Housing and Local Government to reduce an authority's "block grant", subject to the permission of Parliament. In this way, however, the measure of financial control which the Secretary of State now has is less delicate and effective than before 1958 when the Minister could pinpoint for grant aid individual items of an authority's Scheme (though, in fact, he seldom did). In Scotland the Secretary of State himself controls the "block grant" through his Development Department.

Finally, if he thinks fit, either Secretary of State can himself issue direct orders to an authority, or even, as a last resort, take over its duties entirely.

Thus the Secretaries of State are potentially very powerful, at least on paper. In practice, however, they exercise this power only in the spheres of finance and organization, chiefly of finance, and never (at least hitherto) in curricular matters. The intention expressed in the Explanatory Memorandum to the Education Bill (1943) was that there would be no diminution in the responsibility of authorities. The power given to the Minister, said the Memorandum, was to ensure *fairness*, in

> recognition of the principle that the public system of education, though administered locally, is the nation's concern, the full benefits of which should be equally available to all alike, wherever their homes may be.

There is trouble if a Secretary of State tries to act in a manner considered autocratic or arbitrary. Authorities, teachers and voluntary associations embody well organized and influential sections of public opinion; and in the last resort, of course, the Secretaries of State, their Government and their political party are answerable through Parliament to the electorate.

How the local government secures provision

Authorities

In England and Wales, COUNTY, COUNTY BOROUGH and LONDON BOROUGH COUNCILS have set up education committees, health committees and so on, to which they delegate their powers. The pattern of local government is slightly different in Scotland. In either case the EDUCATION COMMITTEE is the effective education authority (LEA), though its decisions need final ratification by the full council. Though mainly composed of members of the council it has power to co-opt non-elected individuals from among teachers, university bodies and other sections of expert opinion. It sets up SUBCOMMITTEES for the various sectors of its education service. Council, committee and subcommittees are helped by a professional staff of advisers, inspectors and administrators under a director of education or chief education officer (CEO). The reports of their meetings ("minutes") are usually confidential in England and Wales, but must be available to electors in Scotland.

Counties in England and Wales may be divided into DIVISIONS, corresponding with smaller local-government areas, within which education is administered by a DIVISIONAL EXECUTIVE. On this sit members of the county council and of the local borough, urban and rural district councils, together with co-opted members. They employ a staff under a divisional education officer (DEO). Their powers are limited to administrative matters, as laid down in the "Scheme of Divisional Administration" drawn up by the county council and approved by the Secretary of State. All deal with primary and secondary education, and some, with the Secretary of State's permission, deal with Further. There are no divisional executives in Scotland.

Boroughs which had a population of over 60,000 on 30th June 1939, or others at the discretion of the Secretary of State, may be made EXCEPTED DISTRICTS. This means that their councils have been "excepted" from the county's Scheme of Divisional Administration within which they would otherwise have been divisional executives. An excepted district has wider powers than a divisional executive; for example, it may levy its own rate for educational purposes.

There are associations of councils, education committees and education officers. Scotland has its own.

Activities and establishments

These are dealt with in later chapters but may be briefly introduced here. The headings under which authorities' Schemes of Further Education are set out, already shown in Chapter 1, give a good idea of them. "Full-time and part-time education" is mainly in institutions which authorities themselves provide. It includes "general provision" which is in technical, commercial and art colleges and departments, domestic-studies colleges and departments, men's and women's institutes and centres, evening institutes, literary institutes, colleges of adult education, working-men's colleges, residential colleges, day continuation schools and centres, recreation centres, community centres, village colleges and village halls. "Vocational training" is mainly in technical, commercial and art colleges and "liberal education" mainly in the others, but both can be provided in the same institution. Extra-mural departments of universities and local committees of responsible bodies can be aided. "Agricultural and horticultural education" is in farm institutes, technical colleges and evening institutes. "County college attendance" has not yet, of course, been introduced, though one authority has maintained a compulsory day continuation centre, and some colleges are aiming at the same kind of education with voluntary students. The county colleges will contain activities of the kind found in any of the others or in youth clubs. They have been thought of as separate establishments, but may have to be housed in other colleges or even in schools; or they may be deliberately joined with existing colleges.

"Social and recreational provision for leisure time" is in youth clubs, youth centres and adult community centres of several types, or in any of the institutions mentioned above. Playing fields, athletics tracks, camping sites, gymnasia, swimming baths, theatres, music rooms, drama and craft centres, concert halls and ballrooms are (or are intended to be) provided. Aided voluntary bodies play a greater part in this sector.

Authorities may also provide or aid special facilities for handicapped or disabled people, patients in hospitals, persons in prisons, Borstal institutions or detention centres or released therefrom on licence, and young people detained in approved schools. The Scottish Act particularly mentions blind people.

Short courses for teachers, youth leaders, wardens and so on may be held in any kind of establishment.

Thus there is much flexibility in the provision and use of establishments, and various combinations of kinds of education may be found in a single one.

Erection of buildings

One authority (Manchester) has had considerable experience of employing its own direct labour for the building of schools and colleges. Most, however, are less enterprising and engage in contracts with building companies. The company's offer, containing the price and estimated time to be taken, is called its "tender". Authorities usually invite the submission of tenders from competing firms in their area, accepting the one they consider the best value. Of course the Secretary of State's approval is needed before the work can start, as already explained.

Much effort has been made by the Ministers and authorities to obtain cheaper and quicker erection of educational buildings and to improve their design. As a result of guidance given to authorities based on the work of the Ministry's Architects and Building Branch it was possible between 1949 and 1956 to halve the real capital cost of each new place provided in schools and to bring about comparable improvements in the design of college buildings.

Authorities have also been taking their own steps, encouraged by the Ministers, to take advantage of the new industrialized methods of building. Several have formed associations or "consortia" in order to bring about economies by increasing the scale of their operations and standardizing their requirements. There are six of these consortia. The first, Consortium of Local Authorities Special Programme (CLASP), formed in 1957, contains twelve English and Scottish authorities, the Departments, the Ministry of Public Building and Works and the University of York. Its purposes are to use and control a prefabricated system reducing the need for skilled labour on the site, to regulate the standardization of components and to develop and extend the system. The buildings are constructed of units using specific materials and design patterns. A Second Consortium of Local Authorities (SCOLA), formed in 1961, contains another nine English authorities. Three others were set up in 1963 : the South Eastern Architects' Collaboration (SEAC), Consortium for Method Building (CMB) and Consortium, Local Authorities, Wales (CLAW); and another in 1965 : Organisation of North Western Authorities for Rationalised Design (ONWARD). There is also a consortium for science equipment (CLEAPSE) and another for school meals equipment (LASMEC).

Following his White Paper of 1963 the Minister of Public Building and Works has set up and aided an independent National Building Agency to advise clients on problems concerned with pooling and collating their building programmes.

Grants to students

In England and Wales before 1st September 1962 authorities had the power, but not the duty, under Section 81 of the 1944 Act and Regulations of 1945 and 1948, to award scholarships and other benefits. These were classified as "major" and "lesser" (or "minor") awards, sometimes called by their older names of "scholarships" and "bursaries" respectively. They are now called "full-value" and "lesser-value" awards. They could be given for courses at any establishment or level.

Authorities varied in their practice. In deciding whether to give an award they were often not satisfied with the simple fact of an applicant's acceptance into his chosen course, but took all kinds of other things into consideration, such as examination marks, head teachers' reports, additional examinations, interviews and (it was commonly believed) age, sex or marital state of applicants; and they were not bound to give any reason for a refusal. Variable too were the amounts given; major awards were on a standard sliding scale based on parental income, but others were not. While university students usually got major awards, those at colleges of Further Education often had to be content with lesser ones or nothing. The Minister drew attention to this injustice in Circular 252 (1952); and in Circular 285 (1955) her successor asked that full-time students pursuing comparable courses at colleges should be given the same rate of grant as those at universities. After consulting with employers through the Federation of British Industries he urged in Administrative Memorandum 567 (1958) that sandwich students whose fees or salaries whilst at college were not being paid by their firms should be given grants too, and that these should be assessed in the same way as those of university students, by ignoring earnings outside the period of full-time study.

By the end of 1958 these recommendations had had some effect: between 1959–60 and 1961–2 the number of students at colleges who were currently receiving full-value awards from their authorities for courses of degree standard rose from over 7,000 to over 10,000, and for lower-level courses from over 12,000 to over 14,000. Current lesser awards rose slightly to 11,000. This was a higher rate of increase than that of the Ministry's own awards. However, in 1961–2 the total number of full-time students from within the UK working for recognized qualifications in the colleges was 67,500 so only just over half were getting any grant; and of this total about 45,000 were in their first year, yet authorities gave under 12,000 new full-value awards and under 6,000 new lesser awards; and no one knows how many did not become full-time students at all because they had been refused a grant.

One suspects that the non-advanced students and those under eighteen were mainly the ones left out; but of course it is very difficult for authorities to judge unqualified applicants for courses where no specific qualifications for admission are demanded.

The matter was next considered by the Anderson Committee. Following the latter's report the Minister in Circular 5/61 asked authorities to give awards automatically to all applicants with certain qualifications who had been accepted into courses of first-degree level, whether at universities or at colleges, and to give generously in other cases also. But this request did not receive universal agreement; and it was not everywhere complied with either, even for university applicants, and even after Ministry intervention in specific cases. Therefore in 1962 it was enforced with a new Act and regulations. At the same time the scales of allowance were raised and the proportion contributed by parents reduced. Loans could also be made, but were intended to be very exceptional.

But in its new regulations (amended in 1963 and twice in 1964, amplified in Circulars 16/64 and 18/64, and replaced with a consolidated code in 1965) the Government did not accede to the Anderson Committee's majority recommendation to abolish the parental contribution altogether. The sliding scale (or "means test"), therefore, remains. The regulations have been criticized on other grounds too. Married students aged under twenty-five or who marry during their course are not entitled to any allowance for dependants. Awards are automatic only to applicants with specific qualifications and for a specific kind of course. On the other hand, to take a few examples : a holder of an Ordinary National Certificate whose marks averaged less than 60 per cent in three main subjects; an applicant accepted to a course of lower than degree level (such as a certificate in social sciences or the Pre-diploma in Art and Design), or shorter than three years full-time or sandwich; a graduate; (before Circular 16/64) an entrant with only the minimum qualifications needed to begin the Diploma in Art and Design; a typical student at a residential college of Adult Education; a candidate accepted at a university through the Matriculation for Persons of Mature Years; an unfortunate who has failed a degree or teacher-training course or has had to repeat a year (perhaps only through illness); or even someone who has already completed two years of full-time study since leaving school (such as a qualified teacher), does not automatically gain an award. All these, however, may be considered for one; and many do get one, although at the discretion of the authority.

How far has the situation changed since the 1962 Act and ensuing regulations? It has been mentioned that just before the Act (1961–2) just over half of the 67,500 full-time students from within UK working for recognized qualifications in the colleges were getting a grant. By 1964–5 this total of students had risen to 113,400; and there were 70,300 current awards in the colleges, or *well over* half. Taking full-time students in their first year of an advanced course, we find that in 1961–2 there were 11,000; whilst authorities made 4,600 new full-value awards for courses of first-degree and comparable standard. In 1964–5 the comparable figures were 18,300 and 11,000, showing a considerable increase in the proportion of full-value grants to students eligible for them. Works-based students taking comparable courses must also be aided where their firms are paying less than the full-value award. According to this rough estimate, therefore, there has been an increase in the assistance given, at least for those actually taking the courses.

Clearly there should be limits to public expenditure, and some think that the system is already too generous. However, it can be seen that in 1964–5 there were still well over one-third of students accepted into full-time advanced courses in the colleges who apparently did not get a full-value grant. An AAI questionnaire showed that not all authorities in 1963–4 gave one for the Diploma in Art and Design (though they must now). This does not take into account the position of the non-advanced or part-time student. Thus there are still plenty of kinds of applicant whose position may be no better than before the 1962 Act. And the suggested reintroduction of loans would increase the difficulties of the poorer ones.

In Scotland, as already mentioned, the Secretary of State gives all awards for university and comparable full-time and sandwich courses, so that authorities are responsible only for grants (called "bursaries") to school pupils, part-time students and those doing non-advanced courses.

Financial resources

To pay for such activities and establishments a county or county borough council has three main sources of income.

First, it receives an annual "block grant" from the Exchequer, through the Ministry of Housing and Local Government or Scottish Development Department. This is adjusted in accord with a formula which makes it up to just over 60 per cent of the council's whole expenditure over a two-year period.

Within the limits of its statutory and other obligations the council can distribute it as it wishes amongst the education and other services it provides, though the obligations render such freedom more apparent than real. The grant is supplemented in the case of poor authorities by a "rate-deficiency" grant.

Second, a council can borrow, either from the Public Works Loan Board or on the open market. Most cases of either sort require the approval of the Minister of Housing and Local Government or Secretary of State for Scotland. They commit the council, of course, to interest charges as well as capital repayment.

Third, within its powers, it can levy its own local property tax or "rates".

In England and Wales a council's education committee has in addition the following subsidiary sources of revenue:

(4) recoupment from a pool (into which all authorities contribute a proportion) of its costs in providing education at the advanced level (including teacher training) and research;

(5) recoupment from another pool of its costs in providing education at the non-advanced level for students who do not belong to the area

of any local authority (such as overseas students or children of parents living overseas);

(6) recoupment from appropriate other authorities of its costs in providing education at the non-advanced level for students belonging to areas other than its own;

(7) repayment by the Prison Commissioners of the full cost of any educational facilities provided for persons in prison, Borstal or detention centre, or released on licence;

(8) contributions from industry and other donations; and

(9) fees and charges.

The pools are regulated by the Secretary of State in accordance with formulæ laid down in his regulations. Capital projects costing between £2,000 and £20,000 which are solely for advanced work may be charged to the appropriate pool instead of to the minor-works allocation if an authority so desires.

In Scotland the cost of all daytime Further Education is pooled; but (7), (8) and (9) are as in England and Wales.

In England and Wales there is no pool for non-advanced courses. What and whom to charge when a student comes into a non-advanced course from an area in which he or his parent pays rates to another authority has therefore been a thorny problem. To charge the student the full cost, which is always much higher than the fees alone, would be unfair to residents in worse-provided areas. Authorities are therefore allowed by the Education (Miscellaneous Provisions) Act of 1953 to recoup the balance of their costs by "extra-district" payments from their neighbours, provided that the neighbouring authority has given its consent to the student's attendance. Refusal of consent, however, has led to injustices to students besides causing much administrative work; some authorities have therefore preferred a system of "free trade" in which it is agreed to allow all applicants a free choice and to accept automatic responsibility for extra-district payments. This was in fact recommended by a special advisory committee set up by the authorities in 1955, and the Minister has tended to favour it. Not all authorities, therefore, take advantage of the right to refuse consent. Some, however, particularly smaller authorities near large county boroughs, fear that their own colleges might be handicapped by "free trade", and residents in such areas have to produce a permit from their home authority before colleges outside will enrol them. Of course the problem does not arise for advanced students because of the pool.

For employed students attending integrated courses of industrial education and training prescribed by industrial training boards (see Chapter 5), authorities are encouraged to charge employers a full "economic" fee.

Fees are not normally charged to full-time students aged under eighteen.

Of the total spent by local government at the time of writing, education takes by far the largest share : about 40 per cent (making £1,223 million in 1964–5); but Further Education takes only about one-tenth of this. Probably about two-fifths of the total expenditure comes out of rates. Although authorities have been allowed to charge what fees they liked since 1959, only about one-fifteenth of their expenditure on Further Education is met by fees. Most of the rest comes from the "block" and rate-deficiency grants which are raised by taxation. These two grants reimbursed authorities in England and Wales with about two-thirds of their educational expenditure in 1964–5. Obviously, therefore, after taking central-government expenditure on education into account, less than one-third of *all* public expenditure on education comes out of rates.

Whether authorities should be fewer and larger than at present may become an important problem with the growth of higher education in the authorities' sector (see Chapter 6).

Voluntary organizations

The third pillar of the system of Further Education is the work of voluntary bodies. Of these there are eight main types : industry and commerce (including nationalized, co-operative and private sectors); associations working for the interests of occupational groups (such as trade unions and professional associations); associations concerned with academic disciplines; consumer-research and advisory bodies; religious bodies; organizations promoting cultural and recreational activities mainly among adults; organizations working similarly among young people; and bodies helping the handicapped and disabled. These are not dealt with specifically in this book but are referred to where relevant.

Advisory bodies

National

It was realized from the outset that in the difficult job of securing the provision of education the Ministers and authorities would need advice. For England and Wales the Board of Education Act of 1899 had set up the CONSULTATIVE COMMITTEE, some of whose reports were to become so well known (the Hadow and Spens Reports, for example); but this body could deliberate only on problems on which it had been asked to deliberate by the President of the Board. In its place the 1944 Act created two CENTRAL ADVISORY COUNCILS FOR EDUCATION (CACE), one for England and one for

Wales and Monmouthshire; and these could advise the Minister not only on matters referred to them but on any other educational matter they liked. Their chairman, secretary and members are appointed by the Secretary of State, who also makes regulations governing their constitution and conduct. The 1962 Act made such a council permissive in Scotland; in fact there is the ADVISORY COUNCIL ON EDUCATION IN SCOTLAND.

The 1944 Act made the Minister keep up another kind of committee too, the so-called BURNHAM COMMITTEES, to advise him on teachers' salaries in England and Wales (which, as mentioned earlier, are imposed by him on authorities). There could be any number of these committees, and have been in fact three : for teachers in schools, Further Education and farm institutes respectively. Each had to contain representatives of teachers and authorities, under an independent chairman nominated by the Minister. There was much argument as to whether the 1944 Act gave the Minister power to *amend* recommendations of the Burnham Committees, as distinct from merely accepting or rejecting them; so the Remuneration of Teachers Act, 1963, gave him this power. The Remuneration of Teachers Act, 1965, gave the Secretary of State direct representation on the committees and laid down that disagreements were to be referred to independent arbitration. Normally the Secretary of State must then implement the arbitrators' decisions; but Parliament can authorize him to substitute his own.

In Scotland, under the 1962 Act, the Secretary of State is not obliged to set up such committees; though he must consult them if they exist (and there is in fact a SCOTTISH JOINT COUNCIL FOR TEACHERS' SALARIES. However, he can at any time make his own salary award without waiting for anyone's recommendation. There is also (since the 1965 Act) a GENERAL TEACHING COUNCIL FOR SCOTLAND which will advise him as to the education, training and supply of teachers and will control their registration and discipline.

These are the *statutory* councils and committees, but several other standing councils have been set up by the Ministers and Secretaries of State (Table 2). They advise in fields such as technical, commercial and art education (NACEIC, NACAE and STECC), the development of the Youth Service (YSDC and SCCYCSS), the training and supply of teachers (NACTST and DCSTS) and the encouragement of amateur sport (SPORTS COUNCIL FOR THE UK).

The education and other Ministers have also set up numerous SPECIAL COMMITTEES, both temporary and permanent, to advise them on particular matters. These committees and their reports are usually named after their chairman.

There are also many advisory bodies set up by industries, professional associations, examining bodies and so on.

TABLE 2

SOME OFFICIAL STANDING COMMITTEES ADVISING THE SECRETARIES OF STATE ON
MATTERS CONCERNING FURTHER EDUCATION, 1965
(with year of establishment)

United Kingdom
Committee on Manpower Resources for Science and Technology (1964)
Council for Scientific Policy (1946)
Interdepartmental Committee on Training for Skill (1964)
Sports Council for the UK (1965)
Standing Advisory Committee on Grants to Students (1961)
UK Advisory Council on Education for Management (1961)

England and Wales
Advisory Committee on Handicapped Children (1945)
Committee on General Studies (1961)
National Advisory Council on Art Education (1959)
National Advisory Council on Education for Industry and Commerce (1948)
National Advisory Council on the Training and Supply of Teachers (1949)
Youth Service Development Council (1960)

England
Central Advisory Council for Education (England) (1945)

Wales
Central Advisory Council for Education (Wales) (1945)
Sports Council for Wales (1965)
Welsh Joint Education Committee (1948)

Scotland
Advisory Council on Education in Scotland (1947)
General Teaching Council for Scotland (1965)
Departmental Committee on the Supply of Teachers in Scotland (1950)
Scottish Joint Council for Teachers' Salaries (1964)
Scottish Technical Education Consultative Council (1959)
Sports Council for Scotland (1965)
Standing Committee on the Supply and Training of Teachers for Further Education
    (1957)
Standing Consultative Council on Youth and Community Service in Scotland (1959)

England: regional
East Anglian Regional Advisory Council for Further Education (1946)
London and Home Counties Regional Advisory Council for Technological Education (1946)
Northern Advisory Council for Further Education (1947)
North-western Regional Advisory Council for Further Education (1947)
Regional Advisory Council for the Organization of Further Education in the East
    Midlands (1946)
Regional Council for Further Education for the South West (1947)
Southern Regional Council for Further Education (1947)
West Midlands Regional Advisory Council for Further Education (1935)
Yorkshire Council for Further Education (1928)
Also nine regional sports councils (1965)

Sources: various.

E

TABLE 3

THE MORE IMPORTANT LEGAL INSTRUMENTS GOVERNING THE PROVISION OF FURTHER EDUCATION IN ENGLAND AND WALES IN 1965

Act of Parliament	Section(s)	Statutory instruments (if any)	Ministerial explanatory documents (if any)	Authority empowered or compelled (amended by Secretary of State for Education and Science Order, 1964)	Power or duty	Function conferred
Education Act, 1921 amended by Education Act, 1944	76, 77, 93 121			Local education authorities which were providing compulsory day continuation schools on 31st March 1947	p	To continue this provision until Section 44 of the 1944 Act (dealing with compulsory county-college provision) shall come into operation
Education Act, 1921 amended by Education Act, 1944	118 121	Social and Physical Training Grant Regulations, 1939, and Amending Regulations, 1940, 1944	Circular 51	Secretary of State for Education and Science	p	To pay grants under prescribed conditions to recognized voluntary associations providing facilities for social and physical training (such as youth organizations, youth clubs and youth centres) towards capital costs, maintenance and incidental expenses and costs of training leaders
Physical Training and Recreation Act, 1937 amended by Education Act, 1944 and by Local Government Act, 1958	3 2 1 (1) and Schedule IX		Circulars 20 (with attached pamphlet), 51 (with attached Memoranda A.W. 1 and A.W. 2 and Addendum No. 1), 350, 11/64	Secretary of State for Education and Science	p	To pay grants under prescribed conditions to voluntary bodies towards capital costs and expenses of providing facilities for physical training and recreation intended primarily for adults (such as community centres, village halls, playing fields)

TABLE 3 (*continued*)

Act of Parliament	Section(s)	Statutory instruments (if any)	Ministerial explanatory documents (if any)	Authority empowered or compelled (amended by Secretary of State for Education and Science Order, 1964)	Power or duty	Function conferred
Physical Training and Recreation Act, 1937	4, 6		Circulars 20, 51, 350, 11/64	Local authorities	p	As above
Education Act, 1944	1, 42, 43, 68, 99			Secretary of State for Education and Science	d	To secure the effective provision of Further Education by local education authorities
Education Act, 1944	7, 41			Local education authorities	d	To secure the provision for their areas of adequate facilities for Further Education
Education Act, 1944	42, 43		Circulars 133, 139 and Addenda	Local education authorities	d	To submit to the Secretary of State for Education and Science for his approval Schemes of Further Education and Plans for county colleges for their areas
Education Act, 1944 amended by Education (Miscellaneous Provisions) Act, 1948	53, 11 (1) and Schedule I, Part I		Circulars 20, 51, 350, 11/64	Local education authorities	d	To secure that facilities for Further Education in their areas include adequate provision for recreation and social and physical training

TABLE 3 (continued)

Act of Parliament	Section(s)	Statutory instruments (if any)	Ministerial explanatory documents (if any)	Authority empowered or compelled (amended by Secretary of State for Education and Science Order, 1964)	Power or duty	Function conferred
Education Act, 1944	77 (2)			Secretary of State for Education and Science	d	To cause inspections to be made of educational establishments provided by local education authorities
	77 (3)			Local education authorities	p	
Education Act, 1944	82, 83, 84		Circular 350	Local education authorities	p	To aid educational research and related activities, and universities
Education Act, 1944 amended by Local Government Act, 1958	100 (1) (a) / 62, 67 Schedules VIII and IX	Milk and Meals Grant Regulations, 1959	Circulars 302, 350, 353	Secretary of State for Education and Science	d	To pay to local education authorities the full cost of providing milk to students aged under eighteen in full-time attendance at direct-grant and maintained establishments
Education Act, 1944	100 (1) (b)	Educational Services and Research Grant Regulations, 1946		Secretary of State for Education and Science	p	To pay grants under prescribed conditions in respect of educational research and other services conducted by persons and bodies other than local education authorities

TABLE 3 *(continued)*

Act of Parliament	Section(s)	Statutory instruments (if any)	Ministerial explanatory documents (if any)	Authority empowered or compelled (amended by Secretary of State for Education and Science Order, 1964)	Power or duty	Function conferred
Education Act, 1944 *(continued)*	100 (1) (b)	Further Education (Grant) Regulations, 1959, and Amending Regulations, 1964 (twice)	Circular 7/59	Secretary of State for Education and Science	p	To pay grants under prescribed conditions in respect of facilities for Further Education provided by bodies other than local education authorities
		Special Schools and Establishments (Grant) Regulations, 1959, and Amending Regulations, 1964	Circular 352			To pay grants under prescribed conditions in respect of facilities provided by bodies other than local education authorities for the education and training of disabled and handicapped persons
Education Act, 1944 amended by Education (Miscellaneous Provisions) Act, 1948	116

11 (1) and Schedule I | | Administrative Memorandum 440 and two Addenda | Local education authorities | p | To provide educational facilities for persons in prison or released from prison on licence, and for young persons detained in Borstal institutions, detention centres and approved schools |

TABLE 3 (continued)

Act of Parliament	Section(s)	Statutory instruments (if any)	Ministerial explanatory documents (if any)	Authority empowered or compelled (amended by Secretary of State for Education and Science Order, 1964)	Power or duty	Function conferred
Education (Miscellaneous Provisions) Act, 1948	5	Provision of Clothing Regulations, 1948	Circulars 183, 350	Local education authorities	p	To lend clothing for physical training to young persons attending maintained establishments or using recreational facilities
Local Government Act, 1948	132			Local authorities	p	To spend up to the product of a sixpenny rate plus net receipts on all forms of entertainment in their areas
Education (Miscellaneous Provisions) Act, 1953	7	Local Education Authorities Recoupment (Further Education) Regulations, 1954, and Amending Regulations, 1955, 1956, 1959, 1965	Circulars 268, 350	Local education authorities	p	To recoup themselves for the cost incurred in providing Further Education at a level up to that of the Ordinary National Certificate or the General Certificate of Education (advanced level) for students not belonging to their area
Housing Act, 1957	93 (1)			Local authorities	p	To provide beneficial facilities for persons for whom housing accommodation is provided

TABLE 3 (*continued*)

Act of Parliament	Section(s)	Statutory instruments (if any)	Ministerial explanatory documents (if any)	Authority empowered or compelled (amended by Secretary of State for Education and Science Order, 1964)	Power or duty	Function conferred
Local Government Act, 1958	1 (4) and Schedule I, Part IV, para. 1	General Grants (Pooling Arrangements) Regulations, 1959	Circulars 270, 350; Administrative Memorandum 11/59	Secretary of State for Education and Science	d	To make arrangements for the pooling of expenditure by local education authorities on the provision of facilities for students who do not belong to the area of any authority on art and technical teacher-training centres; on courses at a level higher than that of the Ordinary National Certificate or General Certificate of Education (advanced level); and on research
Education Act, 1944 and Local Government Act, 1958	48 3 (4)	School Health Service Regulations, 1959	Circulars 352, 11/61	Local education authorities	d	To observe requirements prescribed by the Secretary of State for Education and Science in relation to medical and dental inspection and treatment of students aged under nineteen in maintained establishments

TABLE 3 (continued)

Act of Parliament	Section(s)	Statutory instruments (if any)	Ministerial explanatory documents (if any)	Authority empowered or compelled (amended by Secretary of State for Education and Science Order, 1964)	Power or duty	Function conferred
Local Government Act, 1958	3 (4)	Further Education (Local Education Authorities) Regulations, 1959, and Amending Regulations, 1961, 1964 (twice), 1965	Circulars 351, 5/59, 7/59, 7/59 (Addendum 1), 6/62, 11/66; Administrative Memoranda 545, 3/59; The Building Code; Building Bulletins Nos. 5, 20	Local education authorities	d	To observe standards and general requirements prescribed by the Secretary of State for Education and Science in respect of facilities for Further Education provided or assisted by local educaion authorities
Physical Training and Recreation Act, 1958	1		Circular 11/64	Local authorities	p	To make loans to voluntary bodies towards the capital costs of providing facilities for physical training and recreation intended primarily for adults
Education Act, 1962	1	University and other Awards Regulations, 1965	Circulars 4/66, 14/66; Administrative Memorandum 9/65	Local education authorities	d	To grant awards and other benefits under prescribed conditions to students undergoing first-degree and comparable courses
	2				p	To grant awards and other benefits under prescribed conditions to students undergoing courses other than those of first-degree and comparable standard

TABLE 3 (continued)

Act of Parliament	Section(s)	Statutory instruments (if any)	Ministerial explanatory documents (if any)	Authority empowered or compelled (amended by Secretary of State for Education and Science Order, 1964)	Power or duty	Function conferred
Education Act, 1962	3	State Awards Regulations, 1963	Circulars 4/66, 14/66; Administrative Memorandum 9/65	Secretary of State for Education and Science	p	To grant awards under prescribed conditions to students under-going certain postgraduate and comparable courses and to mature students undergoing certain first-degree courses
Remuneration of Teachers Act, 1965	1			Secretary of State for Education and Science	d	To set up committees to negotiate salaries of teachers
	2	Remuneration of Teachers (Farm Institutes) Order, 1965, and Remuneration of Teachers (Further Education) Order, 1965	Administrative Memorandum 17/65			To make an Order to local education authorities to pay agreed salaries to teachers
	3, 4					To determine teachers' salaries in accord with the decisions of arbitrators in the event of disagreement in a negotiating committee

Regional

In preparing their Schemes of Further Education, authorities were obliged by the Acts to consult with universities, neighbouring authorities and other interested agencies, in order to investigate needs, co-ordinate provision, make the best use of available resources and avoid waste; and the regulations made such consultation a normal part of the post-war system.

Of course the need had been felt before. A Joint Committee for Technical Education had been set up in the west of Scotland in 1901. The Yorkshire Council for Further Education, founded in 1928, was followed by similar bodies in Lancashire, Wales and the Midlands before or during the war. In art education, regional co-ordination has been in operation since 1933. In 1945 the Percy Report recommended such councils for the whole country and a year later the Minister endorsed this proposal in Circular 87.

Nine REGIONAL ADVISORY COUNCILS have been set up by authorities in England (Table 2). Authority representatives form a majority of their members, with representatives of universities, colleges, teachers, industry and HM Inspectorate making up the remainder. Their functions include: ascertaining the educational needs of their region; advising authorities thereon; consulting with industry about the needs of students; publishing information; arranging conferences and courses; encouraging research; making recommendations on the distribution of courses among the different universities and colleges in the region; providing opportunities of consultation among authorities; and maintaining contact with national advisory councils and with the Secretary of State. Since 1957, following the report of a working party, they have prepared regional patterns of advanced courses, on the basis of which they advise HM Staff Inspector responsible for approving these on behalf of the Secretary of State. For these functions they have provided themselves with academic boards and other committees.

In addition there is the WELSH JOINT EDUCATION COMMITTEE, which is a statutory "joint committee" created by the Minister. In Scotland the Secretary of State set up five regional councils in 1948 but in 1959 he replaced them by the single SCOTTISH TECHNICAL EDUCATION CONSULTATIVE COUNCIL (STECC).

In spite of these measures there is little real inter-authority planning in the sense of active co-ordination of Schemes. Joint activities are pursued, however: the building consortia have been mentioned. A considerable amount of consultation takes place through associations of authorities and officers: maintenance awards and free clothing for poor students under eighteen, for example, are worked out regionally.

Local

Authorities often set up their own ADVISORY COMMITTEES. Colleges, too, have them for departments or subjects, particularly where close relations with industry are desired.

Levels of course

Course of study may be classified into three main levels : pre-senior, senior and advanced. PRE-SENIOR courses prepare school leavers for senior ones. SENIOR extend from the first year of apprenticeship, normally at about the age of sixteen, to the ONC or A level of the GCE, inclusive. ADVANCED are above this level. "Preliminary" courses may be entirely pre-senior (as are pre-craft courses) or may overlap with senior courses (as do the G2 and G*; see later).

Because of the extension of preliminary courses leading into ONC and technician courses a new dividing line is also growing up separating the O level of the GCE, or the G2 or G* preliminary, from the start of the ONC or the T2 year.

The main dividing line is the ONC, which separates NON-ADVANCED from advanced. Advanced courses train high-grade technician and professional levels of personnel.

The term "higher education" now covers the same range as advanced but is used in the wider context of all tertiary education, so as to include provision at universities, colleges of education, and so on, as well as in establishments of Further Education. It also includes the final parts of certain technician courses for which the Secretary of State's approval is required. This is quite different from its usage in the 1902 Act, where it included secondary (see Chapter 1).

Notes on further study

For England and Wales the relevant Acts, Orders, Regulations, Circulars and some Administrative Memoranda are set out in Table 3. The main reference work is Taylor and Saunders : *The New Law of Education* (sixth edition, 1965). The Secretary of State's main publications in England and Wales are listed in *Government Publications, Sectional List No. 2,* and his Circulars and Administrative Memoranda current on 1st January are indexed annually in *List 10.* SED publications are in *Sectional List No. 36.* Statutory instruments are listed monthly and annually by HMSO.

For short accounts and introductions to the system see also the *Notes* to Chapter 1. The effects of Further Education (Scotland) Regulations, 1959, were reviewed in Scottish Circular 405 (1959), and those of the Education (Scotland) Act, 1962, in Scottish Circular 514 (1962).

The *Twelfth Report from the Select Committee on Estimates, session 1952–53* and *Seventh Report, session 1956–57* contained useful memoranda on technical education and Youth Service grants respectively, as they were then.

On government and public finance generally there is of course a large literature. Useful recent textbooks are Gladden : *British Public Service Administration* (1961) and Wilson : *The British System of Government* (1963). On paying for education see the Ministry's *Reports on Education*, Nos. 3 (1963) and 13 (1964). Administrative, financial and economic aspects of higher education were gone into in the Robbins Report, especially Appendix Four (1963); see also Appendix Two (A) (1964). Short accounts were in the COI's reference pamphlets.

On the organization and work of the Ministries see Kathryn Heath : *Ministries of Education* (1962) (which contained small errors). The Welsh Department was described in Circular 22 (W) (1958). The new Department of Education and Science was announced in Circular 6/64; for further detail see *Hansard* for 11th and 12th March 1964.

Divisional Schemes of Administration were dealt with in Circulars 5 (1944) and 344 (1958).

Building procedures, cost limits and standards are laid down in the Minister's *The Building Code* which is a collection of regulations, Circulars and Administrative Memoranda thereon; this was introduced with Circular 6/62. Much information and guidance is in Building Bulletins Nos. 5 (1951, 1955, 1959) and 20 (1961). See also reports and pamphlets by authorities : for example, Hertfordshire's *Building for Education 1948–61* (1962), and *Building for Education in Staffordshire 1950 to 1963* (1963). On the use of rationalized building methods see the Wood Report (1944), the two Cleary Reports (1946 and 1948), the Minister's Pamphlet No. 33, especially Appendix 1 (1957), *The Story of CLASP* (Building Bulletin No. 19, 1961), SCOLA's *SCOLA*, the White Paper *A National Building Agency* (1963) and Circular 1/64. The basic recommendations were in the second Cleary Report.

For the Minister's policy on authorities' grants to students in England and Wales before the 1962 Act see Circulars 26 (1945), 104 (1946), 161 (1948), 167 (1948), 247 (1952), 252 (1952), 263 (1953), 285 (1955), 315 (1956), 335 (1958) and 5/61; and Administrative Memoranda 425 (1952), 502 (1955) and 567 (1958). Circular 167 dealt with correspondence courses. Then came the Anderson Report (1960) and the Education Act, 1962. For the Minister's policy after this see Circulars 4/62, 7/62, 9/62 and two

Addenda (1963), 8/63, 11/63, 5/64, 15/64 and Addendum (1965), 16/64, 18/64, 4/66 and 14/66; and Administrative Memorandum 7/63. Circulars 4/66 and 14/66 followed the 1965 regulations, which were amended in 1966.

Grants given by the Secretary of State and research councils in England and Wales were explained in Circulars 5/65 and 14/66. See also the DSIR's (SRC's) annual *Studentships and Fellowships*.

On grants to employed students see the FBI's *Policy Statement* (1958, 1963) and Administrative Memorandum 7/63.

The whole system of student grants in England and Wales was explained in the DES's *Reports on Education*, No. 24 (1965) and in Circulars 5/65, 4/66 and 14/66. The DES also issues an annual *Grants to Students*. The SED, too, issues an annual *Guide to Students' Allowances*. Information about all sorts of grant including charities was contained in Merle Hastings: *Grants for Higher Education* (1964).

Statistics of authorities' grants to students in England and Wales are given in the DES's annual *Statistics of Education, Part 2* and *List 71*.

The NUS case against loans was given in a duplicated report (1965).

For the Minister's policy on authorities' fees before the 1958 Act see Circulars 210 (1949), 242 (1951), 283 (1954) and 307 (1956). Fees for industrial training were discussed in Scottish Memorandum 35/1966.

Details of national and regional advisory councils are to be found in the annual and other reports. Regional councils are listed (with addresses) in works of reference such as the annual *Year Book of Technical Education and Careers in Industry* and *Education Authorities Directory and Annual* and the DES's *Further Education for School Leavers* (1966). Examples of the setting-up of local committees have been reported in the ITC's *Co-operation between Industry and Education* (1960) and discussed in the FBI's *The Technical Colleges and their Government* (1960). A wider study was PEP's *Advisory Committees in British Government* (1960). Shorter accounts of the pattern in England and Wales were the DES's *Reports on Education*, No. 9 (1965) and the Secretary of State's *Education in 1964*, pp. 17–20 (1965). The personnel of STECC and SCCYCSS is given annually in *Education in Scotland in* . . . . The General Teaching Council for Scotland was explained in Scottish Circular 601 (1965).

On professional bodies see Millerson: *The Qualifying Associations* (1964).

Public relations were the subject of Circular 343 (1958) and NACEIC's Alexander Report (introduced with Circular 17/64).

Some important voluntary associations are listed in *Year Book of Technical Education and Careers in Industry*, *Year Book* of NIAE, annual report of SCNVYO, and so on.

The science research councils after the Science and Technology Act, 1965, were described in the DES's *Report on Civil Science* (1966).

CHAPTER 4

ESTABLISHMENTS FOR FURTHER EDUCATION

Definition

An "ESTABLISHMENT" is defined in the Secretary of State's regulations as an organization which has acquired land, buildings, furniture and/or equipment for the principal purpose of providing educational facilities. In this book we are confined to institutions coming within the definition adopted in Chapter 1, namely, those maintained or assisted by the two Secretaries of State or by local education authorities. As already mentioned, however, certain establishments which have until recently conformed to this definition, but now do not, are included for convenience.

Scottish differences

The Scottish system was pioneered by the Central Institutions, large establishments aided by direct grant from the Secretary of State. In England and Wales, on the other hand, authorities have led the way. Another difference is that the Scottish pattern of differentiation of work as between central and local institutions is even more varied than the English; thus the terms "National", "Regional", "Area" and "Local", as used for colleges in England and Wales (see later), would have little meaning in Scotland; and Scottish establishments, as a rule, have no precise English or Welsh equivalents. There is less support from Scottish employers for day release than in England.

These differences arise from the fact that economic development in Scotland has been more uneven than in England and has resulted in concentrations of industry and population in a few places surrounded by large sparsely populated areas. In Scotland a higher proportion of the finance of Further Education comes direct from Exchequer sources. As there has always been a drain of Scots-trained personnel to England, this does not seem unfair.

Scotland: direct-grant colleges

Central Institutions

These date from 1901, when the Scottish Education Department (as it was then), whilst aiding "continuation classes" with grants, began to exempt some of them from direct administrative control. They were given statutory recognition in 1908. There are now thirteen (Table 6), of which ten have continued to be under the SED; but three were transferred in 1912 to the Board of Agriculture for Scotland, which became, in 1928, the Department of Agriculture and Fisheries for Scotland, under which they are now. They enjoy substantial autonomy under independent and widely representative governing bodies, but work closely with the Department concerned. Some are connected with single industries ("monotechnic"), others with a wide range; and some are "national" in character (such as the Scottish Woollen Technical College) whilst others are "regional". They are mainly orientated towards professional qualifications and therefore contain advanced and full-time work and have close links with universities. There were 6,000 full-time students at fourteen colleges in 1964–5. The Robbins Committee recommended that either these links be strengthened or the Institutions be given university status in some other way. As a result, Heriot-Watt College, Edinburgh, was transferred to the University Grants Committee in 1965. Two others had already done this between 1949 and 1951 (see p. 119) and another two in 1964 (see p. 126).

Residential college of Adult Education

There is one only, Newbattle Abbey, Dalkeith, which has been aided since its opening in 1937, and more substantially since the McClelland Report (1952). Its general character resembles that of its English counterparts, the main provision being one-year full-time courses in the humanities for older persons who have missed the chance of higher education at the normal age. There were seventy-one such students in 1963–4. It also runs short courses lasting one or two weeks.

Other direct-grant establishments

There were six smaller establishments directly aided through the SED in 1965 (Table 6).

TABLE 4

TYPES OF EDUCATIONAL ESTABLISHMENT IN GREAT BRITAIN, 1966

I. *Independent*
   Receiving no financial aid from public funds

 1. *Recognized as efficient*
    Governing bodies have sought and obtained recognition by the Ministry of Education—Department of Education and Science as efficient after inspection by HM Inspectors

 2. *Other independent establishments*
    Have not sought or obtained such recognition

II. *Grant-aided*
   Receiving financial aid from public funds

 1. *Direct-grant*
    Aided by payments from central government to governing bodies

    (a) From Department of Education and Science or Scottish Education Department

    (b) From other government departments

 2. *Maintained*

    (a) *By local education authorities*

       (i) *Voluntary*
           Initiative voluntary but receiving financial aid from authority, with or without some measure of control

       (ii) *County*
            Controlled and financed by authority or authorities

    (b) *By other local authorities*

TABLE 5

TYPES OF GRANT-AIDED FURTHER EDUCATION ESTABLISHMENT IN GREAT BRITAIN, 1966

I. *Assisted or maintained by either Secretary of State*

 1. *Providing mainly formal education*

    (a) *Direct-grant*
        Central Institutions (Scotland only)
        The Royal College of Art
        National colleges (England only)
        Agricultural colleges (England only)
        Residential colleges of Adult Education
        Forester training school (Scotland)
        Other direct-grant establishments

    (b) *Set up by organizations promoting liberal education for adults*

       (i) *By responsible bodies*
           Extra-mural departments of universities and university colleges
           Voluntary associations
           Joint bodies

       (ii) *By other national voluntary associations*

 2. *Providing mainly for social and physical training and recreation*

    (a) *For persons aged eighteen and over*
        Community centres
        Village halls
        Playing fields, etc.

Table 5 *(continued)*

    (b) *For persons under eighteen*
       Establishments set up by national voluntary youth organizations
  3. *Providing for the disabled or handicapped*
  4. *Conducting research and other services*

II. *Assisted or maintained by local education authorities*
  1. *With attendance compulsory by statute*
      Day continuation school (Rugby only)
      (County colleges, when introduced, England and Wales)
      (Junior colleges, when introduced, Scotland)
  2. *With attendance not compulsory by statute*
    (a) *Major establishments* (England and Wales only)
       Technical colleges
         Local
         Area
         Regional
       Colleges of commerce
       Art establishments
       Farm institutes
       Residential colleges and centres of Adult Education
       Other maintained major establishments
    (b) Further education centres (Scotland only)
    (c) Farm schools (Scotland only)
    (d) Evening institutes
    (e) *Establishments for social and physical training and recreation*
       Community centres
       Village halls
       Playing fields, etc.
       Youth clubs and centres
  3. *Providing for the disabled or handicapped*
      (None reported at present)

Scotland: forester training school

There were two of these in 1965, under the Forestry Commission (which, as mentioned earlier, is supervised in Scotland by the Secretary of State), but one was to close in July.

Scotland: establishments maintained by authorities

Further education centres

These have been in existence since 1892. In the past most of their classes have been held in the evenings; but there has been much growth of daytime work, particularly full-time pre-employment, first-year apprenticeship and

F

Scottish Certificate of Education (SCE) courses and part-time courses for apprentice craftsmen and technicians. Some of the day work, mainly non-advanced but including advanced, has been taken over from Central Institutions; but there is much local variation, depending partly on the degree of support given by local employers. Courses vary from elementary to degree-level. Centres with their own new or converted buildings are often called technical colleges or institutes; but others operate only in the evenings in school premises as do evening institutes in England and Wales; and a few use the premises of firms. There are about 80 day centres and over 1,000 evening centres. They cannot readily be divided into distinct categories.

Farm schools

There were eight of these in 1965, providing mainly residential courses in agricultural and related subjects lasting from one to four years. Much of their work is secondary; but five cater for young people who have left school.

England and Wales: direct-grant colleges

The Royal College of Art

The only direct-grant college of art in England and Wales opened in 1837 in Somerset House as a school of design under the Board of Trade, and moved to South Kensington in 1857. The Victoria and Albert Museum was an offshoot of the same plan. Its function was intended to be the training of craftsmen in the decorative industries, especially silk, ceramics, furniture and building, but it also developed activities in the fine arts and the training of art teachers. It has passed through many reorganizations, becoming a limited company in 1951. Its present functions are to provide advanced teaching and to conduct research in the fine arts and in the principles of art and design in relation to industrial and commercial processes. It does not now train teachers. It is governed by a council which may found and finance awards, grant diplomas, sell goods and designs, publish and sell literature or acquire land. The Secretary of State appoints the chairman and the majority of this council, who then co-opt the remaining members. The staffing establishment, too, is determined by the Secretary of State, who must also approve the appointment of principal, the salary scales of staff, the fees charged and the overall expenditure. The College is divided into Faculties or Departments of Fine Arts, Graphic and Interior Design, Industrial Design, and General Studies. There were 501 full-time students at the beginning of the 1965–6 year. The Robbins Report recommended that it be given university status.

The College of Aeronautics

This was founded at Cranfield in 1946. Unlike others it was established from the first by the government, the Minister of Education being made responsible for it. Its governing body includes representatives of Commonwealth governments, UK government departments, Services, universities, professional institutions, aeronautical societies and industry. Its chief purpose is to provide scientific, engineering and technical training at postgraduate level for responsible positions in the aircraft industry, civil aviation, the Services, education and research. More recently it has extended its activities into non-aeronautical fields, adding in 1953 a Work Study School, and in 1961 an Advanced School of Automobile Engineering founded jointly by the Minister and the Society of Motor Manufacturers and Traders. There were 289 full-time students in 1965–6. The Robbins Report recommended that it be brought within the ambit of the university grants system, but without degree-awarding powers because of its small size. This was done as from 1st April 1965.

Colleges of advanced technology

The "CATs" were the spearhead of Further Education between 1956 and 1965. Their function was to provide a substantial volume of technological and allied education, done mainly in full-time and sandwich courses, relevant to a broad range of industries, exclusively at a level above that of the Ordinary National Certificate ("advanced"), including graduate and postgraduate work and research. They contained 14,000 full-time and sandwich students and 9,000 part-time students in 1964–5.

Some were nineteenth-century foundations—Bristol goes back to 1856—and until very recent years all have been controlled and largely maintained by authorities. They were selected by the Minister because they were considered ready for special treatment designed to develop them in a relatively short period into national institutions having the quality and status of universities. Although one (Loughborough) had been under direct grant since 1952, it was intended in the White Paper of 1956 that the others would be left under authorities. On 1st April 1962, however, they were put by trust deeds under new independent governing bodies containing representatives of the Ministry, industry and commerce, authorities, higher education, scientific and professional interests and college teachers. The

Minister took over financial responsibility, though the governors were free to spend widely within estimates approved by him. The Minister had to approve fees, new courses, acquisition of land and buildings, purchase of items costing over £1,000 and the establishment of senior staff.

Following the Robbins Report the ten CATs, together with Heriot-Watt College, were transferred to the University Grants Committee on 1st April 1965 and have therefore passed out of our present scope. Nine of these eleven became separate universities and the other two became colleges of existing universities. Most have changed their names, so that there is no longer such a thing as a college of advanced technology.

National Colleges

These are monotechnics supplying certain important industries which need specialized technical and technological manpower but offer too few students to sustain locally provided courses. They may be established when the Secretary of State receives a specific request from an industry, which in return must co-operate by taking a prominent part in the college government, releasing students and staff, paying students' fees and maintenance and providing equipment. Of the seven which have been founded, the first, Horology (opened in 1947), was closed in 1960 and its courses in instrument technology taken over by Northampton CAT, London. The other six have all recently acquired or moved into new buildings; but some are associated with Regional Colleges (as in Table 21). Student numbers have remained small (totalling 800 full-time and sandwich in 1964-5).

Agricultural colleges

These were transferred from the auspices of the Ministry of Agriculture, Fisheries and Food to the Department of Education and Science on 1st April 1964. There are five, all in England; but one (the Royal Agricultural College, Cirencester) receives no aid from public funds (though, of course, many of its students do). They provide mainly one-year, two-year and three-year full-time residential courses to students who have already had practical experience on a farm for a year or more. One (Studley College) is for women only.

Residential colleges of Adult Education

All five of these were established by private effort. They provide full-time residential courses in liberal studies lasting usually one or two years. The students are normally working men and women whose education has been curtailed, many, for example, having left school at fourteen. No formal educational qualifications are required for admission, entrants being selected mainly on their record, references, an interview and perhaps an essay. Fees are charged, but some scholarships are offered by the colleges themselves, by trade unions and other bodies and by authorities. There are formal and informal studies, and great stress is laid on the residential corporate life. Many students continue full-time higher education at universities and other establishments.

Ruskin College, the oldest and largest, is governed by a council representing organizations including the Trades Union Congress General Council, Co-operative Union, Workers' Educational Association and twenty-six trade unions which make a substantial contribution to its funds. There are 120 students at a time, most of whom stay for two years and take a Diploma in Economics and Political Science of Oxford University, but a few take the University's Diploma in Public and Social Administration, and others do a course on literature and related subjects. The College employs its own full and part-time teachers besides using the facilities of the University. There are also correspondence courses. Coleg Harlech offers one-year courses, but some students return for a second year.

In 1964–5 there were 390 students in the five colleges.

Other direct-grant establishments

There are eighteen other major establishments and one evening institute aided by direct grant (Table 6).

England and Wales: major establishments maintained or assisted by authorities

"Major establishments" are those which provide a substantial amount of daytime work. There were 719 maintained or assisted by authorities in 1964–5. Most were maintained, but a few (in London) were only aided.

Technical and commercial colleges

These form the largest group of major establishments. They have originated in six main waves. Some trace their origin back to the mechanics' institutes which started in the 1820s. There was a second burst during the later decades of the nineteenth century, particularly after the Technical Instruction and Welsh Intermediate Acts of 1889 had empowered authorities to levy a rate for technical education. A third group followed the 1902 Act, and the name "municipal college" may reveal a college's origin or takeover by an authority at about this time. Similarly, "day continuation schools" belong to the period after the Act of 1918. Colleges founded after the 1944 Act are often called "colleges of further education"; and a title like "Regional College" shows a designation after 1956.

TABLE 6

DIRECT-GRANT ESTABLISHMENTS OF FURTHER EDUCATION, 1965

(with year of foundation and year of first grant from central education department, if known)

Central Institutions
Dundee Institute of Art and Technology (1888, 1903)
Edinburgh and East of Scotland College of Agriculture (1901, 1901)
Edinburgh College of Art (1908, 1908)
Edinburgh College of Domestic Science (1875, 1908)
Glasgow and West of Scotland College of Domestic Science (1875, 1908)
Glasgow School of Art (1840, 1899)
Leith Nautical College, Edinburgh (1855, 1903)
North of Scotland College of Agriculture, Aberdeen (1904, 1904)
Paisley College of Technology (1900, 1901)
Robert Gordon's Technical College, Aberdeen (1910, 1910)
Royal Scottish Academy of Music, Glasgow (1890, 1938)
Scottish Woollen Technical College, Galashiels (1909, 1922)
West of Scotland Agricultural College, Glasgow (1899, 1899)

National Colleges
National College of Agricultural Engineering, Silsoe (1960, 1962)
National College of Food Technology, Weybridge (1951, 1951)
National College of Heating, Ventilating, Refrigeration and Fan Engineering, London (1948, 1948)
National College of Rubber Technology, London (1948, 1948)
National Foundry College, Wolverhampton (1947, 1947)
National Leathersellers College, London (1909, 1951)

Agricultural colleges
Harper Adams Agricultural College, Newport, Shropshire (1901, 1964)
Seale-Hayne Agricultural College, Newton Abbot, Devon (1912, 1964)
Shuttleworth College, Biggleswade (1946, 1964)
Studley College, Warwickshire (1898, 1964)

Residential colleges of Adult Education
Catholic Workers College, Oxford (1921, 1923)
Coleg Harlech (1927, 1927)
Fircroft College, Birmingham (1909, 1925)
Hillcroft College, Surbiton (1920, 1929)
Ruskin College, Oxford (1899, 1920)
Newbattle Abbey College, Dalkeith (1937, 1937)

Forester training school
Faskally, Pitlochry, Perthshire (1952, 1952)

Other establishments (England and Wales)
Bristol Aeroplane Technical College, Bristol (1938, 1938)
Camborne School of Metalliferous Mining (1882, 1906)
College of the Sea, London (1938, 1947)
Merchant Navy Training Board, London (1935, 1937)

TABLE 6 (*continued*)

Royal College of Art, London (1837, 1856)
Royal College of Nursing, London (1916, 1949)
School of Navigation, Southampton (1935, 1935)
12 sea training schools[1]
Bournville Works Evening Institute, Birmingham

Other establishments (Scotland)
Edinburgh School of Speech Therapy (1947, 1954)
Glasgow School of Nautical Cookery (1907, 1953)
Glasgow School of Seamanship (1950, 1953)
Glasgow School of Speech Therapy (1964, 1964)
Royal College of Nursing (Scottish Board), Edinburgh (1917, 1960)
Scottish Association for Homecraft Training, Stirling (1953, 1953)

Sources: correspondence with DAFS, DES, Forestry Commission, SED and registrars of establishments.

[1] *Sea training schools:* Cardiff School of Nautical Cookery; Cardiff Seamanship School; Gravesend Sea School, Gravesend; Gravesend Sea School, Sharpness, Glos.; Kingston upon Hull School of Nautical Cookery; Liverpool Firemen's Training School; Liverpool Seamanship School; London Seamanship School; Newcastle Firemen's Training School; Southampton Seamanship School; South Shields School of Nautical Cookery; South Shields Seamanship School.

The "polytechnic" or all-embracing industrially orientated large college was the sort of establishment pioneered by scientists, teachers, progressive sections of private enterprise and authorities towards the end of the last century. The county college, too, was comprehensively conceived just after the war. The recent trend, however, has been towards the specialization and differentiation of establishments according to level of work, full-time or part-time provision, and subject matter, but in the White Paper *A Plan for Polytechnics* there were signs of an attempt to reverse this.

TECHNICAL COLLEGES were classified by the Minister in Circular 305 according to level of work and type of timetable. LOCAL COLLEGES were envisaged as providing only non-advanced work, at any rate as far as their vocational courses were concerned, chiefly in part-time day and evening courses. AREA COLLEGES were to provide such work too, which might be in the majority, but in addition varying amounts of advanced work, mainly in part-time day courses. Thus the badge of the Area College would be the Higher National Certificate, though some were expected to provide full-time and sandwich courses and work above this level also. REGIONAL COLLEGES would provide a "substantial amount" of advanced work in full-time and sandwich courses, taking in students from the areas of several authorities in a region; but would not concentrate entirely on such work, as would a CAT.

The Minister and authorities, advised by regional advisory councils, have been trying to carry out this plan. Regional Colleges have been individually designated by the Minister. At first they were taken to be those colleges which after Circular 255 (1952) had provided advanced courses approved for the 75 per-cent grant (see Chapter 6). The White Paper of 1956 named 24 such colleges, and by 1958 there were 30. Eight of these, however, were designated to become CATs; by 1958–9, therefore, 22 Regional Colleges had been named.

However, after the ending of the percentage-grant system the Minister redefined his criteria in Circular 3/61 and has attempted to establish something like a national pattern of Regional Colleges. He had to be satisfied with the volume and range of all advanced full-time and sandwich courses, the facilities for research, the number and qualifications of staff and their conditions of work, the buildings and equipment and the composition of the governing body.

In 1965 there were twenty-five Regional Colleges (Table 7). Over two-thirds of their full-time and sandwich and getting on for one-third of their part-time students were doing advanced work, mainly in technology and commerce. This made nearly 36,000 advanced students in all, of whom two-thirds were part-time. In 1962–3 there were eight colleges with over 500 advanced full-time students each. Some, like some Central Institutions, have

TABLE 7

REGIONAL COLLEGES, 1966 (with year of designation)

Brighton College of Technology (1956)
Glamorgan College of Technology, Treforest (1956)
Hatfield College of Technology (1962)
Huddersfield College of Technology (1956)
Kingston College of Technology, Surrey (1962)
Lanchester College of Technology, Coventry (1962)
Leeds College of Technology (1962)
Leicester College of Technology (1956)
Liverpool College of Building (1956)
Liverpool College of Technology (1957)
London: Borough Polytechnic (1956)
   Brixton School of Building (1956)
   Northern Polytechnic (1956)
   Sir John Cass College (1956)
   The Polytechnic, Regent Street (1956)
   Woolwich Polytechnic (1956)
Nottingham Regional College of Technology (1956)
North Staffordshire College of Technology, Stoke on Trent (1956)
Plymouth College of Technology (1958)
Portsmouth College of Technology (1957)
Rugby College of Engineering Technology (1956)
Rutherford College of Technology, Newcastle upon Tyne (1964)
South-east Essex College of Technology, Barking (1962)
Sunderland Technical College (1956)
West Ham College of Technology, Newham (1956)

Sources: Minister of Education and Secretary of State for Scotland: *Technical Education,* Cmd. 9703 (1956); correspondence with registrars of colleges.

arrangements of various kinds with universities. The Robbins Report recommended that up to ten be given full university status, but the Government rejected this proposal in 1965 (see pp. 126, 293). Instead, it will probably redesignate them for special treatment as "polytechnics" as conceived in the 1966 White Paper thereon.

Area and Local Colleges are not so clearly defined. Some Local Colleges (as in London) do work only up to the G2 preliminary or O level of the GCE (see Chapter 5). In theory, however, the approval of one advanced course in a Local College would make it an Area College. In fact the Minister, authorities and regional councils have tried to concentrate in certain of the remaining colleges those advanced courses which could not be conveniently provided in Regional Colleges. Obviously the distance which students would have to travel is a major factor to be taken into account. Certain colleges, therefore, in fact serve as area establishments, the remainder being local, but the courses may vary from year to year or even from week to week. A considerable amount of advanced work is done in some Area Colleges, which therefore function as regional colleges, but in other areas there may not be one which is pre-eminent. The Robbins Committee said there were "about 160" Area Colleges, containing over 72,000 advanced students, of whom seven-eighths were part-time. There were then believed to be about 350 Local Colleges.

As regards subject matter, differentiation has not come about as a result of deliberate policy until recently. Indeed, technical colleges are still predominantly oligotechnical or polytechnical, offering courses in a number of technologies, relevant to several industries and strongly influenced by the local industrial bias and pattern. A wide variety of other courses is provided.

Indeed it is the all-embracing Area College which most nearly perpetuates the British polytechnic tradition.

However, others have for a long time specialized in single industries, and London has several such monotechnics. Liverpool College of Building, to take an example, separated from Liverpool City Technical College, in which it had been a department, in 1951. Reardon Smith Nautical College did likewise in Cardiff. In other cases, however, there has been amalgamation : Liverpool Nautical College, for instance, became a department of City Technical College in 1925, as did Liverpool School of Pharmacy in 1950.

Courses in subjects traditional to women and girls, whether pre-employment for school leavers, part-time day for employed girls, or evening courses, tend also to be segregated in separate colleges or departments; Liverpool, for example, has two such colleges and Birkenhead one.

About 130 technical colleges are believed to have commerce departments, and most offer some courses which may be more commercial than technical. In other cases, however, there are separate COLLEGES OF COMMERCE. The Department in its annual statistical report lumps these together with Area and Local Colleges as "other major establishments", but the Crowther Report gave their number as 23. At first they benefited little from the new building which followed 1956; in Circular 1/59, therefore, the Minister said they were to be given a higher priority in future. Since advanced work tends to be concentrated in certain commercial colleges for the same reasons as in technical colleges, some are called "regional". This title has been unofficial, however, since Circulars 305 and 3/61 did not apply to colleges of commerce. Indeed, so much commercial education is part-time day and evening that they are really more comparable with Area than with Regional Colleges. The McMeeking Committee (1959) found advanced courses in only 15. In Circular 15/61 the Minister promised to consider some for designation as Regional, though he seemed to favour the integration of commercial with technical education.

The Department reported 497 OTHER MAJOR ESTABLISHMENTS in 1964–5. They accounted for about two-thirds of the full-time and sandwich, over five-sixths of the part-time day, and well over one-third of the evening students in Further Education. According to the Crowther Report about half the students in Area and most in Local Colleges were under nineteen, and nearly all of these attended part-time courses.

Closer co-operation of Area and Regional Colleges with colleges of education has been recommended (for example, by the ATTI).

Art establishments

Art education has tended to separate more sharply than commercial : at first into schools of art under their own principals but still attached to technical colleges; then into separate SCHOOLS or COLLEGES OF ART which have moved into their own new buildings; and occasionally in new foundations. The number of maintained art establishments has decreased from 207 in 1946–7 to 157 in 1964–5. About 70 were believed to be attached to technical colleges. They teach a wide variety of arts and crafts. One-third of their daytime students are full-time. Advanced courses have tended to be concentrated in certain colleges, and there are about 100 which thus serve as area or regional establishments; but further concentration was hinted at in Circular 340, and only 29 had courses recognized for the Diploma in Art and Design when it began in 1963–4. Circular 16/60 promised the latter priority for new building.

Farm institutes

These provide mainly one-year residential and longer part-time day courses for young people wishing to become farm managers or farmers. There

are 40; and as this is fewer than the number of counties, neighbouring authorities often co-operate on their governing bodies. Their
size averaged about 65 full-time and 95 part-time day students in
1964–5.

Residential colleges and centres of Adult Education

Some authorities provide one or more of these, either alone or jointly
with their neighbours; about half are fully maintained. University extra-
mural departments and other responsible bodies co-operate in providing
some of them. Most courses are at weekends, and three-quarters are of less
than four days' duration, so that they are usually unfilled at mid-week.
Generally they relate to leisure-time pursuits, but courses in such vocational
or semi-vocational subjects as youth leadership, management subjects or
horticulture are common too. Great stress is laid on the value of bringing
people together from all walks of life. There were 20 colleges and 9 centres
in 1963–4.

Other maintained major establishments

Some colleges established by industrial firms for their employees are
assisted by authorities, which buy college equipment and consumable
materials and pay the salaries of teaching staff other than trade instructors.
Examples of such WORKS SCHOOLS are Leyland Motors Limited Day
Continuation School, Leyland, and Associated Electrical Industries Limited
Works School at Trafford Park, Manchester. The Crowther Report gave
their number as ten.

The same report also said there were twenty-four NURSERY TRAINING
CENTRES.

England and Wales: evening institutes

There were 7,783 of these maintained by authorities in 1964–5, and one
by direct grant. They contained one million students, of whom over
two-thirds were women. They normally provide evening courses only, under
part-time principals, in the premises of schools which are fully used during
the day; and since 1955 some school buildings have been designed with
this in mind. Others, however, as in the West Riding of Yorkshire, have
offered part-time and even full-time day courses, and may be grouped as
area institutes under full-time principals. Indeed, the employment of full-time

TABLE 8

NUMBERS AND SIZES OF SOME GRANT-AIDED ESTABLISHMENTS OF FURTHER EDUCATION, 1964–5

ENGLAND AND WALES

	No. of establishments		No. of students				
	Direct-grant	Authority-maintained	Full-time	Short full-time	Sandwich	Part-time day (including block-release)	Evening-only
National Colleges	7[1]	—	926	30	152	86	342
Colleges of advanced technology	10	—	5,688	278	8,117	4,072	4,604
Regional Colleges	—	25	12,864	881	6,309	35,231	36,974
Art establishments	1	157	22,136	33	111	41,022	57,275
Agricultural colleges	5[2]	—	1,346	11	—	—	—
Farm institutes	—	40	2,573	39	36	3,889	2,226
Other major establishments	17	497	114,417	6,122	7,447	563,989	676,977
All major establishments	40	719	159,950	7,394	22,172	648,289	778,398
Evening institutes	1	7,783	—	—	—	—	1,131,509
All above establishments	41	8,502	159,950	7,394	22,172	648,289	1,909,907
Residential colleges and centres of Adult Education[3]	5	29	368	56,168	—	—	—

[1] Including the College of Aeronautics, Cranfield.
[2] Including the Royal Agricultural College, Cirencester.
[3] Session 1963–4.

Source: Department of Education and Science: *Statistics of Education, 1964, Part 2*, tables 5 and 32 (1965).

TABLE 8 (*continued*)

SCOTLAND

| | No. of establishments | | No. of students | | |
	Direct-grant	Authority-maintained	Full-time	Part-time released	Part-time not released
Central Institutions under the SED	11[4]	—	5,388	3,810	7,148
Central Institutions under the DAFS	3	—[5]	488	109	565
Further education centres	—	?[5]	10,248	50,242	249,526
All establishments	14	?	16,124	54,161	257,239

[4] Including Heriot-Watt College.

[5] The number is not published.

Sources: Secretary of State for Scotland: *Education in Scotland in 1965*, table 11 (1966) (which included all 14 colleges); correspondence with DAFS, 1966.

principals and organizers is a growing trend. By providing day courses some evening institutes, like City Institute, Liverpool, have evolved into major establishments.

Traditionally their courses are either prevocational or non-vocational. The prevocational or junior "night school", as explained in Chapter 14, has been an attempt to fill the gap between leaving school and entering college. It is now being discontinued by having its technical courses transferred to colleges; nevertheless, in 1964–5 135,000 evening-institute students, nearly one-eighth of their total, were under sixteen, and much preparatory *commercial* training goes on.

Courses cover a wide range of adult interests, mainly non-vocational; and the establishments may be variously called men's, women's, literary institutes and so on. Vocational and semivocational courses, however, may also be provided.

On the whole, the evening institute is changing from a prevocational and vocational establishment for adolescents to a non-vocational one for adults, particularly women.

Establishments for social
and physical training and recreation

These can be provided by authorities or voluntary bodies; and the latter can be aided either by their authority in respect of capital and maintenance costs or by the appropriate Secretary of State in respect of capital and headquarters costs.

Community centres

These are places for leisure-time social, recreational and cultural activities, open primarily to the adult or whole population of an area such as a city ward, block of flats or suburban housing estate. They are of diverse origins; thus they may be in separate premises or not; and may have full-time or even resident wardens. Some also contain health clinics. There are two types according to whether they are used merely as meeting places by unrelated organizations or run as clubs by single bodies such as community associations or miners' institutes; but these may be combined. Either can be provided or aided by an education authority or by a local authority acting in another capacity. The associations can also be aided by the Secretary of State, and they usually raise money by their own activities too. Some take voluntary organizations and even statutory bodies into membership as well as individuals; and some are affiliated to a National Federation (NFCA).

Village halls

These are small community centres in the countryside where the population of a village may not be much more than 400. They are usually run by their own committees. Their sponsors generally use the premises of schools, but some have built their own, with or without aid from the Secretary of State or authority.

Playing fields and the like

According to Section 53 of the 1944 Act, as amended by the Miscellaneous Provisions Act of 1948, authorities must secure the provision of facilities such as playing fields, camps, gymnasia or swimming baths for the use of those engaged in Further Education. Voluntary bodies providing these for other people may not be aided by an *education* authority, though the latter may co-operate with them; but they may be aided by the appropriate Secretary of State under the Physical Training and Recreation Act of 1937, provided that the facilities concerned are made available to the community as a whole. The Secretaries of State also pay grants towards the expenses of national athletic and sporting associations and the salaries of coaches (Tables 1 and 3).

Youth clubs and centres

Youth "clubs" are usually definite *organizations*, however loose, perhaps owning or renting their own premises. Youth "centres" are *premises* provided by authorities for the use of clubs or other groups lacking their own, or merely for casual visitors. Centres may be special buildings, schools, youth "wings" in schools or colleges, or community centres. Clubs may be aided with capital and maintenance grants by authorities or by the appropriate Secretary of State.

Establishments for the disabled and handicapped

At the time of writing there are no Further Education establishments of this kind maintained by authorities. They are run by other government departments and local authorities or by unaided voluntary associations and are therefore outside our present scope; but one received a grant from the Minister in 1961–2.

Research establishments

These are dealt with in Chapter 18.

Facilities provided in other establishments

As mentioned, authorities may provide educational facilities in HM Prisons, Borstal institutions, detention centres, approved schools or hospitals. In 1963 they were employing about thirty full-time tutor-organizers for work in the first three of these.

The internal organization of technical colleges

Governing body

Under the Secretary of State's regulations all maintained major establishments in England and Wales must have a governing body. It must be directly responsible to the authority: it may be, for example, a subcommittee of the education committee or of the Further Education subcommittee. In some cases there may be more than one authority concerned, in which case it would be constituted as a "joint education committee" as defined in the 1944 Act. Only exceptionally, as where a group of small colleges is under a large authority, may there be a single governing body for more than one college.

About one-third of its members must be drawn from industrial, commercial and other appropriate local interests, and, if advanced courses are provided, from universities and professional bodies. Representatives of the authority or authorities need not be in a majority. In Pamphlet No. 8 the Minister recommended representation of the Youth Service, but this is rare. Staff representation, too, is not common. In Circular 7/59 twenty persons was suggested as a suitable size.

The degree of autonomy allowed to governing bodies varies considerably from one authority to another. They are usually permitted to spend within stated limits without further approval, to take part in the appointment of principal and to appoint other staff.

In Scotland the position is different, as further education centres have not had governing bodies but have been administered directly by authorities. However, in 1962 the Secretary of State supported a recommendation of a committee of STECC (in the Dinwiddie Report) that there should be statutory changes to permit the establishment of governing bodies with executive powers and other wide responsibilities. Such bodies, it was hoped, would attract industrialists of standing to take part in college administration. After the amendment of the Local Government (Scotland) Act, 1947 (Section 109), by the Education (Scotland) Act, 1963, the Secretary of State urged authorities to make use of their new discretionary powers to appoint a "board of management" for each day college. This board, he wrote in his Circular 549, should contain substantial representation of employers and trade unionists in appropriate fields, at least two members of the education committee, representatives from other interested educational bodies, and co-opted members able to contribute in a personal capacity. The new Napier Technical College, Edinburgh, was the first to comply.

Staff

The principal acts under the direction of the governing body and is responsible for day-to-day college management and discipline and for the admission of students. He makes an annual report which is usually submitted to the Further Education subcommittee and may become available with other council reports in the local public library or in the college.

Serving under the principal are teaching, administrative, technical and caretaking staffs. Colleges are divided into departments by subject matter, and departments may be divided into sections; each department and section is under the direction of an appropriate senior teacher. Administration operates as a separate department under a registrar. The technical staff is concerned with both the servicing of teaching laboratories and the maintenance of plant in the building. Cleaners work under the supervision of a caretaker.

Advisory bodies

As mentioned earlier, college departments are helped by advisory committees for each of the industries for which they cater, on which sit representatives of local firms with the head of department and perhaps other members of the teaching staff.

The staff may also participate in boards of studies for each of the subjects taught.

Membership of associations

Staff and students

The principal is probably a member of the Association of Principals of Technical Institutions (APTI). Most college teachers belong to the Association of Teachers in Technical Institutions (ATTI), and therefore, through

G

a joint membership scheme, also to the National Union of Teachers (NUT); but a few belong to other bodies such as the Association of Scientific Workers (AScW), Incorporated Association of Assistant Masters (IAAM), Association of Assistant Mistresses (AAM), National Association of School-masters (NAS), or, if the college is a CAT, Association of University Teachers (AUT). Scottish teachers may belong to the Educational Institute of Scotland (EIS), Scottish Secondary Teachers' Association (SSTA), Scottish Schoolmasters' Association (SSA), or in some Central Institutions the Scottish Section of the AUT (AUT(S)). Many teachers are members of professional institutions also. Administrative and clerical staff are likely to be in the National and Local Government Officers' Association (NALGO) and laboratory and other technical staff in the AScW. Porters, caretakers and cleaning staff belong generally to the National Union of Public Employees (NUPE). There may be a college staff association within the college.

Students are generally organized in a college students' union which in a bigger college may have its own building. This finances and oversees general student life in the college. A students' representative council (SRC) is obligatory at a Central Institution. Nationally, full-time students may belong individually to the National or Scottish Union of Students (NUS, SUS), but there is no national body for further-education students as such, nor for part-time students.

Establishments

Establishments which provide higher education in technical subjects are eligible for membership of the Association of Technical Institutions (ATI). The governing bodies of institutions in membership (which here means *establishments*) may appoint representatives, two voting and one non-voting : these usually include the principal and either the chairman of governors or director of education. Several Commonwealth colleges belong. The ATI has a number of committees set up jointly with the APTI.

The Association of Art Institutions (AAI) fosters art education in the same way. Each establishment may appoint three voting representatives which must include the principal, and an authority controlling more than one art establishment may appoint another two.

Notes on further study

The policy of centralizing courses in certain colleges began in Scotland with the Department's *Code of Regulations for Continuation Classes* and accompanying *Memorandum* (1901); and the status of Central Institutions was regularized in Section 34 of the Education (Scotland) Act, 1908. In England and Wales the policy began with art education in the Board's Circular 1432 (1933). The transfer of elementary and local work from Central Institutions to further education centres was recommended in the Fyfe Report (1946).

The idea of a hierarchy of types of authority-maintained college was in the Percy Report and can be traced through the Minister's Circulars 87 and 98 (1946), Pamphlets Nos. 3 (1945) and 8 (1947) and Circular 255 (1952) to the White Paper *Technical Education* (1956). It began to be implemented with Circular 299 (1956) which introduced the White Paper to authorities; the Minister's speech in Parliament on 21st June 1956; and Circular 305 (1956).

The Secretary of State's *Education in Scotland in 1952* and *Public Education in Scotland* (1963) contained short historical accounts, as did West's *Technical Education in Scotland* (ATI, 1959) and Mackintosh's *Education in Scotland Yesterday and Today* (1962) (especially Chapter 9). See also Scottish Circular 405 (1959). Scottish establishments are listed in the SED's free annual *Directory of Day Courses*.

The College of Aeronautics arose from the Fedden Report (1944), National Colleges from the Percy Report (1945), and the pre-Robbins status of the Royal College of Art from Circular 199 (1949).

CATs were announced in the White Paper of 1956 and defined in the appendix to Circular 305 (1956). There was much about them in the Robbins Report (1963) and the DES's *Reports on Education*, No. 10 (1964). See also Chapters 6, 7 and 19 and *Notes*.

Colleges of commerce were dealt with in Circulars 281 (1954), 5/59, 7/59 and 15/61; and colleges of art in Circulars 281 (1954), 340 (1958), 16/60 and 11/62. See also Chapters 7 and 8 and *Notes*.

Farm institutes were listed in the De La Warr Report (1958) and in the DES's *Full-time Agricultural Education in England and Wales (List 185)* (1965). Agricultural colleges were also in the latter. See also Chapter 9 and *Notes*.

Residential colleges of Adult Education are listed annually in the National Institute of Adult Education's *Year Book*.

Evening institutes were described in the Minister's Pamphlet No. 28 (1956) and by Edwards in *The Evening Institute* (1961).

Community centres were the subject of Circular 20 (1944) which had a pamphlet attached. They were defined and discussed in the NFCA's *Creative Living* (1964) and in the SCCYCSS interim report on the linkage of youth and community services (1965). They, too, are listed in the NIAE *Year Book*.

Major establishments were individually named, with information about them, in Venables's *Technical Education . . .* (1955), and are now listed annually in the *Year Book of Technical Education and Careers in Industry* and *Education Authorities Directory and Annual.* Those providing higher education are in the *Year Books* of the AAI and ATI. For Scotland see *Directory of Day Courses.*

Establishments providing for the disabled and handicapped were tabulated in the Ministry's *List 42* (1963).

Direct-grant establishments in England and Wales come under the Minister's *Further Education (Grant) Regulations, 1959*; authority-maintained establishments under *Further Education (Local Education Authorities) Regulations, 1959*; and establishments for the disabled and handicapped under *Special Schools and Establishments (Grant) Regulations, 1959* (Table 3). There are corresponding Scottish regulations.

On governing bodies of colleges see Circulars 98 (1946), 305 (1956), 351 (1959), 5/59, 7/59, 3/61 and 15/61, and of farm institutes the Addendum to Circular 7/59 (1961). For Scottish colleges see Scottish Circular 405 (1959), STECC's Dinwiddie Report (1962) and Scottish Circular 549 (1964). Higher-education establishments were dealt with in the Robbins Report, especially Appendix Four, Part I. See also the FBI's *The Technical Colleges and their Government* (1960) and *Further Education for those in Industry and Commerce* (1961). For some individual establishments refer to the *Instrument and Articles of Government* drawn up by its authority (e.g. Birmingham), in which the constitution, powers and duties of its governing body and responsibilities of its principal are laid down. For a discussion of this aspect of college government see Russell (ATI, 1966).

Much factual material about teaching staffs was gathered in Part III, Appendix Three, of the Robbins Report. On conditions recommended for teachers see the Willis Jackson Report (1957), Circular 336 (1958) and the Robbins Report, Chapter XII.

The annual reports of the Ministers and Secretaries of State, and, for England and Wales from 1961 onwards, *Statistics of Education, Part 2*, give statistical and other information about establishments. For Central Institutions under the DAFS see the Secretary of State's annual *Agriculture in Scotland.* For England and Wales see also the Schemes of Further Education and annual reports of authorities and reports of regional and district advisory councils. For more recent information see the Robbins Report, especially Appendix Two.

Administrative Memorandum 440 (1953, amended 1956 and 1963) instructed authorities on how to deal with the Prison Commissioners and Prison Department of the Home Office.

On libraries see the Minister's Circular 322 (1957) and Building Bulletin No. 5 (1959); the Secretary of State's Scottish Circular 405 (1959) and *School and College Libraries* (extracted from *Education in Scotland in*

1962); the Library Association's *Standards for Library Service in Colleges of Technology* (1959) and *Recommended Standards* (1965); the London and Home Counties Regional Advisory Council's *Libraries in Colleges* . . . (1954 and 1959); the ATI's *Technical College Buildings* (two interim reports, 1962 and n.d.); Neal : *Technical College Libraries* (1965); and Smith and Baxter : *College Library Administration* (1965).

Some colleges have had their histories written; examples of such work are : Brooks (1955) on Woolwich Polytechnic; Ethel Wood (1965) on The Polytechnic, Regent Street; and Smith (1965) on Wigan. See also *The Story of Ruskin College* (anon., 1955). For the situation before the war see Richardson : *The Technical College* (1939).

Finally there are of course the prospectuses of the establishments themselves.

CHAPTER 5

EDUCATION FOR INDUSTRIAL SKILL

Apprenticeship

The growth of organized training

Training for industry has evolved mainly through the institution known as "apprenticeship". This is a sort of contractual relationship between an employer or "master" and his employee or "apprentice" in which the master undertakes to engage the apprentice on agreed terms for a stated number of years and to be responsible for his training, while the apprentice promises to serve the master loyally during the period. There may be a deed of indenture or other strict contract, or a looser form of agreement may suffice. In some trades, notably electrical installation, there is a form known as "custom of the trade". Sometimes a premium may be charged by the employer. In due course the apprentice "comes out of his time" as a skilled worker or journeyman.

Looser forms of arrangement may be called "learnerships" or "traineeships". "Learners" are usually being trained, under a definite understanding with their employers, for semiskilled occupations rather than skilled. "Trainees" are generally beginners in non-manual occupations, but the term is also used for intending craftsmen in government training centres and for craftsmen retraining for other crafts. The word "improver" may mean a learner of an only slightly skilled occupation (as in engineering and shipbuilding, where no definite understanding with the employer is necessarily implied) or the grade next above an apprentice (as in hairdressing). Any of these arrangements may be difficult to distinguish from one another or from apprenticeship.

Apprenticeship was under legal regulation under the Statute of Artificers between 1562 and 1814. But since the industrial revolution employers have become neither able nor willing to impart all of their apprentices' training themselves and have looked to educational institutions to help. The first Factory Act (1802) introduced the principle of compulsory attendance at school during part of the working week. Since then the combination of works training with college education has become a fundamental feature of preparation for industry.

The present system began to take shape after the first world war. Its central feature is that the employer agrees to allow the apprentice time off or "release" for periods of college study during working hours, while paying his wage, generally the college fees and sometimes also a maintenance allowance. The traditional form of release which grew up between the wars was the "part-time day" type, in which the apprentice attended college during term for one day a week, probably supplemented by one or more evenings in his own time. In the engineering industry release for one and two days in alternate weeks was sometimes given. In other cases recruits had to serve a probationary period as "utility boys" for perhaps as long as a year before being taken into apprenticeship. Some firms offered two kinds of apprenticeship—"engineering" and "trade"—the engineering requiring

TABLE 9

PERCENTAGES OF SCHOOL LEAVERS ENTERING APPRENTICESHIPS IN ENGLAND AND WALES SINCE THE CROWTHER REPORT

	Boys	Girls
1959	33·6	7·4
1960	36·0	7·6
1961	37·9	7·2
1962	36·2	6·6
1963	33·5	5·5
1964	36·4	5·7
1965	40·6	6·2

Source: Central Youth Employment Executive.

quite a large premium and leading to a higher level of training than trade; but a small number of trade apprentices were sometimes selected for free engineering apprenticeships as a sort of "scholarship".

Modern trends

There was great development after the second world war. Six trends are noteworthy.

First, there was a growth in the number of apprentices. As mentioned earlier, in 1965 about four-tenths of boys and one-sixteenth of girls leaving school entered regular apprenticeships. The looser forms of learnership have also expanded. The *proportions* of the age group, however, declined between 1961 and 1963 (Table 9).

Second, there was a sharp increase in the number of young workers released. The war had underlined the importance of scientific knowledge at all levels of industry; and the low pre-war birth rate, the raising of the school-leaving age in 1947 and the continuance of national service had led to a scarcity of recruits to skilled occupations. In order to attract keen youngsters, apprenticeship schemes more and more tended to include release as a condition. In 1946–7 there were 167,000 employed students getting various forms of release; but by 1964–5 there were over 624,000. Nearly half of those getting day release in 1964–5 were under eighteen. This represented 31 per cent of boys (under eighteen) employed and 7 per cent of girls (Table 13).

Third, a form of national control evolved within industries. Since the ending of state control in 1819 apprenticeship schemes have been a matter for negotiation between employer and employee and have therefore varied widely. The post-war multiplication of schemes, however, alongside the rise in collective bargaining, led to the formation of joint apprenticeship councils in the important industries. On these are represented employers, trade unions, the Ministry of Labour and in some cases the Departments; they have national and local committees, often with education subcommittees, and develop liaison with regional advisory councils and other bodies. They regulate new agreements, which normally implement the conditions negotiated nationally, and supervise their operation. The National Joint Advisory Council under the chairmanship of the Minister of Labour (mentioned in Chapter 2) was set up to advise the government in 1939.

There were 128 recognized national agreements in 1966. Most were in traditional crafts, of which the following are examples from manufacturing industry :

clothing : cutting;

engineering and shipbuilding : boilermaking, mechanical and electrical fitting, moulding, patternmaking, toolmaking, turning;

printing : composing, machine operation, photomechanical processing;

woodworking : cabinetmaking, coopering;

textiles : engineering maintenance, tackling.

The agreements govern apprenticeships in such matters as length of time (usually five years), number of entrants (usually a fixed proportion of the journeymen already employed) and rates of pay (usually increasing with age but lower than for non-apprentices). Because it has become customary for a worker to qualify for the skilled wage by the age of twenty-one he must begin a five-year training at about sixteen.

A fourth significant though as yet small development has been the appearance of experimental schemes breaking away from established traditional practice. For example, in the "group apprenticeship" scheme, developed mainly in the engineering industry since 1953 (EIGA), firms pool the training and release of apprentices. In this arrangement small firms find that they can reduce the difficulties encountered in taking on and training their full quota of apprentices. Another example is where craft apprentices (mainly in the engineering industry) have spent the first year of apprenticeship as full-time students at technical colleges, following an integrated course of further education and industrial training, but paid normal apprentices' wages by their employers. A further development was an experiment started in September 1962 by STECC in conjunction with the Glasgow authority and twenty engineering firms, under which apprentices spent the first *three* years of their five-year engineering apprenticeship as full-time students at the Stow College of Engineering,[1] with their wages paid by the firms. Thirty-one apprentice toolmakers and turner fitters completed this course. An assessment of the results of this method as compared with the more traditional form of apprenticeship training is being made by a specially appointed committee of assessors from the University of Strathclyde. A second course began in September 1964.

A fifth post-war trend has been the extension of apprenticeship into higher levels of training, with consequent evolution of new forms. As mentioned in Chapter 2, industry has tended to stratify its occupations into five main levels; unskilled or labourer, semiskilled or operative, skilled or craftsman, technician, and professional (technologist, administrator, scientist). These can be subdivided, though the boundaries are neither clear nor static and are often determined as much by tradition as by anything else. Apprenticeships and other learnerships have become divisible in a comparable way. They are not, of course, needed by the unskilled; but, as mentioned, there has been the beginning of a tendency for loose forms of learnership to evolve for semiskilled operatives. For the remainder, five kinds of apprenticeship can be broadly distinguished : craft or trade, student-technician, technical-college student-technologist, university or undergraduate student-technologist, and graduate. These, too, can be subdivided, taking various names, though the "student" grades are the least clearly separable. Student and graduate apprenticeships, preparing for employment at higher levels, are less, if at all, controlled by national agreements. It is among these that the greatest post-war growth has occurred (Table 15).

This growth has led to new forms of release. Between the wars, intending technicians got the same kind of release, if any, as craft apprentices, namely "day", which meant one day a week. Indeed, as technicians in many industries were largely recruited from promising craftsmen, technician apprentices were not always clearly distinguishable at first. But they need more scientific knowledge than craftsmen do; and since about 1953 various other kinds of arrangement, recognizing them earlier and allowing them more time at college, have been growing in popularity. In the case of technologists this need is greater still.

[1] Now Springburn College of Engineering.

Therefore some employers now give more than one day a week. More commonly there are alternating periods of training at work and full-time college study. Thus, in addition to day release, five main kinds of new scheme have emerged :

(a) two-day release, or two days per week instead of one;
(b) "block" release, in which the aggregate of full-time periods at college, over the whole course, averages eighteen weeks per year or less (such as, for example, one full term of twelve or thirteen weeks per year, or one week in every three);
(c) "sandwich" or "thin-sandwich" release, in which the full-time periods at work and at college are of about six months each;
(d) "thick-sandwich" release, in which the full-time college periods are longer than six months (such as nine months at college and three in industry; or a year in industry, followed by a three-year course at a university, and then by another year in industry); and
(e) a kind which might be called "inside-out-sandwich", in which, for example, a full year in industry occupies the second or third year of an otherwise full-time four-year course.

Courses based on block release usually contain periods of day-release or evening-only study between the full-time blocks. Half-and-half thin-sandwich schemes in which the student employees are divided into two equal and alternating groups are called "end-on". In the same way, end-on block release usually contains four consecutive twelve-week college terms, each taking one-quarter of the student employees. Two-day and block release are more recent developments than sandwich but block release is growing rapidly. Thus there were 24,000 students in England and Wales studying for recognized qualifications by block release in 1964–5. The number of students on sandwich courses in England and Wales has risen from 1,400 to 22,000 in the eleven years between 1954–5 and 1964–5. Most sandwich students are, like part-time day students, "works-based", being employed as student apprentices and paid a wage by their firms whilst at college and at work. But a few are "college-based", that is to say, not regular employees at all, but eligible for grant from their authorities whilst at college, and paid a wage only during the works-training parts of their courses. The latter parts are arranged by the colleges in consultation with co-operating firms. There seems to be a growing tendency for authorities to aid works-based students more, and for their firms to aid them less; so that a category of student known as "works-sponsored" has come into recognition.

A self-contained full-time course lasting for eight weeks or less is called "short full-time". Release for such a course may be regarded as a form of block release.

A sixth trend is the return of state control. This is discussed in the next section.

The remainder of this chapter is concerned with the education of operatives, craftsmen and technicians for industry. Their courses are "non-advanced". In 1964–5 in England and Wales they numbered about 840,000, or five-sixths of all students working for recognized qualifications in the colleges. Thus they form what the Crowther Report called the "central core" of Further Education. Just over half are under twenty-one.

Training at work

As mentioned in Chapter 1, this is really outside our definition, but early reference to it is inevitable because of its inseparability from apprenticeship and its close links with Further Education.

The post-war pattern

Skilled men have always been trained chiefly at work. Normal practice has been for craft apprentices to be enabled to learn "on the job", by being put for a time under a craftsman on each type of operation or machine in turn ("watching Joe"). Girls have been trained in the same way ("sitting next to Nelly"). This method can be very potent—after all, it is the way we learnt our mother tongue, and many other things. But in the circumstances of industry it can also be most inefficient; and it has even more serious limitations in the case of a small firm performing only a small range of operations, particularly if the firm is not in any group scheme. The more progressive enterprises, therefore, conduct more systematic courses "off the job". These may include class instructions in basic skills. A few firms, as mentioned, have built and staffed their own apprentice-training centres and works schools; or firms in an industry have got together to do this. In some cases there have been gap-filling courses such as those arranged regionally by the British Iron and Steel Federation.

The Ministry of Labour also provides training courses in colleges, works and government training centres (GTCs). These are of a practical nature and vary in duration between three months and two years. One-year courses for first-year apprentices have been provided. There are also schemes for the disabled, for redundant workers and for those discharged from the armed forces. However, only 8,500 adults completed such courses in 1965, and of these, 2,700 were disabled. Maintenance allowances while training are low : a married man with children, for example, draws only £9 – 10 a week. Nevertheless, the NEDC has suggested a widening of the range of courses offered. Recently the number of GTCs has been raised from 13 to 31; and it is expected to reach 38, taking over 12,000 men, during 1966.

For supervisors and foremen the Ministry of Labour has sponsored since 1944 a scheme called "training within industry" (TWI). It offers five courses : Job Instruction, Job Relations, Job Methods, Job Safety and Office Supervision. They are generally given on a firm's premises by either a Ministry of Labour instructor or a trained officer of the firm. The Ministry of Labour also has a Technical Staff College at Letchworth. Over 140 technical and commercial colleges provided courses for supervisors in 1961–2, enrolling about 9,000 students. A National Examinations Board in Supervisory Studies was set up in 1964.

Thus the general trend is undoubtedly towards the more systematic and formal instruction both of craft apprentices and of foremen trainees.

As mentioned, there has arisen some emphasis on training the less skilled too. Most non-apprentices at present get no systematic training on the job at all, but some firms are introducing planned schemes containing anything from a few weeks of intensive practical work to two or three years of general industrial training with college release. Instruction usually fits the immediate rather than the anticipated future needs of the firms, but more attention to the impact of technological advance, particularly in creating a need for adaptability, has been urged (see Chapter 2).

These trends received further encouragement after 1958 by the formation, following the Carr Report, of an Industrial Training Council (ITC). This had the function of keeping industrial recruitment and training under review and disseminating information thereon. It contained representatives of the British Employers' Confederation, Trades Union Congress, nationalized industries, Ministries of Labour and Education, Association of Technical Institutions and City and Guilds of London Institute, with Lord McCorquodale as chairman. Thus industry was strongly represented on it. It had a Scottish committee. In 1960 it set up a Training Advisory Service (TAS), with a staff of full-time training development officers, to give practical help to employers and joint councils; this was financed partly by government grant and partly by fees. The ITC also administered grants to help the appointment of similar officers by firms.

New moves, 1962–1964

The Carr Report had recommended that the state should continue to leave industrial training to industry. But by 1962 the Government was still not satisfied with the volume or quality of training going on. Provision was lacking in direction, unco-ordinated and unfair to progressive firms. In a White Paper the Minister of Labour announced the intention of establishing "training boards" in different industries to bring about improvements. Unlike the ITC these would have real power. They would be able to assess trends, lay down policy, determine duration of training and age of entry, set content of training, impose standards and tests, provide centres, take on their own trainees, send people to college and reimburse firms' expenses. They would be for industries, not occupations, and would be responsible for everyone working in them, not only apprentices. The cost would be borne by a levy on enterprises in the industry; but very small firms could be excused, and rebates would be allowed to those already spending more than the levy. It was suggested that the full-time training of first-year apprentices with wages paid by the boards should be the first priority.

The Industrial Training Act of 1964 embodies these proposals. In addition it empowers the boards to carry out research. At the suggestion of the TUC it has introduced a Central Training Council (CTC) to advise the Minister of Labour. It gives the Minister of Labour much freedom in appointing the boards. However, it does not empower him or the boards to alter established practices by direct order or regulation. In matters to do with the nature and length of training, the persons to give and receive it, and the standards, testing and further-education provision needed, the boards have power only to publish recommendations. But they are allowed to impose levies, pay grants, obtain information, set up their own training facilities (though not courses of further education), take on their own apprentices, and train them in their own way if need be, always subject to approval by the Minister of Labour.

It is expected that, at least at first, firms will pay all trainees' wages, no firm will be excused levy, and grants will only be paid to firms whose training services fulfil the requirements of the boards. Thus the boards will carry out their functions by "stick and carrot". They will use research, example and persuasion, backed by financial pressure, but not regulation, and probably not direct provision of rival facilities.

The boards are now being set up. Ten were in existence by the end of 1965: engineering, construction, wool textiles, iron and steel, shipbuilding, electricity supply, gas, water supply, ceramics with glass and mineral products, timber and furniture.

The ITC has come to an end since its functions will now be performed by the CTC; but the ITC's Training Advisory Service is continuing as an Industrial Training Service (ITS), loosely attached to the CTC as a sort of field force. The ITS is a non-profit-making company, financed by fees and government grant. In a membership of eleven its board of directors contains one representative of the education service. Links will no doubt be established with regional advisory councils, authorities and other educational bodies. As mentioned earlier, an interdepartmental Committee on Training for Skill has been formed to advise appropriate ministers.

These measures have gone some way in the direction recommended in the third Oldfield-Davies Report (see p. 110). The boards must contain some representation of the education service; both they and the Minister of Labour have powers of financial compulsion; and the CTC can develop a real co-ordinating function. Some fear, however, that the more radical the recommendations of the boards, the greater would be the possibility that they might be opposed by apprenticeship councils, or even that firms might be willing to forfeit their grant rather than carry them out.

Courses for craftsmen and technicians

Courses promoted by examining institutes

At the colleges there is a wide range of subjects available. Most craft and many technician students take "senior" courses and examinations offered by the City and Guilds of London Institute and the so-called "regional" examining unions. These are intended to supplement the apprentices' industrial experience, improve their skill and understanding of their work and make them responsive to technological change. Most are based on a time allowance of one day a week plus one evening, which, assuming eight hours per week for three ten-week terms, is 240 hours per year; usually there has been a recommended minimum of 150 or 200. In every year except the last, students normally take either a college examination or examinations of the regional union of which the providing authority is a member. The regional unions co-ordinate their syllabuses with those of the City and Guilds Institute to make this possible. Most courses are started at the age of fifteen or sixteen.

Until about 1959 the standard pattern of a City and Guilds course was a continuous four- or five-year syllabus divided into two parts : a two- or three-year part leading to an "Intermediate" certificate followed by a two-year part leading to a "Final" certificate. In some cases a further year or more could be spent in gaining a "Full Technological" certificate (FTC) which could sometimes lead into Higher National Certificate studies (see p. 99). A number of courses still follow this pattern : Flax Spinning, for example, or Milk Processing and Control. Most were craft courses, at least at first, but some, such as Flax Spinning and other textile crafts, Machine Shop Engineering or Electrical Installation Work, reached technician standard in the Final stages; and in other cases, as in the building or printing crafts, technician or technologist studies could branch out from them.

It was found, however, that the Final and Full Technological certificates represented levels of achievement which very few craft students attained. Usually those who did so became technicians or managers. The majority, who in fact became competent journeymen, took four or five years to gain an Intermediate, which proved adequate for their needs and was therefore inappropriately conceived and named. On the other hand, the more able students found craft courses too easy at the beginning and could have started earlier on the more scientific and mathematical studies needed by technicians. Yet the distinction between craft and technician levels in City and Guilds courses had not been clear; and the best-known technician courses proper, those for National Certificates, had proved too difficult for many technician students. Thus there was a need for new courses, planned from the beginning to meet the needs of technicians in specific industries, at a level somewhere between those of craft and National Certificate courses.

Since about 1951, therefore, two connected trends have emerged : the recasting of craft schemes to bring them into line with the needs of all apprentices likely to become competent craftsmen, and the construction of new technician courses separate from craft courses from the start. In that year the City and Guilds Institute began a review of its provision for the building industry. In 1953 it changed its scheme for Heating and Ventilating Engineering Practice into a single three-year self-contained craft course, removing some of the science and calculations which had been included for the sake of possible later studies, and putting the main emphasis on the young fitter's practical operations. It followed this with the similarly designed Mechanical Engineering Craft Practice, first examined in 1959. In the same year it altered its courses in building crafts and began to award a "Craft" certificate after three or more years and an "Advanced Craft" certificate after another two. The Full Technological certificate was retained and can lead into the Higher National Certificate in Building. The new scheme (Table 10) is thus a basic course for intending journeymen, with opportunities for special studies thereafter for those aiming at promotion to foremen, technicians, junior managers and above, and with a way open to professional qualification. The same principle has spread to other craft courses such as Patternmaking, Foundry Practice, Sheet Metal Work and Welding, though there are, of course, differences arising from the nature of the industries. In such ways the content of courses is being modernized, broadened and integrated. Non-vocational subjects are being encouraged also, and it is assumed that more time (up to 330 hours per year) is becoming available. Over 40 craft courses were revised between the White Papers of 1961 and the end of 1964.

As with craft courses, technician courses are being made to fit the needs of the average technician; but there is here more scope for advanced studies with a view to promotion. There are two types of technician course : those designed to follow on from a craft course ("end-on") and those designed for technicians from the outset (*"ab initio"*). An example of the end-on type is the Full Technological Certificate in Building, already mentioned. Another

TABLE 10

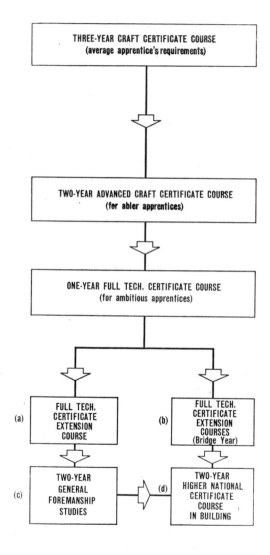

is the two-year Motor Vehicle Technicians' course (No. 170), for which a foundation of craft practice is desirable and easily obtainable in the industry, and which follows the three-year Motor Vehicle Mechanics' course (No. 168). An example of the *ab initio* type is the Mechanical Engineering Technicians' course (No. 293), which is in three two-year parts : Part I provides a broad basis in workshop technology; Part II, while continuing this, also allows specialization in one of six alternative streams; and Part III (a FTC) allows for further specialization to high-grade technician level.

All this change has involved the appearance of many quite new courses. For example, the City and Guilds Institute has introduced two new craft courses in Aeronautical Practice (Nos. 332–3) and five in Motor Vehicle Body Work (Nos. 294–8). Its newer technician courses include two in Telecommunications (Nos. 49 and 300), one Electrical (No. 57), three in Aeronautical Engineering (Nos. 171, 175 and 371), two Metallurgical (Nos. 154–5), one in Construction (No. 314) and the one mentioned in Mechanical Engineering (No. 293, to replace Machine Shop Engineering). All these technician courses are *ab initio*. Others are in preparation and older ones are being redesigned. There were 113 craft and 110 technician courses in 1964.

Indeed, the whole programme of City and Guilds courses is in a state of change. The courses were classified into eleven occupational grades in 1959. In 1963–4 they engaged 405,000 students in England and Wales. Over three-quarters of these were part-time day and most of the remainder attended in the evenings only, but 3 per cent were full-time or sandwich. In round figures, in 1964 there were 198,000 examination entrants from the British Isles and another 27,000 from overseas; 63 per cent passed. This total of 225,000 candidates was nearly five times the 1947 figure. Four subjects together took over one-quarter of them : Telecommunications Technicians, Machine Shop Engineering, Carpentry and Joinery, and Automobile Engineering Practice (in that order); but this proportion is falling. There were 282 subjects offered in 1966–7 (Table 11).

The National Certificate and Diploma schemes

These, too, grew up between the wars, and continue to exercise a powerful influence on the pattern of Further Education. Their structure derives from a three-evenings-per-week system. They appear to satisfy four groups of need : the working apprentices' for a nationally recognized qualification, based on continuous study and assessment, and providing a route to professional status alternative to that of the universities; industry's for technicians trained to a high level in both practice and theory; teachers' for freedom and flexibility in planning syllabuses; and professional institutions' for the control of standards.

H

TABLE 11

CITY AND GUILDS OF LONDON INSTITUTE:
SUBJECTS IN WHICH EXAMINATIONS WERE OFFERED IN 1966

The classification is based, as far as possible, on the Standard Industrial Classification, Central Statistical Office. Each subject, however, is included under one heading only, even although it may have relevance to more than one of the groups.

General Courses
(for intending technicians)

246. General Course in Science
287. General Course in Engineering
313. General Course in Construction
322. General Course in Shipbuilding
354. General Course in Printing

Agriculture and Agricultural Engineering

260. Agricultural Mechanic's Certificate
261. Agricultural Engineering Technician's Certificate
262. Horticulture (Stage I)—General Horticulture
265. General Agriculture (Stage I) (*Old Scheme*)—Crop Husbandry
266. General Agriculture (Stage I) (*Old Scheme*)—Animal Husbandry
267. General Agriculture (Stage I) (*Old Scheme*)—Farm Machinery (Introductory)
268. General Agriculture (Stage II)—Crop Husbandry
269. General Agriculture (Stage II)—Animal Husbandry
270. General Agriculture (Stage II)—Farm Machinery, Operation and Care
271. General Agriculture (Stage II)—Records and Accounts
272. General Agriculture (Stage II)—Farm Maintenance and Repair
273. Horticulture (Stage II)—Principles and Practice
274. Horticulture (Stage II)—Machinery
275. Horticulture (Stage II)—Records and Accounts
276. Horticulture (Stage II)—Foremanship (Local Authority Services)
277. Horticulture (Stage III)—Organization and Management
278. General Agriculture (Stage III)—Organization and Management

Mining and Quarrying

25. Coal Mining Certificate
26. Colliery Mechanic's Certificate
27. Colliery Electrician's Certificate
189. Colliery Mechanic's Advanced Certificate
190. Colliery Electrician's Advanced Certificate
191. Coal Mining Advanced Certificate
196. Iron Ore Operatives' Course
197. Iron Ore Quarrying Certificate
198. Iron Ore Quarrying Advanced Certificate
199. Coal Preparation Practice
252. Sand, Gravel and Quarrying Operative's Certificate
253. Sand, Gravel and Quarrying Certificate
254. Sand, Gravel and Quarrying Advanced Certificate
359. Coal Preparation Technology

Food Technology and Catering

112. Flour Milling (*New Scheme*)
112. Flour Milling (*Old Scheme*)
147. Basic Cookery for the Catering Industry
150. Catering Trades Basic Training Course
151. Cookery for Hotels and Catering Establishments (*Old Scheme*)
151. Cookery for the Hotel and Catering Industry (*New Scheme*)
152. Advanced Cookery for Hotels and Restaurants (*Old Scheme*)
152. Advanced Cookery for the Hotel and Catering Industry (*New Scheme*)
156. Breadmaking and Flour Confectionery
157. Design and Decoration of Flour Confectionery
158. Cocoa, Chocolate and Sugar Confectionery Manufacture
159. Milk Pasteurization and Distribution
160. Milk Processing and Control
353. Kitchen Supervision and Organization

Chemicals and Allied Industry

5. Advanced Fuel Technology
7. Petroleum and Petroleum Products

TABLE 11 (continued)

9. Paint Technology (Old Scheme)
11. Technology of Plastics (Old Scheme)
24. Chemical Plant Operation
120. Rubber Workshop Practice
250. Printing Ink Technician's Certificate
251. Printing Ink Technician's Advanced Certificate
315. Chemical Technician's Certificate
357. Paint Technician's Course (New Scheme)
358. Plastics Technician's Course (New Scheme)

Metal Manufactures

15. Iron and Steel Operatives' Course
61. Patternmaking
62. Foundry Practice
130. Goldsmiths' and Silversmiths' Work
131. Silversmiths' Work—Allied Crafts
132. Jewellery
154. Metallurgical Technician's Certificate
155. Metallurgical Technician's Advanced Certificate
249. Foundry Craft Practice
321. Foundry and Patternshop Technician's Certificate

Electrical Engineering

47. Electronics Servicing
48. Radio and Television Servicing
49. Telecommunication Technicians' Course
51. Electrical Installation Work
52. Electrical Engineering Practice
53. Radio Servicing Theory (Overseas Centres and H.M. Forces only)
55. Radio Amateurs' Examination
56. Industrial Radiography Technicians' Course
57. Electrical Technicians' Courses
58. Electrical Fitters' Courses
113. Illuminating Engineering
300. Supplementary Studies in Telecommunication and Electronics
304. Ordinary Certificate in Electrical Engineering (Overseas Centres only)
305. Higher Certificate in Electrical Engineering (Overseas Centres only)

327. Ordinary Technician Diploma in Mechanical and Electrical Engineering (Overseas Centres only)
346. Electricity Distribution Operative's Course
347. Electrical Craft Practice

Mechanical Engineering

64. Engineering Planning, Estimating and Costing
65. Boilermakers' Work
66. Sheet Metal Work
72. Refrigeration Practice
73. Science and Technology of Refrigeration
74. Welding
79. Instrument Maintenance
176. Fabrication of Steelwork
181. Heating and Ventilating Engineering Technicians' Course
185. Instrument Making
193. Mechanical Engineering Craft Practice
256. Heating and Ventilating Engineering Fitter/Welders' Course (Oxy-Acetylene)
257. Heating and Ventilating Engineering Fitter/Welders' Course (Metal-Arc)
259. Heating and Ventilating Engineering Draughtsmen's Course
293. Mechanical Engineering Technicians' Courses
302. Ordinary Certificate in Mechanical Engineering (Overseas Centres only)
303. Higher Certificate in Mechanical Engineering (Overseas Centres only)
309. Instrument Maintenance Craft Certificate
310. Industrial Measurement and Control Technician's Certificate
311. Instrument Production Craft Practice
312. Instrument Production Technician's Certificate
323. Welding Craft Practice
327. Ordinary Technician Diploma in Mechanical and Electrical Engineering (Overseas Centres only)
339. Heating, Ventilating and Air Conditioning Technician's Certificate
360. Fabrication, Engineering Craft Practice

TABLE 11 (*continued*)

Shipbuilding and Marine Engineering

87. Marine Plumbing
182. Shipbuilding
183. Ship Joinery
184. Yacht and Boat Building
289. Shipbuilding Technician's Certificate
299. F.T.C. in Shipbuilding Crafts

Vehicles

168–170. Automobile Engineering Practice Subjects
  168. Motor Vehicle Mechanics' Work (*Old Scheme*)
  169. Motor Vehicle Electricians' Work
  170. Motor Vehicle Technicians' Work
  168. Motor Vehicle Mechanics' Work (*New Scheme*)
171. Aeronautical Engineering Practice
175. Aircraft Electrical Practice
294–298. Vehicle Body Craft Subjects
  294. Vehicle Body Building
  295. Panel Beating
  296. Vehicle Painting and Industrial Finishing
  297. Vehicle Body Trimming
  298. Vehicle Body Work
318. Vehicle Body Engineering Technician's Certificate
332. Aeronautical Engineering Craft Practice (Mechanical)
333. Aeronautical Engineering Craft Practice (Electrical)
371. Aeronautical Engineering Technician's Certificate

Textiles

30A. Technician's Certificate in Wool Textiles Raw Materials (*New Scheme*)
30A. Woollen and Worsted Raw Materials (*Old Scheme*)
30B. Woolcombing
30C. Technician's Certificate in Worsted Spinning (*Revised Scheme*)
30C. Worsted Spinning (*Old Scheme*)
30D. Technician's Certificate in Woollen Yarn Manufacture (*Revised Scheme*)
30D. Woollen Yarn Manufacture (*Old Scheme*)
30E. Technician's Certificate in Woollen and Worsted Weaving

32. Technician's Certificate in Yarn Production (Short Staple System) (*New Scheme*)
32. Cotton Spinning (*Old Scheme*)
33. Plain Cotton Weaving
34. Technician's Certificate in Weaving (Cotton and Man-made Fibres) (*New Scheme*)
34. Cotton Weaving (*Old Scheme*)
35. Technician's Certificate in Flax Spinning (*Revised Scheme*)
35. Flax Spinning (*Old Scheme*)
36. Technician's Certificate in Linen Weaving (*Revised Scheme*)
36. Linen Weaving (*Old Scheme*)
37. The Manufacture of Silk and Man-made Fibres
38. Jute Spinning (*Old Scheme*)
39. Jute Weaving (*Old Scheme*)
40. Manufacture of Hosiery and Knitted Goods
41. Mill Engineering and Services
42. Industrial Organization
43. Chemistry as applied to the Textile Industry
44. Appreciation of Colour and Design
45. The Dyeing of Textiles
250. Technician's Certificate in Jute Manufacture (*New Scheme*)
330. Worsted Spinning Craft Certificate (*New Scheme*)
348. Craft Certificate in Wool Textiles Raw Materials (*New Scheme*)
349. Craft Certificate in Woollen and Worsted Weaving and Tuning (*New Scheme*)

Clothing, Footwear and Leather

18. Leather Manufacture, Dyeing and Finishing
116. Tailor's Cutting and Tailoring
126. Dress Manufacture
128. Clothing Technology
129. Leather Goods Manufacture
137. Boot and Shoe Manufacture
138. Surgical Shoemaking
139. Boot and Shoe Repairing
279. Rural Saddlers' Work
366. Craft Certificate for Clothing Machine Mechanics

Furniture and Timber

81. Machine Woodworking
103. Furniture Industry

TABLE 11 (continued)

Paper and Printing

165. Paper and Board Making Practice
166. Science and Technology of Paper and Board Making
200. Typographic Design
201. Compositors' Work
202. Line Composition
203. 'Monotype' Composition
205. Letterpress Machine Printing
206. Photogravure Machine Printing
207. Letterpress Rotary Machine Printing
208. 'Monotype' Caster Work
209. Electrotyping and Stereotyping
210. Photo-engraving
211. Photogravure
212. Photolithography
215. Lithographic Printing
216. Craft Certificate in Bookbinding and Printing Warehouse Practice
217. Advanced Craft Certificate in Bookbinding
218. Advanced Craft Certificate in Publishers' Edition Bookbinding
219. Advanced Craft Certificate in Printing Warehouse Practice
221–224. Full Technological Certificate in Printing Subjects
 221. General Survey of the Printing Industry
 222. Technical Processes of Printing
 223. Appreciation of Design and Colour in Printing
 224. Applications of Science in Printing
225. Printers' Costing
226. Printers' Estimating
227. Printing Administration
325. Graphic Reproduction
351. Printing Management

Building

80. Carpentry and Joinery
82. Brickwork
83. Masonry
84. Plasterers' Work
85. Painters' and Decorators' Work
86. Plumbers' Work
89. Builders' Quantities
90. Welding in Relation to Plumbers' Work
91. Structural Engineering
92. Mastic Asphalt Work
93. Concrete Practice
94. Stair Construction and Handrailing
95. Formwork for Concrete Construction
96. Roof Slating, Tiling and Cement Work

97. Furnace Brickwork
98. General Foremanship Studies in relation to the Building Industry
99. Roadwork
110. Concrete Technology (Supervisory Level)
121. Plumbing Design and Quantities
288. Structural Detailing
291 & 292. F.T.C. Qualifying Examination in Building Crafts
306. Ordinary Certificate in Building (*Overseas Centres only*)
307. Higher Certificate in Building (*Overseas Centres only*)
308. Higher Certificate in Civil Engineering (*Overseas Centres only*)
314. Construction Technician's Certificate (Part I) and (Part II)
328. Ordinary Technician Diploma in Building and Civil Engineering (*Overseas Centres only*)
331. Blocklaying and Concreting Craft Certificate (*Overseas Centres only*)
334. Glazing
335. Wall and Floor Tiling
356. Formwork Planning and Technology

Gas, Electricity, Water

12. Gas Utilization
13. Gas Fitting
29. Steam Utilization Practice
75. Boiler Operator's Certificate
76. Boiler-House Practice
77. Combustion Engineering Practice
167. Power Plant Operation
192. Steam Turbine Plant Operation

Distributive Trades

122. Wholesale Textile Distribution
133. National Retail Distribution Certificate
134. Retail Trades Junior Certificate
135. Retail Distributive Trades Junior Course (Scotland)
136. Certificate in Retail Management Principles
188. Solid Fuel Production, Distribution and Utilization

Professional, Scientific and Miscellaneous

107. Photography
117. Dental Technician's Certificate

TABLE 11 (*continued*)

118. Dental Technician's Advanced Certificate
119. Science Laboratory Technician's Certificate & Advanced Certificate
146. Kiln Burner's Certificate
195. Work Study
228. Technical Illustration
229. Technical Authorship
263. Hairdressing, Basic Craft Course
264. Hairdressing, Advanced Craft Course
290. Radiation Safety Practice
317. Traffic Engineering Technician's Certificate
319. Certificate for Computer Personnel
336. Technical and Scientific Editing
361. Glass Manufacture and Processing (Part I)

Teacher's Qualifications

162. Teacher's Certificate in Handicraft
163. Technical Teacher's Certificate
164. Domestic Subjects (Further Education) Teacher's Certificate

Domestic Subjects

231. Embroidery
232. Advanced Embroidery
233. Dress
234. Advanced Dress

235. Millinery
236. Advanced Millinery
239. Ladies' Tailoring
240. Advanced Ladies' Tailoring
241. Home Upholstery and Soft Furnishings
242. Advanced Home Upholstery and Soft Furnishings
243. Domestic Cookery
244. Advanced Domestic Cookery
245. Home Management
247. Hand Loom Weaving
248. Advanced Hand Loom Weaving

SUBJECTS IN WHICH EXAMINATIONS WILL BE OFFERED SUBSEQUENTLY TO 1966–1967

265. General Agriculture (Stage I) (*New Scheme*)—Crop Husbandry
266. General Agriculture (Stage I) (*New Scheme*)—Animal Husbandry
267. General Agriculture (Stage I) (*New Scheme*)—Farm Machinery
320. Advanced Certificate for Computer Personnel (1967–68)
338. Heating and Ventilating Pipe Welding (1967–68)
344. General Photography (1967–68)
345. Photographic Technician's Certificate (1967–68)
365. Technician's Certificate in Smallware Weaving (1967–68)
367. Craft Certificate in Tailoring
368. Advanced Craft Certificate in Retail Bespoke Tailoring
369. Craft Certificate in Women's Light Clothing Manufacture

They are administered by joint committees on which the Secretaries of State, professional institutions and teachers are represented and to which syllabuses must be submitted for approval. The examinations are set and marked by college teachers or (commonly in smaller colleges) by a regional union, but they are assessed by an external examiner appointed by the professional institution concerned and acting under the control of the joint committee. Homework, drawings, notebooks and so on may be called for by the assessors. The Certificates and Diplomas are endorsed by both the Department and institutions concerned.

There are certain differences in Scotland. In most subjects there are separate Scottish joint committees. The subject coverage is not quite the same—for example, Scotland has a joint committee for mathematics but England and Wales has not. One set of rules governs all Scottish schemes. A central co-ordinating and examining body (SANCAD—see Chapter 17) acts for the colleges, devising common syllabuses and examination papers. "Distinction" is higher.

The scheme in Mining, however, applies through the whole UK.

Most have Ordinary and Higher levels (Table 12). The courses for ORDINARY CERTIFICATES (ONC) were until 1963 based on three years of part-time study (S1, S2, S3). Each year had to contain at least 150 hours; and the usual post-war practice has been to allow for one afternoon and two evenings, or one whole day and one evening, per week. The ORDINARY DIPLOMAS (OND) are two-year full-time (OD1, OD2), broader in scope than the ONC, and usually taken in a thin-sandwich course. The HIGHER CERTIFICATES (HNC) need two more years of part-time study (A1, A2 or HC1, HC2) and the HIGHER DIPLOMAS (HND) need three years in a sandwich course or two or three years full-time (HD1, etc.).

The standard of the ONC is about that of the A level of the General Certificate of Education (GCE), and the OND is a little higher. The HNC and HND are usually thought to be at about the level of a university pass degree in the main subjects taken, but the range of subjects, particularly for the HNC, is narrower.

Before 1959 a student aged sixteen could be put into the first year of a National Certificate course if he could satisfy his principal or head of department as to his fitness to do so; there were no formal admission requirements. But to go on to gain a certificate he had then to obtain, *in each class for each year* : at least 60 per cent of possible attendances; at least 40 per cent of possible marks in homework, classwork, laboratory work and an annual examination, considered separately; and in the last year, at least 50 per cent of an overall total of possible marks, worked out in a loaded scheme.

This system was severely criticized by the English Central Advisory Council in the Crowther Report. The Council tried to measure the "wastage" and "retardation" during part-time courses, which had been causing concern for some time and had also worried the Percy Committee fourteen years earlier. By "wastage" was meant the proportion of students who did not gain certificates at all; and the Council found that of all students entering ONC courses without exemptions in 1951, only 26 per cent eventually gained Ordinary and only 10 per cent Higher Certificates. Similar results were obtained from a survey of six City and Guilds five-year craft and technician courses in engineering and building. By "retardation" was meant the proportion of students who did eventually gain certificates but in more than the "standard" time; and the Council found that of engineering students entering ONC courses in 1951, only 11 per cent gained Ordinary Certificates in the standard three years and only 3·3 per cent gained Higher Certificates in the standard total of five years. Wastage and retardation among students exempted from S1 were nearly as high.

The Council came to the conclusion that the two most important causes of these high rates of wastage and retardation were shortage of time, and weakness in the basic subjects, particularly mathematics. The Percy Report had said exactly the same about the HNC in 1945; indeed such comments can be found as early as 1904, long before the National schemes. The Council considered that one day a week did not allow nearly enough time for young people to study for skilled occupations and should therefore be replaced by block and sandwich release. For technicians, it suggested, sandwich courses should become the norm; and there should be a great increase in college-based courses, both sandwich and full-time. Evening study, particularly in vocational subjects, it considered unsuitable for young people. As a minimum immediate reform it recommended that the hours of part-time day release should be increased from the then 220–270 per year to the 330 laid down for county and junior colleges in the Acts and already being worked in some colleges and works schools. Weakness in the basic subjects, it thought, was aggravated by gaps in the passage from school to college. It also held the rules governing annual promotion and the award of

TABLE 12

NATIONAL CERTIFICATES AND DIPLOMAS AWARDED IN 1964

ENGLAND AND WALES

Subject	Year scheme started	No. awarded			
		Certificates		Diplomas	
		Ordinary	Higher	Ordinary	Higher
Building	1929	2,494	1,405	309	114
Business studies	1960	1,504	697	734	163
Chemistry and Applied chemistry	1921	1,756	1,284	—	60
Applied physics	1945	557	391	—	12
Applied biology	1963	—	86	—	—
Aeronautical engineering	1958	—	26	—	4
Chemical engineering	1951	—	90	—	—
Civil engineering	1943	—	700	—	—
Electrical engineering	1923	5,974	2,810	19	333
Engineering	1960	—	—	306	—
Foundry technology	1963	12	—	—	—
Mechanical engineering	1920	9,609	4,018	346	655
Production engineering	1941		648	—	32
Metallurgy	1945	370	341	—	67
Mining	1951	506	151	—	110
Naval architecture	1926	90	52	—	—
Textiles	1934	170	71	—	—
TOTAL		23,030	12,790	1,174	1,550

Source: Department of Education and Science: *Statistics of Education, 1964, Part 2*, tables 26–28 (1965).

TABLE 12 (*continued*)

SCOTLAND

| Subject | No. awarded | | | |
| | Certificates | | Diplomas | |
	Ordinary	Higher	Ordinary	Higher
Building	136	93	—	6
Biology	58	17	—	—
Chemistry and Applied chemistry	213	143	—	—
Mathematics	15	—	—	—
Applied physics	23	23	—	—
Chemical engineering	—	10	—	—
Civil engineering	—	108	—	—
Electrical engineering	386	215	—	4
Engineering	—	—	7	—
Mechanical engineering	782	354	31	8
Production engineering	—	78	—	—
Metallurgy	45	35	—	—
Mining	59	13	11[1]	—
Mining surveying	—	13	—	—
Naval architecture	32	17	—	—
TOTAL	1,749	1,119	49	18

[1] National Diplomas in Mining.

Source: Secretary of State for Scotland: *Education in Scotland in 1964*, table 15 (1965).

Certificates in National schemes responsible for much waste of time. And it wanted to see curricula reorganized to make them broader and more general.

The dearth of courses intermediate in difficulty between craft and ONC had long been felt also, as mentioned already.

In an attempt to meet this criticism changes were made, following the White Papers of 1961 and Circular 1/61. To reduce wastage and retardation there is now more stress on the preparation and selection of entrants to Ordinary Certificates and Diplomas, and in England and Wales there are preliminary courses suitable for part-time day study immediately after leaving school (see p. 105). The ONC courses (including Scottish) have been shortened to two years (O1, O2) which are of at least the standard of the old S2 and S3. The new O1 started in September 1963. The qualifications for admission have been correspondingly raised and standardized at four appropriate O-level passes in the GCE, a sufficiently good performance in one of the new preliminary courses, or the display of exceptional academic ability during at least two years of a technician or three years of a craft course. In Scotland admission to ONC and OND courses is one of the purposes of the new Scottish Certificate of Education (SCE) in which four passes are needed for admission to the OND and three for the ONC. The technician courses are to serve the needs of those not quite able to get into O1. There has been some relaxation of examination rules in National schemes, principals of colleges having been given more power.

The Ministers hoped, too, that employers would give more day, block and sandwich release, particularly to fifteen-year-olds, so that no young student would have to rely wholly on evening study, and preliminary vocational courses at evening institutes could be discontinued.

Like those of the City and Guilds Institute, National courses are also being reorganized, with broadening of their content. For example, Mechanical and Electrical Engineering for ONC and OND have been joined as Engineering. A similar move for Sciences came into effect in England and Wales in September 1965. Much revision of courses is going on, and new subjects are being introduced.

Following Circular 3/63 the hours of attendance are being increased too. The four-session day, containing a "twilight" session between 5 and 7 in the evening, is one way of doing this.

Full-time apprentice courses

The Carr and Crowther Reports urged industry to expand its intake of apprentices sufficiently to take advantage of the bulge in the population of sixteen-year-olds which would reach a peak in 1963. The Carr Committee thought that finding training facilities with firms would be the chief difficulty.

The Central Advisory Council calculated (see Chart 17 in the Crowther Report) that to maintain the post-war rate of increase in the proportion of boys aged sixteen in England and Wales getting release, the number released in 1961–2 would have to be about 105,000; or merely to keep the proportion at its 1957–8 level of 31 per cent without raising it, the number would have to be about 85,000. With a different method of counting, it turned out to be in fact 74,000, which, on the basis of estimation used for the earlier figures, would have been equivalent to about this 85,000.

The Council expected it to fall short, however, and as a temporary measure, recommended one-year full-time introductory and diagnostic courses in Local Colleges. Shorter courses of this kind had in fact been pioneered by colleges (for example Lancaster and Morecambe, Birkenhead) from about 1958. In Circular 9/60 the Minister took up the idea, suggesting the provision of courses integrating education with general training in basic skills, for employed young people, counting as the first year of their apprenticeship. In 1961–2 nearly 3,000 first-year apprentices and learners aged at least sixteen in paid employment attended such courses in 86 colleges arranged by 58 authorities. Similar developments in Scotland followed Scottish Circular 450. Another 300 were accommodated in the 13 training centres run by the Ministry of Labour, mentioned earlier. But the response from firms to both kinds of provision was disappointing. Numbers remained small.

Thus in 1961–2, the line (expressed as the proportion released of one year-group in the population of boys) was only held at just above the 1957–8 level. The post-war rate of advance was not maintained, and it had not been regained by 1964–5 (Table 13). Indeed, the proportion of girls entering apprenticeship is lower now than in 1959 (Table 9).

However, there was an increase in such courses following the White Paper *Industrial Training* (1962), which, as mentioned earlier, recommended them as a first priority. Indeed, they are now no longer thought of as an emergency measure for the population bulge but as a normal development. Nearly 7,000 attended them in 1965.

Courses for women's crafts

These have followed a path of evolution similar to that of men's courses. Where they mainly differ is that there has been less reorganization of syllabuses, and the distinction between vocational and non-vocational subjects is perhaps less clear. Some of them have long been offered in evening institutes. Clearly vocational courses include full-time one- or two-year pre-employment courses (in, for example, dressmaking, millinery, junior nursing, nursery nursing or catering); full-time courses in domestic science or institutional housekeeping; or part-time day courses for hairdressing apprentices, hospital cadets or nursery assistants. These are provided in technical colleges, some of which are specially biased in this direction. Well over half of girl apprentices are in hairdressing. City and Guilds courses at ordinary and advanced craft levels in subjects such as ladies' and children's tailoring, dressmaking, needlework, embroidery, home upholstery, basketry, soft toy making and cookery are widely available by evening study at both technical colleges and evening institutes. Such provision overlaps with Adult Education.

Preliminary courses

Until the end of the summer term 1970 (after which the school-leaving age will be raised to sixteen), pupils who leave school at fifteen experience a gap between the end of their secondary education and the beginning of a senior course at a college. Many sixteen-year-old leavers, too, need further preparation for admission to senior courses. In the past the regional unions have provided PRELIMINARY or "PRE-SENIOR" (PST) syllabuses and examinations, called Pre-National (PNC), pre-technical (PTC) and pre-craft (PCC), to tide school leavers over this period. As mentioned, these have been mainly offered in evening institutes; but wastage has been high.

The colleges, too, have run PRE-EMPLOYMENT and PREAPPRENTICESHIP courses. These have had four main aims : to maintain the habits of study which the intending apprentice or trainee should have acquired at school; to prepare him for his later studies by extending his general education, particularly in mathematics and science; to counteract the ever-present tendency to premature specialization; and to diagnose his abilities, enabling him to be given better guidance into suitable courses. In some cases remission of time to the completion of apprenticeship has been given by employers in recognition of attendance.

Full-time courses (often called "end-on") were started in Glasgow in 1911 and have become well known in Scotland. In England and Wales, too, there are plenty of examples of courses of one and two years for fifteen-year-old students and of one year for sixteen-year-olds, in engineering, building, nautical subjects, catering, commerce, nursing, agriculture, horticulture, textiles, tailoring and other subjects. For example, a course in building began at York in 1950. There is also a good deal of work for the GCE and SCE, with which preapprenticeship courses may link up, particularly since the introduction of the new ONC scheme. Mabel Fletcher Technical College, Liverpool, offers a one-year junior nursing course starting at fifteen, a two-year pre-nursing course at sixteen, some two- or three-year science-technicians' and catering courses at fifteen or sixteen, a one-year course in retail distribution at fifteen, and four two-year needle-trades courses at fifteen or sixteen which are intended to take the place of half of an apprenticeship. Several colleges run one-year pre-building courses for college-based fifteen-year-olds, the national joint apprenticeship council and the National Federation of Building Trades Employers guaranteeing each student an apprenticeship at the end of it with time spent after the age of sixteen remitted. One of these, Birkenhead, has for some time offered a nine-month course in basic workshop training for holders of four GCE passes which must include mathematics and science (thus coming mainly from grammar schools).

To help meet the bulge the Minister encouraged all such studies in Circular 9/60. He had particularly in mind courses precisely defined as follows : one-year full-time, provided in consultation with the Youth Employment Service for non-employed school leavers intending to seek apprenticeship, and designed to take the place of the first year of apprentice training. Courses of this kind had been known in Scotland since 1953 and were commended in the Scottish White Paper of 1961 and Scottish Circulars 450 and 521. In England and Wales about 3,200 young people attended such courses arranged by 83 authorities at 120 colleges in 1961–2.

Part-time day courses lasting one and two years have been even more common. In particular, the introductory and diagnostic GENERAL courses for intending technicians, already mentioned, are a central feature of the pattern announced in the Minister's White Paper of 1961. The first one, in engineering, was introduced in Administrative Memorandum 10/61, with syllabuses drawn up by the Standing Committee of Technical Examining Bodies. It is in two alternatives: a one-year course (G*) for the sixteen-year-old school leaver, and a two-year (G1, G2) for the fifteen-year-old (Table 20). G1 in Engineering started in September 1961, G* and G2 in 1962. G1 in Textiles started in 1962, Mining in 1963 and Science, Shipbuilding and Construction in 1964. A G course in Printing is to start in 1966.

In so far as they are comparable (as in mathematics), the standard intended in G2 and G* appears to be at (or slightly higher than) the level of the former S1.

Evening-only courses in vocational subjects for young people, as mentioned, are supposed to be on the way out. As part of this move the regional unions have withdrawn their preliminary technical schemes. However, without compulsion on employers there are always likely to be many young people who cannot get release. Indeed, during 1963–4 well over two-thirds of all students under sixteen in Further Education in England and Wales were attending in the evenings only. From a Ministry survey it has been estimated that there were about 150,000 students under eighteen taking *vocational* courses in this way. Therefore some colleges are offering the new General courses on three evenings per week for three years—surely a severe prospect for any school leaver.

The G scheme has not been introduced in Scotland, where it is stated that there is already sufficient general education in schools and in full-time courses at further education centres to provide for the needs of intending apprentices.

Courses for operatives

These are of comparatively recent origin. As mentioned in Chapter 2, the growing complexity of industrial processes has created a need for even the semiskilled operator of plant or machinery to receive some organized teaching. It is also recognized that there is more than one grade of operative.

The main aim of an operatives' course is to impart a deeper understanding of the principles underlying the daily jobs and a wider knowledge of the processes of the industry as a whole. Some of these courses, however, can lead to technician standard. Though planned with the needs of young entrants foremost in mind, they are intended to be of value to older workers too. Day or block release are recommended, not evenings.

In 1963–4 the City and Guilds Institute offered twenty-four such courses. Examples were the Boiler Operator's Certificate (for stokers, firemen and the like) and Iron and Steel Operatives' Course. For higher-grade operatives, examples were Flour Milling, Concrete Practice, Boiler-House Practice and Power Plant Operation. There were also new courses in Radiation Safety Practice, Coal Preparation and Boot and Shoe Manufacture. Two-stage courses are coming in, as with craft courses. The degree of support by employers will be crucial.

General studies

With the advance of technology and the growing need for occupational flexibility it has long been realized that courses for operatives, craftsmen and technicians have been too narrowly vocational, mainly because of the shortage of time; and this was emphasized again in the Crowther Report. Courses containing English, physical education and general studies of many kinds have long been known in day continuation schools, day colleges, technical colleges and "county colleges" (see Chapter 10), but on a relatively small scale. In technical colleges "day continuation sections" have been usually in general-studies or commerce departments.

Although such work has been designed mainly for the unskilled, some experience of integrating it with vocational courses for the skilled has also been gained. The White Paper of 1961 encouraged such experiments, suggesting that when the hours of day release for craftsmen and technicians were increased to 330, some of the added time should be given to general studies. This is now being done, the Ministry having insisted on at least sixty hours being so used. In the G course in Engineering some colleges are allotting as much as *all* of the additional ninety hours to English and general studies, and a special committee appointed by the Minister has published notes for their guidance (1962). Similar courses have appeared for operatives and were commended by the ITC (1960, 1962). English and liberal studies are included also in new craft, technician, ONC, OND and other courses. In every case mentioned they need not be examined, and no syllabuses are called for by joint committees; but examinations are available if wanted.

However, the technical content of courses always tends to grow, making pressure on available time even greater. In the colleges there is therefore much criticism of these moves, and the status of general studies tends to be low. On the whole, too, general studies tend to be tacked on as an addition to vocational studies rather than permeating or transforming them.

The expansion of provision

Growing points

The most actively growing parts of the sector can now be recapitulated. In the earlier period after the war there was a marked growth in craft and technician apprenticeship. This usually carried day release, which increased for boys and men in England and Wales from about 41,000 in 1938–9 to 496,000 in 1964–5. But there were only 79,000 girls and women released in 1964–5. For both, the rate of increase suffered a check in 1957. As for the under-eighteens, the number released actually declined between 1956 and 1965. About one-fifth of these young workers got day release in 1964–5, including only 7 per cent of the girls (Table 13). In Scotland less than half the under-eighteens in *skilled* employment were released. Block and sandwich release, however, have recently made their appearance for technicians and to a small extent for craftsmen, and are now growing. Hours at college have been increased by about one-third.

Courses are being reorganized. New ones are becoming available, with a content and structure better adapted to the changing needs of industries, more stress on general studies and a clearer differentiation between levels of difficulty. New provision for the preliminary stage is going some way towards easing the transition from school, postponing specialization, standardizing conditions of admission and aiding guidance into courses. The number of fifteen-year-olds in evening institutes, though still high, is decreasing.

Emergency measures to cope with the population bulge, particularly full-time first-year apprentice courses, failed to maintain the rate of increase in the proportion of school leavers receiving apprentice training. They held it at its 1957–8 figure in 1961–2, but it then fell. Such courses, however, are now becoming normal, and this proportion is rising (Table 9).

Features retarding growth

The most thorough recent reviews were the Crowther and third Oldfield-Davies Reports.

The Crowther Report pointed out that Further Education is not, like secondary, a product of an educational policy, but has grown up as the "handmaiden of employment". This is because, in general, only in so far as young people have needed qualifications for getting jobs or gaining promotion have they sought courses and examinations, and only in so far as employers have wanted their workers trained have they allowed them to attend college during working time.

Many important features of Further Education flow from this fact. For example, day release has been given in the main to apprentices only. But the intake of apprentices depends on employers and the maximum has been limited by agreements with trade unions. And the association of day release with apprenticeship is by no means complete, nor even consistent. In engineering and building, for example, two-thirds of the intake are apprentices; in engineering, where apprenticeship schemes normally do no more than *recommend* day release, three-quarters of men under eighteen get it; but in building, where the schemes make it *obligatory* for firms which meet the conditions of the joint apprenticeship council, only half of men under eighteen get it. On the other hand, mining provides a substantial amount of day release for non-apprentices as well as for all apprentices under eighteen.

Indeed, the provision of release as between industries is extremely inconsistent (Table 13), the "standard pattern" having evolved in only a few. For girls, whose potential value to employers can never be very certain, there is hardly any at all. Block and sandwich release for non-advanced courses are scarce for both boys and girls.

Then the differentiation of accessible courses according to difficulty does not nearly match the range of ability of young people, so that even if a young worker is lucky enough to find an employer who will give release, he or she must still find a suitable course within reasonable travelling distance.

There is a marked difference, too, between completing an apprenticeship and completing a college course. The one does not depend on much intellectual effort; the other needs study and homework. The one follows automatically after the agreed time; the other depends on passing annual examinations. The one may not really need as much as five years to learn what there is to be learnt; the other may need more. During four-fifths of his working time a boy is with one set of workmates, who may have a wide range of ability; but during the other one-fifth he may be with quite different classmates, whose ability may be close to his own. Thus, in the words of the Crowther Report, he finds himself climbing two ladders simultaneously. What is more, his examinations may not be necessary to the completion of his apprenticeship; indeed, they may keep him at college long after this, even perhaps after his release has expired; they may lead neither to promotion nor even to an increase in pay; and his employer may take no interest in them whatever.

Moreover, day release, though better than no release, is an inefficient way of teaching. Particularly where it is unsupported by serious intervening

TABLE 13

PERCENTAGES OF EMPLOYEES AGED UNDER 18 GETTING DAY RELEASE IN DIFFERENT INDUSTRIES SINCE THE CROWTHER REPORT (ENGLAND AND WALES)

Industry	Boys			Girls			All		
	1957–8	1961–2	1964–5	1957–8	1961–2	1964–5	1957–8	1961–2	1964–5
Agriculture, forestry and fishing	3	10	17	2	5	5	3	9	15
Mining and quarrying	64	38	40	8	13	9	61	37	38
Food, drink and tobacco	12	15	19	8	8	7	10	11	12
Chemical and allied industries	54	64	58	23	20	18	35	37	32
Metal manufacture	50	54	56	19	17	21	42	44	47
Engineering and electrical goods	} 74	60	62	} 1	9	8	} 54	40	39
Shipbuilding and marine engineering	}	45	45	}	9	8	}	42	41
Vehicles	38	48	53	8	12	12	31	38	40
Other metal goods	15	22	19	6	5	3	10	15	12
Textiles	15	15	16	3	3	2	7	7	7
Leather, leather goods and fur	4	10	6	1	4	1	3	7	4
Clothing and footwear	16	13	14	3	2	2	5	4	4
Bricks, pottery, glass, cement, etc.		10	10		3	3		7	8
Timber, furniture, etc.	12	18	19	1	2	2	9	14	15
Paper, printing and publishing	37	43	37	2	2	2	17	21	18
Other manufacturing industries	27	21	21	10	5	4	16	11	11
Construction	50	42	44	5	5	5	47	39	41
Gas, electricity and water	80	100	85	25	26	23	64	77	68
Transport and communication	27	25	28	29	22	18	28	24	24
Distributive trades	7	8	7	3	2	2	5	4	4
Insurance, banking and finance	1	2	10	1	1	1	1	1	3
Professional and scientific services	26	29	33	33	26	25	31	27	27
Miscellaneous services	6	23	24	6	8	10	6	15	17
Public administration and defence	83	74	81	73	68	65	78	71	73
TOTAL	33	30	31	9	8	7	21	19	19

Sources: Crowther Report (1959); and Ministry of Education—Department of Education and Science: *Statistics of Education, 1961, Part 2* (1962) and *1964, Part 2* (1965).

I

study and homework, it cannot provide the intensity and continuity of experience which efficient learning needs.

Many contemporary features of apprenticeship itself have been unfavourably criticized also. These include the common insistence on five years, the restrictive limits on the age of entry, the rigid demarcations between different "skilled" occupations, the absence of supervision by any outside authority, the absence of tests of competence, the lack of organized instruction and the dearth of opportunities for girls.

Lastly, the principle of attendance under statutory compulsion, fundamental to primary and secondary education, has still not been applied in further education, despite its provision in the main Acts.

Proposals

Ever since the White Paper of 1943 the Ministers have been very emphatic that Further Education should be regarded not simply as an aid to employers but as a national investment. In the 1956 White Paper they wanted the number of employees given day release (370,000 in 1954–5, including Scotland) to be doubled through voluntary action by 1961. The Carr Report, too, urged a great increase in apprentice intake and the relaxation of restrictive conditions, appealing to both sides of industry to bring these about. None of these happened; indeed, only 536,000· were in fact released in 1961–2. Nevertheless, in Circular 1/59 and in the 1961 White Papers the Ministers were still urging employers to give more *voluntary* day release, and so were the Pimlott working party in 1962 and Henniker-Heaton Committee in 1964. The latter merely urged—by 1970—another doubling of under-eighteens released. As mentioned in Chapter 2, no *reasons* were given for the choice of this particular factor of increase; nor were previous failures analysed.

Indeed, advisory councils have not been satisfied with this recommendation. In the Oakley Report, STECC expressed great dissatisfaction with developments in Scotland and proposed compulsory registration of all young workers in skilled occupations. The Central Advisory Council for Wales went much further in the third Oldfield-Davies Report, proposing that the recruiting and training of craft apprentices be operated through the Ministry of *Education* in accord with a long-term national policy. Apprentices would be admitted to government training centres at or above the age of sixteen where they would take a broadly based three-year course containing at least two days per week at a college. During this period they would be paid a government grant and would not be employed until its completion; and they would continue to be apprentices during the first two years of employment. A national apprenticeship council would be set up to plan and administer the system. This proposal meant (a) a nationally determined apprenticeship policy and (b) the ultimate transfer of responsibility for apprentice education and training from industry and professional institutions to the education service.

The English Central Advisory Council has taken the widest overall view in the Crowther Report. It advocated, by 1979 : all fifteen-year-olds at school (two-and-a-half times the 1959 provision); half of the sixteen-, seventeen- and eighteen-year-olds in full-time or sandwich courses either at school or in further education (four times the 1959 provision); and the other half of the sixteens and seventeens getting day release backed by compulsion (three times the 1959 provision). This would require an increase in volume of provision far greater than any aimed at previously (Table 14).

The Crowther Council suggested that such expansion should be based on three principles : a closer integration between secondary and further stages, the provision of more time for all courses, and the development of what it called the "alternative road". By "alternative road" was meant a broad and humane education centred on the practical applications of science to human needs. "It should be regarded as one of the major tasks before English education", the Council wrote, "to construct a new form of education which would suffer from the defects neither of the part-time route nor of the academic in the old conventional sense". Therefore :

> the long-term aim should be to transform what is now a varied collection of plans for vocational training into a coherent national system of practical education.

Problems

Obviously the programmes proposed in these reports, if they were to be fully adopted (which, up to now, they have not been), would pose many problems, all of which could be aided at least to some extent by research. They can be considered in groups.

One group of problems might be called "understanding the present system better so as to find how best to go forward from it". For example, further studies are needed, particularly psychological and sociological, of the causes of wastage and retardation.

Another group concerns the relative merits of alternative ways of organizing facilities. For example, we need to know more about the educational effectiveness and the advantages and disadvantages to the parties concerned of different kinds of course and of different ways of providing more time. Co-ordination with secondary education would be in this group.

Problems involved in the introduction of compulsion could be the nucleus of a third group. Another would arise from the retraining of adults.

TABLE 14

PROPORTIONS OF THE POPULATION OF ENGLAND AND WALES AGED 15–18 UNDERGOING DIFFERENT KINDS OF EDUCATION, ACTUAL AND PROPOSED (approximate percentages)

	Actual, 1957-8				Actual, 1964-5				Proposed for 1979–80 in the Crowther Report			
Age:	15	16	17	18	15	16	17	18	15	16	17	18
Full-time and sandwich:												
school	37	20	11	4	61	26	14	5	100¹	50¹	50¹	50¹
further education	2	2	2	3	3	5	4	6	0	50	50	50
All full-time and sandwich	40	22	13	8	64	31	18	11	100	50	50	50
Part-time day and block-release	16	24	25	18	6	14	16	13	0	50	50	50
All daytime	56	47	38	26	70	47	34	24	100	100	100	50+
Evening-only	24	25	24	18	15	17	16	13	0 (vocational studies)	0	0	0
None	20	28	38	56	15	36	50	63	0	0	0	0
TOTAL	100	100	100	100	100	100	100	100	100	100	100	50+

¹ Percentages expected to be at school if present trends continue: 99, 57, 22, 7 respectively.

Sources: Crowther Report (1959); Department of Education and Science: *Statistics of Education, 1964, Part 2,* table 3 (1965), and *1965, Part 1,* table 1 (1966).

Then there are problems of teaching method, the use of tutorials and seminars, ways of teaching practical subjects, the linking of college work with training in industry and the induction and guidance of students. There are problems of designing curricula combining a clear differentiation of standards with flexibility of transfer from one course to another, and problems of testing, assessing and examining. More comparative studies of technical education in different countries are also needed.

Perhaps the most difficult are those concerned with *content* of teaching. Curricula must fit the needs of changing productive processes, which implies selecting the principles and operations which are of the most general significance, and planning for occupational flexibility; and they must suit students of diverse ages, abilities and backgrounds. Thus the broader purposes of education must be pursued through forms arising from both these groups of needs, a task which requires constant assessment of the place of English, social studies and so on in technical education. Indeed, the classical problem of designing a "liberal education with science and its applications as the core and inspiration", to quote the Spens Report, is reopened in the complex conditions of further education.

Notes on further study

Earlier relevant reports include the Fyfe Report (1946), the Minister's Pamphlet No. 8 (1947), the Parliamentary and Scientific Committee's *Technical Education and Skilled Man-power* (1950) and the McClelland Report (1952). The Anglo-American Council on Productivity's two reports on the training of operatives and supervisors (1951) aroused interest at the time. More recent ones were Carr (1958), Crowther (1959), Oldfield-Davies (1960 and 1961), Arrell (1962), Oakley (1962) and Henniker-Heaton (1964). See also the annual report of STECC.

The Crowther Report stimulated reforms announced in the Ministers' White Papers *Better Opportunities in Technical Education* and *Technical Education in Scotland: the Pattern for the Future* (both 1961). Further consideration was given to the proposals of this Report by a Special (Pilkington) Committee of NACEIC (1963) whose comments (Pilkington Report) were issued by the Minister as an attachment to Circular 3/63; its most interesting remarks were on induction courses, block release, and sandwich release for technicians. The Oakley Report dealt with day release in Scotland and the Henniker-Heaton Report with England and Wales.

The Crowther, two Oldfield-Davies, Oakley and Henniker-Heaton Reports have been discussed and commented on by many bodies; see, for example, BACIE: *The Implications of the Crowther Report* (1960), *Education for Survival* (1960) and *Policy in Perspective* (1960); the TUC's

Annual Report for 1960; and the ATTI's *The Henniker-Heaton Report* (1964).

Statistical and other information is contained in the annual reports of the Ministers and Secretaries of State, and, for England and Wales from 1961 onwards, in *Statistics of Education*, especially *Part 2*. See also the Ministry's *Reports on Education*, No. 2 (1963).

Government policy has been expounded in Circulars 343 (1958), 1/59, 4/60, 9/60, 1/61, 1/61 (W), 3/63 and 14/64; Administrative Memoranda 10/61, 3/64 and 4/64 (titles of which are indexed in the annual *List 10*); and Scottish Circulars 405 (1959), 450 (1961), 465 (1961), 521 (1963), 558 (1964) and 560 (1964).

Apprenticeship has been the subject of proposals in the Carr, Crowther and two Oldfield-Davies Reports. The ITC's *Craft Apprenticeship* (1962) factually summarized existing provision. General material about apprenticeship is in the *Ministry of Labour Gazette*. Specific information about schemes can be found in brochures of firms, the annual *Year Book of Technical Education and Careers in Industry* (which lists national apprenticeship agreements), reports of apprenticeship councils and the literature on careers (useful examples of which are mentioned in the *Notes* to Chapter 14).

Authoritative studies of problems of apprenticeship include Gertrude Williams : *Recruitment to Skilled Trades* (1957) and *Apprenticeship in Europe* (1963); and Kate Liepmann : *Apprenticeship* (1960). See also Margaret Croft : *Apprenticeship and the "Bulge"* (1960); Wellens : *The Training Revolution* (1963); and Beveridge : *Apprenticeship Now* (1963).

On industrial training see the above, plus the ITC's factual booklets *Training Boys in Industry, the Non-apprentice* (1960), *Training Girls in Industry* (1962), *Group Training Schemes* (1963) and *Training Advisory Services Available to Companies* (1963); and Downie : *The Training of Young People in Industry* (1965). See also the British Iron and Steel Federation's *Report on the Recruitment and Training of Technicians* (1961). For supervisors see the Wilson (1954), Barnes (1962) and Marre (1964) Reports. The Minister of Labour's proposals were in the White Paper *Industrial Training* (1962). Numerous bodies commented on the latter : for example, for a Government-sponsored body see the NEDC (1963), for teachers the EIS (1963) and ATTI (1964), and for the TUC, *Labour* for January 1963; see also BACIE (1963) and Industrial Association of Wales and Monmouthshire (1963). The outcome was the Industrial Training Act, 1964. Much has been said and written about this Act; see, for example, BACIE (1964) and Work (ATI, 1964). It was summarized for authorities and colleges in Administrative Memorandum 4/64 and for employers in the Ministry of Labour's booklet *Industrial Training Act*. See also *Education in 1963*, Chapter III (1964). For the composition of the first five industrial training boards to be set up see *Education in 1964,* p. 56 (1965) and for the next five *Education in 1965,* p. 50 (1966). The annual reports of the boards began to appear in 1965, as did that of the CTC. See also Administrative Memorandum 5/65, and the CTC's *Industrial Training and Further Education* (1965 and 1966) and *Approach to Industrial Training* (1966).

On problems of education for industry see also Wellens : *Education and Training in Industry* (1955); National Institute of Industrial Psychology : *Training Factory Workers* (1956); Venables and Williams : *The Smaller Firm and Technical Education* (1961); and Young : *Technicians Today and Tomorrow* (1965). Mills's *Techniques of Technical Training* (1953) and MacLennan's *Technical Teaching and Instruction* (1963) were guides to teaching method.

For courses, the prospectuses of examining bodies such as the City and Guilds Institute contain syllabuses and regulations. See also their annual and other reports : particularly the City and Guilds Institute's monographs *Further Education for Operatives, Further Education for Craftsmen, Further Education for Technicians* and *Education for the Printing Industry* (all 1964). City and Guilds courses were classified by Wheatley in *Vocational Aspect,* pp. 31–59, Spring 1959. The Secretary of State for Scotland's *Craft Courses in Building, Engineering and Allied Industries* (1963) was an extract from his report for 1962, published separately. See also the Hall Report (1964). National Certificate and Diploma schemes in England and Wales are governed by *Rules 100–133* laid down by the Secretary of State, titles of which are listed in HMSO's annual *Sectional List No. 2* and in the DES's *Further Education for School Leavers* (1966); and there are numerous Administrative Memoranda, for which see the annual *List 10.* These schemes were described more fully in the DES's *Reports on Education,* No. 26 (1965). In Scotland see the Secretary of State's *Rules 1* (1964), introduced with Scottish Circular 560. Information about block and sandwich courses in England and Wales used to be catalogued in the Ministry's *List 182* (1961); for Scotland see the Department's annual *Directory of Day Courses.*

More specific and local information on courses is contained in prospectuses of colleges and evening institutes, reports of authorities—such as the Cheshire Education Committee's *Training for Skill* (1961)—and *Guides* published annually by regional and district advisory councils. See also the quarterly *STECC Newsletter.*

On problems see Venables : *Sandwich Courses* (1959).

The Minister tried to clear up the confusion which had arisen between preapprentice and apprentice courses, as recommended in Circular 9/60, by further explanation in *Education in 1962,* pp. 33–34. On preemployment courses in Scotland see *Education in Scotland in 1959,* pp. 43–55, also issued separately as a pamphlet (1960); the Arrell (1962) and second Brunton (1963) Reports; and Scottish Circulars 450 (1961) and 521 (1963). On full-time preapprenticeship courses in building see Scottish Circulars 226 and 250 (1942), Dickinson's address at York (1959) and the report of the National Joint Council for the Building Industry (1960); for an example in engineering see Siklos : *Partnership Incorporated* (1963).

General studies were the subject of the Ministry's pamphlet *General Studies in Technical Colleges* (1962) and the second Brunton Report (1963). On physical education see Edmundson : *Physical Education in the Technical College* (ATI, 1961). See also *Notes* to Chapter 6.

Wastage in part-time courses has been the subject of studies reported in journals such as *Brit. J. educ. Psychol.* and *Vocational Aspect* (reviewed in *Educ. Res. and abstracted in Tech. Educ. Abstr.*). See also the Watts Report (1959) and the Crowther Report (especially Volume II). For wastage in full-time higher education see the Robbins Report, Appendix Two (A) (1963).

For a more thorough study of developments before 1958, Benge's bibliography *Technical and Vocational Education in the United Kingdom* (UNESCO, 1958) is useful.

On relations between secondary and further education, relations with industry, and educational research see later chapters.

CHAPTER 6

THE EDUCATION OF TECHNOLOGISTS
AND HIGH-GRADE TECHNICIANS

The two rivers of further education

SOME students must earn while they learn; others have chosen their parents more wisely. In mediaeval and mercantilist times ambitious poor boys sought craft apprenticeships; the clerical, professional and merchant classes used the universities to get their sons into respectably learned occupations. After the industrial revolution working men struggling for advancement formed mechanics' institutes; the new middle class founded additional universities. All these four tributaries are traceable in the two rivers of tertiary education today: technical colleges and universities. Both train technologists, but in ways appropriate to the two classes of student; and only one trains technicians. There are different streams, too, within the rivers.

Technical colleges are predominantly for the employed student. Most of their courses, therefore, have been part-time (mainly evening but latterly also day release and sandwich) for the student in apprenticeship or other form of employment. Their periods of academic study have had to be interrupted by or pursued concurrently with earning a living, suffering a consequent limitation of time which has been sometimes severe. Thus, although they may have stressed what the Percy Report euphemistically called the "art aspect" of technology, the colleges have been in fact the "handmaiden of employment". Their inspiration has been explicitly vocational. Their courses have been at all levels of difficulty, and there has likewise been a high degree of variety and flexibility in length of course, entry qualifications, study methods and timetables. Professional training has tended to be of the "concurrent" type, that is—with vocational and academic parts together. The colleges have been supervised, managed and financed by authorities under the Ministers' regulations or directly by the Ministers, and have established close links with professional and other bodies. Their hallmarks have been the City and Guilds and National Certificate schemes and the examinations of professional institutions, all of which have been largely outside their control. Thus they have had very little autonomy. They contained 150,000 advanced students in 1962–3, of whom over two-thirds were part-time.

Universities, on the other hand, provide for students not in regular employment, whose parents, albeit helped to an increasing extent by authorities and other bodies, have been able to maintain them. Their courses are almost entirely full-time, and at levels above the standard of "matriculation". Their tradition has been based on the ideal of knowledge "for its own sake". Their technology students undergo periods of concentrated academic study, stressing what the Percy Report called the "science aspect" of technology, interrupted typically only by vacations spent in industry. Professional training has tended to be the "consecutive" type, that is—with the vocational part following the academic. Universities are self-governing, deriving their powers from Royal Charters or special Acts of Parliament, though receiving over two-thirds of their income from the central government through the University Grants Committee. Their hallmarks have been "degrees", which they themselves award, and pre-eminence in research. They have enjoyed a high level of autonomy and of social prestige. There were thirty-one in 1962–3, containing 118,000 full-time students.

Industrialists have looked mainly to the university river for pure scientists and to a lesser extent for technologists. They commonly regard newly graduated technologist employees as trainees or learners, still needing professional training and experience. Industry has looked mainly to the college river for technicians and craftsmen, as well as for technologists; but, as mentioned, college-trained technologists are more likely to have had some professional training concurrently with their college courses. It has looked to neither river in particular for senior administrators or technical managers, for whom until recently there has been little available in the way of special training; but practice has varied among industries.

The rivers touch in places

There has always been a tendency, however, for technical colleges providing higher education to acquire more sandwich and full-time students, shed their part-time and non-advanced students, and either draw the two rivers together at that point, or (until 1965) cross over from one river to the other.

There are a number of examples of this drawing together. Thus Heriot-Watt College, though continuing to provide for technicians, was, until 1965, affiliated also to the University of Edinburgh, some of whose departments it housed, while retaining much of the character of a technical college. At Robert Gordon's College, Aberdeen, there is a scheme for the teaching of engineering jointly with the University; and similar conditions exist at

Central Institutions for music, art and agriculture. Six Regional Colleges (Northern and Woolwich Polytechnics plus Sir John Cass, West Ham, Liverpool and Sunderland) enjoyed special relationships with neighbouring universities which enabled their students to gain internal degrees thereof. Teaching staff at neighbouring colleges may submit work for higher degrees at the University of Sheffield. At probably over fifty colleges, *external* degrees of the University of London are taken. More recently there has been an increase in the number of college-based students in the colleges, and their sandwiches are growing thicker, so that they come to resemble their university colleagues. Conversely, too, apprentices on sandwich schemes are attending universities, perhaps after a period in industry. In such ways the rivers can approach one another.

In Scotland, universities and colleges have always been closer than in England or Wales. This is partly because of the predominance of Scottish science during the second half of the eighteenth century, which led to the founding of certain institutions a century earlier than their counterparts in England, and partly because of the leading position of the Central Institutions which combine features of both streams. The basic dividing line has been the same, but between Central Institutions and further education centres.

On the whole, the paths taken by employed and non-employed students have remained separate. The greater tendency has been for colleges providing higher technological education to *cross over* from one river to the other with their advanced full-time and sandwich students, leaving the non-advanced and part-time students behind. This trend has been much helped by the growth of three aids which have turned many otherwise part-time students into full-time or nearly full-time ones : thick-sandwich release, authority grants for full-time students at colleges as well as at universities, and aid from authorities for works-sponsored students. Such crossing over has taken place in several stages since the beginning of this century.

The transfer of full-time and sandwich higher education from one river to the other

Leading institutions, mainly pre-war

At first a small number of establishments crossed over. Thus three colleges (Birmingham, Leeds and Sheffield) became universities in the early 1900s. The Central Technical College, South Kensington, passed completely into the University of London in 1908. Two veterinary Central Institutions became university departments in 1949 and 1951. A technical college (Manchester) has since 1955 contained a university faculty of technology, besides providing for technicians.

Recognition: early post-war reports

There has always been a tendency for the technical-college river to divide, advanced full-time courses separating off from the mainstream. At first this was not much noticed. Probably because of the greater prestige of universities, the wide range of work in the colleges and the fact that the bulk of it had been for craftsmen, technicians and office workers, the magnitude of the work done in the colleges at more advanced levels was for a long time relatively unrecognized. At least in England the colleges were often thought of as places where rough young lads spent happy evenings filing lumps of iron. During and immediately after the war, however, the advanced work gained great impetus, and post-war reports drew attention to it. The colleges produced well over half of the wartime output of civil, electrical and mechanical engineers gaining HNC or above, from whom many senior administrators and technical managers were later drawn. In postgraduate work and research between 1945 and 1949, 218 higher degrees were awarded in thirty-one of the larger colleges. In 1949 there were 20,000 day students in the colleges doing work for university degrees alone. These facts greatly influenced the Percy Committee.

Proposals: the Percy Report

As mentioned earlier, the Percy Committee thought that the greatest deficiency in British industry was the shortage of organizer scientists and technologists who could apply the results of research to development. It wanted colleges and universities to share in training these during the first post-war decade, as part of a comprehensive plan of recruitment and training based on estimated national manpower requirements. But this would need, it thought, a considerable effort to free the colleges from their handicaps and to develop and upgrade their opportunities. There should be new courses at graduate and postgraduate level, in both older and newer branches of technology and in industrial management. These should be given more time, in substantial periods of concentrated full-time study of a total length at least comparable with that of an equivalent university course, but containing also a planned programme of works practice. Teachers' activities should necessarily include research. Such work should be developed mainly, though not exclusively, in a small number of selected colleges (about 27) which should receive particular treatment as regards buildings, staffing, finance and degree of self-government. Some of these colleges might contain national schools in certain specialized technologies, which, alternatively, might form special colleges. There should be closer, simpler and more systematic collaboration with industry, industrial research associations and universities. A network of advisory councils with academic boards would be needed : regional councils to regularize consultation and co-ordinate provision in different establishments, and a "National Council of Technology" to advise the Minister and the University Grants Committee. A determined attempt would have to be made to recruit and finance more and abler students, not only from schools but also from industry itself; and regular paths should be formed from industry, at various levels, back to full-time education at both college and university, and each way between college and university. There would need to be new qualifications comparable with the honours degrees, postgraduate certificates and research degrees of universities; these should be examined and awarded by colleges but guaranteed by the National Council of Technology, which would approve and moderate courses, suggest standards and select external assessors. The opinion of the Percy Committee and its chairman was divided on whether the first major qualification should be called "degree", "associateship" or "diploma", but was agreed that the second should be a doctorate.

The Percy Report has been summarized at this length because it was the first and perhaps also the most important of all the post-war educational reports. The essence of its proposals was the idea of a more fully developed form of technical education, to be fostered by separating off a part of the work of the colleges and elevating it to the status and quality of the best university study whilst encouraging the retention of its close connection with industry. This idea included the development of existing forms but also contained important novel elements. It envisaged, for example : new studies and new kinds of study; new arrangements for students; new sorts of qualification; new types of college; new relations with industry and with other sections outside the colleges; and the planning of manpower output in relation to national needs.

Early developments and difficulties: 1946–1951

Some of the Percy Report's proposals were implemented quickly. Following Circular 87 (1946) all ten regional advisory councils with their academic boards had been constituted by 1947, and there were another five in Scotland. Having in 1946 amended her Further Education Grant Regulations so as to enable her to pay all of their cost, the Minister established the College of Aeronautics and in the next year the first National

College. With Circular 137 (1947) her successor introduced technical state scholarships enabling persons employed in industry to enter college or university (100 per year, raised to 120 in 1950), and state scholarships for mature persons who had missed the chance earlier (20, raised to 30 in 1950). After the report of the Hardman Working Party (1947) the National Advisory Council on Education for Industry and Commerce (NACEIC) was set up in 1948 under the chairmanship of Lieutenant-General Sir Ronald Weeks, Chairman of Vickers Limited. However, it was given less than one of the two basic functions proposed : for it was to advise the Minister on national aspects of regional policies, and consult with (though not advise) the University Grants Committee on matters of common concern; but it was not given the job of guaranteeing new qualifications.

Another government move in line with the proposals of the Percy Report was the appointment at the end of 1945 of the Barlow Committee, mentioned in Chapter 2, to estimate the country's needs in scientific man-power. This committee agreed with the main proposals of the Percy Report, which it saw as complementary to the expansion of technology in universi-ties, and it wanted some colleges to be given full university powers.

Meanwhile other people elaborated some of the Percy Committee's remaining suggestions and put forward similar proposals of their own. The Minister, in *Youth's Opportunity* (1945), Circulars 87 and 98 (1946) and *Further Education* (1947), developed her ideas on differentiating the colleges as local, area and regional, raising their status and co-ordinating them with universities. In Circular 94 and Administrative Memorandum 134 (1946) she urged that college teachers be given time and encouragement to do research and to spend short periods in industry. The Parliamentary and Scientific Committee, an unofficial but influential group of parlia-mentarians and scientists (1947), strongly supported the Percy proposals. The Urwick (1947) and Carr-Saunders (1949) Committees recommended the development of management study both in courses of technology and for special qualifications of its own, and the Carr-Saunders Committee proposed a new qualification of graduate standard in commerce. The Anglo-American Council on Productivity (1951) supported the Percy diagnosis of the key importance of the engineer-scientist and development engineer.

The question of the proposed new technological qualifications proved difficult, particularly as to what they should be called and who should award them. On the naming of the first award, a question which had divided the Percy Committee, the Parliamentary and Scientific Committee agreed with those who had wanted it called a bachelor's degree. Both committees wanted the second award to be called a doctor's degree, and both com-mittees wanted *the colleges to award them* (at least soon) and *the new national body to guarantee them*.

The new national body itself (NACEIC), however, advised none of these. In its first report (1950) it suggested a second new body, a "Royal College of Technologists", which would award a first qualification or "associateship", a second or "membership" and a third or "fellowship" of itself. It also recommended sandwich courses, greater financial aid to authorities for advanced courses planned in consultation with industry, the shedding of elementary work by certain colleges and a more generous allocation of building permits. It made no reference to the Carr-Saunders proposal for a commerce award. In its White Paper of 1951 the Government of the day accepted all these recommendations. But it was unable to carry them out, for in the same year it was defeated in a general election.

Delays: 1951–1955

The Conservative Government rejected most of NACEIC's proposals, suspended new college building and in the following year made further building cuts. One proposal, however, it accepted, for with Circular 255 it increased its help to authorities by paying 75 per cent (instead of 60 as hitherto) of the approved net cost of providing advanced courses specifically designed to meet industrial needs, subject to fulfilment of certain conditions by the colleges concerned. By the end of 1955, 616 such courses had been approved in 25 colleges, but this was less than half of those for which application had been made. Another move was Circular 252, already mentioned, in which the Minister asked authorities to give scholarships as generously to college as to university applicants. And in Circular 270 she encouraged short courses for scientists and technologists employed in industry : 83 full-time and 843 part-time courses of this kind were reported during 1955. But the Government directed its main effort towards the expansion of universities, and especially after 1953, of Imperial College, London, for which £15 million was earmarked.

The general lack of progress in technical education at this time was severely criticized. The Advisory Council on Scientific Policy reported serious shortages of trained manpower, yet the total output of qualified scientists had begun to decline in 1951 and of technologists in 1952. In 1953 there was also a fall in the number of candidates for Ordinary and in 1954 for Higher National Diplomas. This was partly due to the absorption of the post-war backlog; even so, by 1953, Further Education building projects to the value of only £4½ million had been completed since the end of the war, and the Select Committee on Estimates (1953) condemned as wasteful the Minister's methods of approving them. The Parliamentary and Scientific Committee (1954) urged the immediate selection of about twenty colleges for "Percy treatment" and repeated its 1947 opinion that the first award should be a bachelor's degree, to be given by the colleges themselves; but these proposals were rejected in the House of Lords in December 1954. NACEIC, too, stuck to its earlier view, which it took up again with a new Minister in 1954: it repeated its 1950 proposals with different names, recommending a "Diploma in Technology" to be given by a "National Council for Technological Awards".

Revival: the Hives Council and the White Paper of 1956

The Government accepted these recommendations in July 1955 and in November the second new national council for England and Wales was set up as an independent self-governing body under the chairmanship of Lord Hives, Chairman of Rolls Royce Limited.

Building had begun to move slowly forward again with Circular 283 and Scottish Circular 296 (1954) which relaxed some restrictions on authorities. In February 1956 the Ministers jointly published a White Paper announcing a five-year programme to increase by about 60 per cent the output of students qualifying from advanced courses and double the number of young people released by employers for part-time studies. In England and Wales new building to the value of £70 million (as compared with £36 million started since the end of the war), together with new equipment worth £15 million, and in Scotland building worth £10 million and equipment worth £2 million, were to be approved. The Hives Council's new award was introduced in May; and on 21st June the programme was debated in the House of Commons, when the Government announced its intention to set up colleges of advanced technology. The annual number of technical state scholarships was raised from 120 to 150, and in the following year to 225; and ordinary state scholarships were allowed to be used in taking courses for the new Diploma in Technology award.

That this programme came none too early was demonstrated by the appearance in November 1956 of the Zuckerman Report *Scientific and Engineering Manpower in Great Britain*, in which, as mentioned earlier, it was estimated that the country's output of qualified scientists and engineers would have to be about doubled by 1970. This clearly implied commensurate increases of craftsmen and technicians, non-engineering technologists and teachers also. In the House of Lords on 21st November, spokesmen stressed the importance which the Government now attached to the part to be played by the colleges.

In October 1958 the Hives Council announced that it would create another new body, the "College of Technologists", to award a higher qualification, to be called, not a doctorate, but "Membership of the College of Technologists". Thus there were now *three* bodies instead of the one recommended in the Percy Report; yet neither these nor the colleges could award degrees.

The Minister's approval in 1958 of the authorities' building projects for 1960–1 completed the programme of approvals for the five-year period since the White Paper and showed that the target of £70 million had been reached. It contained 363 "major" projects (each then costing over £10,000), four-fifths of which were for Area and Local Colleges. In 1960 the rate of buildings completion reached £10 million per year, twice the figure for 1955. Between 1956 and 1962 the total approvals came to even more: around £120 million. In order to maintain the momentum of advance during the next three years, 1961–1964, targets of £45 million to be approved for new building in England and Wales and £9 million for equipment were announced in Circular 1/59. The combined figure for Scotland was about £8 million; and £28 millions-worth altogether had been approved by March 1963. The momentum has been increased by the approval of another £75 million for England and Wales over the three years 1964–1967; and by March 1965, approvals had totalled £180 million. Thus there has been a really big attempt to build technical colleges since 1956.

Meanwhile the advance of the CATs went on. By 1962 ten had been transferred from authorities to the Ministry and had so acquired the status which Central Institutions had enjoyed since 1901; but none of these could give degrees.

Thus, after seventeen years, the Percy concept of building up higher education in technical colleges, separating it from the technical-college mainstream and establishing a recognized place for it as university-type provision had made slight progress, at least with full-time and sandwich courses. The mainstream itself, too, was splitting into Local, Area and Regional Colleges.

New proposals and promises, 1963

The continued shortage of higher education, however, had produced further discontent, leading to the appointment of the Robbins Committee in 1960. Its proposals (1963) carried the process further. The two rivers were to continue, and indeed to be under separate Ministers; but twenty-one direct-grant and maintained colleges carrying on full-time advanced work were recommended for full transfer to the university river with power to award their own degrees, and another one for transfer without this power. In such ways the Robbins Committee continued the thinking of its Percy and Barlow predecessors.

In another White Paper (1963) the then Government accepted these proposals in principle. Two Central Institutions (Royal Technical College

K

and Scottish College of Commerce) had already planned a merger to form the University of Strathclyde. After 1963 these two, together with the College of Aeronautics, Heriot-Watt and the ten CATs (as mentioned in Chapter 4), came under the UGC.

Thus the full-time and sandwich advanced technological student was at last recognized as a university-type animal. But the part-time one was not. Therefore the old division continued, with non-advanced and part-time on one side of the pale, advanced full-time and sandwich on the other. And there were plenty of advanced full-time and sandwich students on the "part-time" side, in the Regional, Area and other untransferred colleges.

However, the student in this "part-time" side did receive one very important proposal. This was that the Hives Council be superseded by a new body or "Council for National Academic Awards", containing strong representation of authority-maintained colleges, to plan and award degrees, diplomas and certificates to candidates in any non-university establishment in the UK, and especially to those in Regional and Area Colleges and Central Institutions. These degrees could be at pass, honours and higher levels, not only in science and technology but in any other subject. They could include degrees of a new type incorporating principles and experience gained from HND, Diploma in Technology and MCT schemes (see later), which, indeed, would probably be superseded too. This new body came into existence in July 1964 under the chairmanship of Sir Harold Roxbee Cox (Chairman of Metal Box Company Limited; now Lord Kings Norton), who was then chairman of the Hives Council.

Permanent separation

Thus the Robbins Committee had envisaged a continuing transfer of colleges to the university stream as their full-time advanced work grew. Meanwhile the colleges were seen as performing a sort of equalizing, reclaiming function, helped by the CNAA, for students inevitably "left behind" in the technical-college stream. Higher education was here thought of as convergent, though hierarchic.

The thinking of the 1964 Government, however, is different. After the twelve which the UGC took over in 1965 (and perhaps also the Royal College of Art) no more are to get university status at least until 1973. Instead, the Regional and other colleges are to be encouraged to develop separately, along their own lines, parallel with but rivalling the universities. They are to expand the concurrent type of professional training, retain their higher technician and part-time courses and remain under authorities. "Promotion" of colleges or merging with universities will be ended. A "limited number", to be called "polytechnics", will be selected for special treatment; and in some areas this may involve merging of colleges. Thus the system will come to resemble a fork rather than a ladder. A dual system will be perpetuated deliberately.

Arrangements for students

Apprenticeship

A major factor in the growth of technological education has been the extension of apprenticeship, as described in the previous chapter, so that it has become a vehicle for advanced training as well as for the training of craftsmen and technicians (Table 15).

STUDENT APPRENTICES at technologist or high-grade technician level are commonly chosen by special selection boards of companies, which may also be ready to promote promising craft and technician apprentices to higher grades. They usually enter at seventeen or eighteen and need passes in several subjects at O level of the GCE, perhaps plus at least one at A; but younger or less qualified entrants may sometimes be accepted for preliminary training, and in some cases there are competitive entrance examinations taken between the ages of sixteen and eighteen or over. An undergraduate apprentice must first have obtained an offer of a university place. Schemes last for four or five years after a six-month probationary period, apprentices attending college on day, two-day, block or sandwich release, or university on thick-sandwich release.

GRADUATE APPRENTICES are taken immediately after leaving university or college. After a short probationary period such schemes generally last for up to two years during which the young graduate (or HN diplomate) learns the work of the firm and perhaps attends short courses or studies abroad. In some firms, overseas candidates are accepted into the graduate schemes only. Postgraduate scholarships may be available.

Time for study

This has been provided mainly through apprenticeship. DAY RELEASE has continued to grow; indeed, the greatest increase has been for students aged eighteen and over. Only about one-fifth of this eighteen-plus group, however, are working for recognized advanced qualifications and only about one-eighth for the HNC. As has been mentioned, day release is now commonly regarded as unsuitable for advanced courses, in any case.

The main increase has been in SANDWICH RELEASE which multiplied 22 times between 1953–4 and 1964–5. Most of this is for men; women have

TABLE 15

SUMMARY OF APPRENTICESHIP SCHEMES

AVAILABLE AT THE DIVISIONS OF BRITISH AIRCRAFT CORPORATION, 1965

Complete flexibility is maintained over the whole scheme to allow apprentices to be regraded according to merit at any stage in their training

Type of apprenticeship	Entry requirements	Arrangements for studies	Duration	Final educational qualification	Career objectives
Graduate	Degree, Diploma in Technology, or Higher National Diploma.	As agreed between the graduate and the Division, depending on the career for which he is preparing.	Up to two years.	Depending on course of study.	Generally as Technologist or Scientists in the Research and Development, Design, or Production Organization (e.g. Designer, Aerodynamicist, Structures Engineer, Systems Engineer, Development Engineer, Electronics Engineer, or Production Engineer). A variety of other opportunities arise from time to time.
Undergraduate	A place on a full-time degree course.	Release to attend University full-time during 2nd, 3rd and 4th years of apprenticeship. (Thick Sandwich Course.)	Five years (studies are counted as apprenticeship served).	University Degree. Graduate Membership of a Professional Institution.	
Student	Admission to a sandwich degree or diploma course, e.g. GCE A-level passes including Mathematics, and three O-level passes, preferably including English Language.	Six months alternately at College and in Industry during four years. (Thin Sandwich Course.)	Five years (studies are counted as apprenticeship served).	Diploma in Technology,[1] or Higher National Diploma.	

[1] Now CNAA degree. Apprentices taking this degree by thin-sandwich release are called "undergraduate".

TABLE 15 (*continued*)

Type of apprenticeship	Entry requirements	Arrangements for studies	Duration	Final educational qualification	Career objectives
Engineering	Four GCE O-level passes including Mathematics, and a suitable Science subject. Preference is given to those with English Language. (Correspondingly higher qualifications for older entrants.)[1]	Part-time day or block release.	Five years.	Higher National Certificate.	A Technician in design and drawing offices, stress office, test laboratory, electronics laboratory, instrument departments, or a planning engineer or jig and tool draughtsman, inspector.
Technician	A successful five-year secondary education, to enable entry to the second year of the General Course in Engineering at a Technical College.[1]	Part-time day or block release.	Five years.	City and Guilds Technicians' Certificate.	

[1]Account will be taken of performance in CSE examinations in accordance with officially recognized standards.

TABLE 15 (*continued*)

Type of apprenticeship	Entry requirements	Arrangements for studies	Duration	Final educational qualification	Career objectives
Craft	Good secondary education.[1]	Part-time day or block release.	Five years.	City and Guilds Craft Certificate.	A skilled craftsman (e.g. Toolmaker, Fitter, Turner and Skilled Machinist, Sheet Metal Worker, Electrician).
Graduate commercial trainee	Usually an Arts degree.	Studies for professional body where appropriate.	Up to two years.	Membership of a Professional Body where appropriate.	Purchasing, Cost and Works Accountant, Commercial Department, Data Processing, or Organization and Methods.
Senior commercial trainee	At least one GCE A-level pass, and several O-level passes, including English Language and Mathematics.	Part-time day or block release.	Five years or to completion of studies.	Higher National Certificate in Business Studies, Membership of a Professional Body.	
Junior commercial trainee	O-level GCE passes to include Mathematics and English Language.[1]	Part-time day or block release.	Two years.	Ordinary National Certificate in Business Studies.[2]	

[1] Account will be taken of performance in CSE examinations in accordance with officially recognized standards.
[2] Also Certificate in Office Studies and City and Guilds Certificate for Computer Personnel.

hardly gained at all so far. Sandwich courses were pioneered in Glasgow in the 1880s and by some English colleges soon after the turn of the century, but their students were all college-based; works-based sandwich courses are a recent growth. The advantages claimed for them have been argued by, among others, the Percy Committee (1945), NACEIC (1950, 1956), Advisory Council on Scientific Policy (1955), Bray and others (BACIE, 1956) and the FBI (1958); they include the closer integration of works with college training and the instillation of students with loyalty to their employers. About 16,000 of the 20,000 advanced sandwich students at colleges in England and Wales in 1964–5 were taking either Dip.Tech. or HND, roughly in the proportion 5:3. College diplomas are often taken at the same time. At the colleges the half-and-half sandwich is normal for the HND and the inside-out sandwich for the Dip.Tech. At universities a five-year thick sandwich, made up of three years' full-time study with a year in the works both before and after, is the usual form, perhaps including day release at a college during the first and fifth years. This depends on the university's holding the apprentice's place open for a year; but if that is not possible, three years at university followed by two in the works is the usual programme followed.

However, nearly one-third of all advanced students in 1964–5 were attending in the EVENINGS ONLY, though this proportion is declining.

Other inducements

FINANCIAL AID has become more easily available than before. Apprenticeship schemes usually involve payments by employers. As mentioned, technical state scholarships awarded by the Minister increased from 100 in 1947 to 225 in 1957, until the scheme was discontinued in 1962. Before 1962, as also described earlier (Chapter 3), authorities were showing increasing readiness to recognize courses at colleges for grants, so that in 1961–2 about two-thirds of full-time students taking courses of first-degree level in colleges were receiving full-value awards. After the 1962 Act and regulations about nine-tenths were receiving them. Works-based students taking courses designated in this Act had to be aided also if necessary.

However, as mentioned earlier, there are still loopholes in these regulations. The grants available to full-time *postgraduate* students (from authorities, SRC and so on) compare very unfavourably with the salaries these graduates could earn in normal employment.

ACADEMIC INDUCEMENTS have increased, as has been seen, through new awards coming into existence. The CNAA will strengthen this trend further.

PUBLICITY, too, has improved—the Minister's free booklets *Britain's Future and Technical Education* and *Further Education for School Leavers* may be instanced—but parity of esteem with universities in the minds of school leavers and their advisers has not nearly been achieved.

Courses and studies

The GCE

There is a good deal of A-level work in mathematics and science subjects taken in the colleges with a view to admission to various university and college courses for scientists and technologists. The usual pattern is a one-year full-time course, containing three main subjects and a small amount of general education. Students are mainly public-school and grammar-school leavers and there are many from overseas, but some are from modern schools. There were about 9,000 students on such courses in 1964–5.

Technician courses

The HNC engages well over a third of all students doing advanced courses and continues to grow steadily. The HND occupies many fewer but their number has been increasing more rapidly. Two-thirds of HNCs and HNDs are awarded in the various branches of engineering, but the proportion is falling. Additional ("Post-National") subjects, such as Industrial Administration, can be "ENDORSED" on them. Sea-going engineers, technicians and deck officers take "tickets" or certificates awarded by the Ministry of Transport; the Chief Engineers' Certificate is regarded as rather lower than HNC. Holders of HNC or HND alone (or their equivalent) are regarded as high-grade technicians.

Courses for technologists

MEMBERSHIP, ASSOCIATE MEMBERSHIP or ASSOCIATESHIP of the scientific and technological institutions which confer "professional" status is the chief avenue of qualification for technologists and is the main alternative to university graduation. A technologist is regarded as "qualified" when he is eligible to become a corporate member of his institution. For example, a "chartered engineer" means a member of one of the engineers' institutions which has a Royal Charter, such as the Institution of Civil Engineers. There are various grades of membership; "corporate" confers full voting and other rights as a member. Eligibility for it is usually reached in two stages : the passing of, or exemption from, examinations (conferring GRADUATESHIP), followed by a period of appropriate experience. Exemption from all or part of the examinations can in many cases be gained by possession of other qualifications. In the case of partial exemption the remaining examinations must be taken, for which some colleges provide special "transfer" courses, sometimes full-time. It is thought that during the early 1960s professional status was gained in this way by about 60 per cent of those awarded HNC or HND; in 1955 the figure was probably nearer 50 per cent. Alternatively, the institution's "direct" examinations can be taken from the start. In yet other cases certain university graduates may be directly elected to membership, or it may be possible to qualify by thesis or published work. Standards of examinations appear to be rising and conditions for exemption becoming more difficult (for example, the Institution of Electrical Engineers; see Administrative Memorandum 570); in some such cases additional qualifications at a lower level (such as LRIC) are being introduced. FELLOWSHIP of an institution may also be awarded for research or other distinguished work.

COLLEGE ASSOCIATESHIPS and DIPLOMAS are usually of about graduate standard, some being recognized by the Secretary of State as of graduate equivalence for computing salaries of teachers in schools. First and second-class honours may be given. These qualifications are particularly sought in Scotland, where the Dip.Tech. scheme has not been used (Table 24). Some can now be converted retrospectively into CNAA degrees. FELLOWSHIPS are also awarded by certain colleges.

COURSES IN NATIONAL COLLEGES are specifically designed for the industry concerned. The Leathersellers College, for example, offers two-year and three-year courses for its Diploma in Leather Technology, entrants to which have to have four passes at the O level of the GCE; following this is a one-year associateship. These courses contain science, technology, management subjects and general studies, and the associateship includes an investigation. All are full-time. The Foundry College has a two-year full-time diploma, entrants to which need at least a pass degree, HNC, HND or City and Guilds advanced certificate in appropriate subjects; and a three-year half-and-half sandwich course for an advanced diploma, entrants to which need two appropriate A-level passes or a good ONC or OND. The Food College has a two-year full-time diploma of about pass-degree standard, a four-year sandwich course for a CNAA degree and three one-year full-time postgraduate courses. Not all courses in National Colleges are advanced, however; the Leathersellers College, for example, provides a one-year certificate for older students with experience in the industry.

Similarly the College of Aeronautics awards a two-year full-time diploma of postgraduate standard in aeronautics (DCAe); and its associated schools run one- and two-year postgraduate courses in such subjects as production engineering, operational research, space technology and management studies, leading to two other diplomas (DAE and DAuE). There are also short full-time courses.

Courses in Central Institutions, too, include provision for particular industries. The Scottish Woollen Technical College, for example, offers associateships and a four-year full-time degree course for the CNAA in textile technology and textile design.

The Diploma in Technology, awarded in England and Wales by the National Council for Technological Awards until 1965, showed a spectacular growth. Its genesis has already been described. Courses began in the autumn of 1956 and the first awards were in 1958. There was a Dip.Tech. (Eng.) for engineering and a Dip.Tech. for other branches of technology. The standard was that of an honours degree, first- and second-class honours being given as well as a plain pass. Admission required at least two appropriate A-level passes and three at O level, or a good ONC or OND. The course had to last at least four years but a student could be admitted at a stage later than the beginning, provided that he still did two years of a full-time or three of a sandwich course. It had to include, during the course (not before or after it), an aggregate of at least one year of planned industrial training, and to contain a requisite amount of science, technology, their application to development and design, liberal studies and principles of industrial organization. About one-tenth of the time was to be devoted to liberal studies. The college submitted schemes to the National Council, which, before approving them, usually sent a party to look into the standards of staffing, equipment, students' accommodation (both for study and residence), staff accommodation, social amenities, libraries, facilities for research and the extent of the college's preoccupation with advanced studies. The college submitted and examined; the Council assessed and awarded.

In 1963–4 there were 124 Dip.Tech. courses at 30 colleges, most of which (but not all) were CATs or Regional Colleges; about three-quarters of the 8,500 students were at CATs. Nearly two-thirds of the students were in branches of engineering, and four-fifths of these were works-based; but of the remainder only half were works-based. All the courses were based on sandwich-release schemes. In 1964 1,150 Dip.Techs. were given.

Of the 472 students who had gained the award up to the end of March 1961, 156 had entered through the ONC, but this proportion was falling. Only 2 per cent of recipients have been women.

The scheme has now been taken over by the CNAA, but will be continued without much change. The name of the award is now a B.Sc. degree. Holders of the Dip.Tech. can have it converted to B.Sc. if they wish. In 1965 there were 66 Dip.Tech. courses at 25 colleges and 4 associateship courses at 2 Central Institutions recognized by the CNAA as leading to a B.Sc. with honours.

Other first degrees in science and technology gained in colleges declined in number until 1959 but are now on the increase; the University of London gave 1,302 in England and Wales in 1963–4. They were taken either externally, or, as already mentioned, by internal students in certain colleges. The chief were B.Pharm., B.Sc. (General), B.Sc. (Special, mainly in Chemistry, Mathematics and Physics) and B.Sc. (Engineering). But college teachers have little or no freedom to modify London University syllabuses; therefore the CNAA will probably prove more suitable to many colleges.

HIGHER DEGREES, like first degrees, have been mainly those of the University of London. A full-time student for one would probably need financial support from his authority, firm, SRC or other source. In 1964–5 there were 1,900 students at colleges in England and Wales taking higher degrees or other research or postgraduate qualifications; 164 higher degrees in science and technology were awarded in 1963–4.

POSTGRADUATE COURSES are numerous and are mainly of short duration (such as one evening a week for twelve weeks). Most are designed for specialists employed in industry and cover a wide range of scientific, technological and management subjects. As mentioned in Chapter 3, students attending longer courses can be aided with "advanced course studentships" by the SRC. The Robbins Report recommended a big increase in postgraduate work of all kinds and especially in full-time courses of one and two years.

RESEARCH is mainly into problems of specific processes and techniques referred to colleges by firms. In some cases arrangements can be made for employees of firms to work under the supervision of college teachers. The Minister complained in his report for 1958 that there was not as much research going on as he had hoped for. Finance is generally the difficulty, but, as mentioned, the SRC awards research fellowships to established research workers. The Whitworth Foundation gives grants worth up to £1,500 per year for research or study in engineering or engineering education; three were awarded in 1964.

MEMBERSHIP OF THE COLLEGE OF TECHNOLOGISTS (MCT) was given for research into a problem related to the needs of industry, extending approximately over three years and carried out under the supervision of members of staff of both technical college and industrial organization. It was thought of as following the Dip.Tech. after an interval of industrial experience and to be of the standard of a Ph.D. degree. By the end of 1964 the College of Technologists had accepted 137 applications for registration. There had been twelve awards by 1964, all to men. Like the Dip.Tech., the MCT has been taken over by the CNAA and will be called Ph.D. in future. Present holders can convert their MCT into a Ph.D.

COURSES IN SOCIAL SCIENCES are on the increase, some being connected with management studies (see below).

"CONVERSION COURSES" in science and technology for entrants qualified in arts subjects are being tried.

SHORT COURSES are many and diverse.

Management studies

As has been mentioned, these were recommended before 1950 in the Percy, Urwick and Carr-Saunders Reports and are included in various training courses for technologists. The Urwick Committee proposed that they should be built up in this country, as they had been in others, into a distinct body of disciplined knowledge which should be not only part of all such training but also given its own separate qualifications. It suggested, too, the setting up of a permanent advisory council on education for management. In 1949 the Minister in consultation with the British Institute of Management (BIM) instituted a part-time Diploma in Management Studies with intermediate and final grades, and in 1953 444 Intermediate and 95 Final Diplomas were awarded. From about that year, short full-time courses lasting one, two and three months in such subjects as work simplification, time and motion study and factory and shop layout began to appear at Acton, Birmingham, Cranfield, Glasgow, Leicester, Loughborough and other colleges, drawing students mainly from industry but also attracting trade-union officials and college teachers. There was at about this time, too, an increase of courses in foremanship and works supervision : mainly part-time day and evening lasting one or two years, or full-time for one month, or in the evenings with about a dozen lectures; for example, the number of courses for the Certificate in Foremanship and Works Supervision offered by the Institute of Industrial Administration had risen from 12 in 1946–7 to 50 in 1953–4. But there was no long advanced course; the Arnold Report (1959) therefore recommended that the final grade of the Diploma in Management Studies should be made a postgraduate or Post-National qualification taken preferably by full-time resident study for at least six months, and that the intermediate should be replaced by a new HNC in Business Studies. The Minister announced his acceptance of these proposals in Circular 1/60 and the Secretary of State in Scottish Circular 429. Together with their Northern Ireland colleague the Ministers set up, early in 1961, a United Kingdom Advisory Council on Education for Management (UKACEM) under the chairmanship of Mr. J. W. Platt, formerly Managing Director of the Royal Dutch Shell Group of Companies; and a new scheme was established by the Ministry and the British Institute of Management. As in National Certificate schemes colleges submit syllabuses to a joint diploma committee which also makes the awards; but they can be exempted from these requirements, and four colleges have been. Indeed the trend is for this Diploma to become a college award with external assessment. There is a separate Scottish joint committee. Fifty-three courses started in the autumn of 1961 at 32 Central Institutions, CATs and Regional Colleges, but only 6 courses were full-time, sandwich or block-release. About 1,000 students enrolled, aged mainly between twenty-five and thirty-five, two-thirds being graduates. The number of students had more than trebled by October 1964, when there were over 90 courses at 45 establishments. First-year enrolments had doubled by 1965. The main support came from larger firms. The *Memorandum* by the committee for England, Wales and Northern Ireland (1965) is the basis of the course outside Scotland. The greatest problem has been to find suitable teachers; and following the first Platt Report (1962) the DES started special one-term full-time courses for these in 1964. Management studies are now coming to be thought of as always postgraduate.

In addition to this National scheme the British Institute of Management (which merged with the Institute of Industrial Administration) and other bodies such as the Institute of Office Management continued for a time to offer their own awards. These examining functions, however, are expected to be passed over to the new National Examinations Board in Supervisory Studies.

RESEARCH started at Regent Street Polytechnic in 1963, followed by SHORT FULL-TIME COURSES for management teachers in 1964.

Liberal studies

Shortage of time has always tended to narrow technical education. With the growth of full-time and sandwich courses from about 1953, however, some colleges began to establish sections or departments of "liberal studies", by which was meant non-technological subjects. This trend was commended in the White Paper of 1956, though the term itself has been criticized as implying either that science and technology are themselves necessarily illiberal or that the "humanities" are necessarily ancillary. In Circular 322 the Minister thought it necessary to recommend the development of libraries in the colleges, suggesting an annual allowance of from £500 to £2,000.

In Circular 323 teachers, examining bodies and employers were urged to foster in students the habits of reflection, independent study and free inquiry into the broader implications of their technical occupations. Five ways of doing this were suggested. Additional "background" or "perimeter" subjects such as human relations, the art of communication, economics or industrial history, or "contrasting" subjects such as music or literature, could be included in the timetable, perhaps taking up to 15 or 20 per cent of the course time; and the teachers thereof should familiarize themselves with the economic and technical background of the students. The specialist subjects themselves could be broadened, particularly so as to emphasize their social and economic origin and consequences. Greater use could be made of project work, directed private study and tutorial methods of teaching. Corporate life and out-of-class activities in the colleges could be encouraged, through fostering students' societies, contact with industrial clubs and provision of communal amenities and residential facilities. And contacts could be developed with institutions abroad.

Some progress has been made along these lines. Liberal studies, as mentioned, are now an established or obligatory part in many technological courses. Collaboration between colleges and responsible bodies for Adult Education has been tried (see Chapter 11). But corporate life in the colleges is still undeveloped, and except at CATs, agricultural colleges and farm institutes there is not yet much residence.

The failure to stress and foster *creativity* was discussed in the Lisborg consultancy is undertaken by some college teachers.

Consultancy

As recommended in the Willis Jackson Report a small amount of consultancy is undertaken by some college teachers.

Developing the colleges

DIFFERENTIATION of colleges has continued as explained in Chapter 4. Its purpose is to foster advanced courses by concentration, so as to make economical use of scarce staff and accommodation. But it requires advanced, Regional and Area Colleges to shed all or part of their lower-level work, depriving them and the Local Colleges of much of the polytechnical character, with all that stems from it, which has been so typical of British further education. Thus the status of colleges has been made dependent on the expulsion of a valuable part of their tradition.

As explained earlier, the Secretaries of State bring differentiation about by controlling the system at two key points : new courses and new building. In England and Wales the 1959 Regulations forbid the commencement of new advanced courses, together with a number of City and Guilds courses which are unevenly dispersed and need expensive equipment, without the Secretary of State's approval. The college submits its proposed scheme to the regional advisory council and to the appropriate HM Staff Inspector. After taking account of the views of the council, which, as mentioned, has worked out a pattern of advanced courses in its region, the Inspector gives a decision on behalf of the Secretary of State. After NACEIC's 1966 Pilkington Report, containing the finding that the great majority of classes in Further Education contained 6–15 students, the Secretary of State made it more difficult to start new courses by raising the number of enrolments needed for a course to be approved. Authorities' expenditure on advanced courses is pooled.

In Scotland the procedure is different. As mentioned, advanced evening courses and all daytime courses must be submitted by authorities to the Secretary of State in their annual amending Schemes; and the costs of all such courses, when approved, are pooled.

Trends in the DESIGN OF BUILDINGS, which, as mentioned earlier, also needs approval, have been inspired by the concept of the CAT as a technological university, with its implications of residence, all-round activity, research and so on. Circular 320 urged the provision of hostel accommodation and suggested that every CAT or Dip.Tech. student should "live in" for at least one year of a full-time course or one term of a sandwich.

Problems of expansion

Thus there has been substantial growth in this sector, particularly since 1956. Clearly the range of problems resembles that of expanding the education of technicians and craftsmen discussed in the previous chapter. There are problems of material provision, of the gains and losses in the stratification of colleges, and of curriculum, status and wastage. Their outline, as we have seen, was drawn in the Percy Report. Both Percy and Crowther Reports diagnosed the same three basic causes of wastage and retardation, urged the need for planned expansion and advocated a new kind of education combining features of older kinds.

Advanced courses, however, are better developed than non-advanced. Employers are more willing to co-operate and governments to spend money on them. NACEIC and other bodies have given them more attention. There is more experience, including that of universities, in matters of teaching method and of looking after full-time students. A greater attempt has been made to work out manpower targets. On the other hand, apprenticeship or release may come to an end before advanced courses are finished, and there is thus a greater problem of getting release for the student aged over twenty-one, or even over eighteen, than for the younger. Problems of staff supply are more acute.

One of the curricular problems is similar for both advanced and non-advanced : to design courses which by integrating theory with industrial practice produce men and women who can usefully apply the results of science at the point of production. But in advanced courses there is a heavier pressure of theoretical work. Much experiment and argument is going on. At present there is criticism that schemes do not allow enough time at college. In the thick-sandwich scheme a long spell in industry between leaving school and starting at college is found to break the momentum of study. In the thin-sandwich scheme it is said that works periods are often arranged to suit employers rather than studies and other college activities. "End-on" sandwich courses, in particular, are unpopular in the colleges since they break up the student body and lengthen the teaching year; if students must be divided, overlapping groups are preferred. In the Russell Report, however, NACEIC, though suggesting further experiment, conditionally supported them in the interests of economical use of capital equipment; and the Minister advocated them in Circular 6/63. Thus at present there is no agreed best sandwich scheme. Another criticism is that some courses are too academic; this is often said, for example, of management studies.

Needing attention now is the position of the part-time student. In the early 1960s the technical-college stream was producing two-thirds of the national output of qualified technologists, one-fifth of its scientists and most of its technicians and craftsmen; and the great majority of these came up the hard way through day release or no release at all. Yet this way is getting harder, through the raising of standards, limiting of exemption routes, scarcity of release and even lack of employment; and separate streams are differentiating within it. Advanced technological education is still the handmaiden of employment, just as surely as non-advanced.

Notes on further study

The main sources have been mentioned. Most important was the Percy Report (1945). After this were the Barlow and Fyfe Reports (1946), the Minister's Pamphlets Nos. 2 (1945), 3 (1945) and 8 (1947), and reports of the Hardman Working Party (1947), Urwick Committee (1947), Parliamentary and Scientific Committee (1946, 1947 and 1954), Advisory Council on Scientific Policy (annually, 1948–1964), Carr-Saunders Committee (1949), NACEIC (1950), Advisory Council on Education in Scotland (1952), Select Committee on Estimates (*Twelfth* and *Fifteenth Reports, session 1952–53*), Committee on Scientific Manpower (1955, 1956, 1959, 1961, 1963), Arnold Working Party (1959), Central Advisory Council on Education (Wales) (1961), UKACEM (1962, 1965), NACEIC's Russell Committee (1963) and Robbins Committee (1963). For two colleges in north Wales see the Chance Report (1958), and for science in Wales the Llewellyn-Jones Report (1965).

The characteristics of technical colleges and universities were discussed in the ATTI's *The Future of Higher Education within the Further Education System* (1965).

Government policy was announced in four White Papers : Labour's in

Higher Technological Education (1951) and *A Plan for Polytechnics and other Colleges* (1966), and Conservative's in *Technical Education* (1956) and *Higher Education* (1963). Implications of the binary system for the colleges were discussed by Russell at the ATI (1966).

Statistical and other information is contained in the annual reports of the Ministers and Secretaries of State, and, for England and Wales from 1961, *Statistics of Education,* especially *Part 2*. See also the COI's *Technological Education in Britain* (1960) and *Technical Education in Britain* (1962).

Relevant Circulars were 87 (1946), 94 (1946), 98 (1946), 137 (1947), 252 (1952), 255 (1952), 270 (1953) and Amendment (1957), 283 (1954), 285 (1955), 299 (1956), 305 (1956), 320 (1957), 322 and Amendment (1957), 323 (1957), 336 (1958), 343 (1958), 351 (1959), 1/59, 1/60, 4/60, 9/60, 3/61, 5/61, 4/62, 6/62, 9/62, 6/63, 7/63 and 10/64 (titles of which are indexed in the annual *List 10*); and Scottish Circular 405 (1959).

Apprenticeship schemes can be studied from brochures issued by firms, the annual *Year Book of Technical Education and Careers in Industry* and the literature on careers.

Details of courses can be found in prospectuses and advertisements of colleges and authorities, *Guides* published by regional and district advisory councils, and reports and memoranda of examining bodies. The regional advisory councils' *Higher Education* (1964), the British Council's *Higher Education in the United Kingdom* (1964) and Watts (editor): *Which University?* (1964) were useful; and Raphael has listed *Full-time Degree Courses Outside Universities* (1964). For details of Dip.Tech.–B.Sc. courses see the Hives Council's *List 16* (1964) and CNAA's *Courses* (1966). National Certificate and Diploma schemes in England and Wales are described in Administrative Memoranda and governed by *Rules* laid down by the Secretary of State, titles of which are listed in the annual *Sectional List No. 2* and in *Further Education for School Leavers* (1966); for Scotland there is a single code—*Rules 1* (1964), introduced with Scottish Circular 560. See also Advisory Centre for Education (ACE): *List of CATs and Technical Colleges in the UK offering full-time courses leading to Dip.Tech. and External Degrees of London University*; and the annual *Year Book of Technical Education and Careers in Industry*. For Scotland see the Department's annual *Directory of Day Courses*.

The CNAA's policy was outlined in its *Statement Nos. 1–3* (1964–5).

Professional bodies publish reports and regulations for admission to membership. Exemptions conferred by the GCE were listed in the DES's *The General Certificate of Education* (1964). Qualifications recognized by the Secretary of State as conferring graduate status were contained in Appendix V of the Burnham Main Report (1965). See also Appendix One, Annex D, of the Robbins Report (1963); and Millerson's study *The Qualifying Associations* (1964).

L

Information about block and sandwich schemes in England and Wales in 1961–2 was contained in the Ministry's latest *List 182* (1961). On the problems thereof see Venables : *Sandwich Courses* (1959), the NUS memorandum to the Robbins Committee (1961), the Russell Report, Circular 6/63 and the ATTI's *Sandwich Courses* (1964), besides many articles in periodicals. Administrative Memoranda 567 (1958) and 7/63 dealt with grants to students on sandwich courses. On the financing of students by industry see the FBI's *Policy Statement* (1958, revised in 1963) and the Minister's *Education in 1958,* pp. 48–50.

Marie Jahoda's *The Education of Technologists* (1963) was a study of Diploma in Technology students at a CAT.

Procedure and criteria for the approval of advanced courses by the Minister were laid down in Administrative Memoranda 510 (1955) and Amendment (1958), 545 (1957) and 3/59; the latter also contained lists of final professional and City and Guilds courses included in the requirement. The criteria were amended in Circular 11/66 which followed NACEIC's (Pilkington) Report (1966). For Scotland see Scottish Circular 422 (1959).

Procedure for the approval of new building was contained in documents assembled in *The Building Code* (1962). For various matters connected with building see also the Ministry's Building Bulletin No. 5 (1951, 1955, 1959). The progress of building work can be found from the annual reports of the Secretaries of State. On design see Barbara Price : *Technical Colleges and Colleges of Further Education* (1959) and the Hertfordshire Authority's *Building for Education 1948–61* (1962). An investigation into *Technical College Buildings* was reported at the 1962 annual general meeting of the ATI. See also *Notes* to Chapter 3. On laboratories see the RIBA's symposium on *Teaching Laboratories* (1958).

On residential accommodation see Circulars 320 (1957), 351 (1959) and 1/59; the Robbins Report (especially paragraphs 587–595 and Appendix Two (A)); and Dorothy Silberston's study *Residence and Technical Education* (1960).

On liberal studies see the National Institute of Adult Education : *Liberal Education in a Technical Age* (1955); Circulars 322 (and Amendment) and 323 (1957); the Yorkshire Council for Further Education : *The Liberal Aspect of Technical Education* (1962); Davies : *Liberal Studies and Higher Technology* (1965); and BACIE's *Symposium* (1965, which contained a bibliography). Job (1965) has also done a bibliography. See also Edmundson : *Physical Education in the Technical College* (ATI, 1961); and the Lisborg Report *Creativity in Technical Education* (1964).

A short account of general progress since 1956 appeared in the Minister's *Education in 1958,* Chapter III. The Ministry's chapter on the UK in the UNESCO/IBE report *Training of Technical and Scientific Staff* (1959) was useful but its authors fell into inaccuracies in their endeavour to present a rosy picture. See also BACIE's conference reports *Education for Survival* (1960) and *The Spectrum of Higher Education* (1962). For a historical treatment of scientific and technical education since 1851 see Argles: *South Kensington to Robbins* (1964).

There is a considerable literature on the education of engineers, much of which appears in publications of professional engineers' institutions : see *Technical Education Abstracts*. For international comparisons see Anglo-American Council on Productivity : *Universities and Industry* (1951); EUSEC : *Report on Education and Training of Professional Engineers* (1960); BACIE : *Continental Comparisons* (1961); the Robbins Report, especially Chapter V (1963) and Appendix Five (1964); Council of Europe : *Engineering Education* (1963); and the Collins Report (1964). For the building industry see the Hall Report (1964).

On management studies see the Urwick Report (1947); Anglo-American Council on Productivity's *Education for Management* (1951); Arnold Report (issued as an attachment to Circular 1/60 and Scottish Circular 429); report of an FBI conference *Stocktaking on Management Education* (1961); first two Platt Reports (1962 and 1965); BIM's *Management Training Techniques* (1962); NEDC's *Conditions Favourable to Faster Growth* (1963); OECD's *Issues in Management Education* (1963); FBI working party's report *Management Education and Training Needs of Industry* (1963); Robbins Report (1963; especially Chapter X); and Franks Report (1963). The BIM's periodic booklet *A Conspectus of Management Courses* (latest 1965) gives a comprehensive review of facilities available. A more recent review, with European comparisons, was Mosson's *Management Education in Five European Countries* (1965). See also Circular 7/63, Administrative Memorandum 8/65 (with attached report of joint committee which replaced *Rules 125*) and Circular 2/66.

On scientific and technological research in colleges the regional advisory councils and academic boards publish reports of projects in progress. See also the DSIR's (SRC's) annual *Scientific Research in British Universities and Colleges*. Earlier references are Circulars 94 (1946), 255 (1952) and 305 (1956); and *Education in 1958*, pp. 51–53. Proposals were in the Robbins (especially Chapter X) and Trend Reports (1963).

On teaching methods in higher education see Appendix Two (B) of the Robbins Report (1964) and the Hale Report (1964). Audiovisual aids were considered in the Brynmor Jones Report (1965).

On wastage in full-time higher education see especially the Robbins Report, Appendix Two (A).

See also *Notes* to Chapter 5.

On more general problems of higher education see Chapters 2 and 19 and *Notes*.

CHAPTER 7

EDUCATION FOR COMMERCE

The time-lag between industry and commerce

PRODUCTS have to be not only produced but also distributed. In an economy of commodities this second field is loosely known as "commerce". It includes three main kinds of activity: trading, organizing the general facilities and consequences of trading, and supplying the special services needed by traders. Examples of the third are banking, insurance and transport. Such activities are carried on both by units which are at the same time engaged in production, and by organizations devoted entirely to them. Thus three main agencies contribute to the conduct of commerce: the commercial departments of agricultural and manufacturing industry, the distributive trades proper, and the specialist services with their professional organizations.

Since they are so closely combined, commerce has followed the same broad pattern of development as industry. In both, the main factor has been the evolution of the large capitalist firm. In both, the decline of the classical apprenticeship system followed by its rebirth in a new form, the growth of the demand for education and training, the advance of specialization and the quest for qualifications, the increasing use made of publicly provided educational facilities and nationally sponsored examination systems, and the emergence of professional organizations have been similar; while levels of commercial occupation roughly comparable with those of industry have become distinguishable.

The progress of commerce, however, has lagged behind that of industry; and there are also specific differences, as will be seen. Post-war scientific advance has had a greater transforming effect on producing than on distributing. The world sellers' market which followed the war has led manufacturers to devote more effort to making than to selling. Variety of commercial occupation has proliferated even more than that of industry and this has hindered rationalization. Industrial careers relative to commercial have lost many of the unattractive features they had before the war, particularly at technician level. The distributive trades are still largely composed of small businesses fed by a pool of unskilled labour.

The post-war growth in apprenticeship at several levels has been but little shared by commerce, in which employers have not given it much support; and on the whole, even what support there has been has come from the larger firms in manufacturing industry. A scheme started in 1946 at Wednesbury[1] College of Commerce, providing five years of day release and designed to train promising young office workers to be professional secretaries or cost and works accountants, had collected in ten years only 63 students from 27 participating firms. Haphazard learning on the job, supported in some cases by evening classes, correspondence courses or even unaided private study, has been the normal practice, and the idea that each individual business had its own *mystique* which could not be applied to any other has been widespread. Courses and examinations have been heterogeneous in the extreme, and their content often little more than narrow and premature vocational training. Therefore there has been much wastage and retardation, accompanied by strain and injustice to students, whilst employers have suffered the inconvenience of a high rate of staff turnover. At the higher levels it has not been easy for university graduates to enter the professional world of business; nor has the business world been responsive to the recommendations of social scientists. The Carr-Saunders Report (1949) produced much less impact that either its elder sister Percy or its younger sister Freeman: its parallel recommendation for an advanced qualification in mercantile studies was not implemented until the CNAA came along; and the ONC and HNC in Commerce made little progress even after their revision in 1951. Bodies like the Committee on Scientific Manpower or the Industrial Training Council have not had to consider such problems, and before 1957 even NACEIC gave its main attention to manufacturing industry.

More recently, however, there have been signs of a change. The world sellers' market has come to an end. More countries are exporting goods once considered typically British. These and others are developing commercial education. Articles to be sold are becoming more technical, needing greater technical knowledge in the sellers. Administrative units grow larger and more complex, creating a need for standardized procedures. Office skills become mechanized. Thus the impact of technological advance in increasing the general demand for highly trained staff begins to be felt just at a time when commercial employers, particularly in retail distribution and in the commercial sections of smaller industrial firms, are also experiencing keener competition from industry in attracting the better recruits.

Following the White Paper of 1956 came the McMeeking Report in which NACEIC reviewed the problems of commercial education at and above the level of the ONC. Some of its recommendations repeated those of the Goodenough (1931) and Carr-Saunders Reports. The main ones were: a much greater development of apprenticeship; expansion of the number of students at this level getting day release to more than double the

[1] Now Staffordshire.

1956–7 figure by 1964; exploration of block release, particularly in certain industries; more release for shop employees in particular; sandwich release for advanced students; wider recognition and use of the ONC and HNC in Commerce; the co-ordination by professional bodies of their examination requirements and the bringing of intermediate syllabuses into closer relation with the ONC; the introduction of an award in Business Studies comparable with the Dip.Tech.; a fresh attack on the teaching of languages; provision of more short courses, research and consultancy in colleges and more use thereof by firms; more courses to supplement private study; "conversion" courses for technically trained staff who switch to commerce; higher priority for developing the colleges and more power for their governing bodies; higher grading and fees for college teachers; and more encouragement for women to train for senior posts. In Circular 5/59 the Minister expressed his general support for these recommendations.

In the Crick Report (1964) NACEIC repeated the Carr-Saunders–McMeeking recommendation for a Diploma in Technology-type award in business studies (but to be given now by the CNAA, not by another "Hives-type" council).

These two NACEIC reports, McMeeking and Crick, together with the Arnold Report (already mentioned) set the background of present trends. The effects of the Industrial Training Act, 1964, have yet to be seen.

Apprenticeship

The Association of British Chambers of Commerce (ABCC) has designed and sponsored a scheme controlled by two commercial apprenticeship boards and run by affiliated chambers of commerce. Based on the original Wednesbury experiment of five years' day release, revised in 1957, it was changed in 1961 to a four- or five-year two-stage scheme. After a three-month probationary period Part I is linked with the new ONC in Business Studies (or Scottish Senior Commercial Certificate; see p. 151) and Part II either with the new HNC in Business Studies (or Scottish Advanced Commercial Certificate) or with the final examinations of certain professional institutions which, as explained later, are willing to grant some exemption from their intermediate requirements. During the first two years the practical training must be in accord with a programme submitted by the firm through its chamber of commerce and approved by the apprenticeship board; after this the firm is free to give what practical training it wishes, provided that training continues under the supervision of a senior member of staff and that a brief outline of it is submitted. Technical training may be included up to a maximum of half of the total time allowed. The Association itself awards a certificate and diploma at the conclusion of

Parts I and II respectively. In 1960–1, 98 new apprentices were registered in England and Wales and 19 in Scotland; there were then about 450 altogether. In August 1962 there were 510, some of whom had two or more GCE A-level passes; 206 schemes had been approved. By 1965 there were 262 schemes but student numbers were nearly the same.

In the distributive trades a successful scheme is that of the National Joint Apprenticeship Council for the Retail Meat Trade. It incorporates day release either for five years or until the apprentice's twenty-first birthday, whichever is the shorter period; the courses taken are those of the Institute of Meat. Since the inception of the scheme in 1954 about 2,000 apprentices in about 80 colleges had been registered by 1962. A similar attempt by the National Association of Retail Furnishers has been less successful. In 1961 the Nottingham Chamber of Commerce introduced a pilot scheme in general retail distribution suitable for selected school leavers.

In manufacturing industries firms now generally offer commercial apprenticeships similar to those given on the production side (Table 15). In other cases, notably banking and insurance, many firms provide their own internal training schemes, though in some of these, college courses are growing.

Courses and studies before employment

Clerk-typists' and secretarial

Office crafts are not quite like those of industry, being narrower in content and best learnt in relatively short bursts of intensive training. Colleges therefore offer full-time pre-employment courses of from two terms to two years containing subjects of general education besides. Most are designed for girls aged fifteen and sixteen and are at different academic levels according to the attainment of the entrants. Mixed classes with less emphasis on office skills are also provided. The most popular of the various examinations taken are perhaps the GROUPED-COURSE and SINGLE-SUBJECT CERTIFICATES of the Royal Society of Arts.

Some colleges also offer secretarial courses for graduates, former Service officers and the like.

Academic subjects

There are a few full-time COURSES IN PROFESSIONAL SUBJECTS such as those required for preliminary and intermediate examinations of bodies like the Chartered Institute of Secretaries or Institute of Cost and Works

Accountants. The most usual, however, is the GCE, which is often combined with secretarial subjects, besides serving as a preparation for commercial and other apprenticeships. There were 41,000 full-time GCE students in colleges of Further Education in 1964–5, of whom two-thirds were working for the O level.

Courses and studies during employment

Office-machine operation

Modern business machines are often too costly either for colleges to install or for firms to use for training purposes. In such cases operators are therefore usually trained in their employer's time by the firms which supply the machines. Such training is outside our present scope.

Office skills

About one-third of all the work done in part-time day and evening commercial classes is in SHORTHAND, TYPEWRITING and BOOK-KEEPING. Much of this is prepared in single-subject entries for the examinations of the Royal Society of Arts which awards certificates in three (or in shorthand, eight) grades of difficulty or speed. GROUPED COURSES are also examined, most containing English as a compulsory subject. The regional unions offer examinations too, linking them with those of the RSA in the same way as they link their technical examinations with those of the City and Guilds Institute. The London Chamber of Commerce awards a diploma for mature shorthand typists. The Scottish Council for Commercial Education (SCCE) also offers courses.

There is far more evening work than day-release.

Academic subjects

GCE and similar courses already mentioned may be taken by part-time day and evening study, and there were over 148,000 students taking the GCE in these ways in 1964–5. There is also much work done in single subjects such as English, arithmetic or languages, with or without examination.

More attention is being given to *spoken* foreign languages, and "language laboratories" (pioneered at Ealing Technical College) are on the increase.

Certificates in the distributive trades

A number of trade associations have for some years offered syllabuses, conducted examinations (either themselves or through the agency of examining bodies) and awarded certificates and diplomas. Courses for these, usually in the evenings, are common in colleges and evening institutes where there is sufficient demand, notably at the College for the Distributive Trades, London, and the School of Salesmanship, Edinburgh. Others may be taken by correspondence. A Retail Trades Education Council was formed in 1956.

There are also the following three certificates, established on the initiative of the Ministers, two of them modelled on National Certificate schemes (Table 23), which are awarded for the study of the principles common to all retailing, combined with training on the job.

The RETAIL TRADES JUNIOR CERTIFICATE is endorsed by the Retail Trades Education Council and is intended for younger entrants to trades other than food. It contains English and calculations besides retailing subjects, and requires attendance for at least four hours per week for two years. Examinations are conducted by colleges at the end of the first year and by the City and Guilds Institute or regional unions at the end of the second. Scotland has its own, also examined by the City and Guilds Institute. The courses are ranked by the Institute as operatives' courses.

The NATIONAL RETAIL DISTRIBUTION CERTIFICATE, also for the "non-food" trades, is awarded by joint committees representing the Retail Trades Education Council, City and Guilds Institute and DES, which approve schemes and establishments and lay down rules. As described in Administrative Memorandum 4/62 it normally follows a two-year course (340 hours) and is intended for entrants who either have a Junior Certificate or have stayed in full-time education till sixteen. The City and Guilds Institute examines externally at the end of the second year, when notebooks may be called for. Conditions regarding attendance, homework and classwork marks similar to those in ONC schemes are imposed. It ranks as a technician course.

The CERTIFICATE IN RETAIL MANAGEMENT PRINCIPLES is for those aspiring to become managers of store departments, shops or area branches, or proprietors of independent shops in both food and non-food trades. It is organized under the same system as the National Retail Distribution Certificate. Entrants must normally be aged at least twenty-one, be educated to a suitable standard and have had not less than two years' experience in a retail trade. Attendance must be for at least five hours a week for two years, or its equivalent (300 hours) in an intensive course. It also ranks as a technician course.

PRE-ENTRY COURSES for admission to any of these may be provided.

The Certificate in Office Studies

This was introduced in Circular 4/63 and began in September 1963. It is intended for young workers who cannot at present fulfil the admission requirements for the ONC in Business Studies, for besides being a qualification in its own right it can qualify for such admission. The course is designed for two years, preferably with day or block release, and entrants must have been in full-time education till at least sixteen. English and General Studies, Clerical Duties and Business Calculations or Book-keeping are three compulsory subjects, to which must be added a fourth chosen from a list including Social Studies, Law and the Individual, Typewriting and Office Machinery. The ONC-type rules of attendance and so on apply, but regional unions or the SCCE conduct the examinations. Preliminary courses can be offered. Single-subject endorsements in specialized branches of office work are possible.

The National scheme in Business Studies

Both Carr-Saunders and McMeeking Reports had commended the National Certificates in Commerce as the first stage in a co-ordinated system, but professional bodies did not accept them for examination exemption and employers gave them little recognition. Pioneer courses in business studies were started, as at Liverpool College of Commerce for Pilkingtons' staff. In Circular 1/60 the Minister announced in England and Wales a new scheme of NATIONAL CERTIFICATES IN BUSINESS STUDIES, with an ORDINARY Certificate replacing the ONC in Commerce and a HIGHER Certificate replacing both HNC in Commerce and Intermediate Certificate in Management Studies. Each embodies two years of part-time study. The syllabuses are broader and more flexible than for the former certificates. Entrants to the ONC must be at least sixteen. At first they had to have three appropriate O-level GCE or SCE passes; or in certain circumstances the Certificate in Office Studies; or (exceptionally) be at least nineteen without paper qualifications; but these requirements have been raised. Entrants to the HNC must be at least eighteen and hold either the ONC, two appropriate A-level GCE passes or certain passes in the Scottish Higher Leaving Certificate; or (exceptionally) be at least twenty-one without. If the A-level passes are in unsuitable subjects "conversion" courses are sometimes provided.

In Administrative Memorandum 7/61 the Minister introduced also an ORDINARY NATIONAL DIPLOMA IN BUSINESS STUDIES for two years of full-time study. Later in 1961 (on 24th July) he announced in Parliament a HIGHER

National Diploma for a further two years' full-time or three years' sandwich study.

Like other National Certificate and Diploma schemes these are administered by joint committees to which colleges submit syllabuses, and regional unions do part of the examining.

Courses for the new ONC, OND and HNC started in the autumn of 1961, and by the end of that year 500 applications had been received for the approval of courses, including over 100 for the Diploma. During their first year there were nearly 10,000 enrolments for the ONC, 1,100 for the OND, and 1,500 for the HNC; in 1964 these figures had risen to 13,000, 5,000 and 3,000 respectively. Eleven of the professional bodies concerned acceded to the Minister's request to recognize passes at "credit" level in the ONC and OND for exemption from the same subjects in their intermediate examinations.

The new HND started in September 1962 with 380 enrolments; there were 1,848 in 1964. The HND and the HNC provide for those who do not intend to join a final professional course, but they qualify for admission to the new Diploma in Management Studies. Three institutions, however, do grant some exemption from their final examination.

These developments stem not from the McMeeking Report, of course, but from the Arnold Report on the reorganization of management studies, described in the previous chapter.

Scottish schemes

The new scheme does not apply to Scotland, which has remained true to its tradition of centralized control of examinations. The SCCE awards a SENIOR COMMERCIAL CERTIFICATE leading to an ADVANCED COMMERCIAL CERTIFICATE through a single system of centrally administered external examinations. Courses for both are normally two-year part-time. The admission requirement for the Senior is four O-level passes; nine professional bodies accept it for intermediate exemption. Other certificates awarded by the SCCE are a SENIOR SECRETARIAL CERTIFICATE, an ADVANCED SECRETARIAL CERTIFICATE, an AGRICULTURAL SECRETARIES' CERTIFICATE and (since 1965) a SCOTTISH DIPLOMA IN COMMERCE parallel with the OND. There is also a CERTIFICATE IN BUSINESS ADMINISTRATION parallel with the Advanced Commercial Certificate but administered by the Scottish Joint Committee for the Diploma in Management Studies (see p. 136), not by the SCCE; both these certificates confer admission to the Diploma in Management Studies. The Junior Commercial Certificate was ended in 1962 when the new system began.

Professional studies

PROFESSIONAL MEMBERSHIP plays an even greater part in commercial than in technical education. It may be sought either as a route to specialist practice or as a general qualification for a commercial career. Institutions are numerous and there is considerable variation among them in the balance of general and specialist studies laid down. While some are not clearly distinguishable from trade associations, others confer qualifications recognized as of graduate status. The oldest is the Institute of Actuaries, founded in 1848.

Unlike those of National schemes such studies are not particularly associated with apprenticeship and do not depend upon attendance at college; indeed, it has been estimated that roughly three-quarters of such work is conducted by correspondence; but colleges do provide courses of different kinds according to the demand. Some institutions open their examinations only to full-time employees, thus forcing them to study in the evenings only.

The pattern of examinations is described in Chapter 17; exemptions can often be gained through passes in other examinations. From intermediate to final commonly takes two, three or four years; but it may be possible to combine the work for membership of more than one body, which may take longer.

As with technological institutions, a period of practice is usually required between passing the final examination and being admitted to membership, and this may be regulated by the imposition of minimum age limits. The normal grade of membership is often called associateship, and there may be a higher grade or fellowship following approved professional experience. The time taken to fulfil all requirements for associateship may be anything from four to twelve years.

College awards

These are numerous. Noteworthy, in the light of the Carr-Saunders, McMeeking and Crick recommendations for an award comparable with the Dip.Tech., were those of the Scottish College of Commerce, Glasgow (now part of the University of Strathclyde), which gave DIPLOMAS in Business Administration, Commerce and Secretarial Science of pass-degree standard, following three years of full-time or sandwich study, and an ASSOCIATESHIP of the College, of honours-degree standard, after another year. Four London colleges (Ealing, Portsmouth, Regent Street and Woolwich) also run four-year courses at degree level.

Some colleges offer their own POSTGRADUATE AWARDS : for example, the Scottish College of Commerce followed its Diplomas with Post-graduate Certificates in Business Management, Marketing and Secretarial Science.

RESEARCH AND CONSULTANCY have been developed in the colleges only to a very small extent.

University studies

Examples of university courses commonly offered by colleges are : London external FIRST DEGREES in such subjects as economics, sociology, law, estate management, geography, history or languages; London DIPLOMAS in public administration or social studies; and the Cambridge Certificate of Proficiency in English for overseas students. In 1964–5 the colleges registered 460 students for external London degrees in sociology and 1,096 in economics; most were full-time.

CNAA courses

The first approved courses for honours degrees in business studies began in 1965.

Short courses

These are numerous and diverse. Examples of subjects commonly offered are : accounting methods, the use of electronic computers, operational research, office organization and methods, export techniques, business law, work study, company procedure, quality control, works statistics. Some are full-time and residential, lasting for a few days to several weeks; another kind is a one-term inside-out sandwich.

*Non-commerce subjects commonly done in colleges and departments
   of commerce*

Examples are : languages, hospital administration, hotel administration, municipal administration, government, social studies, vocational guidance, librarianship, journalism and police work.

Establishments

Publicly provided commercial education is in technical colleges, colleges of commerce, evening institutes, residential colleges of Adult Education, Central Institutions and further education centres. In Scotland the Senior Commercial Certificate is usually provided in further education centres and the Advanced in Central Institutions. A sample survey of the position in England and Wales in 1946-7 appeared in the Carr-Saunders Report. More recently, as already mentioned, the Minister's policy has been to concentrate advanced courses in Area and Regional Colleges and the larger colleges of commerce. However, the McMeeking Committee found that commercial courses at and above the level of the ONC were quite widely spread : in about 170 technical colleges, 15 colleges of commerce and nearly 20 evening institutes.

The Minister's intention of designating some colleges as Regional is mentioned in Chapter 4. In Circular 15/61, however, he agreed with NACEIC that in order to benefit from contact with technology, other factors being equal, the new National Scheme in Business Studies should be provided in technical rather than in commercial colleges. Whether some colleges of commerce will be contained in the new polytechnics is not at present known.

The expansion of provision

Main features at present

To summarize, commercial education is preponderantly either in office skills or for professional membership; courses at the equivalent of technician level are sparsely developed. In office skills most of the work is either in full-time pre-employment courses or in evening classes, and the bulk of the latter is narrow vocational training preparing for single-subject examination entries. Professional studies are pursued, as mentioned, mainly in evening classes, by correspondence, by articled pupilage or altogether unaided; much of the work is either at a relatively low level or vocationally specialized; and there is a multiplicity of requirements. Fewer university graduates, therefore, find it possible to gain professional qualifications than in technology. The relation between professional bodies and colleges is less developed, too, than in technology. A considerable amount of training goes on within firms. And there are many occupations in the commercial world for which no proper training exists at all.

Growing points

In commerce proper, apprenticeship is still in its infancy; but the organization exists, ready for use; the new National scheme in business studies should suit its needs; training boards are to be set up under the new Act; first steps towards common syllabuses and the integration of requirements of professional bodies, at least up to intermediate levels, have been taken; and management studies, particularly at the higher levels, have been reorganized. In some distributive trades apprenticeship has made headway, and new courses are available in general retailing, but there is not as yet agreement on the need for a national retail apprenticeship scheme. The CNAA has begun to approve degree courses.

Features retarding growth

Support for day release is still meagre (Table 13). By industries in November 1964, insurance, banking and finance released only 3 per cent of its employees aged under eighteen (but this was more than double the 1961 figure). In the distributive trades the figure fell from 4·2 per cent in 1962 to 3·7 in 1964. The McMeeking Committee found that most release was given by the larger firms to the younger employees. In Scotland the Oakley Committee found that only 400 out of 9,000 retail firms in 1960 expressed any support for release. To the number of students working for recognized qualifications in the colleges and institutes of England and Wales in 1964–5, "business and administration" contributed 10 per cent of the total, 16 per cent of those attending in the evenings only and 11 per cent of the full-time students; but only 7 per cent of those getting day release and only 5 per cent of those getting sandwich release. Rather over a quarter were taking qualifications classified as advanced. The number of apprentices is small. The overall proportions released, however, seem to be rising slowly.

Thus it can be seen that the features regarding technical education diagnosed in the Crowther Report as resulting from its function as the hand-maiden of employment act with even greater force on education for commerce. The two greatest retarding factors are the lack of time for study and the multiplicity of special interests. The first has secondary effects too. For example, the fact that most commercial education is in the evenings results in a good deal of provision having to be in school buildings which are scattered and probably lacking in suitable accommodation and equipment. It means, too, an excessive reliance on part-time teachers who may be tired, untrained and (of the calibre required, at the remuneration offered) scarce. This extreme lack of time caused NACEIC to find itself extolling the virtues of day release for office and shop workers at the very time that the Central Advisory Council was attacking it as inadequate for the training of craftsmen and technicians. Professional institutions are often unable or unwilling to co-ordinate syllabuses even in common subjects.

NACEIC commented also in the McMeeking Report that full-time teachers of advanced courses often lacked business experience and were not ranked at sufficiently senior grades to inspire the confidence of the business world. Evidently authorities had not been providing their staffs with opportunities for further study and experience as recommended by the Minister in Circular 336. The Report also said that there were not enough links between colleges and local commerce, and firms were not sufficiently aware of the facilities offered. Systematic training within firms, it said, was rare.

Problems

The educational problems thus resemble those that have been discussed in earlier chapters. The main general requirements are : clearer agreed objectives; more analysis of employment needs leading to a national man-power policy; rational integration and planning of courses with greater breadth, later specialization, more sharing of common material, greater flexibility of transfer, better guidance, closer linking of practical and theoretical training, planning of practical experience and mutual fertilization of technical and commercial studies; more generous facilities, especially time; and an objective study of the genuine needs of the technological and economic advance of society as a whole, as distinct from the imagined or real interests of individual employers, the employing class or sections of employees, alone.

Notes on further study

The Fyfe (1946), Carr-Saunders (1949) and McMeeking (1959) Reports reviewed the whole sector and provide a background for a more detailed study. Paragraphs 497–498 of the Crowther Report and 510–512 of the Robbins Report should also be looked at. See also the DES's *Reports on Education*, No. 15 (1964).

Statistical information was contained in the Carr-Saunders and McMeeking Reports, the Robbins Report's Appendix Two, the annual reports of the Ministers and Secretaries of State, and, for England and Wales from 1961 onwards, *Statistics of Education,* especially *Part 2.*

Government policy was referred to briefly in paragraphs 9 of the White

Paper of 1956 and 35–36 of the Scottish White Paper of 1961; expounded in Circulars 98 (1946), 1/59, 5/59, 7/59, 1/60, 15/61, 4/63 and 4/64, and in Administrative Memoranda 510 (1955), 545 (1957), 3/59, 7/61 and Addendum (1962) and 4/62 (titles of which are indexed in the annual *List 10*); and reviewed in the annual reports of the Ministers and Secretaries of State. See also Scottish Circulars 429 (1960) and 563 (1964). On industrial training see the Minister of Labour's White Paper (1962) and the Industrial Training Act, 1964, which apply to commerce and retail distribution. The annual reports of the Association of British Chambers of Commerce provide a useful commentary.

Apprenticeship schemes can be studied from brochures and reports issued on request by firms, apprenticeship boards and councils and the ABCC; and in the literature on careers. Useful surveys of provision with much information and discussion of problems were *Commercial Apprenticeship* by Harman (1958), *Commercial Apprenticeships* by Tonkinson, Thomas and Magnus-Hannaford, edited by Oakley (1962) and the ABCC's *Guide to Commercial Training* (1961).

Details of courses can be found in prospectuses of colleges and institutes, programmes of provision by authorities and *Guides* published by regional and district advisory councils. See also the CNAA's *Courses* (1966).

National Certificate and Diploma schemes and others modelled on them in England and Wales are governed by *Rules* (especially 121, 124 and 128) laid down by the Secretary of State, titles of which are listed in *Sectional List No. 2* and *Further Education for School Leavers*. For Scotland see the annual *Handbook* and other prospectuses of the SCCE.

Professional bodies publish reports and regulations for admission to membership and syllabuses of examinations. Exemptions conferred by the GCE were listed in the DES's *The General Certificate of Education* (1964). Qualifications recognized by the Secretary of State as of graduate status were contained in Appendix V of the Burnham Main Report (1965). For further study see Millerson's *The Qualifying Associations* (1964). The policy of the CNAA was outlined in its *Statement Nos. 1–3* (1964–5).

On business studies see the Arnold Report (1960), the ATTI's *Future of Higher Education* (1962), the ABCC's *Pattern of Business Studies* (1963), and the Robbins (1963), Franks (1963) and Crick (1964) Reports.

For references on management studies see *Notes* to Chaper 6.

On language teaching see the FBI working party's *Foreign Languages in Industry* (1962) and *Foreign Language Needs of Industry* (1964). Russian was the subject of Circular 81 (1946) and the Annan Report (1962). On oriental and other languages see the Hayter Report (1961) and on Latin American studies the Parry Report (1965). Turner's *Language Laboratories in Great Britain 1963–4* (1963) was a useful list. Encouragement and further information was given in Circular 2/64. See also SCCE's *Foreign Language*

M

and Export Courses (Workman Report, 1964) and Scottish Circular 563 (1964).

On the recruitment and training of social workers see the Younghusband Report (1959) and the Minister's *Education in 1962*, paragraph 39 (1963); and for municipal accountants Dickerson's study (1965).

On higher education for commerce in Scotland see the Secretary of State's *Education in Scotland in 1963*, pp. 50–58 (1964); and for Glasgow see Graham : *One Hundred and Twenty-Five Years* (1964).

CHAPTER 8

EDUCATION FOR THE ARTS

Art education since the war

The evolution of art education has mainly involved advanced courses and has been closely connected with changes in the system of professional art examinations. The latter were the first examinations to be reorganized : in 1946. The task was made easier by the fact that unlike those in other subjects they were then conducted by the Ministry; indeed, they had been held by the central education department since 1854. In the change, announced in Circular 4, the three-tiered structure which had existed since 1913 was preserved, as was the centrally organized method of examining. But the first examination, which had been in drawing, was broadened by the addition of several new subjects, including general knowledge, and renamed the Intermediate Certificate in Art and Crafts. The second, which had been in one of four subjects with separate examining bodies, was standardized under one body and renamed the National Diploma in Design (NDD). Thus there was a broad foundation on which rested specialized study to a uniformly high standard. The third or Art Teachers' Diploma (ATD) was retained. All were intended for full-time study, the Intermediate taking two years, NDD two and ATD one; but the examinations could be taken without necessarily completing a recognized course. The NDD supplied industry and commerce with designers, less than half staying for another year to qualify as full-time teachers.

This system lasted for nearly twenty years, though it was modified several times from 1950, following the report of a Committee on Art Examinations under the chairmanship of Mr. F. Bray. In order to encourage greater freedom and initiative in the colleges certain features of the National Certificate schemes in technology were incorporated, such as the approval of syllabuses submitted by colleges, the insistence on minimum attendance and attainment in a definite college course, the demand for evidence of course work and the use of internal examinations with external assessment (see Chapter 5). Not all National Certificate procedures were adopted, however; for example, external assessors were appointed by the Minister, not by professional institutions or joint committees, and the assessors continued to *set* the tests themselves in some subjects. The Bray Committee also proposed a permanent National Advisory Committee on Art Examinations, with representation of professional institutions, to advise the Minister in these matters; and this was set up in 1949 under the chairmanship of Mr. F. L. Freeman. However, in 1951, the first year of the new examination, 50 tons of course work arrived at the Imperial Institute[1]; after which, not surprisingly, demands for such evidence were somewhat reduced.

The growth in popularity of art education in England and Wales during and soon after the war is shown by the fact that between 1937–8 and 1949–50 the number of students in art establishments more than doubled, full-time increasing from 6,000 to 15,000 and part-time from 62,000 to 129,000. Between 1951 and 1955, however, it suffered an even greater setback than did technical or commercial education. From 1953 *all* new art courses had to be approved in advance by the Minister. In 1954–5 the number of full-time students had fallen to 11,000 and evening students too were fewer than in 1949–50. In 1956 and 1957 all courses were reviewed and fewer for the Intermediate and NDD approved. The numbers of full-time students and NDD candidates began to rise again in 1955 and of Intermediate candidates in 1956. However, fifty-three art establishments were closed between 1946 and 1964.

The general move forward with the 1956 White Paper saw the beginning of the end of the NDD system. The National Advisory Committee on Art Examinations wanted the standard raised, suggested still more freedom for the colleges, and considered that centrally set examinations tended to restrict originality. Therefore in its second report (1957) it recommended that the Minister should give up his direct responsibility for art examinations; that the Intermediate be abolished; that the NDD be made a three-year instead of a two-year course, reaching the standard and status of a university first degree; that a new and independent council be set up, with wider functions including awarding the new diploma; and that certain colleges should be freed altogether from any external examination. In Circular 340 the Minister accepted all these proposals except the last, and in January 1959 appointed a National Advisory Council on Art Education (NACAE) under the chairmanship of Sir William Coldstream. The Committee on Art Examinations was dissolved.

The first task of NACAE was to consider its predecessor's proposals further; and in its first ("Coldstream") report it recommended that the proposed award be given a new name—"Diploma in Art and Design"—and be administered not by itself but by a new executive body. The Minister accepted these proposals in Circular 16/60 and in 1961 the National Council for Diplomas in Art and Design was appointed as an independent self-governing body under the chairmanship of Sir John Summerson. It approves syllabuses submitted by colleges and assesses course work and examinations

[1] Now the Commonwealth Institute.

conducted by them. There will be no central examination for any college. Courses for the new diploma (Dip.AD) began in the autumn of 1963. The Intermediate and NDD will come to an end in 1965 and 1967 respectively.

This dual proposal, emanating from the second Freeman Report, for a new award *and* awarding body, obviously resembles those of the Carr-Saunders Committee for commerce in 1949 and of NACEIC for technology in 1950 and 1954 (save that neither of these wanted the existing HNCs or HNDs superseded). The origin of all three proposals is in the Percy Report (see Chapter 6).

Thus there are now two national bodies for art education : advisory (NACAE) and awarding (National Council for Diplomas in Art and Design or "Summerson" Council). They are very similar, both in origin and function, to NACEIC and the National ("Hives") Council for Technological Awards respectively. The commerce wing of the awarding triad was never born (at least in England and Wales, though Scotland has the SCCE). It cannot be born now, since any awarding function at that level in commerce will now fall to the CNAA which has already absorbed the Hives Council. But the Robbins Report made no proposal as to the future of the Summerson Council. The ATTI (1965) wanted the latter, too, to be absorbed into the CNAA. The Robbins Committee did not like *degrees* for art.

In its second report NACAE advocated a greater development of two-year and three-year full-time courses arising from the needs of industry. They would be at a lower level than the Dip.AD, for students aged sixteen and upwards. They would have a local flavour and would lead to awards through internal assessment by colleges either individually or in area groups. The importance of flexibility of transfer with diploma courses was stressed. Closer relations of colleges with industry and commerce, between art and technical colleges, and among colleges themselves, combined with a greater use of day, block and sandwich release, were recommended. The Minister welcomed these proposals in Circular 11/62, and "vocational" courses, as they are called, began to come into the colleges. This development is comparable with that in technical education after the White Paper of 1961.

NACAE's third report (1964) suggested the provision of facilities for Post-Diploma studies, of unrestricted scope, leading to a new higher qualification after one or two years beyond the Dip.AD. Such studies should be provided in up to ten colleges selected and approved by the Summerson Council, which would also give national recognition to the new award. There is here a parallel with the MCT. The Secretary of State approved the proposals in Circular 11/65.

In Scotland development has been different. Since 1901 most of the growth there has been in the four Central Art Institutions, which conduct examinations under their own joint scheme of awards, and to which the Secretary of State delegates his awarding power. In 1939 the Scottish

Academy of Music, too, became a Central Institution. The NDD and Dip.AD have not been commonly taken.

Types of student

Evening-only students constitute nearly half of the total enrolled in art establishments, but this proportion is falling. Probably the majority of evening students, many of them journeymen, are trying to improve their skill as industrial or commercial designers or craftsmen, particularly in areas where there is a staple industry containing an important element of design, such as pottery, metalwork, textiles, glass or furniture. The remainder are mainly amateur enthusiasts; but some are full-time art students gaining additional tuition or practice, or teachers seeking inspiration or practical guidance for their work in schools.

Part-time day students are usually apprentices or articled pupils (as in architecture); but some are housewives.

Sandwich courses are as yet hardly developed at all. But full-time students in 1964–5 were as numerous in art establishments as in National Colleges, CATs, Regional Colleges and farm institutes all put together (Table 8). Most are taking preliminary, professional or "vocational" courses.

Thus there are four types of student: industrial and commercial employees attending mainly part-time day or evening vocational courses; full-time students intending to become professional or industrial artists, craftsmen, musicians, actors, architects, designers or teachers; practising teachers; and persons indulging in leisure-time recreation.

Courses and studies

These are of five kinds : leading to examinations of the City and Guilds Institute or similar body; leading to a professional qualification in art, design, music, drama or architecture; leading to a professional qualification as a teacher of one of these; preliminary; and unexamined.

Craft courses

City and Guilds courses are usually part-time day and evening, taken by employed students, though there are some full-time, taken usually by younger ones. They cover a wide variety of crafts : for example, painting and decorating, cabinet-making, upholstery, tailor's cutting, gold and silversmithing, over a dozen printing crafts, book-binding, embroidery or hairdressing (Table 11). Other subjects are examined by regional examining unions : for example, commercial design and display.

Professional studies

These are for the DES's NDD and its successor the Dip.AD; college certificates and diplomas; membership of professional institutions; or university degrees.

The NDD is open only to students who have gained the Intermediate Certificate in Art and Crafts, except for certain three-year industrial courses. It is taken by full-time study in one or two subjects, which include the fine arts (painting and sculpture) and a wide range of applied arts such as illustration, dress, silversmithing, interior decoration, pottery, typography or commercial design. There were 2,828 candidates in 1964, of whom just over two-thirds passed. The last full examination was in 1965, but two further years are being allowed for failed candidates to repeat papers. The Dip.AD, as mentioned, began in 1963, with 1,400 students. It takes three years of full-time study and is expected to be recognized as of first-degree standard. Normally entrants will have to be at least eighteen, have five O-level GCE passes or their A-level equivalent and have satisfactorily completed a Pre-Diploma course (see below) of at least a year; though these requirements can be waived until 1966. The courses contain fundamental principles of art and design, history of art and complementary studies (taking about 15 per cent of the total time), plus a liberal education in one of four areas : textiles and fashion, three-dimensional (including industrial) design, graphic design or fine art.

COLLEGE AWARDS are at various levels, some high. In Scotland they provide the traditional route to professional status. The Central Art Institutions offer Diplomas in Art (DA) after four or five years of full-time study, two of which are general and two or three specialized. Examination work and classwork are submitted to external assessors appointed by the Institutions themselves, after which the college makes awards which are accepted by the Department. The Royal Scottish Academy of Music gives a Diploma in Musical Education and a diploma of the college (DRSAM), both after three-year full-time courses. It also prepares for external examinations of other bodies and participates in conducting the examinations of the Associated Board of the Royal Schools of Music, besides providing part-time courses. It has a school of drama.

In England the Royal College of Art awards two diplomas, called Associate (ARCA) and Designer (Des.RCA), after two, three or four years of full-time study. Subjects offered are : painting, sculpture, graphic design, graphic print making, television and film design, stained glass, engineering design, furniture design, interior design, printed textiles, woven textiles, ceramics, silversmithing, jewellery, industrial glass and fashion design. The Birmingham School of Music offers awards similar to those of the Royal Scottish Academy.

There are also POST-DIPLOMA COUSES and scholarships for Post-Diploma studies including work abroad.

VOCATIONAL COURSES for full-time students, recommended in the second Coldstream Report, have an industrial or commercial bias. Entrants are aged at least sixteen, have an aptitude for art and have passed a college entrance examination, but are not qualified to start the Pre-Diploma. The courses lead to college awards.

As in technology, certain college awards confer exemption from examinations for PROFESSIONAL MEMBERSHIP. Diplomates in Architecture of the Edinburgh College of Art, for instance, have only to take one further paper and gain one or two years of practical experience to become eligible for admission to Associateship of the Royal Institute of British Architects (ARIBA). At other colleges this Institute's examinations can be taken directly. Examples of art colleges containing departments of architecture are Aberdeen, Edinburgh, Dundee, Leicester, Birmingham, Leeds and Middlesbrough. There were about 2,500 full-time and sandwich and 1,400 part-time day students of architecture in colleges of Further Education in England and Wales in 1964–5. Other institutions conducting examinations are the Town Planning Institute, Incorporated Institute of British Decorators and Interior Designers and Gemmological Association.

UNIVERSITY STUDIES in the arts conducted in establishments of Further Education are uncommon, though they do exist. An example is the University of Edinburgh's MA degree with honours in Fine Art, part of which is taught in the Edinburgh College of Art. The Royal Scottish Academy of Music provides practical courses for music students of the University of Glasgow. External London degrees in music are sometimes taken.

The CNAA has set up a subject board for architecture.

RESEARCH is hardly done at all. In a sense, of course, all creative art is a kind of research; but there is scope for normal research in many fields, such as the properties of materials, or the functionality of designs. Work has been done at the Royal College of Art, for example, on the design of non-surgical hospital equipment.

Teaching qualifications

The ATC, ATD and Scottish teaching certificates are aided under the teacher-training regulations and are outside the scope of this book.

Preliminary courses

These may be general, preapprenticeship or preliminary professional; all of these are full-time. GENERAL ART COURSES of one year are for younger students who hope to enter pre-employment courses in subjects such as commercial design and display, dressmaking, dress design or millinery; but exceptional students can be accepted into a Pre-Diploma course. Besides basic art subjects they contain others such as English, history, biology and physical education. PREAPPRENTICESHIP and other PRE-EMPLOYMENT COURSES would include many of the regional union and City and Guilds courses already mentioned; they may last from two terms to three years, or perhaps two years following a general course. PRELIMINARY PROFESSIONAL COURSES are the two-year Intermediate Certificate in Art and Crafts, due to end in 1965; and the Pre-Diploma course which has been taking its place since 1962. The latter is of one or two years (depending on the student's age and attainment) and is intended to test general art ability. A good GCE (with O-level Art) is normally looked for in candidates for admission, but the course may itself provide GCE subjects in addition to basic art studies, or they may be taken elsewhere. Colleges may also offer GCE classes in art and craft subjects themselves. There are also COURSES PREPARING FOR ENTRANCE EXAMINATIONS to such establishments as the Royal College of Art, Central Art Institutions, Royal Academy Schools or University of London Slade School of Fine Art.

Unexamined subjects

These are many and various, and may be provided in evening institutes and further education centres, if the equipment is available, as well as in major establishments. Amateur courses in drawing, painting, sculpture, pottery, fashion and personality grooming, interior design, hand weaving, women's crafts, music, drama and dancing are always popular.

Establishments

Those providing art education are the Royal College of Art, the 4 Central Art Institutions, the 157 maintained colleges of art (often called "schools of art") in England and Wales (1964-5), a number of Regional and other technical colleges containing art and architecture departments, and further education centres, evening institutes and residential colleges of Adult Education. Hairdressing and other crafts may be offered in technical colleges and departments as well as in schools of art.

For music there is one Central Institution and several colleges maintained by English authorities. In England and Wales, however, most colleges of music, dancing and drama have not come under the ægis of the Minister or Secretary of State and are therefore outside the scope of Further Education as defined in Chapter 1.

As mentioned in Chapter 4, the policy of centralizing advanced courses in certain colleges in England and Wales was tried first in art. With the supersession of the NDD it received a new impetus from the Summerson Council, in that for 1963–4 (as mentioned earlier) only 29 colleges had had 61 courses approved for the Dip.AD. The number of colleges rose to 40 in 1965–6. Three were designated for Post-Diploma studies to begin in 1966. Within the limits of this general policy, however, colleges are supposed to be encouraged to develop freely their own approach and solutions to problems.

Problems of expansion

These are broadly similar to those of industrial and commercial education already discussed. In art, however, as has been seen, the problem of designing a national system of examinations has proved particularly difficult. This is because of the wide range and variety of subjects taken and careers entered, the physical size and weight of some of the work to be assessed, the subjective nature of many of the judgements which have to be made, and the need always to stimulate creative activity and originality. The problems arise from having to allow freedom to colleges and candidates without lowering quality or losing a sense of common standards. Thus the national-diploma scheme has now evolved through two stages: 1946–1951 (when final examinations in all prescribed subjects were both set and assessed centrally), and 1951–1963 (when some prescribed subjects were internally examined but centrally assessed). It is now entering a third: 1963 onwards (when *all* prescribed subjects are internally examined and centrally assessed). In technology, however, the third stage was entered at the beginning of the National and Diploma in Technology schemes.

The Pre-Diploma presents problems of teaching the fundamentals of the arts in a broad context of general education so as to bridge the gap between school and further art studies. No doubt the level of general education of art students ought to be high; but it is questionable whether the GCE, required for admission to the Pre-Diploma course, is a good instrument for this purpose. The functions of the courses have not always been clear; and for this reason NACAE (1966) has proposed their renaming as "foundation" courses, not necessarily intended only for admission to a Diploma course.

The policy of centralizing advanced courses in very few colleges creates difficulties for others. The latter are expected to develop non-advanced work, which involves more students but has attracted less attention. The so-called "vocational" courses orientated towards the needs of industry and commerce are believed to be the main requirement here. There appears to be a growing demand for craftsmen who can design or collaborate with designers, requiring courses combining art with industry; but, of course, some students will continue to work at traditional crafts such as stonecarving or silver-smithing. There is a need, too, to raise standards in the design of common articles; indeed, some attempt to instil an awareness or sense of design should permeate all education.

On this last point there is the all-important problem of developing the contribution of art education to the general life of the community. Its solution will require a deliberate effort of communication by artists, designers, manufacturers and public, aided to the full by public authorities. The Arts Council, Council of Industrial Design and universities, together with consumer organizations, must help here. Above all, authorities are allowed by the Local Government Act of 1948 to spend up to the product of a sixpenny rate plus net receipts on all forms of entertainment in their areas. However, the Institute of Municipal Entertainment (1964) has estimated that this would have come to about £50 million a year in the early 1960s; yet they were actually spending about £3 million, and only about one-sixth of this was for "cultural" activities. Regional and local associations and festivals, permanent arts centres as proposed in the White Paper *A Policy for the Arts*, the work of community centres and many other kinds of activity make up a vast field awaiting development.

Notes on further study

There has been no report reviewing the whole sector since the Minister's Pamphlet No. 6 (1946) and the Fyfe Report (1946), but the main stages of development were mentioned in the annual reports of the Ministers and Secretaries of State. The Board's Circular 1432 (1933) announced the policy of centralizing advanced courses. The evolution of the national-diploma examination system can be traced through the reports of the Bray Com-mittee (1948), National Advisory Committee on Art Examinations (Free-man Reports, 1952, 1957), National Advisory Council on Art Education (NACAE, first Coldstream Report, 1960) and Summerson Council (*First Report*, 1964). Vocational courses at a lower level than the Dip.AD have also been discussed by NACAE (second Coldstream Report, 1962), and at a higher level (third Coldstream Report, 1964). Pre-Diploma courses were reconsidered in an *Amendment* to the first report (1966). The Robbins Report said very little about art education.

On creativity in technical education see the Lisborg Report (1964).

Statistical information is contained in the annual reports of the Ministers and Secretaries of State, and, for England and Wales from 1961 onwards, *Statistics of Education,* especially *Part 2.*

Relevant Circulars have been 4 (1944), 98 (1946), 199 (1949), 220 (1950), 340 (1958), 1/59, 7/59, 16/60, 11/62, 4/65, 11/65 and 12/66; together with administrative Memoranda 510 (1955), 545 (1957), 3/59, 13/61 and 4/65. Titles of those current are indexed in the DES's annual *List 10.*

Details of courses can be found in prospectuses of colleges and institutes, lists got out by authorities and *Guides* published by regional and district advisory councils. Schools of architecture recognized by the RIBA have been listed by it (1965).

The NDD scheme is governed by *Rules 110,* laid down by the Secretary of State. For the Dip.AD see the Summerson Council's Memorandum No. 1 (1961).

Discussion of problems is reported annually in the *Association of Art Institutions Year Book*; see also the ATTI's *Future of Higher Education* (1962) and *The Future of Higher Education within the Further Education System* (1965).

For the present Government's proposals see the White Paper *A Policy for the Arts* (1965); Circular 8/65 and Scottish Circular 589 (1965); and the DES's *Report on the Arts* (1966).

CHAPTER 9

EDUCATION FOR AGRICULTURE

Agricultural education during and since the war

In England and Wales at the outbreak of war, further education for agriculture (using the term "agriculture" to include also horticulture, poultry husbandry, dairying and forestry) was conducted in five separate streams. Four were for full-time students and one for part-time. First, university departments provided three- and four-year degree courses required for careers in advisory, teaching, research and overseas services. Second, agricultural colleges, originally independent foundations, offered two-year diploma courses for training farmers and farm managers. Third, agricultural and horticultural institutes (farm institutes), under county councils, conducted one- and two-year courses for farmers, farm managers, farm technicians and skilled farm workers. There was a considerable overlap between these three, for agricultural colleges, to take an example, often provided courses at above and below diploma level in addition to their diploma courses. All three were aided by the Minister of Agriculture and Fisheries under whom (but in Scotland under the Secretary of State) the Forestry Commission provided a fourth group : full-time schools for the training of foresters. Fifth, a small amount of part-time day and evening work was conducted by local education authorities in technical colleges and evening institutes.

The war brought a new realization of the special importance of agriculture. The Luxmoore Committee, appointed in 1941, began to give agricultural education early and close attention, publishing a report two years later. A joint advisory committee appointed in 1944 by the Ministers of Education and Agriculture under the chairmanship of Dr. T. Loveday produced another three reports dealing with agricultural education in secondary schools (1945), farm institutes (1947) and part-time classes (1949); and another committee appointed by the Minister of Agriculture, also under Dr. Loveday, published one on the work of universities and colleges (1946).

Under the influence of these reports there have been several important changes. First, the numbers of students in all types of establishment have increased considerably. Second, there has been a sharper segregation of levels of work, each to its appropriate type of establishment; thus universities

169

have confined themselves more closely to degree work, colleges to diplomas, and farm institutes to one-year certificates and the teaching of farming skills to young farmers and farm workers. This reorganization, like its counterparts in technology, commerce and art, has been regarded as leading to a more economical use of scarce teaching resources.

Third, all the 38 farm institutes and 5 agricultural colleges have been transferred from the agricultural to the educational service. This move is in accord with the conception of Further Education contained in the 1943 White Paper and the main Acts, and is contrary to the proposal of a majority of the Luxmoore Committee that agricultural education should be provided by a new central authority, under the Minister of Agriculture, separate from the rest of the educational system. The transfer has proceeded in four steps. On 1st October 1946 the education of students in farm institutes, which during the war had been concerned largely with emergency training of Women's Land Army recruits, was recommenced under county education committees, which continued to receive grant-in-aid, however, from the Minister of Agriculture. At the same time the advisory functions of county councils, exercised until then through their war agricultural executive committees, were transferred to a new National Agricultural Advisory Service (NAAS), also under the Minister of Agriculture. Then, after the Carrington Report (1953) and Circular 275 (1954), HMIs began to inspect farm institutes, but reported their findings to the Minister of Agriculture. Next, on 1st April 1959, after the De La Warr Report and Circular 346 (1959), complete overall responsibility for farm institutes was transferred to the Minister of Education. The NAAS remained under the Minister of Agriculture, though continuing to work closely with local education authorities, as had been urged in Circular 123 and again in the fourth Loveday, Carrington and De La Warr Reports and in Circulars 275 and 346. Finally, responsibility for the agricultural colleges was transferred to the Department of Education and Science on 1st April 1964. The 2 forester training schools in England and Wales, however, have remained under the Minister of Land and National Resources and Secretary of State for Wales respectively, through the Forestry Commission.

A fourth trend is the growth of part-time study, some of it linked with apprenticeship, in technical colleges and evening institutes. Provision has been mainly for part-time day and evening vocational students aged from fifteen to eighteen, particularly since 1954; but there have also been some block-release courses, recreational classes and extra-mural work for adult domestic producers.

A National College of Agricultural Engineering opened at Boreham in 1962 and moved to Silsoe in 1964. NACEIC set up a regular committee for agriculture in 1964.

In Scotland the trends have been similar, but four of the five streams (all except forestry) have co-existed in the three agricultural Central Institutions at Aberdeen, Edinburgh and Glasgow. These are under the Secretary of State, but, as recommended in the Fyfe Report, still administered through the Department of Agriculture and Fisheries, not the Education Department. They work closely with adjacent universities, conduct applied research and offer advice to farmers in their regions. There is no separate advisory service. Acting in association with university departments of agriculture they are sometimes called "schools of agriculture". They are now shedding their day-release courses to authority-maintained further education centres. There are no farm institutes but there are 5 farm schools in which courses are provided at further-education level. There are 2 forester training schools which are also shedding courses to authorities. STECC set up a committee for agriculture in 1963 and one for forestry in 1964.

Arrangements for students

Apprenticeship

A national joint apprenticeship council was formed in 1949 and launched a scheme for Scotland in that year and another for England and Wales in 1953. Their organization is similar to that of industrial schemes (see Chapter 5). Applications are received from employers ready to take an apprentice and from people aged between fifteen and eighteen who wish to start a career in agriculture. Apprenticeship with a selected farmer or grower lasts for three years under a deed, conditions being regulated by the Agricultural Wages Board. The apprentice must be released without loss of pay to attend courses, generally at a farm institute or technical college, for a total period of at least sixty days during the three years. After completing his apprenticeship the young worker is entitled to be paid at 10 per cent above the standard minimum wage. However, apprentices make up only a small minority of agricultural students.

The Forestry Commission runs a training scheme with entry at age seventeen, involving compulsory residential attendance at a block-release course followed by admission to a two-year full-time course at a forester training school at nineteen or later.

For non-apprentices

Particularly since 1960, day release has grown more rapidly than apprenticeship. For example, local parks authorities have commonly released unapprenticed employees under eighteen.

About one-third of all students enrolled at farm institutes in 1964–5 were full-time, receiving grants from their authorities; and most of these were in residential accommodation. Rather more than one-third were on day release and rather fewer than one-third attended in the evenings only. Very few got sandwich release. Only about one-eighth of the total were girls. Among all young people employed, however, the proportion given day release has risen sharply in recent years (Table 13). About a quarter of young male entrants in 1965 received daytime education.

A small number of postgraduate students at Central Institutions are aided by the Scottish Department of Agriculture and Fisheries, ARC or NERC.

Courses, studies and establishments

Craft, technician and management courses

Part-time day courses of from one to three years' duration in agriculture, agricultural engineering, horticulture, poultry practice, dairying, farm management and rural domestic economy are provided for apprentices and others at Central Institutions, farm institutes, Scottish farm schools and technical colleges. Evening courses at all of these or at evening institutes may be available for those unable to get release. Some are PRELIMINARY; others lead to CERTIFICATES of a variety of bodies, including regional examining unions, the City and Guilds Institute, colleges themselves and professional institutions such as the Royal Horticultural Society. The City and Guilds Institute, in particular, offers a three-stage system of grouped-course certificates in which stage I is at about the standard of admission to a farm-institute certificate course, stage II to a farm-institute certificate itself (one year, full-time, or three if taken by day release), and stage III to a farm-institute supplementary course (two years; see below).

The Cumberland and Westmorland Farm School takes the Forestry Commission's block-release trainees already mentioned.

PREAPPRENTICESHIP, CRAFT and TECHNICIAN courses in building and engineering with a rural bias, including agricultural engineering up to graduateship standard, are offered at some rural technical colleges. To take an example, Rycotewood College, Oxfordshire, offers full-time courses and others based on block release supplemented by correspondence; residential accommodation is provided.

As yet, however, there is no consistent pattern of part-time courses over the whole country.

Full-time courses at Central Institutions, agricultural colleges and farm institutes cater for young workers who have already had some practical

experience. They range in length from one term to three years, some requiring entrance qualifications in terms of the GCE or SCE. An example is
the one-year NATIONAL CERTIFICATE IN AGRICULTURE (NAC), awarded on
results of the farm institute's own examinations (externally assessed), after
which a second year may be spent in gaining ENDORSEMENT in one or more
supplementary special subjects. Twelve farm institutes offer a NATIONAL
CERTIFICATE IN HORTICULTURE (NCH), and four specialize entirely in horticulture. Although self-contained these can also serve as PRELIMINARY to
agricultural-college or university courses.

Just under half of the entrants to one-year full-time courses at farm
institutes in the session 1962–3 had the qualification recommended for all
such entrants in the De La Warr and first Lampard-Vachell Reports (see
later), namely, a pass at City and Guilds stage I or in three O levels of
the GCE.

Diploma courses

NATIONAL DIPLOMAS in Agriculture, Dairying, Horticulture, Agricultural
Engineering, Poultry Husbandry, Bee-keeping and Forestry (NDA, etc.) are
awarded by professional institutions concerned, and corresponding SCOTTISH
DIPLOMAS by Central Institutions. The Departments do not actively participate in these schemes. Entrants must be aged at least seventeen, have had at
least one year of practical experience and normally have passed in four
appropriate O-level subjects in the GCE or SCE. Two-year and three-year
full-time courses for National or Scottish Diplomas or for COLLEGE DIPLOMAS
are offered by all 3 Central Institutions, all 5 agricultural colleges and 3 of
the farm institutes. Course work in the form of diaries and so on must be
submitted to the examiners.

Professional membership

National Diplomas are recognized by the Institute of Biology as of
roughly HNC or pass-degree standard and so qualify for admission to
ASSOCIATE MEMBERSHIP. Examinations of the Land Agents' Society and
Royal Institution of Chartered Surveyors can be taken at the Royal
Agricultural College, Cirencester.

National College courses

The National College of Agricultural Engineering offers a three-year

N

full-time ASSOCIATESHIP of graduate standard and a number of one-year POSTGRADUATE and POST-NATIONAL COURSES.

University studies

DEGREES, POSTGRADUATE STUDIES and RESEARCH can be done at the 3 Scottish schools of agriculture.

Short courses

These are numerous, and include some for domestic producers. RECREATIONAL CLASSES are offered in some evening institutes.

The expansion of provision

Main features at present

Of course the agricultural industry exhibits general features shared with other parts of the British economy. But in addition it has characteristics of its own, some natural in origin, others economic and social. These tend to make education for agriculture at least as necessary yet at the same time more difficult than for many other industries.

Perhaps the most striking features are the continued shrinkage of both land and manpower available, contrasted with the ever growing home and world demand for food. This contradiction has greatly increased the productivity required from what remains, with obvious implications for technical education. At the same time, isolation of farming people has created a need for *general* education also, offering better opportunities for communal activities than in urban communities.

There has indeed been a marked advance in the technology of agriculture. British food production, in spite of the shrinkages mentioned, is now nearly 70 per cent greater than before the war. The agricultural worker at all levels has been obliged to become more of an all-round technician than in most industries.

But the difficulties in the way of further development are formidable. Perhaps most important, the small productive unit has remained predominant, three-quarters of all full-time workers being engaged at farms worked by ten or fewer people. In consequence, over one-third have management or supervisory responsibility in addition to their technical duties. But paper qualifications have not been highly rated, employers have been neither willing nor able to release workers for daytime study, and there have been no large firms to lead the way in educational policy. In horticulture most holdings are not only small and scattered but specialized too, so that few are varied enough to be able to provide opportunities for all-round experience during training, while movement from one to another is rarely feasible. The industry as a whole has become dependent on permanent government aid, administered through the agriculture ministries, and its educational service has been split between these and the education ministries.

Difficulties of organizing educational provision have been made worse by the sensitivity of hours, tempo and conditions of farm work to natural phenomena, the local variability of circumstances and practices and the scattered incidence of farm dwellings often placed well away from the main centres of population.

Proposals

These features were taken into account by Earl De La Warr's Committee, which wanted agricultural education expanded within ten years into a comprehensive and progressive system embracing in one way or another everyone engaged in the industry. It should be closely linked, said the De La Warr Report, with practical training on the farm or other workplace, should lead to nationally recognized examinations and should contain provision in rural domestic economy for all girls wanting it. It should begin immediately on leaving school, with day or block release for all; and should continue with full-time courses for a selected minority at farm institute, college or university, supplemented by a wide range of part-time courses including advanced ones.

The greatest expansion, thought the Committee, should be in part-time day provision for the fifteens to eighteens. For this to be possible before the introduction of compulsion, far more support from the industry would be needed.

Expansion of full-time provision would then be easier, since the part-time expansion would, among other things, prepare for it. The wide range of attainment of students in farm institutes could then be narrowed, the supply of better-prepared students increased and the institutes relieved of much of their more elementary work. They could then concentrate on what the Loveday Joint Committee had regarded as their main function, the provision of one-year basic courses in general agriculture, designed to train farmers, farm managers, foremen and farm technicians, whether as employers or employees, whilst also offering one-year and shorter supplementary specialized and refresher courses. Admission to the basic course should require either the completion of a recognized three-year part-time course with practical farm training (to the standard of, say, the City and Guilds stage I), or possession of three appropriate O-level GCE passes plus a year's farming experience. The needs of specialized production, as in large poultry units, should be distinguished from those of mixed farming, only the latter being the province of farm institutes. Courses in horticulture should be concentrated in certain institutes only. Farm institutes should not normally provide diploma courses, which were considered appropriate to agricultural colleges. Rural domestic economy should not be done in farm institutes either, being better suited to part-time treatment in technical colleges, evening institutes or special centres devoted to it. The farms attached to farm institutes should be used as teaching aids and not to demonstrate commercial farming practices. The size of existing farm institutes was too small and they should be increased to at least 100 students each.

Voluntary activities, particularly the Young Farmers' Club movement (YFC), have played a big part in agricultural education, and the De La Warr Committee urged authorities to give every encouragement to them.

The Committee also proposed that the educational responsibilities of the Minister of Agriculture be transferred to the Minister of Education. As already described, this has now been completed in the case of the farm institutes and agricultural colleges, but it is not clear whether the forester training schools were meant to be included in this proposal.

The Government adopted the De La Warr Report by publishing it as a White Paper.

In the two Lampard-Vachell Reports NACEIC reconsidered and agreed with nearly all of the De La Warr proposals, adding some of its own. In Circulars 7/60 and 6/61 the Minister accepted them too, as did his colleague at the Ministry of Agriculture. Both these Ministers urged the industry to accept its full share of responsibility in carrying them out, particularly by providing practical training at work and by releasing students to attend courses. The Minister also asked authorities to submit new outline Schemes, as a result of which a special building programme for England and Wales, to last three or four years, was started in 1961. Capital expenditure approved by him for the period 1959–60 to 1964/5 totalled £3·7 million by the end of 1963, which was about half the amount asked for by authorities in their Schemes.

NACEIC looked at agricultural education again in the Dadd Report (1966). Its main proposal, that there should evolve a pattern similar to the rest of technical education, which young people could enter immediately on leaving school, is reminiscent of the De La Warr Report. This pattern would include preliminary, craft, technician, National and degree levels. Although agriculture did not become the subject of any proposal by an official body for a Dip.Tech.-type award, degree courses outside universities were later recommended in the Robbins, Bosanquet and Dadd Reports. However, the CNAA had not set up a board for agriculture by the end of 1965.

Notes on further study

The background reports have been mentioned, namely Luxmoore (1943), four Loveday (1945, 1946, 1947, 1949), Fyfe (1946), Carrington (1953), De La Warr (1958), Crowther (1959; especially pp. 400–403), two Lampard-Vachell (1960 and 1961) and Dadd (1966). For Wales see the second Old-field-Davies Report (1960). The De La Warr and Dadd Reports are the most important of these. For Central Institutions see the Bosanquet Report (1964; especially paragraphs 11–14).

Statistical information is contained in the annual reports of the Ministers and Secretaries of State and of the Minister of Agriculture, and, for England and Wales from 1961 onwards, in *Statistics of Education*, especially *Part 2*. For Scotland see the DAFS's *Agricultural Research, Advisory Services and Education in Scotland* (1965). For information about one-year full-time students at farm institutes in 1962–3 see *Education in 1963*, paragraph 78, p. 49 (1964).

Relevant Circulars have been 25 (1945), 123 (1946), 161 (1948), 275 (1954) and Addenda (1961, 1964), 335 (1958), 346 (1959), 7/59 (Addendum No. 1, 1961), 7/60 and 6/61; and Administrative Memorandum 452 (1953). Titles of those current are indexed in the annual *List 10*. Procedure for the approval of buildings and advanced courses is as for technology.

Apprenticeship schemes (introduced into England and Wales in Administrative Memorandum 452) can be studied in brochures issued by the Agricultural Apprenticeship Council in London and the Scottish Joint Apprenticeship Council for Agriculture and Horticulture in Edinburgh.

Details of courses can be found in prospectuses of colleges and institutes, lists got out by authorities and *Guides* published by regional and district advisory councils. Full-time courses were described in detail in the DES's *List 185* (1965) and the Forestry Commission's *Training as a Forester* (1962).

The National Examination Boards in Agriculture, Horticulture, Dairying, Poultry Husbandry, Poultry Technology, Agricultural Engineering, Forestry and Bee-keeping, sponsored by professional institutions, govern the examinations for National Diplomas and Certificates and have published a booklet *Agriculture as a Career* (1964).

For forestry see the Society of Foresters' Cirencester meeting report *Education in British Forestry* (1965).

TABLE 16

NUMBERS OF STUDENTS AT ESTABLISHMENTS OF FURTHER EDUCATION ENROLLED
IN COURSES LEADING TO RECOGNIZED QUALIFICATIONS (ENGLAND AND WALES,
1964–5) *(thousands)*

	Men	Women	Total
NON-ADVANCED			
GCE			
O level	93·1	51·1	144·2
A level	29·6	15·1	44·6
City and Guilds			
Building	86·4		86·4
Engineering	228·0	0·4	228·4
Other subjects	84·6	38·5	122·2
National schemes			
ONC	68·6	3·1	71·6
OND	5·6	3·8	9·3
Other courses			
Agriculture	3·8	0·6	4·4
Art and design	4·4	4·8	9·3
Business and administration	48·8	8·8	57·6
Catering	2·1	2·8	4·9
Health and welfare	3·4	11·0	14·3
Wholesale and retail trades	4·8	0·4	5·2
Languages	2·3	3·5	5·8
Other subjects	28·0	3·7	31·7
All non-advanced	692·5	147·5	840·0
ADVANCED			
National schemes			
HNC	52·9	1·1	53·9
HND	7·8	0·5	8·3
Art and design			
NDD	1·5	1·5	3·1
Dip.AD	1·5	1·7	3·2
ATC and ATD	0·3	0·3	0·6
Diploma in Technology	9·8	0·3	10·1
Degrees			
First	11·7	2·4	14·1
Higher	1·1	0·06	1·2
Postgraduate and research	4·1	0·1	4·2
Other courses			
Architecture	4·3	0·2	4·6
Business and administration	16·7	2·1	18·8
Engineering	15·2	0·03	15·3
Sciences	4·0	0·4	4·4
Other subjects	13·3	3·3	16·4
All advanced	144·1	14·0	158·1
TOTAL	836·6	161·6	998·2

Source: Department of Education and Science: *Statistics of Education, 1964, Part 2,*
tables 13–14 (1965).

CHAPTER 10

PART-TIME DAY EDUCATION FOR
ALL UNDER EIGHTEEN

An intention unfulfilled

The duty of a civilized society to continue the education of *all* its school leavers, not merely of those who need it for their careers, has been officially admitted for over half a century. Sir Michael Sadler had been greatly influenced by German experience before 1900; and in 1909 the Board's Consultative Committee, of which he was a member, recommended that authorities be given two things : a *duty* to provide daytime "continuation classes" for anyone under seventeen who might ask for them, and a *power* to impose compulsory release and compulsory attendance. Without compulsion, thought the Committee, such education would not reach those needing it most.

The first world war stressed the value of this advice. After the Lewis Report the Education Acts of 1918 and 1921 gave authorities the duty to set up "day continuation schools" for young people who had been obliged to attend, and the power to oblige them to attend. Up to the age of sixteen, later to be extended with certain exemptions to eighteen, young people could be compelled to put in at least 280 hours per year, their employers having to release them for the purpose. This was almost what the Consultative Committee had recommended, but not quite. The duty placed on the authorities was to provide, not for *all* young people who might demand it, but only for those who *had been obliged* to demand it. Thus the duty became operative only if the power were used.

In fact few authorities did use the power, and only one after 1922. Where it was used the schools were opened in no consistent sequence, so that young people and their employers, particularly if near authority boundaries, were faced with anomalies in the operation of compulsion. Also the schools were generally unpopular with employers; there was a scarcity of the right kind of teacher; and few suitable buildings were provided. Obviously the difficulties, disadvantages and costs of the measure had not been correctly appreciated. Public opinion, not least among the young people themselves, was not strong enough to force the overcoming of such difficulties. To make matters worse there was a slump in 1921–2 which brought "economy" cuts. Only in Rugby has compulsory attendance remained until today, and there only to the age of sixteen. In some areas, where there happened to be sympathetic employers, day continuation schools were opened voluntarily, or firms built their own, with or without aid from the Board or authorities. Unemployed people under eighteen could (and still can) be compelled to attend classes. Nevertheless, in 1938 only about one-fifth of the leavers from elementary schools continued to receive any kind of formal education, and of these most attended in the evenings only.

Thus, when Parliament came to look at the problem again after the second world war, it was realized that merely to give *powers* to authorities would not be enough. The Acts of 1944, 1945 and 1946, therefore, set out to guarantee provision by making it *four times compulsory* : on young people and their employers, and on authorities and Ministers as well.

The Acts were explicitly detailed in all four of these directions. Every young person between compulsory school age and eighteen who was not exempt had to be served by his authority with a notice directing him to attend what was to be called in England and Wales a county college or in Scotland a junior college. Normally attendance would be for one day or two half-days in each of forty-four weeks per year; but it could be varied in the light of the young persons' preferences or the needs of their employment, in forms such as eight continuous weeks at a time or two four-week periods, so long as it totalled at least 330 hours in any one year. Only those already receiving education to the satisfaction of the authority, or training or engaged in the mercantile marine or sea-fishing industry, or, of course, in categories to which the duties of local education authorities did not relate, were exempt. If aggrieved a young person could appeal to the Minister.

The employer had to release the young person to attend during working hours, and the period so released had to be counted as working time for purposes of computing limited hours or overtime. The employer had also to tell the authority, as far as he could, the names, addresses and changes of address of all his young employees as they entered or left his employment. A young person, parent or employer could be jailed for breaches or connivance at breaches of these laws.

The authorities had the duty of providing county and junior colleges just as they had to provide schools, in accordance with Plans approved by the Ministers. The provision of medical inspection and treatment, milk, meals, board and lodging, clothing for physical education, financial aid, means of recreation, social and physical training, transport and other facilities and the enforcement of cleanliness were to be very much as in schools. No fees were to be charged, except, in certain cases, for board and lodging, and in the latter the provisions for remission were similar to those for school pupils. The Plans, however, were to be linked with Schemes of Further Education and not with Development Plans for Primary and Secondary Schools (see Chapter 1).

The Ministers had to promote, direct and control the system, approve authorities' Plans, specify the colleges to be set up, make regulations for their conduct and introduce compulsion on an appointed day. They might also make orders binding on authorities regarding various other aspects of college provision.

Most important of all, as it has turned out, the Ministers had to name the dates on which the system was to come into operation. This was to happen in four stages, of which the first had a built-in date-line but the other three had not. Subsection 43 (1) of the 1944 Act said that on a date to be determined by Order in Council, not later than three years after 1st April 1945, the authorities' duty to establish and maintain county colleges would begin. This was to enable authorities to take preliminary steps such as the acquisition of sites. Subsection 43 (2) said that as soon as practicable after 1st April 1945 the Minister would direct authorities to make their estimates and send him their Plans. This was to make sure that needs in each area had been properly assessed. Subsection 43 (3) said that after considering these and consulting with authorities the Minister would make an Order specifying which county colleges were to be maintained by each authority. This was so that the colleges would be ready when compulsion was introduced. And Sections 44–46 defined compulsory attendance, which was to come into operation on a date to be determined by the Minister as soon as practicable after the date named by Order in Council under Subsection 43 (1). This was to ensure a uniform beginning throughout the country.

What actually happened was as follows. First, under the subsection with the built-in date, an order was in fact made (SR & O 1947, No. 527), with the effect that the authorities' *duty began* on 1st April 1947. Next, the Plans were duly called for (in Circular 139) and submitted. Circular 133 had seemed optimistic, but Circular 139 ended with an ominous warning. Indeed, under the third subsection, no orders saying which particular county colleges were to be maintained have yet been made. Thus, although the authorities have been told that their duty has begun, they *have never been told to fulfil their duty*. Naturally, then, as there are no county colleges to attend, no Minister has yet considered it "practicable" to introduce the fourth stage, compulsory attendance. So there are still neither county colleges nor compulsory attendance. In Scotland the indefinite postponement of junior colleges was made explicit in the 1949 and 1962 Acts. We have got no further than stage two.

By these simple devices, despite all the care in the Acts, county and junior colleges have been avoided even more adroitly than were the corresponding provisions of the Act of 1921. As a result, over half of the boys and over three-quarters of the girls aged sixteen and seventeen are receiving no education during the daytime at all. Indeed, these proportions have actually *increased* since the Crowther Report (Table 14). Yet no Minister or Secretary of State has declared an intention of choosing a date for completing a measure intended by Parliament nearly fifty years ago.

The concept of the county college

Classical

In the 1944 Act county colleges were defined as

> centres approved by the Minister for providing for young persons who are not in full-time attendance at any school or other educational institution such further education, including physical, practical and vocational training, as will enable them to develop their various aptitudes and capacities and will prepare them for the responsibilities of citizenship.

Thus the county college was to be for the all-round education of anyone under eighteen who was not already receiving it full-time. During the planning period, as mentioned in Chapter 1, the Minister gave guidance to authorities in Pamphlets Nos. 3 and 8 and Circular 133. Pamphlet No. 3 (*Youth's Opportunity*) remains the classical exposition of the concept. Three principles were put forward :

(1) The scheme must meet the fundamental, as well as the purely vocational needs, of the young people for whom it is to be created.
(2) It must be flexible enough to allow for vocational and non-vocational work to be carried on within it, without artificial and harmful segregation.
(3) It must recognize the fact that the whole field of further education is one.

The county colleges were expected to contain the great majority of the younger school leavers. They were to have close contact with other establishments of Further Education, sending students to them and perhaps sharing buildings and other facilities with them. County colleges would provide vocational courses as required, but these would be subordinate to the fundamental needs of the adolescent. The Minister thought that about one young worker in three would be training for a skill, but county colleges would take both skilled and unskilled, and there should be no segregation of vocational sheep from non-vocational goats. Some vocational courses, however, would need specialized equipment which could be better provided centrally; in the more populous areas, therefore, county colleges should be differentiated as central and branch colleges. The larger ones should be self-sufficient and some might function primarily as feeders to the bigger technical colleges whilst others might be housed within technical colleges. County colleges were expected to transform the evening institutes by reducing the demand for some studies and increasing it for others, besides stimulating other forms of adult education and youth activity. Community and youth centres should therefore share their buildings with county colleges or be near to them. County colleges should be sited in the home area rather than in the work area, for cheapness and to ensure occupational mixing of students. Residential accommodation would be necessary in thinly populated areas, where an eight-week block-release system would probably prove the most useful, and where the cost of playing fields and gymnasia might make it necessary for a county college to be incorporated as an annexe to a secondary school.

The Minister thought that a suitable size for a county college would be between 300 and 400 students a day. Student groups should be small— normally of not more than 20—and the sexes should not be artificially segregated. Attendance would be from the date stated on the college attendance notice until the end of the county-college term in which the student became eighteen. Thus most students would be under eighteen, but every effort should be made to encourage them to remain beyond the time at which they could leave. The day would be $7\frac{1}{2}$ hours long, which is more than in schools and many colleges at present but less than in industry; and there would be eight weeks of vacation, which is less than in schools and most colleges at present but more than in industry. The Minister hoped that during this holiday period young people would continue to be released so that they would have these days free.

The curriculum of the county college, said Pamphlet No. 3, should contain a wide range of studies and activities, classified not as vocational and non-vocational but as physical, practical, general and elective. As a rough estimate these groups should occupy respectively $1\frac{1}{2}$, 3, 2 and $1\frac{1}{2}$ eighths of the day's time; but they should be organized flexibly, with periods when students chose and planned their own activities, and without a rigid weekly timetable. Some activities might need to be followed intensively for a time and then dropped, or projects might be undertaken. Physical education, broadly conceived, should be compulsory for those fit for it. Practical education should offer a wide range of crafts and every student should gain some mastery of at least one. General education should include the "basic" subjects approached in new ways and linked with the other groups. Elective activities should be freely chosen and informally conducted. Teaching methods would have to be different from those which had become traditional in schools, and there should be a rich provision of voluntary societies for leisure-time activities. As mentioned in Chapter 2, a detailed list of curriculum aims was suggested.

Works schools, wrote the Minister, were desirable only in exceptional circumstances. Although often both purposeful and well disciplined they were usually too small, tended to be over-dominated by the firms providing them and did not bring students into a sufficiently varied social intercourse. In the words of Pamphlet No. 8 :

> The county college will be the focal point in the plans for further education, and a corner-stone of all part-time education for young people under 18.

By and large the authorities adopted this concept in their Plans (Table 17), though there were numerous individual departures from it. They planned the colleges in close relation with the rest of their Further Education provision, intending to house them sometimes in technical colleges, sometimes in school buildings whose original occupants had been moved elsewhere and sometimes in new buildings of their own. Some expected the colleges to provide full-time courses, or to absorb the junior evening institutes. They tended to choose a smaller size, however, than the Minister had recommended, such as 300, 200 or even fewer students a day. They

TABLE 17

DIAGRAMMATIC REPRESENTATION

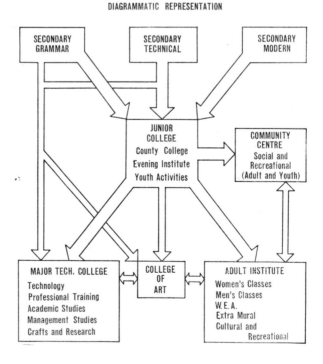

tended, too, to feature vocational courses prominently in the curriculum; thus Blackburn decided :

> The curriculum of the County Colleges will be both general and vocational in approximately equal proportions. In special circumstances, students will be allowed to take vocational work in the other Further Education Institutes, but it is anticipated that, in general, the County Colleges will provide courses up to and including the S2 stage. . . . Indeed, the County Colleges could well become Branch Colleges for Further Education.

The Central Advisory Council for Wales (1951) largely agreed with Pamphlet No. 3. But it, too, favoured a smaller size of college. It did not like the idea of central and branch colleges, which might lead to an invidious hierarchy; and it wanted colleges to have their own new buildings, in which residential accommodation would be more important than in England. It thought that colleges should have close relations with the Youth Employment Service but did not commit itself on the recommendation of the Ince Committee that the Service should be housed in the colleges.

Modern

Perhaps, if things had gone as intended, the technical and other colleges would have taken only full-time and sandwich students and those over eighteen. But things have not gone as intended. If the county colleges were to have been the cornerstone of part-time Further Education for the under-eighteens, then such education has had to develop without its cornerstone. The Youth Service has not developed on anything like the scale expected either. In fact the part-time education of the under-eighteens has fallen mainly to Area and Local Colleges, many of which were conceived originally as county colleges but have developed differently. Further Education on the voluntary basis has remained overwhelmingly vocational.

Thus the county college can never now be a focal point. Instead, it will be a newcomer into a well established system. Since young people aiming at skilled occupations now attend vocational courses it has come to be assumed that county colleges will take those with less pronounced vocational needs. The voluntary system will already have "selected" some of the brighter, more ambitious and more fortunate students, leaving the county colleges, like modern rather than comprehensive schools, to gather up the rest. The Minister's prediction of one-third as the proportion of school leavers requiring to be trained for skill has proved about right for boys, but the segregation of these vocational sheep from the two-thirds of non-vocational goats, against which she warned, has happened.

For how long this would continue under universal compulsion is problematical. Technological advance increases the demand for both general and vocational education, each stimulating the other. And there are sure to be some young people, particularly girls, among those who at present get no further education at all, who would take opportunities of vocational advancement if these came their way. By 1960 the Minister's expectation of the proportion of young people needing vocational courses had risen to over half. Moreover, the boundary between skilled and unskilled is neither static nor clear.

Nevertheless, it seems probable that, at least at first, the county colleges would contain a higher proportion of the less ready, willing and able than was originally envisaged. So the concept of the county college has changed into something for the education of the *unskilled*.

This is the concept adopted by the Central Advisory Council for England in the Crowther Report, whose recommendations differ significantly from those of the Minister fourteen years earlier. Though no less insistent on the need, the Crowther Council was less confident and less explicit in suggesting how it should be satisfied, and stressed the difficulties more.

The Council did not much like the idea of the county college being a part of a larger college because of the danger of its being handicapped by a feeling of inferiority, but it did not commit itself to any other particular form of organization. Nor did it put forward specific curricular proposals but confined itself to discussing the general and educational needs of adolescents (see Chapter 2). It thought that very little was known about how to deal with the future county-college student. Not much could be learned from Rugby whose experience had been with an age group that would be kept in school when the compulsory school age was raised. It considered the experience gained in voluntary "county colleges" to be of little direct relevance either, since all such work had been done by pioneering teachers, helped by enlightened employers, and with young people either attending willingly or free to change their job; and none of these would be typical in the real county college. Nor had the Youth Service been able to provide much guidance, and for the same reasons, namely the absence of the most significant element—compulsion—and the consequent failure to reach the majority of young people in semiskilled and unskilled occupations. Thus the core of the problem had not been touched. The need for a new kind of teacher or "tutor", perhaps more akin to a youth leader than to a school teacher or further-education lecturer, was also stressed, as was the problem of recruiting and training the 20,000 who would be needed. A much stronger Youth Service than at present was seen as an essential complement.

It may be remembered (see Chapter 5) that the Council also recommended that half of all sixteen- and seventeen-year-olds ought to be getting full-time or sandwich education by 1979. If this should come to pass through the use of existing establishments (schools, etc.), perhaps supplemented by a new type of institution (the "junior college" which was also suggested—see Chapter 14), the function of the future county college might well shrink still more.

The way to the county college

The Crowther Council did not believe that the immediate or sudden introduction of county colleges would be feasible. So it put forward a coherent programme linking the task with another unfulfilled promise—the raising of the compulsory school age to sixteen.

The relation between these two measures had not been greatly appreciated during the earlier period, when it had been generally assumed that the colleges would come first. Thus authorities when drawing up their Plans had expected a sudden drop of about one-third in county-college attendance when the age came to be raised. The problem began to be more widely discussed in the 1950s when it was still commonly thought that this was the better sequence. That it would have meant either providing buildings which would later become too large or handicapping the colleges during their early years by overcrowding tended to be overlooked. The Crowther Council wanted to avoid both these dangers; it pointed out, too, that raising the age would need far less new building than providing colleges (especially as new schools were already being built for a full five-year course anyway); and that raising the age would help the colleges but providing colleges would not help the raising of the age. For these reasons it proposed that county colleges should come *after* the age had been raised.

The Council's selection of the period 1966–1969 for the raising of the age, because the population of fifteen-year-olds would then be at a minimum, therefore determined the timetable for introducing the colleges. Three phases were suggested, to which the teacher-training and building programmes would have to be adjusted.

First, there should be a period of voluntary growth. The Council thought that expansion had been inhibited in the past by a widespread lack of belief in any serious intention to introduce compulsion. The key to the opening of this phase, therefore, would be an announcement by the Minister that he intended to do his duty on an early and specified date. During this first phase the Minister and authorities would be fully occupied with raising the age. Teachers would gain increased experience with the three main categories neglected at present: skilled trainees in industries where day release is not normally given, the semiskilled and unskilled, and girls in general. Properly designed studies should be conducted of problems, such as the effectiveness of different incentives, or ways of recruiting and training teachers.

The second phase should begin soon after the raising of the age and last for not more than five years. It would be the main experimental period. Compulsion would now be introduced, not everywhere, but in a few carefully selected large areas, each containing a variety of occupations so as to form a relatively self-contained economic microcosm clearly bounded by what might be called employment watersheds. These areas would not necessarily correspond with the territories of local government, so that co-operation among authorities would be needed. In this way it was hoped to avoid as far as possible the anomalies which followed the Act of 1921. Teachers would then learn something about handling the whole of the age group under compulsion. The apathetic or angry attenders, the youngsters without any vocational interest, the frequent job-changers, the juvenile unemployed, the unwilling employers, the hostile foremen, the seasonal industries, the difficult work situations, the awkward parents and many other incidences would create problems to be studied. The merits of separate colleges versus departments of Local Colleges could be compared. The Youth Service in these areas should be given extra aid. Special legislation and financial arrangements would be necessary.

In the third phase compulsion would be quickly spread by planned steps over the whole country. This might take three or four years.

These proposals are remarkable for their progressive, integrated, tightly phased timetable; their emphasis on the need for continuous trial, experience and research; and the high degree of centralized planning and direction which they would require.

Voluntary part-time day and residential education for the unskilled

Courses and establishments

As mentioned, some "county-college type" education has been conducted voluntarily : in day continuation schools, day colleges, "county colleges" and technical colleges (usually Area or Local, whose buildings, where new, may have been planned with some eye to later expansion along these lines). Thus there is experience of work both in separate establishments and in departments of bigger colleges. Pioneer work with voluntary day-release classes began in London in 1916; and Birmingham, Liverpool, Nottingham, Wolverhampton and York spring also into mind as authorities helped by progressively minded employers in whose areas such work has become well known. According to the Crowther Report, however, it has reached no more than about $1\frac{1}{2}$ per cent of the age group and now reaches rather less than this.

The usual curriculum pattern, as at Childwall Hall County College,

Liverpool, contains "basic" and "elective" subjects. The former group includes English, social studies, hygiene (for girls) and arithmetic; while the latter covers a wide range containing, for example, first aid, family care, home making, current affairs, local surveys, map reading, languages, speech training, drama, sciences, gardening, car and cycle maintenance, art, photography, various crafts, music, film appreciation, film making and accident prevention. Physical education may be in either group. Experimental courses on topics such as "new horizons", "personal living" or "home and work" are frequently tried. Vocational studies, mainly commercial or technical, may also be fitted in as required, and examinations such as RSA, GCE, Civil Service or Retail Trades may be taken. At London day colleges there are elementary, intermediate and advanced "optional" courses. Some colleges invite firms to apply for the services of college teachers who are prepared to visit premises of firms to conduct classes for employees. At Childwall there have been one-week "leadership" courses in the Lake District supported by firms, and weekends devoted to film making. In all cases use is made of flexible class grouping and timetabling, tutorial and informal teaching methods, a wide range of sources and materials, audiovisual aids, visits, free discussion, individual and group assignments and projects, visiting speakers, holiday and residential courses, foreign travel, links with work and self-governed student activities. There is some difference of opinion as to the best method, if any, of assessing students' work and progress.

Similar work is done in some evening establishments such as London junior commercial and technical colleges.

Short residential adventure-type courses for young workers of both sexes are run by some authorities with the co-operation of employers (as, for example, Liverpool's at Colomendy Camp School, Denbighshire). There are also unaided establishments doing similar work (such as Brathay Hall, Ambleside), but these are outside our present scope.

Problems of expansion

An important group of problems arises from the need to gain the support of employers. There are also peculiar administrative problems, such as those concerned with a variable and sometimes unpredictable intake of students, the absence of co-ordination among employers of the day of the week chosen for release, the maintenance of a full staff complement through the year and a student attendance which can vary in response to economic fluctuations.

Curricular problems abound. In London experience has been recently reviewed by a committee appointed by the authority, whose report (Briault Report) can be regarded as a step towards the first-phase research urged in

o

the Crowther Report. It is expected that in London day release will centre on Local Colleges (which are to undertake work only up to the O level of the GCE).

Most teachers in this field are enthusiastic about it and recall with pride their successful students. In London (and elsewhere), however, it may be found that technical-college teachers are unused to the unskilled student. There is a dearth of career rewards in this type of work.

Should the county college now be an entirely separate establishment, or should *all* kinds of further education be provided in existing types of college? The sixth Oxford conference *The Young Worker* (1956), the ATTI (1958) and the Ministry (for example Sir David Eccles at BACIE in 1960) favoured the latter course; but there is much to be said on both sides.

The general task is to design an education which will be of real value to the student (and therefore contain a vocational element) whilst at the same time being genuinely general, not limited by the wishes of employers nor by narrow craft or professional requirements. This must take the young worker as a young learner, not as a unit of labour power.

General studies for the skilled

Experience of general education with the unskilled is of obvious relevance to the problems of general education for the semiskilled and skilled, discussed in Chapter 5, in which there has been a marked renewal of interest since the Crowther Report. The student's life in the contemporary world is its theme.

Notes on further study

Most of the basic references have been mentioned in the chapter. The fundamental arguments for compulsory part-time day further education were stated by Sir Michael Sadler in *Continuation Schools in England and Elsewhere* (1907) (especially Chapter 25 where earlier advocates were quoted); and by the Board's Consultative Committee in its *Report on Attendance, Compulsory or Otherwise, at Continuation Schools* (1909). They were repeated in the Lewis Report (1917), in the White Paper *Educational Reconstruction* (1953) and by the Advisory Council on Education in Scotland (1953). See also YCFE : *The Reconstruction of Further Education* (1943).

This thinking underlay the attempts to legislate it into existence in the Education Act, 1918, Sections 3, 10–12; Education Act, 1921, Sections 13, 75–79; Education Act, 1944, Sections 43–46; Education (Scotland) Act, 1945, Sections 29–31; Education (Scotland) Act, 1946, Sections 39–42; and

Education (Scotland) Act, 1962, Sections 45–48. The government was urged to give a lead to employers in the Assheton Report (1944).

For earlier experience (after the 1918 Act) see Wray and Ferguson : *A Day Continuation School at Work* (1920); Edith Waterfall : *The Day Continuation School in England* (1923); and Ferguson and Abbott : *Day Continuation Schools* (1935).

Experience at Rugby was described by P. I. Kitchen in *From Learning to Earning* (1944). For the modern descendants of the Rugby courses see now the prospectus of the East Warwickshire College of Further Education. See also Silberston : *Youth in a Technical Age* (1959).

The post-war ("classical") concept of the county college was expounded in the Minister's Pamphlets *Youth's Opportunity* (1945), *Further Education* (1947) and *Citizens Growing Up* (1949); the Central Advisory Council for England's *School and Life* (1947); and the authorities' Schemes of Further Education and Plans for County Colleges (1948 onwards). The Ministry's Welsh Department's views were in *Education in Rural Wales* (1949) and the Welsh Central Advisory Council's in *The County College in Wales* (1951). The Scottish junior college was discussed in the Fyfe Report (1946).

The change in the concept of the county college can be traced in the *Twelfth Report* of the Select Committee on Estimates for the session 1952–3 (1953); the reports of Oxford University Department of Education's series of conferences under the title *The Young Worker* (especially the *Sixth*, 1956); King George's Jubilee Trust's *Citizens of To-morrow* (1955; especially Part III); and an article by C. E. Gurr in *Times educ. Suppl.* for 29th July 1955. For a discussion of this change see V. G. Hutchinson (unpublished, 1965).

The Crowther Report (Part IV) restated the case for compulsory day release and attendance, tentatively sketched a "modern" concept of the county college and proposed a phased programme for implementing the relevant sections of the 1944 Act. The "modern" concept was also used in the first Albermarle (1960) and third Oldfield-Davies (1961) Reports. German practice was reported in the Crowther Report.

Firms were urged to release their young employees for non-vocational day courses in the Assheton (1944), Carr (1958), Oakley (1962) and Henniker-Heaton (1964) Reports, among others; and in Circular 14/64.

The LCC's *On From School* (Briault Report, 1962) reviewed experience and made proposals on voluntary general education for fifteen-to-eighteens in London; and in *General Studies in Technical Colleges* (1962) the Ministry's Committee on General Studies made similar suggestions for developing general education among young people preparing to be operatives, craftsmen and technicians. Much of the Newsom Report (1963) is also relevant. The ITC's *Training Boys in Industry, the Non-apprentice* (1960) and *Training Girls in Industry* (1962) contained background information and proposals on training at work for the unskilled and semiskilled. These reports all derived their immediate inspiration from the Crowther Report (especially Chapter 17) and the White Paper *Better Opportunities in Technical Education* (1961).

More detailed information about voluntary provision of general education can be found in prospectuses and student magazines of day continuation schools, day colleges, "county colleges" and some Local Colleges.

There were useful bibliographies in the reports of the first four Oxford conferences on *The Young Worker*.

For a more general discussion see Downes and Flower: *Educating for Uncertainty* (1965).

CHAPTER 11

ADULT EDUCATION

The meaning of the term

Non-vocational education for persons aged eighteen and over is what is meant here by "Adult Education". In accordance with our initial definition it is limited in this book to that which is secured under the auspices of the Secretaries of State.

As mentioned earlier, it was regarded in wartime thinking as one of the four basic kinds of Further Education. It is the adult part of the "leisure-time occupation" which the Acts divided into "cultural training" and "recreative activities". The same division appeared in the Schemes of authorities under the headings "liberal education" and "social and recreational provision for leisure time".

The term "adult education" has never been defined in a statute and is often used loosely. An examination of the literature shows that it can have at least six meanings. These are :

(1) *All* education for persons aged eighteen and over. This distinguishes it from most secondary education, from further education for the younger student and from much of the Youth Service.

(2) All *non-vocational* education for persons aged eighteen and over. This is how it was used in the Smith Report (1919) and is its common use —though it may be extended into (1), as Kelly did in his *Bibliography*, by including forms of vocational education as in mechanics' institutes or the armed forces. It includes general education provided as part of a vocational course.

(3) Non-vocational education *of the more "cultural" kinds* for persons aged eighteen and over. This is the sense used in the Central Office of Information's Reference Pamphlet *Education in Britain*. It includes all forms of cultural training, by whomsoever provided, but excludes recreative activities as in community centres.

(4) Non-vocational education for persons aged eighteen and over *as secured under the control of the Minister of Education or either Secretary of State*. This is the sense used in the annual reports of the Ministers and Secretaries of State and in this book. It includes both

cultural training and recreative activities, but only those which enter the statutory system of education. It excludes general education provided as part of a vocational course.

(5) Non-vocational education *of the more cultural kinds* for persons aged eighteen and over *as secured under the control of the Minister of Education or either Secretary of State*. This is the sense used in the Minister's Pamphlet No. 8 and in the Robbins Report. It is the overlap between (3) and (4), that is : cultural training as statutorily secured. It includes informal activities such as the use by authorities or responsible bodies of libraries and broadcasting, but not recreative activities.

(6) Non-vocational education of the more cultural kinds for persons aged eighteen and over as secured under the control of the Minister of Education or Secretary of State for Education and Science *by responsible bodies*. This is the sense used in Further Education Grant Regulations, 1946, No. 18; and 1959, No. 19; and in the Ashby Report.

Thus even the Ministry has from time to time used the term in at least three different meanings (4, 5 and 6).

Post-war development

Cultural training

The English pattern was built up during the later years of the nineteenth century and the early years of the twentieth, following many decades of working-class struggle. It is a partnership between universities, voluntary bodies, authorities and the central government. "Extension lectures" provided by universities for public audiences were started at Cambridge in 1873. "Tutorial classes" formed for the purpose of giving closer attention to individual students began to be organized by universities co-operating with voluntary bodies, beginning at Oxford in 1907. Chief of the voluntary bodies was the Workers' Educational Association (WEA), founded in 1903. The Board began to aid the work with grants towards teaching and other costs in 1907, and from 1924 such universities and voluntary associations were called "responsible bodies". Authorities also played a big part, providing and aiding classes and other forms of activity from 1889 onwards.

The post-war changes did not greatly alter the pattern. Responsible bodies continued to receive grants from the Minister as they had done from the Board, but new regulations gave them greater freedom than before. A third type of responsible body was recognized : the "joint body", on which representatives of universities and voluntary responsible bodies sat with those of authorities. Joint bodies had been known since before the first world war; but only two have survived: the Cornwall and Devon Joint Committees for Adult Education. Authorities found their responsibilities increased by the new Acts, for, as already explained, they now had the duty to secure adequate provision, to consult with other interested parties and to submit Schemes to the Minister. In Schemes reviewed in the Minister's annual report for 1949 the ninety-five authorities which had assessed the cost of their proposals for the period 1948–1953 estimated a total of £10 million for sites, buildings and equipment for adult and youth services, or rather under 7 per cent of their total estimates for all Further Education. The Schemes contained all sorts of interesting adult centres, both cultural and recreative.

But the Minister warned: "The state of the national economy precludes development at such a pace." In fact nothing like £10 million was made available. The authorities have had to carry on as best they could. A couple of dozen residential colleges have been established; but $1\frac{1}{4}$ million students were enrolled in evening institutes in England and Wales in 1965–6.

Growth of the work of responsible bodies has been uneven and unspectacular: the number of students attending all their courses rose from 138,000 in 1946–7 to 179,000 in 1960–1, jumped to 210,000 in 1961–2, had only reached 212,000 in 1963–4, but jumped again to 219,000 in 1964–5. The early post-war wave reached its peak in 1948, after which a decline was aggravated by government stringency culminating in actual cuts in Ministry grants in 1952. Public protest prevented worse and led to the appointment of the Ashby Committee.

The latter recommended the continuation of the existing system, helped by a new national advisory committee, but urged a more rational, flexible and generously aided programme of development through responsible bodies. In 1955 the Government accepted these proposals (except the one for an advisory committee). Since then the programmes of responsible bodies have been more closely assessed but more money has been given. Grants to headquarters of national associations were made triennial from 1961. But deputations from authorities and associations to the Minister in that year were told that no major advances would yet be approved.

Scottish development has been slightly different. Its origins were earlier: in the eighteenth century. But as admission to secondary schools, Central Institutions and universities was believed to be easier than in England or Wales, the need for adult education was thought to be less. Under the Physical Training and Recreation Act of 1937 the Secretary of State aided associations providing recreative activities; but not until 1953, after a recommendation by the Advisory Council on Education in Scotland, did he make regulations enabling him to pay grant to voluntary organizations for cultural training. But he still does not aid their *teaching* costs. Thus the term "responsible body" has no statutory application in Scotland. Authorities are regarded as the providing bodies, whether acting independently or relying on the WEA or university extra-mural departments to form classes. They may also help towards the salaries of tutor-organizers. The Secretary of State aids the headquarters-administrative expenditure, but not teaching costs, of Glasgow and St. Andrews Universities Extra-mural Committees and the three Scottish districts of the WEA.

Recreative activities

The Ministers and authorities before the war had powers deriving from the Housing (Scotland) Acts of 1925 and 1935, the Housing Act of 1936 and the Physical Training and Recreation Act of 1937 to aid and establish community centres, village halls, playing fields and other facilities for physical and social recreation. Some authorities, following the initiative of Cambridgeshire from 1924, had already begun to combine community centres with schools, youth centres and evening institutes into integrated village colleges; and these were commended in the Scott Report (1942). Thus, when the Education Acts from 1944, without prejudice to this earlier legislation, brought all such provision fully into the education service, two parallel series of statutes were brought into being. The Minister, as explained in Circular 51, preferred to use the more flexible 1937 Act rather than the Education Act, and to aid associations' capital costs, not their recurrent expenses; and so did the Secretary of State for Scotland.

Nevertheless, community centres and village halls were regarded at that time as essential elements of Further Education provision. This was seen in the Minister's early pamphlet *Community Centres*, as well as in Circular 20 and Pamphlet No. 8. Over 2,000 were proposed in the Schemes of authorities in England and Wales. Voluntary associations, of which there were nearly 200 affiliated to the National Federation of Community Associations in 1948, were also pressing for them. Finding accommodation was the biggest problem. There were then only 250 community centres in England and Wales, of which only 115 had their own premises. Assistance with capital costs was particularly needed. In rural communities with less than 4,000 inhabitants, authorities and local voluntary associations could obtain, through the Village Hall Grants Committee of the National Council of Social Service, grants from the Carnegie United Kingdom Trust and interest-free loans from the Treasury advised by the Development Commissioners. Associations in larger communities could apply either to the Minister or to their authority under the 1937 Act, and could ask the authority for maintenance as well as capital costs. If allowed by the Minister, authorities also had their duty under Sections 41 and 53 of the

1944 Act to provide adequate facilities. Or authorities acting in their capacity as housing authorities could use Section 80 of the 1936 Act or Section 4 of the 1937 Act. The situation in Scotland was similar. So in 1944 there were plenty of channels through which aid could be sought and provision secured.

The Carnegie grants came to an end, however, in 1945. From then until 1949 the Minister aided associations in respect of 148 community centres and village halls; but in 1949 he stopped doing this, and because of scarcity of building resources would not allow authorities to build them either. Between the end of 1950 and 1955 some grants to associations were made, on condition that the recipients could find their own labour and raise a proportion of the capital cost themselves. Authorities helped them on the same conditions too, as in the "Bristol scheme" in 1954, in which Bristol City Council provided an association with a site at nominal rent, advice with plans and a capital grant of up to three-quarters of the cost of a centre. But an improvement in 1955 (following Circular 283) was followed by quite a big cut in 1956–7.

The position improved then, but was still uneven. Local authorities other than education authorities were given powers to provide recreational facilities under several Acts, notably the Local Government (Scotland) Act, 1947, Local Government Act, 1948, National Assistance Act, 1948, and Housing (Scotland) Act, 1950. Not only has the legislative dichotomy continued, therefore, but there may have been a temptation for education committees to leave the provision of such facilities to other committees. Certainly there has seemed to be a tendency for the community service to be separated from the rest of the education service (including the Youth Service) and to be relatively neglected.

Nationally, too, provision has been uneven. Between 1955–6 and 1961–2 the Minister made 190 offers of capital grant for community centres, 1,404 for village halls and 90 for playing fields and the like; but the numbers dropped again in 1962–3, and only playing fields increased in 1963–4. They dropped again in 1965–6. In rural areas combined-purpose buildings are being mainly used. In Circular 350 the Minister announced a relaxation of *financial* control over authorities following the Local Government Act of 1958 (while, of course, retaining his power of approval of the annual instalments of their Schemes). The Physical Training and Recreation Act of 1958 empowered authorities to lend. But all this did little more than scratch the surface of the problem. The Government of the day refused to take any comprehensive action on the Wolfenden Report *Sport and the Community* (1960) which recommended an extensive development of facilities for physical recreation; but it later tried to stimulate authorities with Circular 11/64 and Scottish Circular 550, with an interdepartmental committee set up in 1963, and with grants to local voluntary bodies trebled between 1963 and 1964. The new Government set up a network of sports councils in 1965 (Table 2), and the situation now seems rather better.

Present provision

Establishments

Residential colleges of Adult Education, evening institutes, community centres, village halls, playing fields and so on are briefly described in Chapters 3 and 4. Technical colleges, too, offer facilities for non-vocational activities. General studies as part of vocational courses are described in Chapters 5, 6 and 10.

Some aided establishments have a distinguished history under voluntary control : the Working Men's College, St. Pancras, for example, celebrated its centenary in 1954. Apart from music, speech and drama, the courses at this college are for men only. Its teachers have been largely unpaid.

Responsible bodies, as mentioned earlier, are of two main kinds : voluntary associations, and the extra-mural departments of universities. They are characterized by the fact that they arrange, publicize and administer classes for which they also recruit and pay their own teachers. In this way the members of voluntary associations, who include many potential students, decide their own programmes. The most important is still the WEA. Responsible bodies also employ some full-time tutor-organizers. For accommodation they usually use rooms in schools or evening institutes lent by authorities, or share in the use of authorities' residential colleges. Universities also use the premises of their extra-mural departments : for example, Liverpool University took over the building of the Liverpool Royal Institution in 1948 and gave it to its Extra-mural Department in 1960; and Manchester maintains its own short-term residential college.

There are believed to be about 1,700 community associations in England and Wales and 150 in Scotland; 472 are affiliated to NFCA. It is not known how many have their own centres.

Courses and studies

AUTHORITIES provide the largest share, mainly in evening institutes and to a lesser extent in technical and residential colleges. The change in the character of evening institutes has been mentioned in Chapter 4. The proportion of their class entries in the group containing women's subjects, handicraft, art, music, drama and physical activities, taken as single subjects, has been steadily rising; and students doing these now outnumber all others by nearly three to one. Women aged over twenty-one form the largest single group of students in evening institutes. There is still plenty of vocational provision, however.

A two-year training course for community-centre wardens began at Westhill College of Education, Birmingham, in 1963.

Courses and studies offered by RESPONSIBLE BODIES were classified in Further Education (Grant) Regulations, 1959, into six kinds:

(a) tutorial, normally lasting for three academic years, each containing not less than 24 meetings of at least two hours duration;
(b) sessional, lasting for one academic years and containing not less than twenty meetings of at least one-and-a-half hours duration;
(c) terminal, containing not less than ten meetings of at least one-and-a-half hours duration;
(d) other courses, not conforming to any of these three;
(e) training courses for teachers in adult education; and
(f) residential.

The "tutorial" class, usually provided jointly by a district committee of the WEA and the extra-mural department of a university, and addressed to an undifferentiated audience, is perhaps the best known. Students participate in the choice of subject and tutor; class numbers are limited; the course goes on for long enough to make serious study possible; and the students personally undertake to attend regularly and do reading and written work under the guidance of the tutor. Such classes have never greatly reached manual workers, however, and in recent years have declined in popularity with middle-class students too. Shorter, more intensive courses, including residential ones such as "linked weekends", have proved more appropriate to modern circumstances, particularly where they have been planned to meet the needs of special groups of student. The place of work has tended to replace the neighbourhood as a source of recruitment.

As in evening institutes a wide variety of subjects is offered by responsible bodies. Some courses, as for example at London and Leeds Universities, lead to the award of certificates and diplomas, but this is not typical. The most popular groups of subject in 1963–4 were social studies, languages and literature and history, as always the case with responsible bodies; but interest in the natural sciences has been growing and leapt up sharply between 1961–2 and 1962–3.

Interesting developments in the work of responsible bodies have included classes on world problems for miners released for one day a week; weekend residential courses for trade-union members; afternoon courses for shop stewards; high-level specialist short courses for social workers, scientists and other professional groups; courses on management and other industrial studies; training and refresher courses for tutors, wardens and youth leaders; collaboration with CATs and technical colleges in providing liberal studies for technical students (see Chapter 6); exhibitions of paintings by class members; music and poetry recitals; joint library-service/adult-education committees; international summer schools; study tours and residential courses abroad; a weekend course on "Opera" at Glyndebourne; courses for special groups such as young wives (aided by a baby-sitting service) or old-age pensioners; and visits of university teams of tutors to remote areas.

All courses at advanced level need the Secretary of State's approval, just as in other sectors of Further Education.

Finance

In England and Wales the SECRETARY OF STATE partly maintains the five direct-grant residential colleges, which also rely to a varying extent on students' fees. He has not in the past made *capital* grants to them, but began to do so in 1965, as recommended in the Robbins Report. He pays rather less than three-quarters of the salaries, fees and travelling expenses ("teaching costs") of tutors employed by responsible bodies; this, the largest item, rose more than threefold between 1946–7 and 1960–1. He also helps to cover the general expenditure of several national associations, which may or may not be responsible bodies. On the recreational side he makes capital grants to voluntary bodies for community centres, village halls, playing fields and similar sports facilities, and headquarters and coaching grants to national athletic and sporting associations. He also aids bodies providing research and other services. Finally, as mentioned earlier, he awards up to thirty university scholarships a year to persons aged over twenty-five who were unable to take a university course at the normal time (Tables 1 and 3).

In some cases village halls are paid for by the DEVELOPMENT COMMISSIONERS.

The practice of AUTHORITIES varies, but besides maintaining their own establishments all give some form of assistance to voluntary effort; and some help substantially with teaching costs of responsible bodies and give grants to students.

Thus RESPONSIBLE BODIES have to find the cost of organizing classes, the balance of teaching costs and the balance of headquarters costs. University extra-mural departments do this from the general resources of the university, aided by students' fees and perhaps grants from authorities. Voluntary bodies do it by means of subscriptions and donations, fees and the fact that much of their work is unpaid. Overall, the Ashby Committee calculated that the total costs of responsible bodies in England and Wales in 1951–2 were met in the following shares : Ministry 51 per cent, Treasury (via University Grants Committee) 20, local rates 9, voluntary funds and fees 20.

NATIONAL ASSOCIATIONS, whether responsible bodies or not, may be aided also, as mentioned above.

Scottish differences have been mentioned.

The expansion of provision

Main features at present

The British system of Adult Education is thus characterized by its strongly local and voluntary character; its freedom and variety; the prominence of authorities and universities; the presence of classes over which students exercise a measure of control; and high academic standards in some classes. It has brought universities into closer contact with their local people. It has been encouraged by governments, at least with words.

But it has developed unevenly and has reached only certain categories of the population. It has not enjoyed government financial support in proportion to its needs. It has not achieved a status comparable with that of other kinds such as primary, secondary or technical. Thus much of the work of the schools has not been followed up.

Trends of change

There are many influential factors. The advance of technology, the increase in material standards of living and the spread of communications and transport have led to changes in leisure-time pursuits and brought new opportunities to the countryside. The improvement of primary and secondary education and the growth of specialization have stimulated new interests. Changes in family pattern and in the position of women, the increase of social mobility and the expansion of international relations have brought demands from new groups of people.

Adult Education has come to be sought less by the underprivileged as an instrument of social change, and more as a source of new interests in a world of enlarging opportunities. This change has happened to adult education before : between the 1850s and 1880s, for example. Today it particularly affects women. It now becomes, too, a potential counterweight to such modern horrors as strident commercialism, spoilage of natural resources, indoctrination by "mass media", unplanned expansion and urban ugliness.

The new demands are reflected in the trends of change already mentioned in students and studies and in the development of closer links with general cultural agencies such as the library, museum and broadcasting services. Residential colleges and non-vocational courses in evening institutes, both provided by authorities, are the main post-war developments.

Proposals

Some of the more important of the many proposals which have been made are : that the Secretaries of State should *regularly* give capital grants to the direct-grant residential colleges and maintenance grants to suitable students thereat; that the government should initiate a planned building programme enabling major projects to be started; that the Schemes of authorities in respect of Adult Education be brought up to date to take advantage of this; that trade unions and similar bodies be drawn into closer participation in the system; that release be used more; that democratic forms of control of broadcasting and other "mass media" be evolved; that more consultation, information, financial uniformity, planning and research be developed within Adult Education; and that Adult Education be unified into a single system. The expansion of sport, for example, needs co-ordination of the various bodies concerned.

Problems

The rate of social change is increasing and with it the responsibility which rests upon the citizen. Primary, secondary and technical education, though improving, have still a long way to go to reach the objectives put forward in 1943. And even where the education of young people has fulfilled the demands placed upon it there remains much that cannot be understood by the immature. The need for Adult Education, therefore, is at least as great as ever, and the Robbins Report stressed this.

The field is enormous. New categories of student to be reached include employees in single industries or specific professional groups, the elderly, the less educated and the great number of people with "lowbrow" interests. New techniques include television. But accommodation, as in halls, theatres, libraries, workshops, community centres, village halls, playing fields and residential colleges, remains scarce and expensive; while governments seem always to be tempted to find higher priorities elsewhere. Hopes have been raised by the White Paper *A Policy for the Arts* (1965), but lowered by economic policies.

Notes on further study

Basic to an understanding of the purposes of adult education is the Smith Report (1919; also called the "1919 Report"). For this see also

Waller : *A Design for Democracy* (1956). Recreational facilities in rural areas were urged in the Scott Report (1942).

The Minister's views at different times have been expressed in Pamphlets : for example, *Community Centres* (1944), *Further Education* (No. 8, 1947) and *Evening Institutes* (No. 28, 1956).

Much factual material is contained in the annual *Year Book* of the NIAE (which in 1965 had a Scottish section) and in UNESCO's *International Directory of Adult Education* (1952). A short account was in the Robbins Report's Appendix Two (B) (1964).

Subjects and student numbers in England and Wales were analysed for evening institutes in Pamphlet No. 28, and for responsible bodies in the annual reports of the Minister and Secretary of State, including, from 1961 onwards, *Statistics of Education, Part 2.*

More specific information can be found in annual and other reports of statutory bodies, authorities, responsible and other voluntary bodies and community associations; in the half-yearly calendar *Residential Short Courses* of the NIAE; in guides and programmes published by authorities and adult-education committees; and in prospectuses of residential colleges, evening institutes, university extra-mural departments and other establishments.

The Minister's policy on recreational facilities was expounded in Circulars 20 (1944), 51 (1945), 57 (1945), 51 (Addendum No. 1, 1948), 210 (1949), 283 (1954) and 11/64; on homecraft in Circular 117 (1946); on governing bodies of residential colleges in 7/59; on mature state scholarships in 12/61; on the financing of responsible bodies by authorities in Administrative Memoranda 248 (1947), the Addendum thereto (1948) and 526 (1956); on the education of immigrants in Circular 7/65; on the approval of advanced courses in Administrative Memorandum 545 (1957); on accommodation and staffing in Administrative Memorandum 6/63; and in *The Building Code.* On recreational facilities see also Scottish Circulars 56 (1946), 550 (1964) and 598 (1965). For the new Government's general policy on the arts see the White Paper of 1965, Circular 8/65 and Scottish Circular 589 (1965), and the DES's *Report on the Arts* (1966). Its moves to foster sport were described in *Education in 1965,* pp. 77–83 (1966).

Problems of adult education have been discussed in a large number of reports, among the more important of which the following may be mentioned : Bussière : *Summary Report of the International Conference on Adult Education at Elsinore, Denmark* (UNESCO, 1949); Advisory Council on Education in Scotland : *Further Education* (McClelland Report, 1952); WEA Working Party : *Trade Union Education* (1953); the Ashby Report (1954); UK National Commission for UNESCO : *The Universities and Adult Education* (1957); Raybould (editor) : *Trends in English Adult Education* (1959); WEA Working Party : *Aspects of Adult Education*

(1960); for rural Wales the second Oldfield-Davies Report (1960); the Wolfenden Report *Sport and the Community* (1960); Universities Council for Adult Education : *The Universities and Adult Education* (1961); TUC : *Promotion and Encouragement of the Arts* (in *Annual Report* for 1961); the Pilkington Report on broadcasting (1962); AScW : *Science and Adult Education* (1963); UNESCO : *Second World Conference* (1963); NFCA : *Creative Living* (1964); and the Fife authority's Connelly Report (in *Scottish Adult Education,* September 1964). They were touched on in the Robbins Report (1963). A report of an inquiry by NIAE into accommodation and staffing appeared in *Adult Education* for January 1963. On community associations in Scotland see the interim report by SCCYCSS (1965).

Noteworthy post-war studies by individuals include : Marks : *Community Associations and Adult Education* (1949); Peers : *Adult Education, a Comparative Study* (1958); Mabel Tylecote : *The Future of Adult Education* (1960); Edwards : *The Evening Institute* (1961); Allaway : *The Educational Centres Movement* (1961); Elsdon : *Centres for Adult Education* (1962); Cleugh : *Educating Older People* (1962); Raybould : *University Extramural Education in England 1945–62* (1964); and Hunter : *Residential Colleges* (n.d.). Frances Banks's *Teach Them to Live* (1958) was a study of education in English prisons.

Notable periodicals are *Adult Education* (published by NIAE), *Scottish Adult Education* (SIAE), *International Journal of Adult and Youth Education* (UNESCO), *The Highway* (WEA), *Common Room* (Educational Centres Association), *Social Service* (National Council of Social Service Inc.), *Community News Bulletin* (NFCA) and *The Village* (Rural Community Councils).

For those desiring to pursue a more thorough study or research *A Select Bibliography of Adult Education in Great Britain,* edited by Kelly (1963), with annual supplements in NIAE's *Year Book,* are essential. For history see especially Harrison : *Learning and Living 1790–1960* (1961) and Kelly : *A History of Adult Education in Great Britain* (1962).

CHAPTER 12

THE YOUTH SERVICE

Definition and functions

The Youth Service is the system by which a threefold partnership of voluntary organizations, authorities and central government departments provides facilities for the social and physical training and recreation of persons between the ages of fourteen and twenty inclusive. Actually such facilities are used by young people on either side of these limits, a practice for which it has been permissible to employ public funds since the Physical Training and Recreation Act of 1937. Young people can benefit also, of course, from facilities intended primarily for adults, described in the previous chapter.

Its foundations were laid by the work of voluntary bodies for nearly a century before 1939. The 1918, 1921 and 1937 Acts had empowered the Board and authorities to pay grants to youth organizations and groups, and some authorities had set up committees on which they and the organizations were represented locally. The fusion of all three elements into a single system was hastened by the outbreak of war. In Circular 1486 of November 1939 the Board asked all major authorities to set up committees of this kind in order to develop "the foundations of an ordered scheme"; it also announced the formation of a National Youth Committee (soon succeeded by the Youth Advisory Council) to give central guidance and leadership thereto. And in the next year in Circular 1516 it stated the aim of this new system, which was to promote the social and physical training of young people for the responsibilities of citizenship.

Thus the Youth Service exists to offer to young people opportunities, entirely without compulsion, for leisure-time activities complementary to home, work and formal education.

Development

Despite the obvious difficulties the Service expanded considerably during the war. Furthermore, the experiences of war strengthened the nation's realization of its deep reliance on youth to rebuild the country afterwards.

Thus the 1943 White Paper stressed that the Service should not be regarded as simply a wartime expedient but "should take its place as an integral part of the national system of education". Accordingly the main Acts made it a duty of authorities, subject to the approval of the Ministers, to secure such facilities as part of their educational provision. The Minister drew the attention of English and Welsh authorities to this duty in Circular 51, and in the Pamphlets elaborated ways in which the Service could be co-ordinated with county colleges and otherwise integrated into Further Education. Authorities carried this thinking into their Schemes. Great interest and enthusiasm was aroused.

However, the impetus was not maintained into the 1950s. By 1952–3 clubs and centres were closing. There were two main reasons : shortage of accommodation and shortage of trained leaders. Both depend on the priority and financial resources allotted to them by the central government. Accommodation needed money on a scale beyond the means of voluntary effort; but the Minister made cuts in grants from the end of 1949. Youth leadership had been recognized in the McNair Report as a profession comparable with teaching, and the Jackson Committee (1949) and National Advisory Council on the Training and Supply of Teachers (in the Fletcher Report, 1951) had made recommendations for getting and training the recruits needed; but in 1955 training courses were running only at University College, Swansea, and Westhill Training College, Birmingham, with a combined total of eighteen students. The Ministry was severely criticized by the Select Committee on Estimates (1957) for showing lack of interest and for what the Committee considered its meagre, confused, misleading and unfair system of grants. All this led to the appointment of the Albemarle Committee in November 1958. This Committee calculated that of every pound spent on education by the Ministry and authorities in England and Wales in 1957–8 only a penny had gone to the Youth Service; that voluntary effort had probably contributed four or five times as much as this; and that the Ministry's direct expenditure thereon, in real terms, had actually fallen by about a quarter since 1945–6. The Committee thought that at the end of the 1950s the Service was reaching only about one-third of young people aged between fifteen and twenty-one.

But "the line has at least been held", wrote the Albemarle Committee; therefore what was needed was an "imaginative leap". The Committee urged that the Minister should initiate a ten-year development programme, to be planned and phased under the surveillance of a national development council, aimed at expanding the Service and bringing it fully into Further Education. Starting in 1960 this should fall into two parts : five years of "blood transfusion" followed by a five-year plan of long-term measures.

The Albemarle Committee's report (1960) had a considerable impact. Early in 1960 the Minister accepted in principle most of its proposals. The

Development Council (YSDC) was quickly set up with the Minister as chairman, and was reconstituted in 1963. More capital was allowed for building: a £7 million programme for 1960–1963 (about half of what the authorities had asked for) was launched with Circulars 3/60 and 11/60; and another £4 million was promised for 1963–4, £4½ million each for 1964–5 and 1965–6 and £2½ million for 1966–7. The number of capital grants by the Ministry to local youth-club projects increased from 157 in 1962 to 514 in 1964. Spending by authorities on the Service nearly doubled between 1960–1 and 1963–4. With the Bristol authority the Minister set up a study group to work on the design of youth-club premises, and this produced the design for Withywood Club, Bristol. In January 1961 an emergency National College for the Training of Youth Leaders was opened at Leicester with 98 students taking a one-year course. This is to continue at least until 1971; and in 1964 it opened an information centre to gather and disseminate research findings. In addition 2 universities (at Swansea and Manchester), a college of education (Westhill) and 2 national organizations (the NABC in collaboration with the University of Liverpool, and in London the National Council of YMCAs) offer main courses for full-time youth leadership; and in 1960 11 colleges of education started optional courses in youth leadership for teachers in training. A Joint Negotiating Committee for Youth Leaders was set up, agreed on qualifications and fixed new salary scales. In Circular 12/62 the Minister commended the proposals of the Bessey Committee on the training of part-time youth leaders, and progress in this field was reviewed in another ("third") Albemarle Report (1965).

There has been expansion in Scotland, too, where the Secretary of State accepted the main principles of the first Albemarle Report in Scottish Circular 436. A Standing Consultative Council, under the chairmanship of Lord Kilbrandon, had already been set up in 1959, and a one-year leaders' course had started at Moray House College of Education, Edinburgh, in the following year. In 1963 (following the Noble Report) a basic full-time leaders' course of two years began at Moray House and in 1964 and 1965 a similar course at Jordanhill College, Glasgow. The Kilbrandon Council has concentrated mainly on four things: encouraging authorities to develop better facilities, getting improvements in the training of youth leaders, exploring new ways of approaching young people and studying ways of co-ordinating youth and community services with the rest of the education service. It was the motive force behind "Scottish Study of Leisure", a two-and-a-half-year research project begun at Glasgow University in 1963. It broadened its terms of reference and changed its name to include community service in 1964 (SCCYCSS).

Thus there have been significant steps recently. The *scale* of operations is still small, however, in comparison with the size of the need.

Present provision

VOLUNTARY ORGANISATIONS are the backbone of the Youth Service. As mentioned, some of them have been active for over a century. The main types are : boys', girls', mixed, uniformed, church and pre-service. Over 2 million members under the age of twenty-one belong to them. In England and Wales 27 of the larger ones (together with 6 associate-member organizations, and 20 observer organizations including the DES and some adult bodies) have formed a Standing Conference of National Voluntary Youth Organisations (SCNVYO) which considers means of strengthening the voluntary principle and makes recommendations to the Secretary of State and others (Table 18). There are similar Standing Conferences for Wales only (SCWVYO) and for Scotland (SSCVYO). Contact with organizations abroad is maintained through the British National and Scottish Committees of the World Assembly of Youth.

In most localities there are local organizations and groups, and local branches and committees of national organizations. They are usually represented on and by a local standing conference (of which there were 44 in 1963–4); but the pattern varies, and there may be a youth-organizations committee set up by the authority, or a federation of youth organizations. On these may be co-opted representatives of such agencies as teachers, the YES, police and the probation service. Such committees have advisory and liaison functions.

AUTHORITIES help in many ways, though there is still much variation among them. Building is more closely controlled for the Youth Service than for other sectors, capital projects of over £2,500 (not £20,000 as for the rest of education) needing specific approval by the Secretary of State (see Chapter 3). Other ways of helping voluntary effort include : paying a share (such as four-fifths) of the salaries of qualified youth leaders; helping with expenses (by paying, for example, half of maintenance costs); making loans; providing teachers, instructors and trainers; laying on courses; offering the services of organizers and advisers; allowing free use of premises, playing fields, camping sites and the like; lending equipment; helping with information and publicity; and organizing festivals, international camps and other large-scale events. Authorities may also provide their own youth centres, though many do not. Some arrange play and recreation centres for younger children in school premises outside school hours.

About half the authorities administer the Service through a direct sub-committee of the education committee (as recommended in the first Albemarle Report); others do it through the Further Education sub-committee.

The SECRETARIES OF STATE can offer capital and maintenance grants

TABLE 18

THE STANDING CONFERENCE OF NATIONAL VOLUNTARY YOUTH ORGANISATIONS
OF ENGLAND AND WALES, 1966

Constituent members:
Army Cadet Force Association
Association for Jewish Youth
Boy Scouts Association
Boys' Brigade
British Red Cross Society
Catholic Young Men's Society
Church Lads' Brigade
Co-operative Youth Movement
Girl Guides Association
Girls' Friendly Society
Girls' Guildry
Girls' Life Brigade
Grail
Methodist Association of Youth Clubs
National Association of Boys' Clubs
National Association of Youth Clubs
National Council for Catholic Youth Clubs
National Federation of Young Farmers' Clubs
Pony Club
St. John Ambulance Brigade
Salvation Army
Sea Cadet Corps
Welsh League of Youth
Young Christian Workers
Young Men's Christian Association
Young Women's Christian Association
Youth Hostels Association

Associate members:
Campaigners
Christian Alliance of Women and Girls
Church Army
Covenanter Union
Girls Venture Corps
Union of Maccabi Associations

Observers:
Air Training Corps
British Council of Churches
British National Committee of the World Assembly of Youth
Central Council of Physical Recreation
Christian Endeavour Union
Church of England Youth Council
Congregational Youth
Department of Education and Science
Duke of Edinburgh's Award
Free Church Federal Council
International Voluntary Service
King George's Jubilee Trust
National Association of Youth Service Officers
National Catholic Youth Association
National Federation of Women's Institutes
National Playing Fields Association
Outward Bound Trust
Toc H Men's Section
Toc H Women's Association
Youth Service Association

(under Social and Physical Training Grant Regulations, 1939) to national and local organizations and branches for administrative expenses, costs of training full-time leaders, costs of premises and equipment and financing of special developments and experiments (Table 1). Since Circular 51, however, the Minister has not made *maintenance* grants to local branches of national organizations (and the first Albemarle Report recommended that after five years he should also discontinue *capital* grants to local branches). The Secretary of State for Scotland does not normally aid local facilities but has done so exceptionally since 1961.

The work of HM Inspectorate, advisory councils and the YSDC and SCCYCSS may again be mentioned here (Table 19).

The expansion of provision

Main features at present

Recent surveys have been reviewed by the Central Advisory Council in the Crowther Report; the following are some of the conclusions to which the evidence points. The very great majority of boys and girls belong to some youth organization during their schooldays but this changes radically when they leave school. After the compulsory school age, uniformed organizations in particular (such as Scouts, Guides or pre-service cadets) become much less popular. Cultural and political societies begin to attract most of their members from about eighteen onwards. The children of semi-skilled and unskilled parents take less part than do others, and girls less than boys. Boys and girls from selective schools, and those taking part in further education, are more likely to belong to clubs than are others. Dance clubs with no other activities account for one-quarter of all the clubs to which girls who have attended non-selective schools belong. Team games are popular among boys, about one-third of whom continue to play for at least three years after leaving school.

The Albemarle Committee was deeply impressed by the volume of genuine concern for the welfare of young people shown by voluntary helpers, which is regarded as the strongest feature of the present system. But it criticized other features, particularly the prolonged financial stringency, patchwork machinery of government grants and lack of guidance or encouragement from the Ministry. Local provision, it thought, was too heterogeneous. Voluntary organizations had not made enough effort to try new methods or to break new ground, and wrong approaches to young people were often still being used. There was too little co-ordination between organizations and authorities. Youth leadership still enjoyed no proper professional structure nor public esteem. The Service was reaching

TABLE 19

Administrative framework of the Youth Service (England and Wales, 1966)

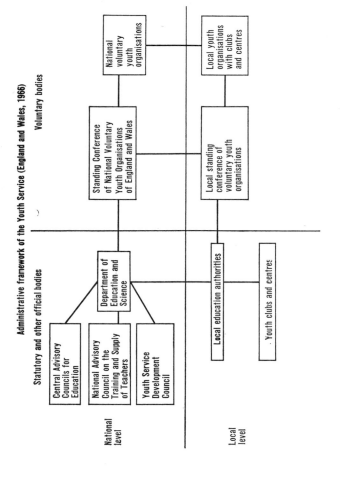

too few young people overall, and in particular, was neglecting those most in need.

Proposals

The Albemarle Committee's general proposal for a ten-year development plan and the Government's response have been mentioned. The Committee made several other important recommendations. It accepted the present aim of the Service as provision for the social and physical needs of young people. It wanted the official age range to be from fourteen to twenty inclusive, thus including on the one hand pupils in their last year at school, and on the other the older members able to provide leadership; this proposal was adopted. Most of these young people, it thought, would be at work, over half receiving no organized education, and the majority having interests which could not be described as intellectual; to attract them, therefore, activities should continue to be (as now) informal, conducted during leisure time, conceived as complementary to home, work and formal education, and, of course, entirely voluntary. They should contain three elements : *association* or doing things together in groups of their own choosing; *training*, particularly in judgement, standards and choice; and *challenge*. Young people themselves should be drawn into active leadership of the Service. Authorities should therefore bring their Schemes up to date with respect to the Service, including imaginative building programmes, and should also allow for its needs in planning new secondary schools. No new legislation, but a lot of new thinking about adolescents in the modern world, would be required. In particular, communication between the generations should be greatly improved.

Notes on further study

The basic thinking was contained in the Board's Circular 1486 (1939), Circular 1516 (1940) and White Paper (1943). Also important were the Youth Advisory Council's *The Youth Service after the War* (1943) and *The Purpose and Content of the Youth Service* (1945); the Welsh Youth Committee's *The Post War Youth Service in Wales* (1945); the Scottish Youth Advisory Committee's *The Needs of Youth in these Times* (1945); the Standing Conference's *Partnership in the Service of Youth 1945* (1945); and the Central Advisory Council's *School and Life* (1947).

The more important relevant enactments are the Physical Training and Recreation Act, 1937 (now used mainly for adults); Education Act, 1944 (especially Sections 7, 41, 42 and 53); and Education (Scotland) Act, 1962 (especially Sections 1, 4, 6 and 7). The Social and Physical Training Grant Regulations, 1939, which are still in force, prescribe conditions under which the Secretary of State for Education and Science is prepared to offer capital and maintenance grants to national and local youth organizations and groups in England and Wales.

The Minister's views were expressed in Circular 51 (1945) and in Pamphlets Nos. 2 (1945), 3 (1945), 8 (1947) and 16 (1949); and the Welsh Department's were in *Education in Rural Wales* (1949). Those of the Advisory Council on Education in Scotland were in the McClelland Report (1952).

The recruitment and training of youth leaders was dealt with in the McNair (1944), Jackson (1949), Fletcher (1951), first Bessey (1962), Noble (1962), third Albemarle (1966) and Inches (1966) Reports and by SCCYSS attached to Scottish Circular 487 (1961). Administrative Memorandum 16/61 defined the qualifications accepted for full-time status, after which see the four reports of the Joint Negotiating Committee for Youth Leaders (1961, 1962, 1963 and 1965). See also the Minister's Circulars 36 (1945), 53 (1945), 116 (1946), 224 (1950) and 351 (1959), and Scottish Circulars 436 (1960), 469 (1961) and 487 (1961).

The Service was kept under regular review at the Oxford University Department of Education's conferences (reported under the title *The Young Worker*). Proposals were made by King George's Jubilee Trust in *Youth Service To-morrow* (1951) and *Citizens of To-morrow* (1955), especially Part IV. The TUC's evidence to the first Albemarle Committee was in its *Annual Report* for 1959.

Kuenstler's *Youth Work in England* (1954) was a useful compilation of documentary material.

The Ministries were criticized in the *Seventh Report from the Select Committee on Estimates, session 1956–57* (1957) and the Ministers' replies were in the *Third Special Report, session 1957–58* (1958).

On the work of authorities in the middle 1950s see Button (editor): *Youth Service* (n.d.).

Investigations were reviewed in the Crowther Report (1959) and the whole Service was discussed in the first Albemarle Report (1960). These two are the most important recent reports covering the Service, but the Newsom Report (1963) also had some relevance. For Wales see the second Oldfield-Davies Report (1960). On relations between youth and community service see SCCYCSS (1965) and the second Bessey Report (1966).

Youth Organisations of Great Britain, edited by D. Cooke (1963), was a directory. See also SCNVYO's *Annual Report and Directory, Young People Today* (1960) and *The Work of a Local Standing Conference* (1964). For other countries see UNESCO's *New Trends in Youth Organizations* (1960).

The Minister's policy after the first Albemarle Report was expressed in Circulars 3/60, 11/60, 17/61, 1/62 (W), 12/62, 10/63, 7/65 and 16/66; and in Administrative Memoranda 12/61 and Addendum, 16/61, 17/61 and 2/62. See also Scottish Circular 436 (1960). On youth leaders, Circulars 36, 224 and 351 are still current. *Youth Service Building: General Mixed Clubs* (Building Bulletin No. 20, 1961) contained recommendations of the Ministry-Bristol study group on the design of club premises and *Youth Club Withywood Bristol* (Building Bulletin No. 22, 1963) reported progress. For a review of development see the Ministry's *Reports on Education,* No. 5 (1963). A short account was the COI's *Youth Services in Britain* (1963).

The Police and Children described Liverpool's atypical scheme of police juvenile liaison officers.

Annual and other reports of authorities (such as Cheshire's *The Service of Youth,* 1961) and publications of voluntary bodies should also be consulted. There is a considerable production of periodicals.

CHAPTER 13

FURTHER EDUCATION FOR THE DISABLED AND HANDICAPPED

Work of the Secretaries of State

The powers given to and duties imposed upon the Secretaries of State and authorities by the Education Acts apply to handicapped and disabled people just as to the more fortunate ones. Very little has been done by the education services for those who have left school, however. At national level the initiative has been left largely to other government departments, and locally to the health authorities; while voluntary associations have been active at both levels. For example, of the several rehabilitation and resettlement workshops and training centres, thirteen are run by the Ministry of Labour and the remainder by voluntary bodies.

In 1961–2 the Minister of Education made no capital grants, one maintenance grant and thirteen grants to cover half the cost of the employers' contribution to teachers' superannuation, in Further Education establishments in England and Wales run by voluntary bodies for the handicapped or disabled. In 1965 the British Sports Association for the Disabled was added to the list of organizations in England and Wales receiving national administration and coaching grants from the Secretary of State.

Most of the provision, however, is outside our present scope.

Work of authorities

Local education authorities contribute in five main ways. First, they pass to the health authorities information about school leavers who may need care or guidance, at the same time telling the parents what is being done. This is particularly important for the mentally handicapped school leaver, for the training of whom the local health authorities bear the primary responsibility.

Second, they provide special facilities in their own establishments. One authority, for example, holds classes for educationally subnormal leavers from a boarding special school in selected outside centres conducted by a

BRITISH FURTHER EDUCATION

teacher from the school. In another case classes of this kind are held for leavers from day special schools. Another provides an evening institute in the premises of its day special school, and another a social club likewise. Two Scottish authorities run classes in commercial and craft subjects for severely handicapped girls aged over sixteen, with residential accommodation. There are probably some unreported remedial classes being provided in ordinary evening institutes.

Third, authorities provide facilities for patients in hospitals. These may take the form of correspondence courses, lessons or classes conducted by visiting teachers, loan of books and other materials or transport for walking cases to classes in ordinary establishments. Normal fees are charged, and the balance of the authority's costs recouped from the pool for students not belonging to the area of any authority (see Chapter 3). Voluntary bodies such as the British Council for Rehabilitation of the Disabled sometimes collaborate.

Fourth, authorities pay the fees for tuition and maintenance of students attending further-education establishments conducted by voluntary bodies. There were 9 of these listed by the Ministry in 1963 : 3 were for blind students, 1 for deaf and 5 for people otherwise physically handicapped; most were residential. A wide range of remedial work, daily care, curative treatment and vocational training is provided for them.

Fifth, authorities may themselves provide establishments for handicapped people who have left school. None have yet done so, but in 1965 approval was given to the Coventry authority to build such a one.

All establishments aided or used by the Secretaries of State or by authorities must conform to regulations made by the Secretaries of State.

Finally, the Youth Employment Service is available to handicapped and disabled school leavers, some authorities employing specialist officers wholly devoted to this side of the work. After reaching the age of eighteen the young person can apply to be registered as disabled, in which case he or she becomes the responsibility of the Disablement Resettlement Officer. In some areas there are after-care committees to watch over the welfare of such people.

An underdeveloped field

The total provision of such facilities, however, is very small. Of the work which has been done a large share has been by voluntary organizations.

Assimilation of the handicapped and disabled as far as possible into the normal life and work of the community has been the primary aim; and this has implications for the education of normal students likely to come into contact with handicapped colleagues. Finding employment for them is perhaps the greatest problem encountered. In the case of educationally subnormal adults the boosting of morale is of prime importance, and this bears on the problem of whether or not provision should be in separate establishments.

Some think that responsibility for the education and training of handicapped people should be transferred entirely to the education service. In Scotland, occupational training centres for "ineducable" but "trainable" mentally handicapped children are run by education authorities and inspected by HMIs, but authorities do not provide such facilities for adults.

Notes on further study

The Minister has expounded his policies in Circulars 68 (1945), 164 (1948), 300 (1956), 12/60, 11/61, 8/64 and 9/66; and Administrative Memoranda 94 (1945), 511 (1955) and 527 (1956). See also Scottish Circular 300 (1955). Circulars 15 (1945) and 312 (1956) dealt with authorities' duties towards patients in hospital. The Ministry's *List 42* (1963) contained particulars of special schools and establishments approved as conforming to Handicapped Pupils and Special Schools Regulations, 1959, which may therefore be used by authorities. To receive grant themselves from the Secretary of State the establishments must also conform to Special Schools and Establishments (Grant) Regulations, 1959. In Scotland the SED's *List G* (1965) listed special schools and occupational centres, but contained no establishments of Further Education.

Rehabilitation, retraining and resettlement were the subject of the Tomlinson (1943) and Piercy (1956) Reports.

For factual information see the National Council of Social Service : *The Welfare of the Disabled* (1957); Nicholson : *Help for the Handicapped* (1958); Central Council for the Care of Cripples : *Disabled? Enquire Within* (1960); Ministry of Labour : *Services for the Disabled* (1961); British Council for Rehabilitation of the Disabled : *The Handicapped School Leaver* (1963); DES : *Careers Guidance in Schools* (1965); and for Scotland, Montgomerie : *The Handicapped Person* (1958).

On the problems of provision for particular handicaps see publications of voluntary and other bodies; for example : Ministry of Labour Working Party : *The Employment of Blind Persons* (1951) and *Workshops for the Blind* (1962); National Institute for the Deaf : *1960 Conference on Care of the Deaf* (1960); National Spastics Society : *After School, What?* (1959); British Council for the Welfare of Spastics : *Spastic School Leavers Employment?* (1961); for mentally handicapped the Fraser Report (1957) and Gunzburg : *Senior Training Centres* (NAMH, 1963). See also Aphra

Hargrove : *The Social Adaptation of Educationally Subnormal School Leavers* (1954).

For history see Pritchard : *Education and the Handicapped 1760–1960* (1963) and Aphra Hargrove : *Serving the Mentally Handicapped* (1965).

CHAPTER 14

RELATIONS WITH SECONDARY EDUCATION

Present pathways from school to vocational further education

The pattern is complex; only some of the better-worn paths into daytime provision will be sketched as examples. These sketches are highly generalized and may not precisely fit every case (see also Tables 20 and 21). The majority lead to courses in engineering, building, other applied sciences, commerce or art (described in Chapters 5–9); but ways into other sectors within the broad field of tertiary education will also be mentioned.

Obviously there are two sorts depending on whether they lead through immediate or postponed employment.

For employed students

Channels open to pupils entering as works-based students may be considered in seven groups according to their starting point at school.

1. Pupils leaving school at fifteen without much in the way of a paper qualification constitute over half of their age group. Of these, only about one-fourth of boys and one-sixteenth of girls got day release in 1964–5. A student in this released group would be accepted into a pre-craft course, or into the first year of a craft (C1), operatives' (Op. 1) or general-education course, depending on what career, if any, he or his employer had in mind for him, and on what were available in his locality. If his employer were willing to sponsor him he might be able to get on to a full-time pre-apprenticeship course for a year, but this would be unlikely.

2. A pupil leaving at fifteen with, say, a local school-leaving certificate, would find the chances better. A boy with day release, particularly if his mathematics were good, could be admitted to a preliminary general course (G1; not in Scotland), or a girl to a commercial course. Full-time preapprenticeship courses are available for boys in some areas.

3. A boy leaving at sixteen without an academic qualification but showing aptitude in practical subjects might get a craft apprenticeship and

be put into the second year of a craft course (C1). If there were one available in his area he might be given full-time release for the first year of a full-time apprentice course. A girl accepted as a nursing cadet might be given two-day or block release to work for the GCE or Part I of the Preliminary Examination of the General Nursing Council (to be abolished). Girl craft apprentices attend clothing, hairdressing and other courses.

4. A pupil leaving at sixteen, particularly from a selective school or Local College, or with a qualification such as a school certificate of a regional union, a Certificate of Secondary Education or a GCE or SCE with one or two O-level passes, would have a wider range of opportunities, though this is a difficult group to place through the Youth Employment Service. If he (or she) were able to get day release and had done some technical drawing he could be put into the one-year preliminary general course (G*; not in Scotland), or, if his mathematics were not good enough for this, the first year of a technicians' course (T1), or even G1. Alternatively, he would be a strong candidate for a craft apprenticeship (going into C1), or for full-time release for up to a year. With day or block release he could start the Certificate in Office Studies.

5. A leaver with three or four suitable passes at O level could be taken straight into an ONC (O1) if given day, two-day or block release, or into an OND with sandwich release. Student nurses are accepted at eighteen. There are also full-time courses available—at, for example, National Colleges.

6. A student apprentice or trainee with some O-level and one or two A-level or equivalent H-grade passes would probably go into the second year of an ONC or OND (O2), where he might have to do extra work on subjects of which he had not done enough, such as, perhaps, technical drawing; but cases have been known in which boys who had studied heat engines before leaving school were admitted into the HNC or HND in Mechanical Engineering. With two appropriate passes the HNC or HND in Business Studies and other subjects could be entered.

7. With two or more suitable passes at A level a student apprentice or trainee might be put on to a sandwich course, leading, for example, to : a degree at a university; a college diploma, college associateship or HND at a Central Institution; professional graduateship or HND at a CAT, Regional College or Area College; a CNAA degree; or a National College qualification.

For non-employed students

Pathways at four more levels are commonly followed by school leavers entering full-time or sandwich courses as college-based students, of whom

TABLE 20

Pathways from school into technical courses in establishments of Further Education (England and Wales, 1966)

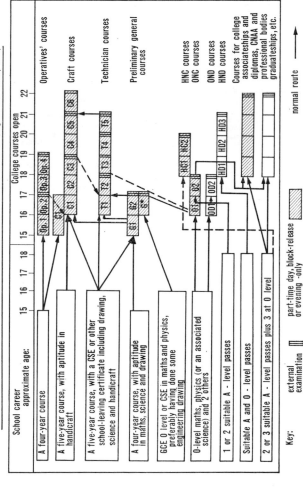

Notes: This is a generalized pattern and does not precisely fit every case. Postgraduate courses have not been included, nor have full-time preliminary.

TABLE 21

ADVANCED COURSES AT A REGIONAL COLLEGE, 1966–7.

	Chemical Engineering		Chemical Technology		Electrical Engineering		Applied Physics		Food Science		Sociology	Applied Biology	Food Science	Applied Chemistry
No. of 'A' Levels needed	3		2		2		2		2		2	1	1	1
COURSES	Chemical Engineering		Chemical Technology		Electrical Engineering		Applied Physics		Food Science		Sociology	Applied Biology	Food Science	Appl Chem
AWARD	B.Sc.		B.Sc.		B.Sc.		B.Sc.		Associateship of Borough Polytechnic		B.Sc. or B.A.	Higher National Diploma	Higher National Diploma in Applied Chemistry	High Natio Diplo
AWARDING BODY	University of London		Council for National Academic Awards		Council for National Academic Awards		Council for National Academic Awards		Borough Polytechnic		University of London	Dept. of Education & Science	Dept. of Education & Science	Dept Educa & Sci
DURATION	3 Years		4 Years		4 Years		4 Years		4 Years		3 Years	2 Years	2 Years	2 Ye
Full Time or Sandwich	Full Time		Sandwich		Sandwich		Sandwich		Sandwich		Full Time	Full Time	Full Time	Full T
SUBJECTS AT 'A' LEVEL	Compulsory	One from	Compulsory	One from	Compulsory	One from	Compulsory	One from	Compulsory	One from	2 'A' Levels in any subject plus 3 'O' Levels in any subject *or* 3 'A' Levels in any subject plus 1 'O' Level in any subject plus Interview	One from	Compulsory	Compulsory
Chemistry	•		•						•				•	•
Biology										•		•		
Botany										•		•		
Zoology										•		•		
Physics	•				•		•			•				
Mathematics (Pure & Applied)		•		•		•		•		•				
Mathematics (Pure)		•		•		•		•		•				
Mathematics (Applied)		•				•								
Other Requirements	4 Subjects at 'O' Level plus Interview		English and 2 others at 'O' Level plus Interview		English Language and 2 others at 'O' Level plus Interview		English, Chemistry and 1 other at 'O' Level plus Interview		3 Subjects at 'O' Level plus Interview			Chemistry studied Post 'O' Level. English, Maths and Physics at 'O' Level plus Interview	English, Maths & Physics or Biology at 'O' Level Physics or Biology must have been studied Post 'O' Level. Plus Interview	English, Physics & Maths at 'O' Level. Physics and …

	Foundry Technology	Environmental Engineering	Heating & Ventilating Engineering	Refrigeration Engineering	Mechanical Engineering	Production Automation	Baking Technology	Institutional Management	
No. of 'A' Levels needed	1	1	1	1	1	1	1	1	**No. of 'A' Levels needed**
COURSES	Foundry Technology	Environmental Engineering	Heating & Ventilating Engineering	Refrigeration Engineering	Mechanical Engineering	Production Automation	Baking Technology	Institutional Management	**COURSES**
AWARD	Higher National Diploma	Higher Diploma	Diploma in Heating and Ventilating	Diploma in Refrigeration	Higher National Diploma	Higher National Diploma	Higher National Diploma	Diploma	**AWARD**
AWARDING BODY	Dept. of Education & Science	National College	National College	National College	Dept. of Education & Science	Dept. of Education & Science	Dept. of Education & Science	Institutional Management Association	**AWARDING BODY**
DURATION	Years	3 Years	2 Years	1 Year	3 Years	3 Years	2 Years	3 Years	**DURATION**
Full Time or Sandwich	Sandwich	Sandwich	Sandwich	Full Time	Sandwich	Sandwich	Full Time	Full Time	**Full Time or Sandwich**
SUBJECTS AT 'A' LEVEL	One from	One from	Compulsory	Compulsory	One from	One from		One from	**SUBJECTS AT 'A' LEVEL**
Chemistry	●							●	Chemistry
Biology								●	Biology
Botany								●	Botany
Zoology								●	Zoology
Physics	●	●	●	●	●	●		●	Physics
Mathematics (Pure & Applied)	●	●			●	●		●	Mathematics (Pure & Applied)
Mathematics (Pure)	●	●			●	●		●	Mathematics (Pure)
Mathematics (Applied)	●	●			●	●		●	Mathematics (Applied)
Other Requirements	Chemistry one of these must have been studied to 'A' Level—plus Interview	English and 3 others at 'O' Level one of which must be Maths or Physics plus Interview	English, Maths and 2 others at 'O' Level plus at least 1 years experience in the Industry plus Interview	English, Maths and 2 others at 'O' Level plus at least 1 years experience in the Industry plus Interview	4 subjects at 'O' Level one of which must be Maths or Physics, studied to 'A' Level plus Interview	4 subjects at 'O' Level one of which must be Maths or Physics, studied to 'A' Level plus Interview	Chemistry, Physics and 1 other at 'O' Level. One Science must have been studied to 'A' Level. Plus 6 months in Industry and Interview. January entry	1 'A' Level any subject, English and 2 other 'O' Levels or 2 'A' Levels, English and 1 other 'O' Level plus Interview	**Other Requirements**

Table 22

Some examinations and qualifications, 1964–5.

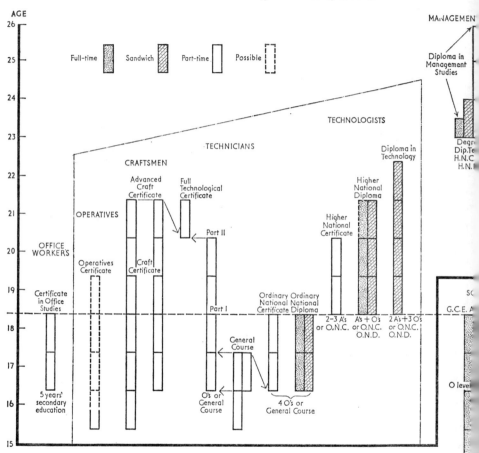

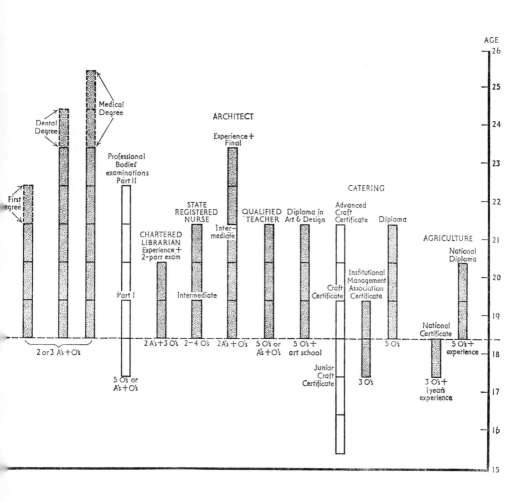

some (mainly the older ones) may be receiving awards from their authorities.

8. For the leaver at fifteen or sixteen there are GCE, typists' and secretarial, pre-craft, pre-technician, Pre-National, junior nursing and pre-nursing, preliminary art and agricultural, catering and first-year or first-two-year craft courses. They vary in length between two terms and two years; usually contain about one-third general education; and may (a) increase the student's chance of getting an apprenticeship, (b) gain him or her remission of time therefrom, and/or (c) qualify for entrance to a higher course.

9. With the right number of O-level passes, usually four or five, a student may start a course for the OND in various subjects, do a National Certificate or Diploma in Agriculture at a farm institute or a Scottish Diploma at a Central Institution, begin a Pre-Diploma course at a college of art or be admitted to an education, drama or music college; but competition for entry to any of these may make A-level passes necessary as well.

10. Those with at least one A-level pass and usually five at O level may be able to get into college-based courses, including two-year and three-year full-time and three-year sandwich courses, leading to various HNDs, LRIC and other qualifications not ranking as degree-equivalent.

11. Finally, for those with two or more A-level (or equivalent H-grade) passes there are courses at Central Institutions, colleges of art and music, universities and colleges of education, and college-based places at technical colleges. These may lead to degrees, diplomas, college awards, graduateship and membership qualifications or teaching certificates. Between the end of the post-war backlog and about 1956 it was often possible to get into university with a bare two passes (80 marks) at A level; but competition then began to increase, so that by 1962 applicants commonly needed a total of 120 marks if two subjects had been taken or 150 if three. Not very many sixth-formers go into art colleges as yet.

In some establishments there are preliminary or "conversion" courses for entrants with the "wrong" subjects. Or a student may have spent a period in employment or abroad before resuming full-time education. In medical, engineering and other departments great stress is sometimes laid on the value of a general or even arts-specialist education before admission.

Return to school

In some areas students who have passed in the requisite O-level subjects at a college may be transferred to the sixth form of a school. Such reflux, however, is rare.

Gaps in the pathways

Education, said the 1944 Act, was to be organized in three "progressive" stages. This implies continuity; nevertheless, since needs change, some breaks there must be.

For many reasons the break between secondary and further or tertiary education is greater than the one between primary and secondary. The age range of further-education students is much wider than that of secondary-school pupils, and it includes many adults but no preadolescents. Most further-education students have made a vocational choice or are actually employed; therefore further education is far more closely connected with employers, professional associations and other bodies outside the education service than are secondary or primary. Further education is voluntary, and therefore many people do not experience it at all, or lose time between secondary and further; but all must go to school, at least till they are fifteen. Thus there are differences of motivation as between further-education students and school pupils; for one thing, the objectives of further education are usually more obvious to its students. Further education may be full-time, block or sandwich, part-time day, part-time residential or evening-only; and it is nearly always short of time; but all schools are full-time. Colleges are generally larger and more complexly organized than schools, and the students are more various. The DES's cost limits on building are looser; and staff–student ratios tend to be higher. Yet authorities have less freedom to design further education than they have with their schools. Therefore there are bound to be differences in teaching method, personal treatment of students, discipline, curriculum, pace of work, facilities, hours of attendance, out-of-class activities, staff training and background, educational guidance, finance and many other spheres; yet in other ways there is continuity. There are, and ought to be, areas of continuity and areas of discontinuity between secondary and tertiary stages.

Of course secondary education has its own job to do which is not and should not be subordinate to that of tertiary. Further education should therefore continue from wherever secondary education has reached. In general there should be continuity, as implied in the Act. Any discontinuities should be deliberate and co-ordinated. At present, however, most discontinuities are just accidents. Some are inevitable or even desirable; but others are wasteful, unjust or both.

Gaps of the latter kind were regarded in the Crowther Report as a major source of subsequent educational wastage and retardation. Five, in particular, have received attention : breaks in the habit of daytime study and consequent loss of impetus and time; lack of continuity in the content of studies; weaknesses in the system of guidance into courses; heterogeneity and rigidity of apprenticeship requirements; and confusion in admission procedures into full-time establishments.

Closing the gaps

The gap in time

Before the war a boy leaving elementary school at fourteen had two years to occupy before being allowed to start a craft or ONC course. Day release during this interim period was rare; many therefore enrolled for two or three evenings a week at junior evening institutes, for which regional unions, as explained in earlier chapters, offered preparatory schemes. Wastage was high.

For a few this gap could be closed in one of two ways, or partially closed in another way. First, some could stay at school until sixteen. In England there were junior technical schools within many colleges, providing two-year or three-year industrially biased courses for entrants transferred from elementary schools at thirteen. From these junior classes (J1, etc.) most boys passed at sixteen into the senior college (S1, etc.) where the abler ones who were probably already known to the principal were accepted without examination into the first or even second year of an ONC course. There were also junior commerical and art schools. Alternatively there were central schools and classes, rather more academically biased, continuing "elementary" education from fourteen to sixteen; and also grammar schools. Second, there were some colleges which ran full-time preliminary courses for fourteen- and fifteen-year-olds. Third, there were a few continuation schools offering part-time courses based on day release.

The raising of the leaving age to fifteen on 1st April 1947 closed this two-year gap by one-half. The other half has since been partially closed by voluntary staying-on (the "trend"). Technical, commercial, art and central schools have generally become fully fledged secondary establishments keeping most of their pupils until at least sixteen, while technically orientated courses lasting to this age have also been growing in modern, all-age, grammar and comprehensive schools. Courses lasting beyond the minimum leaving age in modern, all-age and comprehensive schools have come to be called "extended" courses.

End-on full-time and day-release courses in colleges (described in Chapters 5–9) have again helped to close the gap, especially for the modern-school leaver.

Another move was in the Education Act of 1962 which established two leaving dates per year—Easter and Summer—instead of three. This lengthened by at least one term the school life of those who would otherwise have left at Christmas. The problem of timing college entrance to reduce the gap still further is under discussion, especially since the Minister in Circular 3/63 encouraged experiments to find practicable arrangements. The English Central Advisory Council and NACEIC (1963) really wanted *one* leaving date per year, but they recognized its practical difficulty, especially when the leaving age became sixteen.

However, the fact that in 1959–60 only 4 per cent of modern-school leavers had completed five years of secondary education moved the Central Advisory Council to urge the raising of the compulsory age to sixteen by not later than 1968. In the Crowther Report the Council allowed that, so long as it were compulsorily full-time, such provision need not necessarily be in school; but in the Newsom Report it wanted all provision till sixteen to be at least school-based.

The gap in content

Here, too, co-ordinating measures are afoot from both school and college.

In the schools there has been the swing to science, maintained at least until 1963. "Biased", "special" or "alternative" courses, once familiar, as mentioned, in junior technical, commerical and art schools especially, are again growing in popularity, particularly in modern and comprehensive schools. Engineering, building, seamanship, hotel and catering, agriculture and rural studies, commerce, art, domestic subjects and retail distribution are examples of "biases" or "centres of interest" around which secondary-school studies can readily be designed. Such courses usually entail a full fifth year, which may contain "day release" at a college or even participation in actual work. They help to make the pupil aware of the world of occupations, the scope of careers in his chosen bias, the qualities needed in them, the significance of his special studies and the value of his general education at school. Experiments along these lines were encouraged in the second Brunton and Newsom Reports, of which the latter said that the school programme in the last year ought to be "deliberately outgoing" into the adult world. There has been some growth in polytechnical integration too; though the polytechnical idea in an explicit form is not yet understood in this country; and there are crucial shortages of staff and accommodation. Between 1954 and 1960 High Pavement Grammar School, Nottingham, experimented with a sixth-form engineering course containing half a day's attendance at Nottingham and District Technical College[1] and conferring admission to the HNC, but the Institution of Mechanical Engineers withdrew its support. There is still much criticism of subtle and cumulative pressures exerted against technology in secondary schools, particularly in grammar schools.

[1] Now Nottingham Regional College of Technology.

In the colleges the wider range and scope of courses and the introduction of liberal studies have increased the possibility of achieving continuity of content, particularly since the White Paper of 1961; though, in general, courses are still very narrow. College participation in school examination schemes helps co-ordination.

There still seems to be much repetition in college, however, of work already done at school—an *overlap* rather than a *gap*. An overlap in one subject (such as mathematics) accompanied simultaneously by a gap in another (perhaps technical drawing) is common. The Secretaries of State do not allow courses for the OND to be provided in schools; and some think that conversely the GCE should not be offered full-time in colleges. In such ways repetitious overlaps might be reduced, while concentrated courses could narrow gaps. But flexibility is the prime need, and opportunities absent or lost at one stage must be available later.

The gap in guidance

By "educational guidance" is meant the leading of students into curricula most suited to them. In school it is usually based on a thorough knowledge of the pupil, gradually acquired, but at college it has to begin when the student first enrols. Enrolment week at a technical college is an unforgettable experience. In those few days thousands of diverse and bewildered entrants are interviewed by college teachers who collect their forms and fees, allocate them to courses and make up their timetables. In the case of day-release students the criteria of allocation are commonly two only : what course has been agreed with the employer in the light of whatever release he is willing to give; and whether the examinations, if any, already passed by the student fulfil the regulations for admission to the chosen course or otherwise indicate an ability to complete it. Such a system of guidance neither needs nor gets much information about the aspirations, tastes or abilities of the young people themselves. Nor is the student sure of much pastoral attention as his course proceeds. Even with younger students there is little liaison with parents.

But this state of affairs, too, is changing; and three component trends may be discerned.

(a) THE SYSTEM OF SECONDARY-SCHOOL EXAMINATIONS is evolving, albeit painfully, into something more informative, about a wider range of leavers. Since the ending of the School Certificate scheme in 1951 the situation in England and Wales has been dominated by the GCE. This university-controlled single-subject examination was devised by the Secondary School Examinations Council for the small minority in English and Welsh public and grammar schools who were to be admitted to universities and certain professions. Its papers at the three levels "Ordinary", "Advanced" and "Scholarship" were intended to be taken by candidates not below the age of seventeen. It was hoped that most pupils would work at their main subjects directly to A level without bothering to take them at O level; and their other subjects were expected to thrive better by not being examined externally at all. The Minister adopted this system in Circular 168 and for some time actively discouraged or prohibited the use of any other external examination in secondary schools.

However, this policy ignored one of the fundamental functions of examinations—to provide the pupil with a goal or target. The consequent need for a general school-leaving examination for the ordinary pupil continued to be felt. In fact, therefore, secondary schools at large turned to the O level to fulfil this need. The O level has grown strongly in further education too, where it is mainly taken by those who have not had or have missed the chance of taking it at school. Following the first Brunton Report it has inspired the appearance in 1962 of a Scottish equivalent, the SCE, intended largely for purposes of further education. It has also spread to overseas territories, even where the old School Certificate has remained. The O level of the GCE and SCE attracted half-a-million candidates in the summer of 1963; and 76,000 of these were in Further Education establishments in England and Wales.

These moves were the opposite of what had been intended. It is not surprising, therefore, that the O level has been found unsatisfactory as a school-leaving examination, a function for which it was not designed. It has proved difficult even for the top one-fifth of the age group, and has been altogether beyond the reach of the majority of pupils in secondary schools. It has been accused of encouraging early specialization, tempting head teachers into an unbalanced use of teaching resources, perpetuating didactic teaching methods, giving too little incentive to creative activity, speech and practical and technical studies, hardening subject boundaries, stereotyping courses and inhibiting curriculum experiment. Because of the late publication of A-level results the O level has also been used sometimes to help in university selection, a function which conflicts with that of being a general school-leaving test. The A level has been attacked also. Only in fulfilling the purely formal requirements of university matriculation and faculty requirements and of professional institutions has the GCE operated somewhat as originally intended.

Attempts to organize alternative sysems of external assessment, therefore, have been frequent in England and Wales. They have been of six kinds, and most have tried to offer opportunities below the O level. First, examinations offered by various bodies in specialized subjects such as music or nursing studies have been taken in schools. But this has often encouraged too early specialization. Second, preparatory examinations in technical and commercial subjects provided for junior evening institutes by London and regional examining bodies have spread since 1947 into the fifth and then into the fourth year at modern schools. But these have not proved reliable predictors of success in National Certificate examinations. On this and other grounds the practice was strongly criticized in the Crowther Report; and technical schemes (though not yet commercial) have been discontinued since the White Paper of 1961. Third, schools individually or in groups have arranged external assessment for their own internal examinations which have been taken often in the fourth year; this has been tried, for example, at modern schools in Kent. Fourth, authorities have awarded their own certificates, usually on results of a fourth-year examination conducted by local boards either with representation of technical-college principals, as at Harrow, Luton, Reading, Southampton, Bootle, Widnes and Wallasey, or without, as at St. Helens and Scunthorpe. In either case college teachers have participated in the operation of the schemes. But the Crowther and Beloe Reports damned them with faint praise, and the Newsom Report was against all external examinations taken earlier than the fifth year. Fifth, connected with the increase of pupils completing a fifth year, the "school certificates" introduced during the 1950s by London and regional bodies have become very popular, mainly in modern, technical and comprehensive schools. Most of these, unlike the GCE, were grouped-course examinations, that is—requiring a pass in several subjects in order to gain a certificate. The Crowther Report was non-committal on these but the Beloe Report attacked them. However, the LCC started its own new scheme. Finally, the SSEC at last recognized the need for a general school-leaving examination, suited to ordinary pupils aged around sixteen, and designed to generate good not bad feedback effects on teaching. Following the Beloe Report the new teacher-controlled nationally current Certificate of Secondary Education (CSE) started in 1965.

Thus it is to be hoped that teachers will develop the CSE into a system whose effects on school curriculum and organization are desired rather than undesired, that it will provide more valuable information about candidates than at present, and that it will embrace *all* pupils likely to proceed to further education. To do these tasks properly it will have to reach candidates whose relative attainment is lower than the third quintile, and this is the intention; but it should not be based on any theory of fixed ability, and should be adaptable to the needs of the most able children also. New techniques of examining will have to be evolved. Thus it is to be hoped, too, that its bold growth will not be inhibited by competition with GCE or G schemes, nor by university requirements (for which the A levels —with their S papers, modified if necessary—should be the complementary indicators). Indeed, the arrival of the CSE strengthens the already strong case for the early abolition of the O level of the GCE.

In Scotland, however, the second Brunton Report advised against any external examination at national level below the SCE.

INTERNAL assessment and recording of pupils' school careers on school-leaving certificates has also developed; and the Newsom Report recommended the use of these for all pupils leaving after a five-year course, as a counterweight to external examinations. The second Brunton Report recommended confidential school-leaving reports.

(b) CONTACT BETWEEN SCHOOL AND COLLEGE, with the aim of getting to know one another better, is developing. This need has received much attention, specially since the Willis Jackson Report. Authorities have called conferences, distributed publicity material, organized visits of school pupils and teachers to colleges and vice versa, arranged exhibitions and careers conventions, established joint advisory committees, set up examination schemes requiring collaboration between school and college teachers, conducted inquiries and encouraged informal contact between staffs. Farm institutes have organized residential courses for school pupils. Schools have approached colleges in many ways : modern and (more rarely) grammar schools, for example, have introduced college attendance into their courses, as mentioned. Sometimes college principals and teachers have taken great pains to seek information about entrants from contributory schools. This is more possible with intending full-time students, who can be interviewed before leaving school, and for whom the college may set its own entrance tests; but part-time students are sometimes seen at their place of employment. University institutes of education, the YES, ATI and other bodies have also helped to bring school and college representatives together. All such liaison has increased the means of acquiring that knowledge of each student as a whole person which is essential for his educational guidance.

However, there is much more to be done, as was shown by HMIs in their report *Forward from School*. Relationships are haphazard and have still to be regularized before the problems can be tackled systematically. For example, school teachers and college lecturers do not study one another's methods in order to improve their treatment of the student and ease transition. Colleges rarely inform schools of the progress of their former pupils. Careers teachers in schools are not given enough time to do their job properly. There is sometimes rivalry between college and school, school heads regarding college courses as temptations for pupils to leave school. There have been many complaints that grammar-school heads and teachers are slow to establish contact with colleges and that some even regard them with hostility. And action hitherto has been on too small a scale. The Willis Jackson, Crowther, two Brunton, Newsom and Robbins Reports (as, indeed, the Hadow Report as long ago as 1926) called for the strengthening of links between secondary and further education. The Robbins Report recommended experiment in the use of aptitude tests and collaboration between college and school teachers in the revision of school syllabuses and textbooks (as already practised in USA). The ATTI has suggested an "education liaison service". Perhaps regional advisory councils could also help.

(c) INTRODUCTORY COURSES IN COLLEGES are taking on a more strongly diagnostic function. End-on full-time academic, preliminary, pre-employment and apprentice courses have been described; all have this function to some extent. The problem is more difficult with part-time students; therefore the Crowther Report and NACEIC (1963) recommended that all part-time courses should be prefaced by a one-month full-time "induction" period, to introduce the student and college to one another. Experiments with such measures are sometimes reported. The problem of their timing to accord both with the two school-leaving dates and with the start of the regular college courses has been mentioned. Co-ordination with firms' own induction courses is another need.

Attention is also being given in colleges to the selection of teachers for recent entrants, the training and further training of teachers, staff interchange with schools, and the use of tutorial and other methods of teaching and pastoral care. It is commonly believed, however, that there is still too much "lecturing" in colleges, particularly to younger students, and that other bad teaching practices are prevalent.

The apprenticeships mix-up

For many school leavers apprenticeship is the only means of getting day release. The decision on whether to seek an apprenticeship or to stay at school is therefore all-important. If a boy takes the former course his difficulties are not over, for there is a contradiction in the conditions which he must consider when deciding the time at which to leave school. On the one hand many craft apprenticeships are fixed to start at sixteen and be completed by twenty-one. In some industries it may become impossible for a boy to begin after sixteen. He must therefore be accepted before his sixteenth birthday, and may believe his chances to be greater if he can become established with a good firm for a short period even before this. He will therefore take the first promising opportunity, which will almost certainly make him leave school as soon as he can. On the other hand, there are industries, such as some branches of engineering, in which an entrant with passes at the O level of the GCE is welcomed and may be offered a student apprenticeship; but if he stays at school in the hope of this, and fails to get the passes or the apprenticeship, he may be too late for the other group. If he later regrets his choice he will not be able to rectify it. Many have urged relaxation of admission-age conditions and shortening of the total apprenticeship period, particularly for those who have stayed longer at school, and there are some examples of this having been done; but not a great deal has been achieved. Such problems will no doubt be considered by industrial training boards.

The admissions mix-up

Further Education does not contain a means of organizing applications for admission to colleges. On the other hand colleges of education have had a "clearing house" system since the 1930s, under which applicants make a single application to the college of their first choice, at the same time stating their second and further choices. If unsuccessful at the first-choice college the application is automatically sent by the Clearing House to the second choice and further if necessary, no additional application being required. To end the chaotic state of their own admissions procedures, universities introduced a similar scheme in 1962–3—the Central Council on Admissions (UCCA). Oxford, Cambridge and the CATs joined it in 1964. Three Scottish universities and the London medical schools, however, are not in the scheme, and it does not apply to applicants from overseas. There is no scheme for Further Education establishments.

Since applicants do not of course know whether they will be accepted at their first-choice institution, many have no alternative but to apply to several. There is still a great deal of uncertainty, confusion and luck before such applicants either confirm an acceptance or are finally rejected. There are also many industry-sponsored applicants. The Robbins Committee recommended that applications to all universities and CATs be channelled through UCCA; and this proposal presumably applied also to the Royal College of Art and certain Central Institutions and Regional Colleges which the Committee had recommended for university status. But it left the rest of Further Education out of account.

The difficulties are made worse by the shortage of time between the publication of A-level results (August) and the start of the higher-education year (September or October). This shortage of time also tends to cause too much reliance to be placed on interviewing as a means of selecting applicants. Examination requirements for admission to courses of higher education vary chaotically from one establishment to another. However, in Administrative Memorandum 8/66 the DES announced the formation of an information service to help applicants for higher-education places in colleges.

School links with non-vocational provision

Many schools share buildings with evening institutes, community centres, youth clubs or youth centres; and new school buildings may be planned with this in view. In such schools pupils are bound to become aware of the adult and youth activities going on; and some no doubt become interested in this way, though others may be antagonized. In such cases the evening institute or centre, whether sharing the whole building or occupying its own wing, is usually a separate establishment under its own principal, warden or leader, even where the latter, as is frequently the case, is a member of the staff of the school.

In the village college, however, as in Cambridgeshire, Derbyshire and some other counties, three spheres of activity are pursued in a single establishment. The principal or "warden" is helped by an "adult tutor" and a "youth tutor"; and his day-school teachers, too, are asked on appointment whether they are willing to do evening work. Staff can combine duties more easily; school pupils are more intimately aware of the programmes; and there is little or no conflict of interest between the three spheres. Youth activities are available from the age of fourteen, as recommended in the first Albemarle Report, and the resulting overlap with school is found to help recruitment to them. Youth *centres* are usually found to be more successful than youth *clubs*. The premises are also available for outside hire.

Where a school caters for a single neighbourhood a youth club or centre provided in a youth wing of the building can approximate in membership to the junior section of a former (or "old") pupils' association.

On a more general level, of course, voluntary youth organizations commonly recruit from young people still at school. Play and recreation centres for younger children may also introduce the club habit to school pupils. However, there are very few contacts between schools and *adult* sporting organizations.

Proposals for junior colleges

The proposal to divide secondary education at sixteen by concentrating sixth-formers into separate "sixth-form colleges" is well known. Commonly associated with the Croydon authority, it envisages these colleges as following rather traditional grammar-school lines, with definite O-level admission requirements and strongly geared to university entrance. It is really a variant of the general idea of the so-called "two-tier" secondary system.

However, the Crowther Report proposed experiments with something more like a further-education establishment—the "junior college". This would offer a much wider range of courses than would the sixth-form college. Containing all kinds of full-time student aged sixteen to nineteen it would have "the adult atmosphere of a technical college but with a much wider range of curriculum and with terms of reference nearer to those of a school".

Mumford (1965) has suggested that such a college could be further broadened to take in *part-time* students in the same age group. Richly provided with facilities for practical work, this could combine some of the best features of secondary and further education and provide a link or overlap between the two.

Notes on further study

Some of the general problems have been discussed in Reports, notably Percy (1945), Willis Jackson (1957), Crowther (1959) (especially Chapters 30, 32 and 33), Arrell (1962), Newsom (1963) (especially Chapters 5 and 9) and Robbins (1963) (especially Chapter VII). The most comprehensive reviews have been the two Scottish Brunton Reports *Curriculum of the Senior Secondary School* (1959) (introduced with Scottish Circular 412) for the abler pupils and *From School to Further Education* (1963) (introduced with Scottish Circular 520) for the less able.

The need to do something to solve the problems inspired the Ministry's free booklet *Britain's Future and Technical Education* (1958) (issued with Circular 343); the DES's *Further Education for School Leavers* (1966) and *Signposts to Higher Education* (1966); the wall chart *Your Future in Industry* (issued with Circular 4/60); the Scottish White Paper of 1958; the White Papers of 1961; the report of NACEIC's (Pilkington) committee on the Crowther Report (issued with Circular 3/63) and (Alexander) committee on public relations (issued with Circular 17/64); Circulars 9/60, 11/62 and 12/66; Administrative Memorandum 8/66; Scottish Circulars 450 (1961), 521 (1963) and 558 (1964); brochures issued to school leavers by authorities (such as Bolton's annual *Reach for the Top*); and the White Paper of 1962 and consequent Industrial Training Act, 1964.

For a discussion of secondary-school reorganization with implications for further education see Mumford : *16–19, School or College?* (ATI, 1965).

An excellent survey of attempts to forge links was the Ministry's *Forward from School*, introduced with Administrative Memorandum 6/62. See also addresses at ATI by Henthorne, Lewis and Whitehouse (1961), Selley (1962) and Thompson (1964); and BACIE : *New Routes to Further Education* (1961). The flow of school leavers in England and Wales was analysed in *Statistics of Education, 1963, Part 3* (1964).

For specific information about channels of transfer the literature on careers may be consulted. Notable are the Central Youth Employment Executive's *Choice of Careers* new series (especially No. 1, 1960) and *Careers Guide* (1962); the NUT's *Annual Guide to Careers for Young People;* the *Year Book of Technical Education and Careers in Industry;* and the SED's annual *Directory of Day Courses.* See also Wheatley (editor) :

Industry and Careers (1961); Goldsmith: *Careers in Technology* (1963); Eva Murray-Browne: *Going to University and Technical College* (1963); and Labovitch (editor): *Directory of Opportunities for School Leavers* (1965). The NUT's *University and College Entrance, the Basic Facts* is another useful annual. For girls see the British Federation of University Women's survey (1957) and *Final Report*.

There is a consumer-research body called Careers Research and Advisory Centre (CRAC), as well as ACE.

A study of recruitment channels was reported in Oxford University Department of Education's *Technology and the Sixth Form Boy* (1963). See also the FBI's *Public School and Grammar School Boys in Industry* (1954), *Industry and the Public and Grammar Schools* (1956) and *From Sixth Form to Industry* (1963). A more recent study was the Dainton Report (1966) which contained a bibliography.

On school examinations, the pure theory of the GCE was expounded in the Norwood Report (1943) and the *First Report* of the Secondary School Examinations Council (1947). For later development see the SSEC's *Second* (1952), *Third* (1960) and *Sixth* (1962) *Reports*. The Minister's policy thereon can be traced in Circulars 103 (1946), 168 (1948), 251 (1952), 256 (1952), 289 (1955), 326 (1957) and 9/61; and in the leaflet *The General Certificate of Education* (1953) and pamphlet *The General Certificate of Education* (1964). See also Circulars 151 (1947) and 205 (1949) which dealt with school records, internal examinations and objective tests. GCE results were analysed in *Statistics of Education, 1962, Part 3* (1964) and *1963, Part 3* (1964). For the SCE see the first Brunton Report (1959); Scottish Circulars 412 (1959), 424 (1959), 452 (1961) and 30 (annual); the Education (Scotland) Act, 1963; and Scottish Certificate of Education Examination Board Regulations, 1963. Professional bodies' requirements in terms of the GCE were listed in Circulars 227 (1950), 338 (1958) and 5/62 and the DES's pamphlet *The General Certificate of Education* (1964). School-leaving examinations other than the GCE and SCE were reviewed in the Beloe (1960) and second Brunton (1963) Reports respectively. The CSE was the subject of the SSEC's *Fourth* (1960), *Fifth* (1962), *Seventh* (1963) *Reports;* and of Circulars 326 (1957) and 9/63. See also the Ministry's *Reports on Education,* No. 4 (1963).

Apprenticeship schemes are advertised in brochures of firms, described in careers literature and summarized in the annual *Year Book of Technical Education and Careers in Industry*. The ITC's *Craft Apprenticeship* (1962) was a short factual survey of known schemes. Problems posed to boys still at school were discussed in the Crowther Report (especially Chapter 30). For other references see *Notes* to Chapters 5–9.

The Youth Employment Service was the subject of the Ince Report (1945) and second Albemarle Report (1965). Annual Reports of the

National Youth Employment Service and local youth employment committees provide a commentary on progress in matters connected with employment. More recently see the DES's *Careers Guidance in Schools* (1965).

The growth of the polytechnical idea was traced by the present writer in *Brit. J. educ. Stud.*, May 1963.

Carter: *Home, School and Work* (1962) and Thelma Veness: *School Leavers, their Aspirations and Expectations* (1962) were studies of school leavers; see also Surrey Educational Research Association's *School Leavers* (1964).

CHAPTER 15

CO-OPERATION WITH INDUSTRY AND COMMERCE

Its importance

Since most students in Further Education are employed, the extent and nature of its co-operation with industry (using that term in the broadest sense to include commerce, applied art, agriculture and the public services) is a major factor determining the quantity and directions of growth of Further Education. Industrial bodies are therefore the most important of the non-governmental agencies concerned with its provision. This is recognized in the insistence of the Secretaries of State on industrial representation on governing bodies and advisory councils.

Government services, nationalized boards, co-operative societies and larger companies in England have been the most active in this direction, Welsh and Scottish employers and smaller firms generally having tended to lag behind. Bodies such as the CBI, trade associations and boards frequently have an education organization. Commerce falls far behind manufacturing industry.

However, the possibilities are enormous.

Fields of co-operation

Supplying students

Until day or block release becomes compulsory the growth of daytime courses for employed students depends on two things : the intake into apprenticeship schemes containing release as a condition, and the willingness of employers to give release in other cases. Firms normally pay wages and in some cases fees of their released employees, or fees may be charged initially to the student but partly or wholly refunded at the end of the session if he has maintained a satisfactory standard. The broad policies of employers in regard to recruitment, training, promotion and so on have to be taken into account by industrial training boards.

In all cases of release there is a strong element of selection. Authority or college staff may be drawn into interviewing, examining, testing and other procedures, or company staff into college enrolment. In some cases college enrolment takes place on company premises in the presence of company staff.

Consultation on courses and research

Industry is very much responsible for the courses initially chosen, since these must satisfy the needs of both employer and employee. Forward thinking by firms is valuable here, since it gives colleges time to assemble resources. Through the regional and local advisory machinery and industrial training boards the opinion of both sides of industry is available. The subject, duration, conditions of entry, type of release, timetable, syllabus, standard and integration of works training with college teaching can be planned in consultation by members of college and company staffs.

Research problems, too, arise from industrial practice, and the CNAA doctorate (which replaced the MCT) is designed to encourage collaboration thereon.

Supervision of students

Firms can keep track of their released employees by receiving attendance and progress reports from colleges. In some cases their representatives visit colleges to see students and discuss their progress with teachers. Conversely, teachers sometimes keep track of students' progress in the works.

Supply and further training of college teachers

Individuals employed in industry commonly teach of their own accord at evening classes, but in some cases they may be specially released for teaching during the day. Conversely, college teachers occasionally go into industry for study or research during their vacations, or authorities release them for this purpose during term. Industry commonly provides facilities and expenses for all kinds of studies. The Willis Jackson and other Reports recommended a great development of such staff interchange.

Regional advisory councils organize refresher courses; and they and other bodies such as the CBI or BACIE call conferences of college and industrial representatives. The British Employers' Confederation has run courses on industry for teachers. Industry collaborates, too, in running the Further Education Staff College at Blagdon.

Participation in governing, advisory and examining bodies

Both sides of industry are well represented on governing bodies and subject advisory committees of establishments, advisory councils and examining bodies.

Provision of premises, equipment and finance

Much machinery and other expensive equipment and financial assistance towards new building in colleges is given by firms : the National Colleges may be mentioned as examples. Conversely, the Secretary of State or authorities aid some works schools, as already described.

Firms sometimes give scholarships, research grants, prizes and gifts towards student welfare. They also make and supply visual aids. Companies' premises may be used by college-based students, while firms' staffs have used college library and other facilities. Since 1923 the Scottish Woollen Technical College, though aided by the Secretary of State, has been administered by the Association of Scottish Woollen Manufacturers and owns a mill which carries out commission work for the industry. In Crawley there is an apprentice-training school run jointly by the college and local employers. Many other examples could be quoted.

Vocational guidance

Firms provide information for and generally co-operate with agencies of vocational guidance and placing. These include the appointments boards of universities and public schools; the Technical and Scientific Register of the Ministry of Labour, which particularly deals with scientists, engineers, architects and surveyors; the Youth Employment Service, whose officers visit schools and help school leavers; and the National Institute of Industrial Psychology, which offers a service of guidance.

Other joint activities

Exhibitions, conferences, careers conventions, open days, visits and many other activities draw representatives from the worlds of industry and education into joint activity.

Special staff

Since 1963, four Central Institutions have appointed industrial liaison officers to their staffs, at senior-lecturer level, with special responsibility for this field of work. One of their functions is to encourage the interest of industry in innovation, development and research, especially among smaller firms. The idea has spread to England and Wales under a DSIR–DES joint scheme; ten were appointed in 1964–5, and more are expected.

Problems of expansion

Co-operation of public and professional bodies with industry is clearly necessary to education and presents a vast field for experiment. For example, the Robbins Report suggested more joint research arrangements and freer movement of staff between colleges, firms and research establishments.

Too much influence on education by industry, however, has dangers. Firms already determine the money and leisure which many students have, and often decide the level and type of course to which they are allotted, besides having a strong influence on their curriculum, timetable and discipline. Cases have been known (fortunately not commonly) in which employers have tried to restrict students' participation in college and union activities, or have withdrawn satisfactory students from courses, or have limited students' choice of optional studies, or have resisted the temporary transfer of students for part of their industrial training to other firms better able to provide it. It is possible for a few large firms (or even one) to control the life of a college. Or gifts and bequests may contain limiting conditions. Large-scale patronage of students, libraries, research and equipment, besides providing authorities with an excuse for "economies", could subtly influence or limit freedom of mobility, expression, promotion, inquiry, publication, curriculum or even thought itself, perhaps leading to a narrowing or distortion of effort in favour of sectional or social-class interests.

There is also, of course, the opposite danger, that the education service might over-ride or ignore the genuine needs of industry.

Notes on further study

Early reports were Percy (1945), Urwick (1947) and Carr-Saunders (1949); and the Minister's *Further Education* (1947), especially paragraphs 53–58. More recent commentaries, each emphasizing different aspects, were in the Wilson (1954), Willis Jackson (1957), Carr (1958), De La Warr (1958), Arnold (1959), Crowther (1959), McMeeking (1959), third Oldfield-

Davies (1961), Coldstream (particularly the second, 1962), Arrell (1962), Barnes (1962), Oakley (1962), two Platt (1962 and 1965), second Brunton (1963), Pilkington (1963), Robbins (1963), Henniker-Heaton (1964), Marre (1964) and Alexander (1964) Reports; in the White Papers of 1961; and in the Minister's Circulars 343 (1958), 1/60, 4/60, 9/60, 3/63, 6/63 and 17/64. See also the annual and other reports of DSIR, ACSP, etc.

The FBI has published reports of national and regional conferences it has organized on technical colleges and industry, notably at Ashorne Hill (1954), Loughborough (1955), London (1957), Cambridge (1958), Windsor (1958) and Chester (1959). See also its *Industry and the Technical Colleges* (1956), *Policy Statement* (1958, revised 1963), *The Technical Colleges and their Government* (1960) and *Invest in the Future* (1961); and BACIE: *The Implications of the Crowther Report* (1960) and *The Spectrum of Higher Education* (1962).

The seconding of teachers to industry was recommended by the Minister in Administrative Memorandum 134 (1946) and Circular 336 (1958), the latter following the Willis Jackson Report.

General Government policy on the co-ordination of industrial training with education was expounded in the Minister of Labour's White Paper (1962) which led to the Industrial Training Act, 1964. On problems of such co-ordination see Venables: *Sandwich Courses* (1959); Venables and Williams: *The Smaller Firm and Technical Education* (1961); the National Council for Technological Awards ("Hives" Council): *Memorandum on the Industrial Training of Students Following Courses Recognised as Leading to the Diploma in Technology* (1960); and the CTC's *Memorandum No. 1* (1965) and *4* (1966). The ITC's booklets *Training Boys in Industry: the Non-apprentice* (1960), *Training Girls in Industry* (1962) and *Craft Apprenticeship* (1962) also had something to say on this topic for the semiskilled; as had the Wilson (1954), Barnes (1962) and Marre (1964) Reports for supervisors. See also E. G. Edwards's address *The Interaction of the Work of Colleges and Industry* (at Moscow, 1962); McVey's article in *British Universities Annual 1963* (AUT, 1963); and Work's address *Industrial Training* (ATI, 1964).

The ITC's *Co-operation between Industry and Education* (1960) and *The Training Specialist in Industry* (1964) were useful short factual reviews, full of examples. The Minister's annual reports have also recorded interesting cases, as in those for 1949, 1950 and 1954. Methods of co-operation were described more generally in *Education in 1958*. Annual and other reports of regional advisory councils should also be looked at, such as East Anglia's *Links with Industry* (1961), and, of course, newspapers and journals. For the latter see *Technical Education Abstracts*. For the scheme at Crawley see Siklos: *Partnership Incorporated* (1963). See also the annual reports of the CTC and industrial training boards.

The FBI's *Education in Transition* (1965) summarized seven reports and the Industrial Training Act and discussed their implications for industry.

For international comparisons see OECD's *Inventory of Training Possibilities in Europe* (1965) and the ILO journal *Training for Progress in Europe and the World*.

On dangers see NUS: *Memorandum to the Committee on Higher Education* (1961) and ATTI: *Future of Higher Education* (1962).

On political implications see Chapter 19 and *Notes*.

CHAPTER 16

COMMONWEALTH RELATIONS OF BRITISH FURTHER EDUCATION

Scope

As founder member of the British Commonwealth the government of the United Kingdom has responsibilities whose discharge brings its education system into relationship with citizens, organizations and governments of other Commonwealth countries. The latter include, besides UK, about a score of sovereign or nearly sovereign states with their dependencies, containing a total population of around 600 million, and the dependencies of UK itself, with about another 10 million.

UK Dependencies are of two kinds : Colonies and Protectorates. They are ruled, at least in theory, by the British Parliament, and administered by the UK government through the Colonial Office or Commonwealth Relations Office. As mentioned earlier, the Secretaries of State consult with their colleagues in charge of these departments when educational matters are concerned.

In this book we deal not with the UK contribution, as such, to Commonwealth educational co-operation, but with the interactions of such co-operation with British Further Education.

Government-financed schemes of mutual aid

General schemes of direct aid

British Further Education is influenced in one way or another by most government schemes of Commonwealth aid. Broadly there are two kinds of assistance : "technical", which includes provision of education and training facilities in the donor country and sending of experts and supplying of educational equipment for use in the receiving country; and "capital", which means giving capital grants. Since technical assistance from the more to the less advanced countries is an aim of most aid schemes, *technical* education is the commonest sector of UK education to be affected.

The COLOMBO PLAN, begun in 1950, is an attempt to promote economic development in south and south-east Asia. Taking part are : Ceylon, India, Malaysia and Pakistan within the region; Australia, Canada, New Zealand and UK outside it; and several non-Commonwealth countries including Japan and USA. Assistance is given directly according to bilateral agreements negotiated between member governments. There is an annual conference. Nearly 2,500 new training places were provided in UK during the eleven years 1950–1960 for students from Ceylon, India, Malaya and Pakistan. In 1961–2, 667 from these countries were in training in UK, principally in administration, communications and transport, engineering, industry and trade, medicine and health and various other technical and general subjects, including mining, textile and oil technology and forestry. UK experts were also provided for service overseas. Equipment has been supplied for specific projects such as the building of a telecommunications training unit at Haripur, West Pakistan, and a new Engineering College at Delhi, India. Many smaller projects have been undertaken. Capital assistance is frequently included.

The SPECIAL COMMONWEALTH AFRICAN ASSISTANCE PLAN (SCAAP), begun in 1960, applies the principles of the Colombo Plan to the African region, but contains Commonwealth countries only. SCAAP trainees in UK numbered 141 in 1961–2 and 438 in 1962–3.

The FOUNDATION FOR MUTUAL ASSISTANCE IN AFRICA SOUTH OF THE SAHARA (FAMA) is supported by independent countries in Africa and by UK. It helps to provide teachers and technical experts and train African students in UK.

The OVERSEAS SERVICE AID SCHEME (OSAS) helps Commonwealth governments to meet the excess cost of employing expatriates.

General schemes of indirect aid

The United Nations Organization (UNO) and its specialized agencies (UNESCO, ILO, FAO, WHO and IAEA) give technical assistance to underdeveloped countries. Most of this is provided under UNO's EXPANDED PROGRAMME OF TECHNICAL ASSISTANCE, UNO's SPECIAL FUND for manpower education and training, or UNESCO, which has sponsored three large-scale plans (Karachi, Addis Ababa and Santiago) for educational development. Through these agencies, grants and other aid can be given for approved projects of technical development. Commonwealth countries contribute to many of these projects, financially and otherwise, and some also have benefited from them. In 1959, 575 fellowships for study in UK were given to overseas Commonwealth nationals, out of a total of 5,700 awarded under UNO technical-assistance programmes; and 499 experts from UK were serving overseas under these programmes. A UK National Commission supervises the work of British delegates to UNESCO.

Separate agreements

The UK government also has MUTUAL-ASSISTANCE AGREEMENTS with Ghana, Nigeria and Sierra Leone, under which training places in further-education establishments, teachers, advisers, equipment and capital assistance are provided in one another's countries.

Special aid for UK Dependencies

For many years British teachers have served under governments of dependent territories in HM Colonial Education Service and later in HM OVERSEAS CIVIL SERVICE. Today they still act as teachers, inspectors, advisers, administrators and so on, in further education as well as other branches, pending the training of local personnel. As mentioned, their expatriate costs may be borne by OSAS, or by ECC (see later).

Financial assistance is provided under COLONIAL DEVELOPMENT AND WELFARE SCHEMES (CD and WS) brought into being by six Acts from 1940 to 1959.

The COMMONWEALTH (formerly Colonial) DEVELOPMENT CORPORATION (CDC), set up in 1948, aids private-enterprise ventures by providing training programmes for employees, both locally and in UK. Two-thirds of its commitments are in Africa.

The Colonial Office also organizes CONFERENCES, creates ADVISORY BODIES and arranges VISITS OF EXPERT MISSIONS to help dependent governments in educational matters. Until 1964 there was also an Overseas Research Council.

Educational conferences

Much specifically educational co-operation has stemmed from special conferences of Commonwealth officials and educationists. The Board was involved in one in 1907 and again in 1911, 1923 and 1927. The series was intended to be quadrennial but was disrupted by wars and economic depressions. At the instigation of the Commonwealth Trade and Economic Conference at Montreal in 1958 it was resumed in 1959, 1962 and 1964.

Among measures adopted at the 1959 conference at Oxford was a COMMONWEALTH SCHOLARSHIP AND FELLOWSHIP PLAN (CSFP) under which over 1,000 awards, mostly postgraduate, were promised by Commonwealth governments, that of UK offering 500. The conference also reviewed Commonwealth educational co-operation generally, stressed the importance of technical education and expressed alarm about the shortage of teachers. The UK Government undertook to provide 4,000 extra places for overseas Commonwealth students in UK technical colleges during the next decade, and to persuade 400 additional experienced UK teachers to take key posts in developing Commonwealth countries by 1964. Also at the 1959 conference a recommendation that serving teachers and other educationists in developing countries should attend refresher courses in UK led to a COMMONWEALTH BURSARY SCHEME FOR TEACHER TRAINING. A Commonwealth Education Liaison Committee (CELC) was set up under the chairmanship of Sir Philip Morris, Vice-Chancellor of the University of Bristol, to help improve co-operation; and there is a Commonwealth Education Liaison Unit (CELU).

At the 1962 conference at Delhi the UK Government offered 40–50 bursaries a year under the Commonwealth Bursary Scheme for training students from developing countries in UK to be teachers of craftsmen and technicians. These bursaries were to be for special two-year courses divided between a technical college, industry and a technical teacher-training college. The scheme began in September 1963; 20 applicants were offered bursaries and 17 accepted. There were 59 technical bursars in UK in 1965–6, out of 490 bursars under the whole Bursary Scheme.

In 1963 the 500 limit on awards held in UK under CSFP was removed, and there were 520 in 1964–5. In 1964–5 also, the target of 1,000 awards was reached (1,048); more than one-quarter were to candidates from India and Pakistan. Only 104 were to undergraduates.

A third post-war conference was held at Ottawa in 1964, at which a Commonwealth technical teacher-training plan was suggested, and this was followed by a conference of experts on technical education in UK in 1966.

There have also been conferences on adult education and community development called by the Colonial Office.

Thus educational co-operation has become re-established as a regular feature of Commonwealth relations. However, there is as yet no major scheme of co-operation in technical education as such.

UNESCO and the International Bureau of Education (IBE) hold many conferences attended by Commonwealth representatives: for example, two on adult education were held in 1949 and 1963; and UNESCO started an international committee on adult education in 1960.

Facilities provided by private enterprise

UK firms in Commonwealth countries, though operating, of course, for commercial profit, frequently offer training schemes, found scholarships or supply equipment to local educational establishments; and some of these activities are on quite a large scale.

Nationals of overseas countries also come to work in UK, though this may have become more difficult since the Commonwealth Immigrants Act of 1962. It has been estimated that some 9,000 people from overseas each year obtain experience and training in British industry, many of whom are from Commonwealth countries; and some firms have special schemes. Under the FBI's overseas scholarship scheme 170 Commonwealth scholars came to UK between 1950 and 1961 for courses of training of up to two years duration. Between 1959 and 1962 there was an Advisory Council on Facilities for Commonwealth Trainees in UK Trade and Industry responsible to the President of the Board of Trade; but from 1962 its functions have been taken over by the new Council for Technical Education and Training for Overseas Countries (TETOC), under the ODM, which co-ordinates all UK effort in this field.

Under the Industrial Training Act of 1964, industrial training boards which pay UK firms to train overseas students who are not employed or intending to be employed in UK may be reimbursed by the Ministry of Labour, and not from the board's levy on the industry.

Voluntary service overseas

There are several UK voluntary bodies interested in promoting service to the community in other countries, and some of these touch on further education. For example, the African Development Trust, Co-operative Union Limited, National Adult School Union, National Federation of Women's Institutes and NIAE work for adult education, the BIM and Industrial Welfare Society for management education, the British Red Cross Society, British Society for International Health Education and NAMH for health education, the Committee on Overseas Service for sending young graduates abroad for periods of at least a year, the NUS, SUS and World University Service (WUS) for helping higher-education students and teachers, the SCNVYO for youth service, and Voluntary Service Overseas for arranging for young people to serve as teaching, welfare and other auxiliaries. These and other bodies are affiliated to the Standing Conference of Voluntary Organisations Co-operating in Overseas Social Service (VOCOSS).

Spreading knowledge of the
Commonwealth in UK establishments

The Minister was urging direct teaching about the Commonwealth at least since Circular 2/59, and has run short courses for teachers to this end.

The Secretary of State for Education and Science aids the Commonwealth Institute, of which he is a trustee. Founded in South Kensington in 1887 the latter moved into new buildings at Holland Park, London, in 1962. It has a Scottish Committee and a gallery in Edinburgh. Among its activities it offers a permanent exhibition, cinema and library, supplies teaching aids and provides a visiting lecture service and journal. Other bodies also help, notably the Royal Commonwealth Society, League for the Exchange of Commonwealth Teachers, Royal Overseas League, and, of course, Commonwealth government offices in UK. The use made of such services in UK Further Education establishments, however, is small.

Interactions with British Further Education

As a result of all these activities, the principles of curriculum and organization of British Further Education exert their influence on Commonwealth educational co-operation and on Commonwealth further education in particular. The converse is also true, though to a much smaller extent. There is also much mutual stimulus and cross-fertilization of ideas. This interaction operates through three main channels : overseas students in UK; exchange of teachers and other experts among Commonwealth countries; and co-operation between UK and overseas institutions.

Overseas Commonwealth students in UK

A citizen of the Commonwealth, or, indeed, of any country, can apply for admission to a British further-education establishment just like a British citizen. He or she may experience difficulty, however, unless the application is backed by an authoritative local influence, such as the appropriate overseas government office; and this may mean going through the ODM or other UK government department.

In 1960–1 there were around 36,000 nationals of other Commonwealth countries studying full-time in UK establishments, about 9,000 more than in 1957–8. Of these about 7,000 were at universities, 1,200 at colleges of education and 8,000 in Further Education; the remaining 19,000 were at unaided establishments. About 8,000 were student nurses, including 6,500 from UK Dependencies. The largest contributors to the overall total were Nigeria (6,800), Ghana (3,800), India (3,400), Jamaica (nearly 3,000) and Malaya (2,200).

By 1964–5 the number enrolled in full-time and sandwich courses in Further Education in England and Wales had risen from 8,000 to 11,000. Nearly half were taking advanced courses, which was about one-eleventh of all advanced students on full-time and sandwich courses. First degrees absorbed the largest single group. Of non-advanced students the largest single group was the two-fifths who were working for the GCE, and this proportion is rising. Business and administration occupied more students than any other field of study, with engineering next. These two, plus the GCE, took two-thirds of the 11,000. There were also about a couple of dozen in residential colleges of Adult Education. Nigeria, India and Ghana were again the largest single contributors, with Malaysia fourth; and there were substantial numbers from east Africa and the Caribbean. If part-time students are included the total was over 17,000.

Many Commonwealth students in UK pay their own way, whilst others are financed by their governments. It must be remembered, of course, that since fees cover only a small proportion of the cost of providing courses, all students are to that extent UK state-aided. Yet others hold fellowships, scholarships, bursaries and other awards, for which there are numerous schemes. An example already mentioned is the Commonwealth Scholarship and Fellowship Plan, mainly for graduates, launched at the Montreal and Oxford conferences in 1958-9. The Commonwealth Scholarships Act of 1959 set up an independent Commonwealth Scholarship Commission to select, place and supervise the 500 scholars and fellows in the UK; and, as mentioned, it was amended in 1963 to allow the award of more than 500. Of the 924 holders in 1963-4, 505 were in UK. The great majority were at universities, but in 1962-3 four awards were taken at technical colleges and one at a college of Adult Education. Another arrangement already mentioned is the Commonwealth Bursary Scheme for overseas serving teachers. UNESCO and other UNO agencies, Colonial governments, the UK government (under Colombo Plan, CD and W, SCAAP and other schemes), the British Council, private firms, the CBI, private trusts and foundations (such as the Rhodes Trust, trade-union scholarships, Ford Foundation, etc.) and many other organizations also offer awards. Apart from those given to candidates from Dependencies, where facilities for higher education are often meagre or lacking, the majority are at postgraduate level.

The wives of overseas students also frequently enrol in further-education courses whilst in UK.

The International Association for the Exchange of Students for Technical Experience, set up in 1948, sponsors exchanges for eight weeks' paid work as trainees during the summer vacation.

Welfare of overseas students in UK is a responsibility of the British Council, which makes arrangements to meet recommended students on arrival, finds or gives guidance on accommodation and offers general help and advice. It maintains facilities in twenty or so towns for social and cultural recreation, organizes courses, conferences, visits and similar functions so as to help students to be happy whilst in UK, and runs an English Teaching

Information Centre in London. Some colleges appoint teachers to act as welfare officers and run induction courses for overseas entrants. Voluntary bodies, too, such as NUS or YMCA, do much to help, as do Commonwealth governments and the offices of Dependencies themselves. Despite their handicaps most Commonwealth students are well liked in the colleges.

In 1964–5 the Secretary of State recognized as efficient thirty-five private establishments in England and Wales teaching English to overseas students.

Money for 5,000 extra college hostel places was allocated in 1961, but Commonwealth students are not segregated among themselves. The consequent mingling ensures for British education a major impact on Commonwealth development.

Exchange of teachers

It has been estimated that in the early 1960s, 2,500 UK teachers a year took up temporary or permanent service in overseas Commonwealth countries; and presumably some of these went from Further Education establishments. They were recruited by various agencies, notably governing bodies of Commonwealth private establishments, the British Council, church missionary societies, TETOC, the Women's Migration and Oversea Appointments Society, the UK government's ODM (for HM Overseas Civil Service, short-term contracts and exchanges), UNESCO and other international bodies (for short-term assignments), the Crown Agents for Oversea Governments (for instructor posts) and Commonwealth governments themselves. Officially sponsored exchange schemes with Canada, Australia, New Zealand and other Commonwealth countries (and USA) have also taken some.

The Oxford Conference provided a further stimulus, the UK Government, as mentioned, promising to encourage another 400 experienced UK teachers to take key posts in developing Commonwealth countries. In Circular 10/60 and Scottish Circular 443 the Ministers announced a six-point plan which included the setting-up of a National Council for the Supply of Teachers Overseas (NCSTO), a code of secondment from UK employment guaranteeing against loss of salary increments, a code for terms of appointment overseas, expense and expatriation allowances where necessary, end-of-service gratuities and an interview fund to aid subsequent reappointment or promotion in UK. The new Council was appointed in 1960 under the chairmanship of Sir Charles Arden-Clarke, formerly Governor-General of Ghana; and it has a Scottish Committee. It contains representatives of authorities, teachers, recruiting bodies, churches and interested government departments; and its main function is to assist the recruitment of UK teachers for overseas service and their resettlement on

s

return. The response, said the Minister in his 1962 Report, was disappointing; only 174 posts were approved by him for allowances in that year.

This scheme is called the COMMONWEALTH SUPPLY OF TEACHERS SCHEME. Together with the Commonwealth Scholarship and Fellowship Plan and Commonwealth Bursary Scheme for Teacher Training (both mentioned earlier) it makes up what is often called the programme for EDUCATIONAL CO-OPERATION IN THE COMMONWEALTH (ECC or CEC). ECC was transferred from the DES to the ODM at the end of 1964.

Thus the expatriate portions of the salaries of UK teachers serving abroad are often borne out of grants paid by the UK government to Commonwealth governments under OSAS or ECC. In the case of UK experts working under technical aid programmes, however, the whole salaries are usually paid directly by the UK government.

The number of teachers from overseas Commonwealth countries serving in UK Further Education is not published, and is probably very small. Some may be on exchange schemes such as the one organized by the League for the Exchange of Commonwealth Teachers (called until 1963 the League of the British Commonwealth and Empire). Cost-of-living grants are available from the education Departments for UK teachers going to Canada on such schemes, and travel grants for those going to Commonwealth countries in the southern hemisphere.

There is no unified career service for educationists in the Commonwealth as a whole.

Co-operation between institutions

DIRECT LINKS BETWEEN ESTABLISHMENTS have been known for many years, that of Fourah Bay College, Sierra Leone, with the University of Durham being a well known example. Such contact used to be fostered by the Council for Overseas Colleges of Arts, Science and Technology, which made available UK experience, and dispensed technical assistance and capital grants under CD and WS to institutions such as the Malta and Jamaica Colleges of Arts, Science and Technology and the Royal College, Nairobi. This council, however, has now been superseded by TETOC. There is also a Commonwealth University Exchange Scheme administered by the British Council.

Professional, examining and other bodies have developed Commonwealth relations too. For example, candidates in approved Commonwealth establishments are in many cases allowed to take examinations of UK bodies. About one-eighth of candidates and a rather smaller proportion of passes in City and Guilds Institute examinations are at overseas centres; and the Institute has its own Committee on Work Overseas. Twenty-one Commonwealth establishments were members of the ATI in 1964–5.

Problems of expansion

Expansion of the Commonwealth relations of British Further Education depends on the rate and nature of growth of (a) Commonwealth education and (b) Commonwealth co-operation; or in other words, on what Commonwealth countries do themselves and on how they help one another to do it.

Problems contained in the first of these groups are now receiving much attention. What place has education in the economy of a country, particularly of an underdeveloped country? What is its contribution in economic terms? What share of a nation's overall investment should it receive? What sectors within it should be given priority? How may solutions to such problems be both theoretically determined and actually carried out? How can the efficiency of an enducational system be measured? Such questions are of obvious urgency in underdeveloped countries but they pose themselves in the more advanced ones too. An awareness of their importance in Britain, for example, permeates the Crowther, Newsom, Robbins and Heyworth Reports.

Of the other factor—Commonwealth co-operation—the most obvious problems are those arising from the sheer size of Commonwealth poverty. The achievements so far look pitifully small against the wants of 650 million people, many of whom need urgent help on a large scale after decades of distortion of their economies. Thus the value of aid from the UK government to its Dependencies under CD and WS during this scheme's first twelve years (£66 million from 1940 to 1952) was of the same order of magnitude as the profits *taken out* of colonial territories by a typical large UK company in a single year. Falls in the prices of their exports can also involve poorer countries in heavy losses. Furthermore, the benefits of aid programmes have often been more than counterbalanced by other aspects of government policy, such as the accumulation of frozen sterling balances owed to Dependencies by the UK, or by political and military policies.

UK measures have also been criticized as complex, short-term, piecemeal and unplanned. Because of past neglect to plan ahead, even the post-Robbins expansion of intake of overseas Commonwealth students into UK higher education is now expected to be impeded by the urgent needs of school leavers from within UK itself. Rethinking, reorganizing, strengthening CELC and CELU and establishing a regular Commonwealth Education Service have been proposed (for example, by PEP, 1964).

The mode of solution of such problems is bound to have an impact on British Further Education.

Notes on further study

Useful official summaries were the COI's *Educational Co-operation Within the Commonwealth* (1961) which described the situation between the Oxford and Delhi Conferences, and *Britain and Education in the Commonwealth* (1964) between Delhi and Ottawa. See also Overseas Development Institute : *British Aid—3* (1963).

UK government policy was outlined in White Papers such as *Technical Education* (1956; paragraph 5), *Overseas Information Services* (1959), *Commonwealth Scholarship and Fellowship Plan* (1959), *Commonwealth Educational Co-operation* (1960), *Technical Assistance from the United Kingdom for Overseas Development* (1961), *Technical Co-operation* (1962), *Recruitment for Service Overseas* (1962), *Aid to Developing Countries* (1963) and *Immigration from the Commonwealth* (1965).

For the conferences see the official *Report of the Commonwealth Education Conference* (1959), *Report of the Second Commonwealth Education Conference* (1962) and *Report of the Third Commonwealth Education Conference* (1964). For the first, see also Heaton : *The Commonwealth Education Conference* (ATI, 1960); and for the third, English : *Commonwealth Co-operation in Technical Education and Vocational Training* (ATI, 1965). Officially sponsored scholarship and fellowship schemes were listed in the FBI's *Overseas Trainees in United Kingdom Industry* (1960). See also UNESCO's *Study Abroad XVI* (1965); the British Council's biennial handbook *Higher Education in the United Kingdom*; and annual reports of the Commonwealth Scholarship Commission, Colombo Plan and other schemes.

For problems in particular areas see reports, such as, for Central Africa the Carr-Saunders Report (1953), for the British Caribbean the Petter Report (1957), for Nigeria the Ashby Report (1960) and for Northern Rhodesia (now Zambia) the Keir (1960) and Lockwood (1963) Reports. See also UNESCO's *The Development of Higher Education in Africa* (1963). An earlier commentary on higher education in the colonies was the Asquith Report (1945).

Overseas Commonwealth students in UK were analysed in the Minister's *Statistics of Education, 1961, Part 1* (Table 32), *Statistics of Education, 1961, Supplement to Part 2* (Table 14), *Statistics of Education, 1962, Part 2* (Table 21) and *Statistics of Education, 1963, Part 2* (Table 17); in Appendix Two (A), Part 7, of the Robbins Report (1963); and in the British Council's *Overseas Students in Britain* (1964). There were short chapters or sections in the COI's *Technological Education in Britain* (1960), *Technical Education in Britain* (1962) and *Britain and Education in the Commonwealth* (1964). See also annual and other reports, handbooks and yearbooks of

Commonwealth governments and their education departments. Interesting studies were : PEP : *Colonial Students in Britain* (1955) and *New Commonwealth Students in Britain* (1965); Carey : *Colonial Students* (1956); and Livingstone : *The Overseas Student in Britain* (1960). On student welfare see the Minister's Circular 332 (1958) and Amendment (1960), which listed responsible officers, followed by Circular 2/63 with Revised Appendix 1 (1963). On the education of immigrants in UK see Circular 7/65.

The Minister's moves to encourage UK teachers to serve overseas were announced in Circular 10/60 and Addenda (1964 and 1965) and Administrative Memorandum 18/61; they followed principles already expounded in Circulars 277 (1954) and 330 (1957). The Secretary of State for Scotland's were in Scottish Circular 443 (1960) and two Addenda, which followed 291 (1954) and 370 (1957). Administrative Memoranda 19/61 and Amendment, 7/62, 8/63, 8/64, 14/65 and 7/66 were on teacher interchange. See also the Minister's booklet *Why Not Teach for a Time Overseas?* (1963), leaflet *A Call from Overseas for Technical Staff* (n.d.) and Circular 11/63; the DTC's *Teaching Opportunities Overseas* (1963); and the ODM's *Study and Serve Overseas* (1965) and *Opportunities Overseas for Teachers* (1965). The situation was examined in PEP's *Teachers for the Commonwealth* (1964). On the impact of the Robbins Report on the supply of teachers for higher education in developing countries see Williams's article in *British Universities Annual 1964* (AUT, 1964). The constitution of NCSTO was given in Addendum No. 2 to Circular 10/60 (1965).

On voluntary service overseas see the *Directory* by VOCOSS (1963) and, of course, publications of appropriate voluntary bodies.

On dissemination of information about the Commonwealth, much in the Minister's Circular 2/59 and Pamphlet *Schools and the Commonwealth* (1961) was relevant to further-education establishments.

The general background of problems was discussed in addresses by Elvin : *Education and the End of Empire* (1957) and Lewis : *Partnership in Oversea Education* (1959).

The COI's *Research and the United Kingdom Dependencies* (1958), *Education in the United Kingdom Dependencies* (1959), *Commonwealth Education: Britain's Contribution* (1961) and *Community Development: the British Contribution* (1962) were concise factual pamphlets written from the UK government official viewpoint.

Needless to say, all official material needs to be read along with critical commentaries if a balanced assessment of UK government measures against a deeper perspective is to be made. See, for example, Dutt : *The Crisis of Britain and the British Empire* (1953), though this needs, of course, to be brought up to date.

For general background information see prospectuses and reports of the British Council, Commonwealth Institute, Royal Commonwealth Society,

Nuffield Foundation (especially *Sixteenth Annual Report*, 1961), City and Guilds of London Institute (especially *Annual Report*, Parts I and VII), ATI, CELC (six annual reports to 1965–6) and other bodies. See also prospectuses of UK and Commonwealth establishments.

On the strategy of educational advance and economic growth see *Notes to Chapter 2*.

CHAPTER 17

EXAMINATIONS IN FURTHER EDUCATION

THERE is much about examinations in earlier chapters, but in view of their all-pervading influence in Further Education it has been thought useful to abstract it into a short summary.

Examining bodies

Regional examining unions

"Regional" here means outside London. There are : the UNION OF LANCASHIRE AND CHESHIRE INSTITUTES (ULCI; founded in 1839), covering Lancashire, Cheshire, Caernarvonshire, Denbighshire, Flintshire and the Isle of Man; the UNION OF EDUCATIONAL INSTITUTIONS (UEI; founded in 1895), covering a midland area bounded by Cornwall, Devon, Hampshire, Huntingdonshire and Staffordshire; the EAST MIDLAND EDUCATIONAL UNION (EMEU; founded in 1911), covering Derbyshire, Leicestershire, Lincoln-shire, Northamptonshire, Nottinghamshire and Rutland; the NORTHERN COUNTIES TECHNICAL EXAMINATIONS COUNCIL (reconstituted in 1924), cover-ing Cumberland, Durham, Northumberland, Westmorland and Redcar in the North Riding of Yorkshire; the WELSH JOINT EDUCATION COMMITTEE, covering the rest of Wales, which (since 1952) has added examining to its other functions; and the YORKSHIRE COUNCIL FOR FURTHER EDUCATION, which did likewise in 1962, covering Yorkshire except the Redcar district.

These bodies have each a council, advisory committees and moderating committees, and employ a staff of examiners. The councils determine policy; they contain a majority of representatives of "institutes" or "institutions" (which in this case now means *authorities*). The advisory committees design syllabuses; on them sit teachers, HMIs and representatives of local industries and professional institutions, with teachers in the majority. The moderating committees approve draft examination papers set by examiners and main-tain standards.

A wide range of technical, commercial, art, domestic and general subjects is examined and certificates awarded. Most are for day-release and evening students, but school-leaving certificates were awarded too until the advent of the CSE. Other bodies such as the City and Guilds Institute accept appropriate passes as exempting from their own examinations. The unions also look after some GCE subjects for matriculation boards (see below), and act as agent for colleges in the earlier stages of National Certificate courses. Their examinations are entirely "external" (see below). Most are at non-advanced level.

London examining bodies

The CITY AND GUILDS OF LONDON INSTITUTE (founded in 1878) is the most important of the bodies examining technical subjects, particularly at operative, craftsman and technician levels. Advisory committees, widely representative of appropriate industries, industrial research associations, professional institutions, teachers, regional unions, authorities and government departments (including the DES and SED) design the 280 or so courses offered. Direct co-ordination with the regional unions has existed since the "concordat" of 1933. There is a Standing Conference of Regional Examining Unions which invites the City and Guilds Institute to its meetings. Since 1955 there has been also a Standing Committee (now Council) of Technical Examining Bodies. The latter prepared, for example, the syllabus in General Engineering (G) published by the Minister in Administrative Memorandum 10/61. By agreement, students usually take annual examinations of regional unions in the earlier years of their courses and final examinations of the City and Guilds Institute at the end. As mentioned in an earlier chapter, syllabuses are co-ordinated. The concordat was revised in 1965.

The ROYAL SOCIETY OF ARTS (RSA; which began to examine in 1856) occupies a position in commerce and administration similar to that of the City and Guilds Institute in technology. Like the latter it works closely with the regional unions.

The LONDON CHAMBER OF COMMERCE (which began to examine in 1890) conducts commercial examinations.

The PITMAN EXAMINATION INSTITUTE offers certificates in commercial subjects.

Examinations of all these bodies are external.

Joint committees in National schemes

Ordinary and Higher National Certificates and Diplomas (started in 1920) are administered by joint committees representing the Departments, appropriate professional institutions and teachers. In agreement with these committees the Secretaries of State make *Rules* governing the courses and examinations. Syllabuses are submitted by colleges (or in Scotland by SANCAD—see below) and approved by the committees. Papers are set and marked by college teachers, a regional union or SANCAD, but draft papers and marking have to be seen by assessors under the control of the committees. This method of examining is called "internal with external assessment". The assessors also take account of marks obtained for work done during the course ("continuous assessment"). In engineering a certain amount of merging of joint committees is going on.

Joint committees in schemes modelled on National schemes

These include, for example, those for the National Bakery Diploma, Retail Distribution and Management Certificates and Diploma in Management Studies (Table 23).

TABLE 23

SOME EXAMINATION SCHEMES MODELLED ON NATIONAL CERTIFICATE AND
DIPLOMA SCHEMES (ENGLAND AND WALES, 1964)

	No. awarded
National Bakery Diploma	98
Higher National Bakery Diploma	4
National Craftsman's Certificate for Motor Vehicle Service Mechanics	1,542
National Diploma in Hotel-Keeping and Catering	140
National Retail Distribution Certificate	368
Certificate in Retail Management Principles	56
Diploma in Management Studies (new scheme)	498

Source: Department of Education and Science: *Statistics of Education, 1964, Part 2*, table 30 (1965).

Scottish co-ordinating bodies

The North-East Scotland Co-ordinating Committee, West of Scotland Committee for Technical Education and South-East Scotland Committee for Certificates in Technology came to an end on 1st April 1963 and handed their duties to the SCOTTISH ASSOCIATION FOR NATIONAL CERTIFICATES AND DIPLOMAS (SANCAD) which had been set up in October 1962. This body acts on behalf of colleges involved in National schemes in Scotland; it offers syllabuses, conducts common examinations and submits candidates to joint committees.

National Councils

At the time of writing there are three of these actually operating and another which has been appointed recently.

The COUNCIL FOR NATIONAL ACADEMIC AWARDS (CNAA) received its Royal Charter in September 1964. As explained in Chapter 6 it superseded both the National Council for Technological Awards (Hives Council) and the College of Technologists. It will operate over a wide field, being empowered to award ordinary, honours and higher degrees, as well as certificates and diplomas, in any subject, to candidates in non-university establishments over the whole UK. It is expected to develop its work along lines pioneered by the Hives Council in connection with the Dip.Tech. and Dip.Tech.(Eng.). Thus colleges will submit schemes and assess candidates, while being subject to control by the Council. Professional training will tend to be of the concurrent type, sandwich courses being favoured. For 1966–7 the Council has recognized 105 courses, some of which were preparing for the Dip.Tech., as leading to a B.Sc. degree with honours, and has accepted registration for the MCT as leading to a Ph.D. It accepts 17 for a B.A. It has invited existing holders of Dip.Tech. and MCT to convert them into the new degrees. There are boards of studies for each of the main subject groups, composed of nominees of the APTI, ATTI, professional institutions and so on, together with co-opted specialists and assessors from the DES and SED; but all serve in an individual capacity and not as representatives.

The NATIONAL COUNCIL FOR DIPLOMAS IN ART AND DESIGN (NCDAD, Summerson Council), set up in 1961 (as described in Chapter 8), gives the Dip.AD. It covers colleges in England and Wales only.

These two Councils have adopted four of the basic principles pioneered by National schemes, namely: internal (college) design of curricula with external (Council) control; internal examination of candidates with external assessment; consideration of course work as well as examination results; and external approval of standards of facilities in the colleges.

In contrast the SCOTTISH COUNCIL FOR COMMERCIAL EDUCATION (SCCE), appointed in 1961, devises courses and conducts external examinations. Besides keeping the whole field of commercial education in Scotland under review, it awards certificates in commerce, secretaryship, office studies and office skills.

The new body is the NATIONAL EXAMINATIONS BOARD IN SUPERVISORY STUDIES, set up in 1964. It contains representatives of industry, commerce, professional institutions, the CGLI and the Departments, and covers the whole UK. It will take over and develop existing schemes in foremanship and supervision, and from 1966 will offer its own qualifications.

Government bodies

The CIVIL SERVICE COMMISSION and LOCAL GOVERNMENT EXAMINATIONS BOARD conduct examinations for recruiting and promoting central- and local-government employees.

Entrance examinations for HM FORCES can also be taken, usually at school or after end-on courses at colleges.

The DES appoints assessors for the NDD, but only until 1967. The SED has examined for the SCE but this, too, is being shed (see below). The SED controls some associateships awarded by Central Institutions.

Professional institutions

As explained earlier, corporate membership of a "professional" institution is a mark of "professional" status. Millerson (1964) listed about 160 qualifying associations. There are about 80 in science and technology, 50 in commerce, sociology and law and another dozen or so in agriculture. Some have Royal Charters giving considerable autonomy. About 120 conduct their own examinations; and at least 75 award qualifications after courses classified by the Robbins Committee as "higher" education.

Their chief functions are to maintain standards and regulate recruitment. These are mainly done, not by teaching or even insisting on pupilage or apprenticeship, but by offering examinations and "recognizing" colleges as fit to prepare candidates therefor. The examinations are externally conducted but exemptions are allowed. They are usually organized in three stages : preliminary, intermediate and final. The preliminary is meant to be a test of general education and exemptions are commonly given for passes at O level in the GCE or SCE. Complete or partial exemption from intermediate and final subjects may be given for qualifications such as GCE A level, ONC, HNC, endorsement, Dip.Tech. or degree. The balance of general and specialist studies in the syllabuses varies considerably. Passing the final examination confers what is usually known as "graduateship", after which complete eligibility for corporate membership generally requires a period of professional practice. In commerce it is thought that about three-quarters of candidates for such qualifications study by correspondence.

Professional institutions also participate in joint arrangements, such as the National schemes already described. In agriculture and agricultural engineering, although there are certificates and diplomas called "national", the Departments do not take an active part; instead, farm institutes conduct examinations which are externally assessed by joint examination boards appointed mainly by the professional institutions concerned. In other agricultural technologies the examinations are external. The Dadd Report recommended a new co-ordinated pattern for the agricultural technologies.

In 1962, thirteen engineering institutions set up a joint council to merge their requirements.

Colleges

There are many college awards. Central Institutions, the Royal College of Art, National Colleges, the College of Aeronautics and certain technical colleges are examples of establishments whose associateships and diplomas are now well known. They are very popular in Scotland (Table 24). Central Institutions run joint examination boards for some subjects; and something like this (by areas) has been proposed by NACAE for "vocational" courses in art and design.

Internal college examinations for admission, assessment or promotion are of course innumerable.

TABLE 24

ADVANCED QUALIFICATIONS AT CENTRAL INSTITUTIONS, 1964

	Entries	Successes
University degrees		144
College associateships and diplomas	1,346	1,236
College associateships and diplomas (supplementary certificates)	38	38
HNC	1,828	1,119
HNC (supplementary certificates)	1,091	777
HND	23	18
SCCE Advanced Commercial and Secretarial Certificates	208	96
Diploma in Management Studies		13
Certificate in Business Administration		19

Source: Secretary of State for Scotland: *Education in Scotland in 1964*, p. 55 and table 15 (1965).

School examination boards

These award the GCE and SCE, the chief function of which is to qualify for "matriculation" which is the minimum requirement for admission to a course for a degree at a university.

In England and Wales these boards are university-controlled, although representatives of teachers sit on them. The use of their examinations in schools and Further Education establishments is subject to approval by the Secretary of State advised by the Schools Council. In recent years there have been sharp rises in the numbers of entries in science subjects. About 17 per cent of candidates for the GCE in summer 1964 were in Further Education establishments. Syllabuses are prescribed by the boards, though establishments may submit their own for approval. Examinations are external.

There are 8 GCE boards :

OXFORD AND CAMBRIDGE SCHOOLS EXAMINATION BOARD,
OXFORD DELEGACY OF LOCAL EXAMINATIONS,
CAMBRIDGE UNIVERSITY LOCAL EXAMINATIONS SYNDICATE,
SOUTHERN UNIVERSITIES JOINT BOARD,
UNIVERSITY OF LONDON ENTRANCE AND SCHOOL EXAMINATIONS COUNCIL,
NORTHERN UNIVERSITIES JOINT MATRICULATION BOARD (JMB),
WELSH JOINT EDUCATION COMMITTEE and
ASSOCIATED EXAMINING BOARD (AEB).

The University of Durham School Examination Board came to an end in 1964.

The SCOTTISH CERTIFICATE OF EDUCATION EXAMINATION BOARD was set up in 1963 to take over the conduct of the SCE from the Secretary of State.

The SCOTTISH UNIVERSITIES ENTRANCE BOARD prescribes the Attestation of Fitness for admission to Scottish universities.

Universities

These award degrees, diplomas and certificates, either to their own students ("internal") or to those enrolled at other establishments ("external"). Several have arrangements with colleges by which college students rank as internal. The University of London is the only university in UK offering external degrees; these are taken in about fifty colleges.

The Certificate of Secondary Education

How far the CSE will come into Further Education establishments, as did the GCE, is not yet known; but it can be expected therein until 1972 at least.

The genesis of the CSE is described in Chapter 14. It is intended as a nationally current school-leaving certificate for the industrious pupil of average ability after completing five years at a secondary school in England and Wales. There are 14 regional boards on which teachers in schools providing the candidates are in a majority. Examinations started in 1965, or in some regions in 1966. They are conducted in any of three *modes* which are :

> *Mode 1:* an externally set, externally marked paper, on a syllabus drawn up by a subject panel of the board;
>
> *Mode 2:* an externally set, externally marked paper, on a syllabus submitted by a school or group of schools and moderated by a teacher appointed by the board; and
>
> *Mode 3:* an internal assessment within the school, of work performed according to a scheme submitted by the school, both scheme and assessment being externally validated by the board.

It is hoped that a "Grade 1" in the CSE will be accepted as equivalent for admission purposes to an O-level pass in the GCE. Some bodies have already said that they will accept it (at the time of writing, they include 16 universities, 14 joint committees and 41 professional associations).

Types of examination

As explained already, INTERNAL examinations are set, marked and assessed within an establishment. Examples are the entrance, terminal, sessional and college-diploma examinations taken within colleges, conducted entirely by college teachers. Groups of colleges may act collectively.

INTERNAL EXAMINATIONS EXTERNALLY ASSESSED are set and marked by college teachers, but question papers, samples of answer scripts, scripts of borderline quality and perhaps candidates' course work are seen by assessors appointed by a body outside the college who have the final say in determining results. This is the dominant form of examining used in higher education today (though universities appoint their own external assessors from other universities without intervention from an outside body). Examples are the schemes for National Certificates and Diplomas, the Dip.Tech. and the Dip.AD. As mentioned, the CNAA is expected to use this method too. Bodies such as SANCAD or a regional examining union may act as agent for colleges.

EXTERNAL examinations are set, marked and assessed entirely by the examining body, and not at all by college teachers (though in some cases, as in the GCE, the latter may be asked to give an estimate which is said to be taken into account in borderline cases). Examples are : the certificates of the City and Guilds Institute, RSA, SCCE and regional unions; the GCE and SCE; the direct examinations of professional institutions, GNC, NNEB and other bodies; and the external degrees and diplomas of universities.

The internal assessment of course work as it proceeds ("continuous assessment") and the use of oral examinations ("vivas") are common in higher education, but objective tests are not much used. The greatest stress has always been, and still is, on traditional essay-type written examinations, with or without practical tests.

There is nothing in Further Education comparable with the Schools Council for the Curriculum and Examinations, which guides the work of the schools in England and Wales.

Problems

Very little research has been done on the efficiency or effects of this system. Research is particularly needed into techniques of assessing practical subjects, particularly with candidates deficient in writing ability.

Examinations have been used mainly for selecting candidates for scarce opportunities, rather than for generating desired feedback effects on teaching, evaluating curriculum designs or motivating less able students.

Notes on further study

The functions of examinations in further education were discussed in the Atholl Report (1928), and more recently in paragraphs 67–72 of the Minister's Pamphlet No. 8 (1947). The Atholl Report surveyed the whole field as it was then.

Professional institutions for technology were shortly described in the COI's *Technical Education in Britain* (1962) and in the annual *Year Book of Technical Education and Careers in Industry*. Their functions were discussed in the Carr-Saunders Report (1949; especially on pages 1, 2 and 7) and more fully in Millerson's *The Qualifying Associations* (1964). There was a brief outline of examining bodies in the FBI's *The Technical Colleges and their Government* (1960) (Chapter IV).

A useful general account was Pedley's *A Parent's Guide to Examinations* (1964). A more theoretical treatment was by Holmes and Dryland at the ATI meeting for 1965. See also Leese's article in *Technical Education and Industrial Training* for May 1965. A much larger study was Montgomery's *Examinations* (1965).

General information is contained in annual reports of the Ministers and Secretaries of State, and, for England and Wales from 1961 onwards, *Statistics of Education, Parts 1, 2* and *3*. See also the DES's *Reports on Education,* No. 14 (1964; reproduced as Table 22).

The National Certificate and Diploma schemes were started by the Board's Circular 1029 (1920). In England and Wales they and several other schemes modelled on them are governed by *Rules 100–133* laid down by the Secretary of State, listed in *Government Publications Sectional List No. 2* and also in *Further Education for School Leavers* (1966). Scottish National schemes are administered under a single set—*Rules 1* (1964)—introduced with Scottish Circular 560. See also the DES's *Reports on Education,* No. 26 (1965).

Examinations have also been the subject of numerous Administrative Memoranda, indexed in the DES's annual *List 10*. Professional bodies' requirements in terms of the GCE were set out in Circulars 227 (1950), 338 (1958) and 5/62 and the DES's *The General Certificate of Education* (1964).

The evolution of art examinations from external to internal is described in Chapter 8.

For references on the GCE, SCE and CSE schemes see *Notes* to Chapter 14.

Specific information such as syllabuses, regulations and statistics can be found in prospectuses and reports of examining bodies, professional institutions and colleges. The annual report of the City and Guilds Institute is in eight parts; see also its monographs *Further Education for Operatives* (1964), *Further Education for Craftsmen* (1964) and *Further Education for Technicians* (1964). On the Dip.Tech. and Dip.Tech.(Eng.) schemes see the National Council for Technological Awards : *Report 1955–7; Report 1957–9; Report 1959–60; Report 1960–1; Report 1961–2; Memorandum on the Industrial Training of Students Following Courses Recognised as Leading to the Diploma in Technology* (1960); *The Diploma in Technology and Membership of the College of Technologists* (1961); and *List 16* (1964). These should be brought up to date with the CNAA's *Courses* (1966). On the Dip.AD see the National Council for Diplomas in Art and Design : *The Diploma in Art and Design : Memorandum No. 1* (1962); and *First Report* (1964). Examinations in agriculture were in the DES's *List 185* (1965) and the Dadd Report (1966).

For the CNAA see Circular 10/64 and Administrative Memorandum 9/64; Cox : *The Coming of the Council for National Academic Awards* (ATI, 1964); the DES's *Reports on Education,* No. 30 (1966); and, of course, its own reports, statements and memoranda.

The revised "concordat" between the CGLI and regional unions was attached to Administrative Memorandum 2/66.

CHAPTER 18

RESEARCH INTO
FURTHER EDUCATION

Approaches

In a sense all intentional practice from which it is hoped that something new can be learned is research. In any scientific sense, however, research should contain an element of objective assessment, evaluation or measurement contributing to a judgement of the relative merits of alternatives. It can be "operational", where processes are studied in the situations in which they occur, or "experimental", where artificial situations are contrived. The latter is the more rigorous and leads to more conclusive results, but is more difficult, or in many cases impossible, to carry out. There are, of course, gradations between the two.

In the past a considerable amount of operational work has gone into the collection and preparation of statistical and other returns, such as those of the Departments. The DES's Architects and Building Branch, medical officers, HMIs and authorities' inspectors have carried out special studies of certain topics from time to time. Such work has generally been designed for administrative or financial rather than research purposes, however, and the amount of fundamental knowledge which can be gleaned from its results is limited. Therefore, it is not usually regarded as research.

In its more agreed sense, research has been carried out by people seeking higher degrees at universities, many of whom have been busy practising teachers or training-college lecturers doing it in their spare time. Much has been in fields such as history or psychology, on topics suited to individuals working alone.

Recently there has been greater use of more organized methods. Several universities now have well established units working in specific fields such as educational economics, recruitment to science and technology, programmed learning or day-release courses; and additional grants were offered by the UGC in 1963. Groups of teachers are in a few cases working under the guidance of a university institute of education. The Central Advisory Councils have conducted researches, notably into early leaving from school and wastage in the further education of fifteens to eighteens; the Committee on Scientific Manpower and its successor have studied the supply and demand for scientists and engineers; NACEIC has inquired into wastage, public relations and technical-college resources; and the Robbins Committee has examined higher education. Technical education came into the purview of the National Foundation for Educational Research, in the secondary field with the appointment of a Research Officer (Technical Education) in 1955, and in further education in 1956. Conferences have been called and working committees set up by authorities, university institutes of education, regional advisory councils, professional institutions and NIAE. There has also been a small growth of sponsored team-work projects financed by industrial trusts, such as those under the Nuffield Foundation at the London School of Economics and the Birmingham[1] and Brunel CATs. Industry has conducted investigations, as have examining, professional and other bodies and the Service Ministries. In 1961 the Ministry of Education set up a Research and Intelligence Branch, expanded its statistical service, increased its aid to the NFER and put up a fund to aid research. Later it started a Curriculum Study Group, which in 1964 was absorbed into the new Schools Council for the Curriculum and Examinations. Ninety projects were receiving aid from the DES at the end of 1964, with about £900,000 promised. In 1964 a research and information centre for youth work (mentioned earlier) was started at the National College, Leicester. Industrial training came under the attention of the DSIR which aided six projects, all at universities, in 1962. The Scottish and DSIR–DES schemes for industrial liaison officers have been mentioned; these are intended to encourage research. Research is also a function of industrial training boards. A committee on research in the social sciences under the chairmanship of Lord Heyworth has reported, as a result of which a Social Science Research Council has been formed. A Society for Research into Higher Education was set up at the end of 1964.

Thus significant moves are now going on, even though the scale of operations is small.

Establishments

The Scottish Council for Research in Education (SCRE) was formed in 1928. It is financed and governed by a council representing authorities, teachers' organizations, certain professional associations, universities and the SED. It employs a director, secretary and office staff. Its function is largely aiding, co-ordinating and publishing research.

The National Foundation for Educational Research in England and Wales (NFER) is constituted similarly, but is much larger. It employs a director and nineteen full-time professional research staff. It conducts investigations (some of which are planned on a large scale to extend over

[1] Now the University of Aston.

five years or more), maintains an information and consultative centre, supplies standardized tests and publishes two journals. Most of its work is done in consultation with authorities.

The NATIONAL INSTITUTE OF ADULT EDUCATION (NIAE) is a federation of authorities, universities and voluntary bodies. Its main function is to promote co-operation by giving advice; but it also encourages experiment in adult education, initiates and publishes research and acts as an information centre. It has no permanent research staff but engages associates for specific projects. It publishes three periodicals.

The SCOTTISH INSTITUTE OF ADULT EDUCATION (SIAE) performs similar functions in Scotland.

The NATIONAL INSTITUTE OF INDUSTRIAL PSYCHOLOGY (NIIP) is run by a council representing its members, who are drawn from the professions, both sides of industry and the SRC. This delegates much authority to an executive and research committee. It employs a staff of six whose main study is the adjustment of people to their work; and it offers a service of vocational guidance. It is aided by the SRC.

Weaknesses

A principal aim of educational research is to obtain evidence with the help of which the effectiveness of different educational operations can be compared. This is true at all levels from problems of classroom technique to the planning of a national system. For this purpose it must, of course, be based on sound foundations of psychology and sociology, which stand in a similar relationship to education as physics and economics do to engineering; research in psychology and sociology, therefore, is inseparable from educational research. And to be sure of isolating the subject of study from the other numerous and complex factors which influence education, the work must be done with samples large enough and over periods long enough to give valid results. Such work is generally beyond the resources of single individuals or even groups. Yet, of the 233 studies registered at the NFER in 1960, 121 were being carried out by people working solo and mainly part-time for higher degrees, and only 76 were by university departments, authorities or teacher groups.

Thus the main weakness of the work has been its small-scale and scattered nature. There has also been a lack of feedback into practice and policy of such results as have been obtained. There has been a dearth of guidance from the Ministries; a scarcity of workers trained in techniques such as interviewing, test construction or statistical analysis; and poor liaison between, on the one hand, practitioners and policy-makers who know the problems but lack time or training to conduct research, and, on the other, research workers who may not be fully in touch with the problems. There were only ten research fellowships in education at universities in 1962–3, and most of these were poorly paid. In the same year the SCRE had only one full-time professional researcher on its staff. Technical colleges and colleges of education do not normally employ trained full-time educational research workers; nor do they possess the resources needed for large-scale investigations. Research carried out by individuals often suffers from a lack of skilled collaboration or advice; but technical-college teachers do not commonly look to university institutes of education for help; and even where they do, it is difficult to recruit the right teams. "Commercial" research by firms and surveys by professional bodies are designed mainly for a limited use. Even government departments have come under heavy criticism for the paucity of their statistical services. Above all, financial backing was described in the Crowther Report as "pitiable"; and the Parliamentary and Scientific Committee estimated that in 1960–1 only 0·014 per cent of expenditure in education went to research, as compared with nearly 1 per cent in medicine and 4 per cent in industry; yet even the meagre amounts available for individual research, according to the Oliver Report (1960), were not being fully drawn.

Obviously basic attitudes, both among teachers and in society at large, are not yet as favourable to educational research as they are to research in many other fields.

Proposals

Organization of resources

The McNair Committee (1944) proposed an educational research council similar to those already in being for medicine and agriculture, on which the Minister, authorities, universities, training colleges, schools and others should be represented. More recently the Parliamentary and Scientific Committee has developed this proposal in more specific terms, but suggesting that its work should be independent, and not, as with the NFER, SCRE and NIAE at present, under the control of the users; therefore it should have an independent chairman under the direction of a committee of the Privy Council, and should report to Parliament through the Lord President of the Council. For the same reason the heads of university departments and institutes of education thought that its constitution should be representative not of organizations but of individuals. The Labour Party's Taylor Committee also supported this. However, in 1963 the Minister did not agree with the idea, preferring to keep the disposal of any additional funds under his own control. The Robbins Report contained no comment on this problem but urged joint enterprise. The Heyworth Committee turned down the idea of a separate research council for education because it thought this might lead to its isolation from the mainstream of social science; but it recommended a social-science research council within the machinery of which education would have its own board.

Other important proposals were the Oliver Report's suggestion that the chief centres of work should be the technical training colleges, aided by university institutes of education and the NFER; and the Judges Report's stress on the need for a policy for the recruitment, training and employment of research manpower.

Subjects needing investigation

A classified list of suggested topics in technical education appeared in the Judges Report. They were arranged in five groups : entry to education and training; methods of teaching and training; relations between education and training; comparative studies; and broader problems. The Robbins Report contained suggestions too, particularly urging continuation of its own operational investigation of the national system of higher education.

No comparable lists are known for commercial or art education, Adult Education or Youth Service, but the NIAE has drawn attention to important areas of ignorance, such as the motivation of the part-time non-vocational adult student.

Notes on further study

Completed research is reported in journals, of which the most important are *British Journal of Educational Studies, British Journal of Educational Psychology, Occupational Psychology, The Vocational Aspect of Secondary and Further Education, Adult Education* and *BACIE Journal.* The latter has detachable bibliographical supplements which have been republished : Volume 1 (1962); Volume 2, Part 1, with index (1963). There are also the research reviews of Birmingham, Durham, Hull, Newcastle and Leeds University Institutes of Education. Articles are listed in *British Education Index* and in the American *Education Index.* Reviews appear in *Educational Research* and abstracts in *Technical Education Abstracts* (but the latter has been guilty of omissions). On Adult Education see Kelly's *Select Bibliography* (1962) (with annual supplements). For completed individual projects for higher degrees see Blackwell : *List of Researches in Education and Educational Psychology* (1950) (with regular supplements). Sparrow has abstracted those dealing with technical education into a separate list. ASLIB publishes an annual *Index to Theses*. . . . For more general articles see also *Forum* and *New Education*; *Forum* for Spring 1965 was a special number on further education. Manpower surveys were listed on p. 43 of *The National Plan* (1965).

Researches in progress are listed from time to time by regional advisory councils, colleges of education (technical) and in the NFER's *Current Researches in Education (Occasional Publications)* of which see especially No. 8 (1965). See also annual reports of the NFER, SCRE and other bodies, and the NFER's *Notes on the Work . . . for 1963–4*. Projects aided by the Secretaries of State were listed in Appendices H and I of *Education in 1965* and Appendix 4 of *Education in Scotland in 1965*.

For proposals on organization and on topics needing investigation see the McNair (1944), Willis Jackson (1957), Crowther (1959), Oliver (1960), Judges (1962), Robbins (1963) and Heyworth (1965) Reports, the Parliamentary and Scientific Committee's *Memorandum on Educational Research* (1961) and reports of conferences called by regional advisory councils and academic boards, professional associations, NFER, SCRE, NIAE, NIIP, ATI, AAI, BACIE, UNESCO, IBE and other bodies. On the scope of educational statistics and other problems of educational planning see the Robbins Report, especially Appendix Four (1963).

The proposal for an educational research council was expounded by D'Aeth in an article in *Nature* for 12th October 1963.

On industrial training see Hilary Clay: *How Research can help Training* (1964); and CIRF's quarterly journal *Training for Progress*.

Establishments for research in the social sciences, other than universities and colleges, were listed in Appendix 3 of the Heyworth Report.

See also prospectuses and annual reports of the bodies mentioned, particularly the Nuffield Foundation's *Eighteenth Annual Report 1962–3* (1963).

The Ministry's *Reports on Education*, No. 9 (1964), reviewed developments, mainly since the Crowther Report.

CHAPTER 19

ASSESSMENT OF THE SYSTEM IN ITS BACKGROUND

Twenty-year retrospect

Intentions

To recapitulate briefly, the aims for the statutory system of education officially enunciated between 1943 and 1947 were to bring up a healthy and happy population, to train a balanced team of workers able to develop a prosperous economy, and to rear a people eager to advance its civilization and culture. Everyone was to have the means of developing his or her talents to the full.

Further Education was to be the third progressive stage of this system. Its erstwhile reliance on evening study was to be ended. Compulsory day-time attendance till eighteen was to be its core; and this would be complemented by a fully developed Youth Service, continued by daytime vocational studies, and enriched by a liberal provision of facilities for adult recreation and culture.

Educational aims were not to be pursued separately in these sectors, however, but in all of them together, despite differences of emphasis. Therefore the system was meant to be planned as a unity, to fulfil the needs of the community as a whole. There was to be diversity, but not at the expense of social cohesion nor equality of opportunity.

We now return to the question posed at the end of Chapter 2 : how far have these intentions been realized?

Achievement in Further Education

There is much to be proud of. Authorities and voluntary bodies are as active as ever. There are able teachers and plenty of keen students. A great deal of change is going on. Features often admired by overseas observers as characteristic of British education have continued or even grown : such as the absence of government dictation of curricula, syllabuses, classroom methods or textbooks; the widespread use, for examining purposes, of internal marking externally assessed, with course work as well as written papers taken into account; the possibility of transfer between courses; and the action of Further Education in reclaiming overflows from other sectors of education.

A great deal has been achieved. The number of daytime students in 1963–4 was treble that of 1946–7. Of students working for recognized qualifications the proportion attending by evenings only has been more than halved from the pre-war three-quarters to less than three-eighths. Many good developments have been described in earlier chapters. New types of college, course and qualification have been evolved. There has been an immense amount of new building and new building design, aided by combination among some authorities to rationalize their dealings with contractors so as to take full advantage of new techniques. In some matters— as perhaps the rate of growth of sandwich release, or new kinds of activity in Adult Education—achievement may have exceeded intention.

After delays between 1951 and 1956, one sector in particular—technological education—made a great advance. The UK output of qualified scientists and engineers grew from 10,300 in 1955 to 16,530 in 1961, of which the college share rose from 1,300 to 7,600. Of the 1961 output of engineers the colleges produced two-thirds, mostly through the HNC. The official target of 20,000 scientists and engineers was expected to be reached well before 1970, with colleges and universities contributing about equally. Of the college share, many more will have used full-time and sandwich courses than in the past. In fact by 1962 the output of qualified scientists and engineers had about quadrupled since the end of the war.

In some sectors there have been important spurts quite recently. Integration between further and secondary education received a new impetus in 1959. After standing still at the back of the queue since the end of the war the Youth Service moved forward in 1960. Research into Further Education, though still small-scale and scattered, has grown markedly since about the same time. A $2\frac{1}{2}$-times expansion of higher education during eighteen years has been started. Machinery is at last being established for the radical reform of industrial training, which has been returned to government control for the first time (in peace time) since the repeal of the Elizabethan statute in 1814. Thus the first half of the 1960s has seen more growth than any comparable period.

These achievements, however, must not blind us to the bad things. There are other sectors which have not shown comparable growth. The earlier increase in day release was not maintained (despite warnings); in consequence the education of operatives, craftsmen and technicians has been hampered, and commercial education severely handicapped, by lack of time. Indeed, commercial education has lagged behind in many ways; for example, there was no Hives-type award until the CNAA came to the rescue. Art education has been subject to actual cuts, and only 2,250 advanced places were approved for 1965–6 in England and Wales. Adult Education has been a victim of fluctuation in government policy and has grown only slightly, particularly on its recreational side. What further education there is for the disabled and handicapped has been brought about very much by private effort. Compulsory day attendance for the under-eighteens, or even release on demand, seem as far off as ever; therefore the system has developed differently from what was intended, and the opportunity of the county college as originally conceived has been lost. The raising of the school-leaving age is to be delayed until 1970. Facilities for training teachers in further education are scarce. The examinations system remains chaotic.

Release from employment is a key factor. In England it has shown three phases of evolution. The general arguments for *day* release were developed from the 1909 Report to the 1943 White Paper; and this form of release began to show substantial development from 1945. Then the Percy Report, perhaps inspired by Scottish experience, popularized the idea of *sandwich* release, and for technologists this form began to grow rapidly after 1956. Then the Crowther Report proposed *block* and *sandwich* release not only for technologists but for all advanced and technician students not already studying full-time, with at least day release for the rest; and the Industrial Training Act has made it possible to impose these forms for all training for skill. The Crowther proposals are far from realization at present, however. Release for courses in commerce has not even completed the first of these three phases.

Scotland has led England and Wales in aspects of higher education. It has pioneered, for example, with Central Institutions, college awards, sandwich courses, full-time pre-employment courses, co-ordination between colleges and universities and co-operation of colleges with industry. It has used central control more : in examinations, for instance. But it has lagged behind in day release, vocational provision by authorities and state aid for Adult Education. Wales has lagged in advanced technology, and in much else too.

Thus only a part of one of the four major sectors has shown substantial development. And even there, full-time and sandwich courses did not arrive until so late that in 1962–3 half the nation's newly qualified technologists (not to mention nearly all its trained commercial personnel, technicians, craftsmen and operatives) were still coming up by the part-time route. Partly because of lack of time, courses for these groups have generally remained narrowly vocational in content.

The official manpower targets of technologists, too, have been considered too low by some, while the assumptions and methods underlying

TABLE 25

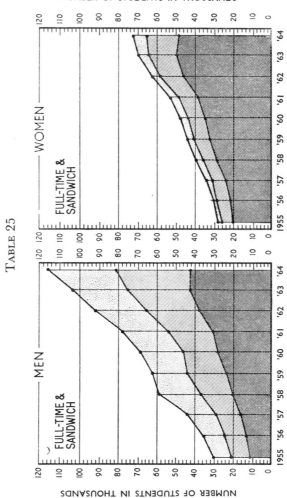

NUMBER OF STUDENTS IN THOUSANDS

TABLE 25 (continued)

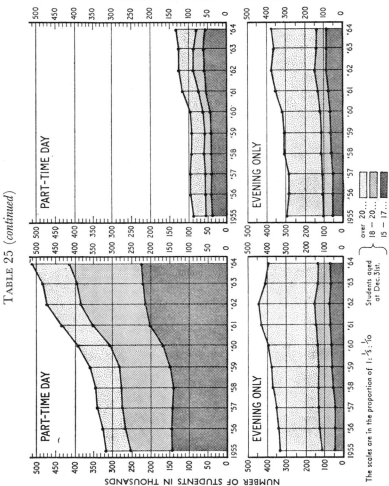

NUMBER OF STUDENTS IN THOUSANDS

PART-TIME DAY

EVENING ONLY

PART-TIME DAY

EVENING ONLY

NUMBER OF STUDENTS IN THOUSANDS

over 20....
18 – 20....
15 – 17....

Students aged at Dec. 31st.

The scales are in the proportion of $1 : \frac{1}{3} : \frac{1}{10}$

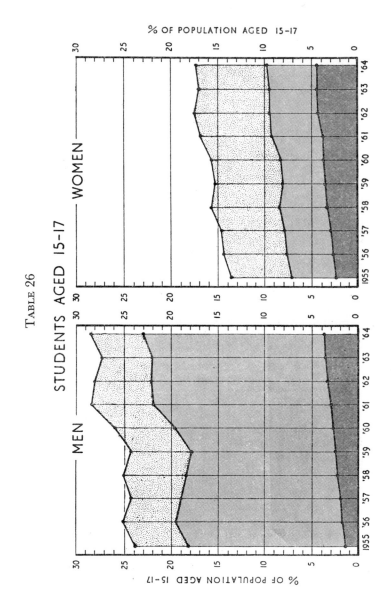

TABLE 26

STUDENTS AGED 15-17

% OF POPULATION AGED 15-17

WOMEN

MEN

% OF POPULATION AGED 15-17

TABLE 26 *(continued)*

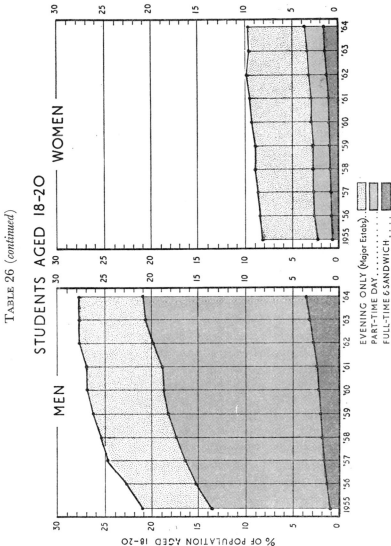

them have been disputed. The Committee on Scientific Manpower itself thought in 1962 that it had underestimated demand in the past, that there would be a shortage of mathematicians and electrical engineers by 1965 and that long-term supply was still far from balancing demand. And there is still no unified national manpower policy including technologists, technicians and craftsmen. With the output of scientists and technologists twice doubled yet still as scarce, one is reminded of what the Red Queen said to Alice : "A slow sort of country ! It takes all the running you can do to keep in the same place. If you want to get somewhere else, you must run at least twice as fast as that !"

Thus development has been uneven. Overall, the Schemes and Plans of authorities and recommendations of councils and committees remain only partially fulfilled.

Features of tertiary education as a whole

To assess its more general features we must look at Further Education as a part of the whole provision for school leavers. This general pattern is admired by overseas critics for the high proportions of higher-education students who are aided out of public funds and of entrants to full-time advanced courses who satisfactorily complete them. But it also retains three notable, older, interconnected features : it is scarce, piecemeal and inegalitarian.

SCARCITY is shown by the fact that in England and Wales in 1964–5, nearly half[1] of the population aged fifteen and over, but under nineteen, got no organized education at all. Only four in every ten sixteen-year-olds got any kind of *daytime* education (Table 14). According to the Robbins Report the proportion of the appropriate age groups entering full-time advanced courses in 1962 was $8\frac{1}{2}$ per cent, which, though difficult to compare with precision, is certainly lower than in USA, Canada, Australia or some European countries; and the rate of increase is much lower than in USSR. There is intense competition for places in higher-education establishments, apprenticeships, employment carrying release, and in some areas, even for jobs at all.

In higher education the Government lost valuable time during the 1950s and early 1960s. As a result it failed to take full advantage of the bulge in the population who became eighteen in 1965. After the Robbins Report in 1963 it tried to atone by raising its target of higher-education places to the figure therein recommended, which meant bringing forward the 1973–4 target to 1967–8; but this rate of growth turned out to be lower than the universities, given the funds, would have been willing to undertake of their

---

[1] Thirteen out of every thirty-one.

own accord; and many regarded it as too little and too late. Even if the Robbins Committee's 1980 target is attained Great Britain will yet send a lower proportion of its population into full-time higher education in 1980 than Canada or Sweden are expected to do during the 1960s; and it will be no easier to get into a British university than it was in 1955. Moreover, the grants made available in September 1964 (and confirmed by the new Labour Government) cast doubt on whether even the 1967–8 targets would be reached.

For the *part-time* student, left out of account in these calculations, the attitude of professional bodies is all-important. Most of these associations are by tradition exclusive, and their preoccupation with standards of admission, necessary enough in itself, can reinforce restrictive policies. At non-advanced levels the part-time student relies greatly on apprenticeship in its various forms, but youth employment officers report the existence of many more suitable candidates than vacancies for them.

All these scarcities exert pressure on one another, besides having very bad effects on secondary and primary education.

HETEROGENEITY lies in the fact that, although there is a considerable overlap in the functions of their different types, establishments vary widely in respect of wealth, social status, mode of governance, degree of autonomy, facilities for advanced study and research, qualifications offered and general richness of provision. For the most part they are rigidly separate, with little overall co-ordination.

The content of higher education, too, is usually specialized and narrow, whether directly vocational or not. Apart from a few notable exceptions (such as at the University of Keele) little deliberate attempt has been made to link studies deeply together by using a consistent general approach or theory; and for the most part "liberal studies", where they have been introduced, have operated merely as an added rather than transforming agent.

INEQUALITY applies in respect of class, sex, age and place. The spectrum of establishments, from Cambridge and Oxford at one end to evening classes for those unable to get day release at the other, contains a distribution of students which closely follows a social-class pattern. Some of this is due to the existence of private fee-paying routes through the system. Even within the publicly provided majority fraction, however, working-class children tend to do progressively worse than their middle-class contemporaries as they pass through. A result is that pupils are gradually sorted into streams which broadly correspond with their class origin. For example, putting together results given in the 1951 Census, in *Early Leaving* (1954) and by Kelsall (1957), it has been shown that in England during the 1950s children of manual workers formed more than *three-quarters* of the general child population, *two-thirds* of the most able entrants to maintained grammar schools, *half* of the most successful pupils therein, and *one-third* of those who passed into universities. The decline was more marked among girls than boys. Only 9 per cent of entrants to Cambridge were children of manual workers. Much similar recent research (such as that reported in Volume II of the Crowther Report, for example) has shown in more detail the close connection between academic and social inequality; and this has been found in Further Education as in other stages. All forms of educational wastage tend to increase as the social-class hierarchy is "descended". Educational establishments have become spread out into a similar hierarchy, which is therefore as much social as intellectual. And although it is commonly believed that such social-class inequalities are decreasing, the Robbins Committee's investigators found no evidence to show that the manual worker's child's relative chances of getting a higher education had increased during the preceding three decades. Indeed, they may even have fallen. Thus selection by success within the class-structured system helps to reinforce the class structure.

Girls have slimmer chances of getting higher education than boys have. Although outnumbering men by 2 to 1 in colleges of education they contribute only one-quarter of university students and one-fifth of full-time and sandwich students aged over eighteen in technical, commercial and art colleges. In the aggregate of higher-education entrants they are in a minority of about 1 in 4. Their chances of apprenticeship, release and so on are also much smaller than those of boys.

Opportunities also fall off markedly as people get older, so that the chance to try again or change occupation tends to fade away. Older people cannot get apprenticeships, even if they could live on the pay and lose pension rights; and it is much harder for them to get release. Only up to thirty state scholarships for mature people can be awarded each year, a number which has not been increased since 1950; and they are given only for "liberal" studies in universities. There were only 390 students in the 5 long-term residential colleges of Adult Education in 1964–5, and it has been estimated that over one-quarter of authorities do not assist students to attend them; yet in 1961–2 Ruskin College had 400 applications for 70 places. The education system is particularly unsuited to the needs of older women. Thus people are enslaved by their place in an age and occupational pattern from which few escape.

Chances vary, too, as between Wales, England and Scotland; between northern and southern England; and between rural, urban and metropolitan types of area.

Imperfect achievement overall

All this must add up to a prodigal waste of ability. It can only mean that the aims of abundance, cohesion and parity in education remain unrealized. Everyone in Britain does *not* have the opportunity to develop his or her talents to the full.

Of course it is questionable whether such aims can ever be realized in any absolute sense. A relativist approach is the only useful one. What is important is : have we done as well as we intended? And if not, why not? These questions take us into a controversial field, where judgements are bound to be somewhat speculative; but they cannot be shirked if an assessment, however tentative, is to be attempted.

The post-war background

An impetus lost

In 1943–1947 there was determination to build a better Britain after the war. The continuance of goodwill between the allied nations and of centralized planning based on public power seemed natural conditions for this renascence. Ministers had already been given controlling powers during the war; and early reports had urged the strengthening of local authorities also. These intentions were given explicit political direction by the general election of 1945, after which sections of industry were taken into public ownership.

In Further Education a good start was made. The Percy Committee had already been appointed and the 1944 Act had become law before the end of the war in Europe. Two years later came the County Colleges Order, the first instalment of the raising of the school-leaving age and the beginning of the authorities' work on their Schemes. The Government set up NACEIC in 1948 and accepted its recommendations for technological awards in 1951. There was a marked growth of day release at this time, too. Unfortunately, however (as mentioned in Chapter 2), the Government blundered in school education by recommending tripartitism and by discouraging all external examinations other than the eleven-plus and GCE. At first it even recommended a reduced intake into selective schools. Thus the middle- and upper-class domination of the channels to higher education was retained. The opportunity of opening up *then* a far broader road to higher education was lost, and incalculable harm was done to future manpower resources.

Then 1947 saw the onset of the "cold war". The build-up of military forces and weapons began to take precedence once more over social reconstruction. Centralized planning began to acquire a "totalitarian" flavour and to be regarded as unsuitable to "free" countries. Nationalization came to an end with four-fifths of the nation's capital resources, including land and the building and building-materials industries (except steel), still in private hands; and industrial training, on which depended the supply of all-important skilled labour, was left to a class-divided industry. Zeal for social reform began to fade and the impetus of the early years was lost.

It was not regained during the 1950s and 1960s. Industrial production actually fell in 1951–2 and again from 1955; there were nasty recessions in 1957–8 and 1963; and according to Colin Clark the annual rate of increase between 1954 and 1963 averaged only 1·3 per cent. By the end of 1964 the balance of overseas payments showed a deficit of £700–800 million, and the public services were always short of money; yet spending on defence had risen to £2,200 million a year and overseas military expenditure was running at £350 million a year.

Some consequences affecting education

A few examples must suffice to suggest how such a politico-economic environment can affect Further Education.

LACK OF ACCOMMODATION, a major obstacle to expansion, has obvious economic roots. Supply of buildings depends on four factors : (a) the overall capacity of the building and building-materials industries; (b) the share thereof obtained by public bodies as customers; (c) the proportion of this share allotted to education; and (d) the pattern of priorities within educational policy. As explained in Chapter 3, (c) and (d) are tightly regulated by the government, and some sectors of Further Education have done relatively well. But the limits have been set by (a) and (b), and these are subject to uncontrolled economic factors. In fact the supply of buildings has lagged far behind demand. The nation's efforts have been like trying to multiply buildings without the power to multiply the capacity to put them up. Rising prices and interest rates have added to the difficulties, particularly of authorities. In particular the high price of land plus loopholes and delays in the compulsory-purchase machinery have defeated the intentions of the Scott, Uthwatt and Cleary Committees that authorities should have real power to acquire quickly the sites they needed.

SCARCITY OF APPRENTICESHIPS has been in the nature of things too. Trade unions must maintain their bargaining power and protect their members from redundancy, whilst employers must keep down costs in order to remain competitive and accumulate capital for modernization. Even during a boom period each must keep in mind the next slump, or the possibility of government measures to curb credit or spending. Thus a heavy engagement of apprentices carries risks for both sides. Since there has been an endemic shortage of skilled workers since the war, recruitment figures based on existing employment have merely perpetuated scarcity. However, according to Gertrude Williams, unions have usually been willing to waive agreed limits; but more often employers, particularly the smaller ones, have kept down the intake. In 1960 the Minister of Labour complained that employers were not making enough use of government courses for apprentices either, and he also found the increase of group apprenticeship schemes disappointing. In commerce and agriculture employers have never given apprenticeship very much support. Fears have been expressed that even advanced technological education might be limited by a scarcity of training places in industry, especially for college-based students. As already mentioned (as in Chapter 5), many other features of the apprenticeship system have also been severely criticized. Without apprenticeship, however, there has been for many workers no guarantee of training at all. Thus the Industrial Training Act can only be called belated. Whether the Minister of Labour will use ruthlessly the new system still remains to be seen, for his powers are only permissive. Those of the boards are only financial. There is a danger that industrial training may still be left too much to the same people who have made such a mess of it hitherto.

SHORTAGE OF TIME FOR STUDY is a consequence of its reliance on conditions of employment. Not only is release too scarce for younger people, but more than one-third of all students aged twenty-one and over attending part-time day courses in 1962–3 were doing so in their own time. The percentages both of school leavers entering apprenticeships and of workers aged under eighteen released by their employers actually declined after the Crowther Report (Tables 9 and 13). Yet in 1962 the Government decided not to make day release a right of young employees because the demand might be too great. Moreover, day release itself is now regarded as inadequate for skilled trainees. Even for the new postgraduate scheme in management studies UKACEM was disappointed at the response of employers in granting release.

UNEMPLOYMENT among young people, bugbear of an unplanned economy, has returned. "The education system cannot be blamed", said the Crowther Report, "for failing to provide courses which could not, under present circumstances, be profitably used." The *fear* of unemployment or underemployment is at the root of many kinds of restrictive practice. The problem of finding jobs for handicapped people is exacerbated by it. Firms show little disposition to retrain older workers whose skills have become redundant; pay scales at government centres are low; and economic fears influence the attitude of trade unions to other aspects of retraining. There is no planned redeployment, with accompanying re-education and re-housing programmes.

An explosion of demand

However, the progress that has been made is real enough. As a proportion of the UK gross national product, educational expenditure rose from 2·3 per cent in 1946 to 4·9 in 1963 and is expected to go on rising. In real terms total current and capital outlay from public funds on education and higher education in UK multiplied 2·7 times between 1952 and 1962, and there has been an undoubted spurt since about 1960. Much thought has been given to making the best use of available investment.

The chief reason for this growth is, of course, the unparalleled explosion of demand for education. Technological advance, international competition, the pressure of the underprivileged, the increase of social mobility and the rising birth rate have all played a part in creating it. What educational advance could have been achieved in a more favourable economic and ideological environment can only be imagined.

Thinking about the future, 1954–1964

By non-political bodies

For the UNDER-NINETEENS the Crowther Report must still be the basis of most current proposals. Real reforms, its authors believed, could come only as a coherent, properly phased development programme, extending by timed and calculated steps a long way into the future. In a similar vein its Welsh sister, the third Oldfield-Davies Report, suggested public control of apprentice training exercised through the education service. In Scotland the Oakley Report proposed compulsory registration of skilled employees under eighteen. Earlier the Ashby Report had advocated a national advisory council on Adult Education, and the Wolfenden Report a development council for sport. The first Albermarle Report urged a ten-year plan for the Youth Service. These proposals have all been mentioned in earlier chapters. Their general tenor is clear.

Provision for the OVER-SEVENTEENS is inseparable from the broader field of higher education, in which the Robbins Report is still influential, despite the Labour Government's departures from it. The Robbins proposals were based on the following principles : that a highly educated population is a national necessity; that higher education should be available to anyone qualified and wishing to pursue it; that there should be equal awards for equal performance, irrespective of the status of institutions; that provision should be in an ordered system; that institutions should be encouraged to develop as freely as would be consistent with this ordered system; that institutions performing similar functions should suffer similar limitations; and that academic standards and freedom should be safeguarded. These principles can be traced, too, in evidence given to the Robbins Committee by many organizations. The Committee suggested increasing the number of full-time and sandwich students taking advanced courses in UK from

216,000 in 1962–3 to at least 560,000 by 1980–1, without lowering standards or lengthening courses. This would double the proportion of the appropriate age groups entering higher education and would treble the cost. The Committee ridiculed the theory that expansion would be limited by a fixed "pool of ability"; but did not take account of possible changes in secondary education, such as the growth of comprehensive schools, which might raise the demand even more.

Unification of the system and the breakdown of hierarchic divisions was another theme in the evidence to the Robbins Committee. In similar vein the Committee itself recommended against creating new types of institution, preferring where possible to develop existing ones. Thus, although 6 wholly new university foundations were proposed, 23 more were to be evolved from existing establishments, making some 60 altogether; and this would include 5 special technological institutions called SISTERs (or giant CATs—*sabre-tooths?*). Degrees were to be available in non-university establishments through the CNAA.

The Committee also recommended forward planning over ten-year periods and advised authorities to budget for three years ahead instead of one; but it did not advocate a national manpower policy.

For EDUCATIONAL RESEARCH the Parliamentary and Scientific Committee proposed a new research council which would conduct, in a series of three-year plans, studies designed to provide an objective basis for the far-reaching decisions of the decade; and the Heyworth Committee broadened this to include all the social sciences.

Covering the WHOLE FIELD, the 1963 Campaign for Education, a loose association of 68 voluntary organizations, did not succeed in its aim of getting the Government to make a definite promise in 1963 to implement the rest of the 1944 Act; but it is continuing its efforts as a more permanent Council for Educational Advance (CEA), and there is a Scottish CEA (SCEA) too. In many localities parents and others have formed Associations for the Advancement of State Education (AASE), 120 of which are affiliated to a national Confederation (CASE).

By political parties before the 1964 general election

Bodies like those mentioned did not pose the question of whether such developments would be possible without accompanying political and economic changes. Such matters were left to political parties. The latter either expressed definite policies or set up committees to submit documents for discussion.

The Conservative Party (which had been in power since 1951) promised a massive enlargement of educational opportunity at every level; but was opposed to direct planning by the government, preferring the use of monetary measures to maintain a balance. The Conservative Government had, of course, brought in the Industrial Training Act and had accepted the basic principles of the Robbins Report, each of which contained a measure of government control by financial pressures mainly.

The Smyth Committee of Conservative MPs found the Conservative Government's educational record impressive and thought that education already enjoyed a high priority among national investments. It did not agree with the Crowther Report's emphasis on centralized planning but would rather the government retained "the power of manoeuvre". It thought that day release should be given as a right to young workers who asked for it, but not made compulsory on all.

On the other hand the Liberal and Labour Parties (in opposition to the Conservatives) proposed advancing the priority of education beyond its position in 1964. The Liberals, advised by their Pattison Committee, wanted a ten-year programme, implemented through firmer use of their powers by the Secretaries of State.

The Labour Party's Taylor Committee on higher education recommended a five-year crash programme of emergency measures, to start simultaneously with a full ten-year plan. It estimated that 80 universities would be needed within the next twenty years, of which about 45 would be new.

In similar vein the Communist Party (which, however, had no Parliamentary representation) advocated an integrated single (not dual) system of higher-education institutions of equal status, financed and planned by a national commission aided by regional commissions.

These three parties also urged the early introduction of compulsory day release, with a *right* to release established *interim*. Labour and Communist favoured the restoration of the percentage-grant system and the total abolition of fees. Thus there was a wide measure of agreement between these three.

Where they mainly differed was in the parallel political and economic changes considered necessary. Labour and Communist Parties believed that planned educational expansion on the scale required would be impossible without planned economic expansion; and both supported public ownership of industry as a means to this. The Labour Party, however, did not propose any very far-reaching measures in that direction. It said that it would re-nationalize steel, set up a commission to buy land, bring down interest rates and be ready to reimpose building controls; but nationalization of the other building industries was turned down at its 1963 Conference. The Liberal and Labour Parties did not say much about how they would find the money for the vast expenditure involved; the Taylor Committee thought that economic expansion would be enough to cope. On the other hand the Communist Party wanted nationalization of key industries and most urban land, heavy cuts in arms expenditure and the ending of costly NATO and other military policies.

Plaid Cymru (Welsh Nationalist Party) wanted self-government for Wales, with membership of UNO, and a separate educational system. It would strengthen scientific, technological and management education, set up a CAT in north Wales, give both languages equal use and status, and make generous grants towards the arts and industrial training. It would spend money on such measures instead of on nuclear weapons. It did not greatly commit itself on domestic economic matters.

Tasks of the new Government

Promises

Thus education figured prominently in the 1964 general election. And so the responsibility of carrying out its pledges now rests with the Labour Government. In its election manifesto the Labour Party promised to work out "a phased and costed plan for the whole of education". To assure the funds, it would restore the percentage-grant system and increase the share to be borne by the central government. It would develop new techniques for forecasting manpower needs. It said that in many firms, technicians and technologists were being held back by "the social prejudices and anti-scientific bias of the old boy network". Therefore it would combine educational reforms with a "revolution" in industrial training. All employees would get a "Charter of Rights": including rights to compensation for loss of job (caused, for example, by technological advance), to "first-rate" industrial training, to day and block release for the young worker, to re-training for adult workers and to full transferability of pension entitlements (during retraining, for example, or change of job). Labour would also carry out a programme of "massive expansion" in higher and further education. It would "end parsimony in the supply of public funds" for outdoor recreation; develop the national parks; protect the coast from pollution and unplanned development; set up a Sports Council to consult with authorities and voluntary bodies and to supply equipment and facilities; develop the Youth Service; "give much more generous support" to the Arts Council, the theatre and so on; and help independent film makers. It would also promote wider educational, cultural, scientific and technical contacts within the Commonwealth, and create more opportunities for overseas voluntary service. "Immigration control", however, would be retained.

A notable omission was any clear promise to bring in compulsory day release and county colleges. The manifesto merely said: "As the first step to part-time education for the first two years after leaving school, Labour will extend compulsory day and block release". But the meaning of this is not clear, since one cannot extend what does not exist. Thus only the "right" of young workers to day and block release is definitely promised as yet; and there must be doubts as to how far this is a practicable idea.

Other notable omissions were any proposal to abolish the parental contribution to students receiving grants from authorities, or to reorganize local government for it to cope better with the expansion of maintained higher education, or to strengthen the powers of the Minister of Labour or industrial training boards.

Actions

A number of new bodies have been formed. These include : ministries (Technology, Land and Natural Resources, Wales, Overseas Development); research councils (NERC, SSRC); Parliamentary undersecretaryships at the DES (one for the arts and another for sport); and advisory councils (the Sports Councils and Council for Curriculum Renewal and Educational Development Overseas). The Minister of Labour has told industrial training boards that he will not approve their schemes unless they insist on day release for all trainees who need a substantial period of training. In the arts, good intentions were expressed in a White Paper which approved of

the growing revolt, especially among the young, against the darkness, uniformity and joylessness of much of the social furniture we have inherited from the industrial revolution. This can be directed, if we so wish, into making Britain a gayer and more cultivated country.

However, there are a number of disquieting features of the Government's policies at the time of writing. *The National Plan* announced an intended increase of 32 per cent in total real public spending on education during the five years from 1964–5 to 1969–70. But, as mentioned earlier, between 1952 and 1962 this spending multiplied 2·7 times. Therefore the announcement meant that there would be substantial reduction in the rate of growth of educational expenditure.

Looking at the rates of increase intended for particular sectors we see that Further Education got the highest, 58 per cent, compared with 55 for teacher training, 33 for universities and 27 for the schools. The annual rate of capital expenditure for Further Education was to be doubled. The number of students in Further Education was expected to increase by about one-third, of whom full-time and sandwich students doing advanced courses would go up from 40,000 to 70,000, a greater expansion than that proposed in the Robbins Report. However, *The National Plan* was never really a plan, but only hopes.

Recent Government moves in higher education have aroused alarm.

The dual system of universities and colleges has been given permanent form. Thus no more colleges or Central Institutions are to be made into universities before 1973, though the Robbins Committee recommended up to ten; and the merging of Coventry's Regional College with the new university was not allowed. Instead, the maintained colleges have been promised that a few of them will be chosen for parity of esteem with universities, while retaining their own characteristics under authorities. But the money for this has not been promised; and, indeed, so much would be needed to put 25 Regional and perhaps another 5 Area Colleges on to a genuine par with modern universities (with comparable research, residential and social facilities) that it is impossible to take the policy seriously. Thus the only thing that the Regional and Area Colleges have certainly got from the Robbins Report is the CNAA.

An actual postponement of new building for half a year was announced in Parliament on 27th July 1965 and in Circular 12/65. This did not augur well for the future; and the Minister of State's proposal at the NUS conference in October 1965 to reintroduce loans instead of grants to students provoked a furore of anger.

The need for social purpose and perspective

The importance of the economic and political environment has been stressed. Whether even the modest programme of the 1964 and 1966 elections is to be attained, therefore, will depend on the Government's policies in a wider field. This poses again, as in Chapter 2, the need for some sort of theory or strategy of social advance. This has been conspicuously absent from the policies of all post-war governments and is absent now from the so-called *National Plan*. Such a theory, however rough, would surely render us less vulnerable to prejudices and pressures. It would surely help us to approach our problems and learn from our mistakes more objectively and radically than hitherto.

Society is changing, whether we like it or not. Changes in our *natural* environment are being brought under control in so far as the growth of scientific attitudes and knowledge enables people to agree about what to do. The next task is to bring *social* changes under similar human control.

Notes on further study

Critical reviews of technical education were: Venables and others: *Technical Education* . . . (1955); Cotgrove: *Technical Education and Social Change* (1958); Payne: *Britain's Scientific and Technological Manpower* (1960); and Argles: *South Kensington to Robbins* (1964). For access to higher education, see Lauwerys's article in UNESCO's *International Study of University Admissions* (1965). The Crowther and Robbins Reports contained much general material.

On educational wastage and its social-class roots (which has been studied mostly at secondary level hitherto) see especially : Lindsay : *Social Progress and Educational Waste* (1926); Hogben (editor) : *Political Arithmetic* (1938); SCRE : *Social Implications of the 1947 Scottish Mental Survey* (1953); Simon : *Intelligence Testing and the Comprehensive School* (1953); Central Advisory Council for Education (England) : *Early Leaving* (1954); Glass (editor) : *Social Mobility in Britain* (1954); Floud, Halsey and Martin : *Social Class and Educational Opportunity* (1957); Kelsall : *Report on an Inquiry into Applications for Admission to Universities* (1957); Marsh : *The Changing Social Structure of England and Wales 1871–1951* (1958); Vaizey : *The Costs of Education* (1958); Furneaux : *The Chosen Few* (1961); Jackson and Marsden : *Education and the Working Class* (1962); Peers : *Fact and Possibility in English Education* (1963); Douglas : *The Home and the School* (1964); the Crowther Report (especially Volume II); the Newsom Report; the Robbins Report (especially Appendices One and Four); and the Minister's *Statistics of Education, 1961, Supplement to Part 2* (1963). Work by Scott, Nisbet, Bernstein, Ethel Venables, Douglas and others was discussed by Bernstein in : Halsey and others (editors) : *Education, Economy and Society* (1961) and in Appendix One of the Robbins Report. See also Floud and Halsey : *The Sociology of Education : a trend report and bibliography* (1958).

The following is a sample of reports representing pre-Robbins thinking about tertiary and higher education among important non-party circles of educational opinion : AAI : *Written Evidence Prepared for the Committee on Higher Education* (1961); AScW : *Science and Education* (1960); ATTI : *Future of Higher Education* (1962); AUT : *Submissions to the Committee on Higher Education* (1961); BACIE : *The Spectrum of Higher Education* (1962); EIS : *Observations to be submitted to the Committee on Higher Education* (1961); Fabian Society : *The Structure of Higher Education* (1961); FBI : *Higher Education—Evidence to the Government Committee* (1961); 1963 Campaign for Education : *A Manifesto* (1963); NUS : *Memorandum to the Committee on Higher Education* (1961) and *Interim Report on Adult Students* (n.d.); TUC : *Memorandum of Evidence* (in *Annual Report* for 1962); and WEA : *Memorandum of Evidence to Committee on Higher Education* (n.d.). See also the 1963 Campaign for Education's *The Case for Advance* (1963).

The Robbins Report followed, to which the then Government's response was the White Paper *Higher Education* (1963). The ATTI commented in *Is Robbins Enough?* (1964) and *The Future of Higher Education within the Further Education System* (1965).

Of political programmes before the 1964 general election see : Conservative and Unionist Association : *The Next Five Years* (1959); Committee of Conservative MPs : *The Rising Tide* (Smyth Report, 1961); Liberal Party : *Education* (Pattison Report, 1962); Peterson : *Investment in People: a Liberal Design for Education* (1962); Labour Party : *Signposts for the Sixties* (1961); Labour Party's Study Group : *The Years of Crisis* (Taylor Report, 1963); Communist Party : *Higher Education in the Nuclear Age* (1959) and *The Development of Higher Education in Britain* (1961); and Plaid Cymru : *Plan for a New Wales* (n.d.).

Then there were also the manifestoes prepared by the parties for the elections themselves. Labour's was *Let's Go With Labour for the New Britain* (1964).

Among the new Government's White Papers were *A Policy for the Arts* (1965) and *Immigration from the Commonwealth* (1965). Its policy for a dual system of higher education was explained by the Secretary of State for Education and Science in the House of Commons on 25th March 1965 and again at Woolwich Polytechnic on 27th April 1965. The latter speech was circulated with Administrative Memorandum 7/65. The policy was further expounded in another White Paper *A Plan for Polytechnics and Other Colleges* (1966).

For the more general policies see *The National Plan* (1965) and the DES's *Reports on Education*, No. 25 (1965). It is not yet clear how much of *The National Plan* has been officially abandoned or postponed.

APPENDIX 1

GLOSSARY OF ABBREVIATIONS USED IN THIS BOOK

A	advanced level (of the GCE).
A1, A2	a level comparable with the first and second years above an ONC or OND.
AACP	Anglo-American Council on Productivity.
AAI	Association of Art Institutions.
AAM	Association of Assistant Mistresses in Secondary Schools.
AASE	Association for the Advancement of State Education.
ABCC	Association of British Chambers of Commerce.
ACE	Advisory Centre for Education.
ACSP	Advisory Council on Scientific Policy [*now CSP*].
ACU	Association of Commonwealth Universities.
AEB	Associated Examining Board.
AEC	Association of Education Committees.
APTI	Association of Principals of Technical Institutions.
ARC	Agricultural Research Council.
ARCA	Associate of the Royal College of Art.
ARIBA	Associate of the Royal Institute of British Architects.
AScW	Association of Scientific Workers.
ASE	Association of Science Education.
ASLIB	Association of Special Libraries and Information Bureaux.
ATC	Art Teacher's Certificate.
ATCDE	Association of Teachers in Colleges and Departments of Education.
ATD	Art Teacher's Diploma.
ATI	Association of Technical Institutions.
ATTI	Association of Teachers in Technical Institutions.
AUBC	Association of Universities of the British Commonwealth [*now ACU*].
AUT	Association of University Teachers.
AUT(S)	Association of University Teachers (Scotland).
BA	Bachelor of Arts.
BACIE	British Association for Commercial and Industrial Education.
BBC	British Broadcasting Corporation.
BC	British Council.
BCC	British Council of Churches.
BCRD	British Council for Rehabilitation of the Disabled.
BCWS	British Council for the Welfare of Spastics. [*now SS*].
BEC	British Employers' Confederation [*now CBI*].
B.Eng.	Bachelor of Engineering.
BFUW	British Federation of University Women Ltd.
BIM	British Institute of Management.
BISF	British Iron and Steel Federation.
B.Pharm.	Bachelor of Pharmacy.
BPsS	British Psychological Society.
B.Sc.	Bachelor of Science.

297

B.Sc.(Econ.)	Bachelor of Science (Economics).
BSI	British Standards Institution.
C., Cd., Cmd., Cmnd.	Command paper.
C1, C2 (etc.)	the first two years (etc.) of a craft course.
CACE	Central Advisory Council for Education.
CASE	Confederation for the Advancement of State Education.
CAT	college of advanced technology.
CBI	Confederation of British Industry.
CCCC	Central Council for the Care of Cripples.
CCPR	Central Council of Physical Recreation.
CDC	Colonial Development Corporation.
CDWS, CD & WS	Colonial Development and Welfare Scheme.
CEA	Council for Educational Advance.
CEC	programme for educational co-operation in the Commonwealth [also EEC].
CELC	Commonwealth Education Liaison Committee.
CELU	Commonwealth Education Liaison Unit.
CEO	chief education officer.
CGLI, C & GLI	City and Guilds of London Institute.
CIRF	International Vocational Training Information and Research Centre.
CLASP	Consortium of Local Authorities Special Programme.
CLAW	Consortium, Local Authorities, Wales.
CLEAPSE	Consortium of Local Education Authorities for the Purchasing of Scientific Equipment.
CMB	Consortium for Method Building.
CNAA	Council for National Academic Awards.
COI	Central Office of Information.
CoID	Council of Industrial Design.
CRAC	Careers Research and Advisory Centre.
CREDO	Council for Curriculum Renewal and Educational Development Overseas.
CSE	Certificate of Secondary Education.
CSFP	Commonwealth Scholarship and Fellowship Plan.
CSP	Council for Scientific Policy.
CTC	Central Training Council.
DA	Diploma in Art.
DAE	Diploma in Advanced Engineering.
DAFS	Department of Agriculture and Fisheries for Scotland.
DAuE	Diploma in Automobile Engineering.
DCAe	Diploma in Aeronautics [of the College of Aeronuatics].
DCSTS	Departmental Committee on the Supply of Teachers in Scotland.
DEO	divisional education officer.
DES	Department of Education and Science.
Des.RCA	Designer of the Royal College of Art.
Dip.AD	Diploma in Art and Design.
Dip.Tech.	Diploma in Technology.
Dip.Tech.(Eng.)	Diploma in Technology (Engineering).
DRSAM	Diploma of the Royal Scottish Academy of Music.
DSIR	Department of Scientific and Industrial Research.
DTC	Department of Technical Co-operation [now ODM].
EARACFE	East Anglian Regional Advisory Council for Further Education.
ECA	Educational Centres Association.
ECC	programme for educational co-operation in the Commonwealth.
EIGA	Engineering Industries Group Apprenticeship.
EIS	Educational Institute of Scotland.
EMEU	East Midland Educational Union.
ESN	educationally subnormal.

ETC	elementary technical course.
EUSEC	Conference of Engineering Societies of Western Europe and the United States of America.
FAMA	Foundation for Mutual Assistance in Africa South of the Sahara.
FAO	Food and Agriculture Organization [*of UNO*].
FBI	Federation of British Industries [*now CBI*].
FTC	full technological certificate.
G1, G2	the two years of a part-time general preliminary diagnostic course at a college.
G*	the one-year part-time general preliminary diagnostic course at a college.
GCE	General Certificate of Education.
GNC	General Nursing Council.
GRO	General Register Office (London); General Registry Office (Edinburgh).
GTC	government training centre.
H	higher grade (of the Scottish Leaving Certificate).
HM	Her Majesty's, His Majesty's.
HMI	Her Majesty's Inspector.
HMSI	Her Majesty's Staff Inspector.
HMSO	Her Majesty's Stationery Office.
HNC	Higher National Certificate.
HND	Higher National Diploma.
IAAM	Incorporated Association of Assistant Masters in Secondary Schools.
IAEA	International Atomic Energy Authority [*of UNO*].
IAU	International Association of Universities.
IBE	International Bureau of Education.
IEE	Institution of Electrical Engineers.
ILEA	Inner London Education Authority.
ILO	International Labour Organization [*of UNO*].
I Mech.E	Institution of Mechanical Engineers.
IMEnt.	Institute of Municipal Entertainment.
IMTA	Institute of Municipal Treasurers and Accountants.
I Prod. E	Institution of Production Engineers.
ITC	Industrial Training Council [*now CTC*].
ITS	Industrial Training Service.
IUC	Inter-University Council for Higher Education Overseas.
IWS	Industrial Welfare Society (Inc.).
IYEO	Institute of Youth Employment Officers.
J1, J2	before 1944, the two years of a course in a junior technical school preceding admission to a senior course in a college.
JMB	Northern Universities Joint Matriculation Board.
JTS	junior technical school.
KGJT	King George's Jubilee Trust.
LA	Library Association.
LASMEC	Local Authorities' School Meals Equipment Consortium.
LCC	London County Council.
LEA	local education authority.
LHCRACTE	London and Home Counties Regional Advisory Council for Technological Education [*formerly for Higher Technological Education*].
LRIC	Licentiate of the Royal Institute of Chemistry.
MCT	Member of the College of Technologists.
MP	Member of Parliament.
MRC	Medical Research Council.
NAAS	National Agricultural Advisory Service.
NABC	National Association of Boy's Clubs (Inc.).
NABE	National Association for Business Education.

NACAE	National Advisory Council on Art Education.
NACEIC	National Advisory Council on Education for Industry and Commerce.
NACTST	National Advisory Council on the Training and Supply of Teachers.
NALGO	National and Local Government Officers' Association.
NAMH	National Association for Mental Health (Inc.).
NAS	National Association of Schoolmasters.
NATO	North Atlantic Treaty Organisation.
NCA	National Certificate in Agriculture.
NCDAD	National Council for Diplomas in Art and Design [*Summerson Council*].
NCH	National Certificate in Horticulture.
NCSS	National Council of Social Service Inc.
NCSTO	National Council for the Supply of Teachers Overseas.
NCTA	National Council for Technological Awards [*Hives Council*].
NDA	National Diploma in Agriculture.
NDD	National Diploma in Dairying; National Diploma in Design.
NEDC	National Economic Development Council [*Neddy*].
NERC	Natural Environment Research Council.
NFCA	National Federation of Community Associations.
NFER	National Foundation for Educational Research in England and Wales.
NIAE	National Institute of Adult Education (England and Wales).
NID	National Institute for the Deaf [*now RNID*].
NIIP	National Institute of Industrial Psychology.
NJCBI	National Joint Council for the Building Industry.
NNEB	National Nursery Examination Board.
NUPE	National Union of Public Employees.
NUS	National Union of Students.
NUT	National Union of Teachers.
O	ordinary level (of the GCE); ordinary grade (of the Scottish Leaving Certificate).
O1, O2 (etc.)	the first two years (etc.) of an ONC course.
OD1, OD2 (etc.)	the first two years (etc.) of an OND course.
ODI	Overseas Development Institute Ltd.
ODM	Ministry of Overseas Development.
OECD	Organisation for Economic Co-operation and Development.
OEEC	Organisation for European Economic Co-operation [*now OECD*].
ONC	Ordinary National Certificate.
OND	Ordinary National Diploma.
ONWARD	Organisation of North Western Authorities for Rationalised Design.
Op. 1, Op. 2 (etc.)	the first two years (etc.) of an operatives' course.
OSAS	Overseas Service Aid Scheme.
OUDE	Oxford University Department of Education.
P1, P2 (etc.)	the first two years (etc.) of a preliminary course.
PCC	preliminary craft course.
PEP	Political and Economic Planning.
PNC	preliminary national course.
PSC	Parliamentary and Scientific Committee; pre-senior commercial.
PST	pre-senior technical.
PTC	preliminary technical course.
RACOFEEM	Regional Advisory Council for the Organization of Further Education in the East Midlands.
RASE	Royal Agricultural Society of England.
RIBA	Royal Institute of British Architects.
RIC	Royal Institute of Chemistry.
RNID	Royal National Institute for the Deaf.

RSA	Royal Society of Arts.
S1, S2 (etc.)	before 1961, the first two years (etc.) of a senior course; in Scotland, the classes in a secondary school.
SANCAD	Scottish Association for National Certificates and Diplomas.
SCAAP	Special Commonwealth African Assistance Plan.
SCCE	Scottish Council for Commercial Education; Schools Council for the Curriculum and Examinations.
SCCYCSS	Standing Consultative Council for Youth and Community Service in Scotland.
SCCYSS	Standing Consultative Council on Youth Service in Scotland [*now SCCYCSS*].
SCE	Scottish Certificate of Education.
SCEA	Scottish Council for Educational Advance.
SCNVYO	Standing Conference of National Voluntary Youth Organisations of England and Wales.
SCOLA	Second Consortium of Local Authorities.
SCRE	Scottish Council for Research in Education.
SCSS	Scottish Council of Social Service.
SCWVYO	Standing Conference for Wales of Voluntary Youth Organisations.
SDD	Scottish Development Department.
SEAC	South Eastern Architects' Collaboration.
SED	Scottish Education Department.
SIAE	Scottish Institute of Adult Education.
SIO	Scottish Information Office.
SISTER	Special Institution for Scientific and Technological Education and Research.
SRC	Science Research Council; student's representative council.
SRCFE	Southern Regional Council for Further Education.
SS	Spastics Society.
SSA	Scottish Schoolmasters' Association.
SSCVYO	Scottish Standing Conference of Voluntary Youth Organisations.
SSEC	Secondary School Examinations Council [*now SCCE*].
SSTA	Scottish Secondary Teachers' Association.
STECC	Scottish Technical Education Consultative Council.
SUS	Scottish Union of Students.
T1, T2 (etc.)	the first two years (etc.) of a technician course.
TAS	Training Advisory Service [*now ITS*].
TETOC	Council for Technical Education and Training for Overseas Countries.
TUC	Trades Union Congress.
TWI	training within industry.
UCAE	Universities Council for Adult Education.
UCCA	Universities Central Council on Admissions.
UEI	Union of Educational Institutions.
UGC	University Grants Committee.
UK	United Kingdom of Great Britain and Northern Ireland.
UKACEM	United Kingdom Advisory Council on Education for Management.
ULCI	Union of Lancashire and Cheshire Institutes.
UNESCO	United Nations Educational, Scientific and Cultural Organization [*of UNO*].
UNO	United Nations Organization.
USA	United States of America.
USSR	Union of Socialist Soviet Republics.
VOCOSS	Standing Conference of Voluntary Organisations Co-operating in Overseas Social Service.
WEA	Workers' Educational Association.
WFSW	World Federation of Scientific Workers.

x

WHO	World Health Organization [*of UNO*].
WUS	World University Service.
YCFE	Yorkshire Council for Further Education.
YEB	youth employment bureau.
YEO	youth employment officer.
YES	Youth Employment Service.
YFC	young farmers' club.
YMCA	Young Men's Christian Association.
YSDC	Youth Service Development Council.

APPENDIX 2

CLASSIFIED LIST OF WORKS
MENTIONED

Synopsis

Bibliographies, etc.

Command papers ("White Papers")

Statutes

Statutory instruments
  England and Wales
  Scotland

Circulars and administrative memoranda
  Circulars: England and Wales
  Administrative memoranda: England and Wales
  Circulars: Wales
  Circulars: Scotland
  Memoranda: Scotland

Other central-government publications
  Of education departments
    Booklets and pamphlets
    Books
    Building bulletins
    Lists
    Reports on education
    Statistical reports published separately
    Miscellaneous (leaflets, etc.)
  Of other departments

Publications of local education authorities

Reports of committees, etc.

Miscellaneous annual publications
  Reports of central government departments and committees
  Reports of other bodies
  Prospectuses, regulations, guides, etc.
  Yearbooks

Addresses at meetings

Other books and pamphlets

Articles

Subappendix. Committee reports known by chairman's name

Note: Except where otherwise stated: (a) items are arranged first in alphabetical order of
    authors, then by chronological order of publication; (b) the place of publication is
    London.

Bibliographies, etc.

ARGLES, O.M.V. *and* **VAUGHAN, J.E.** British government publications concerning education: an introductory guide. Liverpool, University of Liverpool Institute of Education, 1966.

ASSOCIATION OF SPECIAL LIBRARIES AND INFORMATION BUREAUX. *Index to theses accepted for higher degrees in the universities of Great Britain and Ireland.* Vol. 1–. [In progress.] ASLIB.

BARON, G. A bibliographical guide to the English educational system. University of London Press, 1965.

BENGE, R. C. Technical and vocational education in the United Kingdom: a bibliographical survey. *Educational studies and documents*, no 27. Paris, UNESCO, 1958.

BLACKWELL, A. M. A list of researches in education and educational psychology presented for higher degrees in the universities of the United Kingdom, Northern Ireland and the Irish Republic from 1918 to 1948. Newnes, for NFER, 1950.

Ibid. Second list . . . 1949, 1950 and 1951. Newnes, for NFER, 1952.

Ibid. Supplement I . . . 1952 and 1953. Newnes, for NFER, 1954.

Ibid. Supplement II . . . 1954 and 1955. Newnes, for NFER, 1956.

Ibid. Supplement III . . . 1956 and 1957. Newnes, for NFER, 1958.

BLAUG, M. A selected annotated bibliography in the economics of education. *Education libraries bulletin*, supplement 8, 1964.

Ibid. Economics of education; a selected annotated bibliography. Oxford, Pergamon Press, 1966.

BOARD, Beryl. The effect of technological progress on education: a classified bibliography from British sources, 1945–1957. I Prod.E, 1959.

BRITISH ASSOCIATION FOR COMMERCIAL AND INDUSTRIAL EDUCATION. Bibliography of publications in the field of education and training in commerce and industry. Supplement to *BACIE journal*. Monthly. *See* **Appendix 3.**

CHOYNOWSKI, M. The psychology of adolescence. *Education abstracts*, vol. 14, no. 4. Paris, UNESCO, 1963.

FLOUD, Jean *and* **HALSEY, A. H.** The sociology of education: a trend report and bibliography. *Current sociology*, vol. 7, no. 3, 1958, pp. 165–235.

HER MAJESTY'S STATIONERY OFFICE. *Catalogue of government publications . . . .* HMSO, annual.

Ibid. *Government publications: Ministry of Education sectional list no.* 2. [–1963.] HMSO, annual.

Ibid. *Government publications: Department of Education and Science sectional list no.* 2. [1964–.] HMSO, annual.

Ibid. *Government publications: Scottish Education Department sectional list no.* 36. HMSO, annual.

Ibid. *List of statutory instruments . . . .* HMSO, annual.

Ibid. *List of statutory instruments for the month of . . . .* HMSO, monthly.

JOB, D. E. A list of books and periodical articles concerned with liberal education. *Liberal education*, summer 1965, pp. 27–29.

KELLY, T. *(ed.).* A select bibliography of adult education in Great Britain. NIAE, 1963.

LELLO, J. The official view on education: a summary of the major educational reports since 1944. Oxford, Pergamon Press, 1964.

LIBRARIANS OF INSTITUTES OF EDUCATION. *British education index.* [In progress; 3 vol. have appeared.] LA. *See* **Appendix 3.**

MINISTRY OF EDUCATION—DEPARTMENT OF EDUCATION AND SCIENCE. *Index to Ministry of Education circulars and administrative memoranda current on 1st January.* List 10. HMSO, annual.

NATIONAL FOUNDATION FOR EDUCATIONAL RESEARCH IN ENGLAND AND WALES. *Technical education abstracts from British sources.* [Irregular; 3 vol. have appeared, covering papers published between September 1960 and June 1963.] NFER. *See* **Appendix 3.**

PETERS, A. J. Published sources for the study of contemporary British further education. *British journal of educational studies*, vol. 13, no. 1, November 1964, pp. 71–86; vol. 13, no. 2, May 1965, pp. 170–187.

Ibid. A guide to the study of British further education: published sources on the contemporary

system. National Foundation for Educational Research in England and Wales: *Occasional publication* no. 15. Slough, NFER, 1966.
TOASE, Mary (*ed.*) Guide to current British periodicals. LA, 1964.
UNITED NATIONS EDUCATIONAL, SCIENTIFIC AND CULTURAL ORGANIZATION. Educational periodicals. Paris, UNESCO, 1963.

Command papers ("White Papers")

CHANCELLOR OF THE EXCHEQUER *and others.* Higher technological education. Cmd. 8537. HMSO, 1951.
CHIEF SECRETARY TO THE TREASURY. Aid to developing countries. Cmnd. 2147. HMSO, 1963.
FIRST SECRETARY OF STATE AND SECRETARY OF STATE FOR ECONOMIC AFFAIRS. The national plan. Cmnd. 2764. HMSO, 1965.
MINISTER OF EDUCATION. Better opportunities in technical education. Cmnd. 1254. HMSO, 1961.
Ibid. Report of the Second Commonwealth Education Conference. Cmnd. 1655. HMSO, 1962.
MINISTER OF EDUCATION *and* **SECRETARY OF STATE FOR SCOTLAND.** Technical education. Cmd. 9703 [with NACEIC report as Appendix B.] HMSO, 1956.
MINISTER OF LABOUR. Industrial training: Government proposals. Cmnd. 1892. HMSO, 1962.
MINISTER OF PUBLIC BUILDING AND WORKS. A national building agency. Cmnd. 2228. HMSO, 1963.
PRESIDENT OF THE BOARD OF EDUCATION. Educational reconstruction. Cmd. 6458. HMSO, 1943.
Ibid. Education Bill: explanatory memorandum. Cmd. 6492. HMSO, 1943.
PRIME MINISTER. Higher education: Government statement on the report of the committee under the chairmanship of Lord Robbins 1961–63. Cmnd. 2165. HMSO, 1963.
Ibid. A policy for the arts: the first steps. Cmnd. 2601. HMSO, 1965.
Ibid. Immigration from the Commonwealth. Cmnd. 2739. HMSO, 1965.
SECRETARY FOR TECHNICAL CO-OPERATION. Technical co-operation: a progress report by the new department. Cmnd. 1698. HMSO, 1962.
Ibid. Recruitment for service overseas: future policy. Cmnd. 1740. HMSO, 1962.
SECRETARY OF STATE FOR COMMONWEALTH RELATIONS. Report of the Commonwealth Education Conference. Cmnd. 841. HMSO, 1959.
SECRETARY OF STATE FOR COMMONWEALTH RELATIONS *and* **SECRETARY OF STATE FOR THE COLONIES.** Commonwealth Scholarship and Fellowship Plan. Cmnd. 894. HMSO, 1959.
Ibid. Commonwealth educational co-operation. Cmnd. 1032. HMSO, 1960.
SECRETARY OF STATE FOR EDUCATION AND SCIENCE. Report of the Third Commonwealth Education Conference. Cmnd. 2545. HMSO, 1964.
Ibid. A plan for polytechnics and other colleges: higher education in the further education system. Cmnd. 3006. HMSO, 1966.
SECRETARY OF STATE FOR FOREIGN AFFAIRS *and others.* Overseas information services. Cmnd. 685. HMSO, 1959.
SECRETARY OF STATE FOR SCOTLAND. Education in Scotland: the next step. Cmnd. 603. HMSO, 1958.
Ibid. Technical education in Scotland: the pattern for the future. Cmnd. 1245. Edinburgh, HMSO, 1961.
SECRETARY OF STATE FOR THE COLONIES *and others.* Technical assistance from the United Kingdom for overseas development. Cmnd. 1308. HMSO, 1961.

A number of Reports of committees, etc. and Miscellaneous annual publications were Command papers.

Statutes

(in alphabetical order)

An Act . . . for Artificers . . ., 1562. 5 Eliz. 1, ch. 4 ["Statute of Artificers"].
An Act to amend . . . [above Act], 1814. 54 Geo. 3, ch. 96.
Board of Education Act, 1899. 62 & 63 Vict., ch. 33.
Commonwealth Immigrants Act, 1962. 10 & 1963, ch. 21.
Commonwealth Scholarships Act, 1959. 8 Eliz. 2, ch. 6.
Commonwealth Scholarships (Amendment) Act, 1963. 1963, ch. 6.
Education Act, 1902. 2 Edw. 7. ch. 42.
Education Act, 1918. 8 & 9 Geo. 5, ch. 39.
Education Act, 1921. 11 & 12 Geo. 5, ch. 21.
Education Act, 1944. 7 & 8 Geo. 6, ch. 31.
Education Act, 1962. 10 & 11 Eliz. 2, ch. 12.
Education (Miscellaneous Provisions) Act, 1948. 11 & 12 Geo. 6, ch. 40.
Education (Miscellaneous Provisions) Act, 1953. 1 & 2 Eliz. 2, ch. 33.
Education (Scotland) Act, 1908. 8 Edw. 7, ch. 63.
Education (Scotland) Act, 1945. 8 & 9 Geo. 6, ch. 37.
Education (Scotland) Act, 1946. 9 & 10 Geo. 6, ch. 72.
Education (Scotland) Act, 1949. 12 & 13 Geo. 6, ch. 19.
Education (Scotland) Act, 1962. 10 & 11 Eliz. 2, ch. 47.
Education (Scotland) Act, 1963. 1963, ch. 21.
Health and Morals of Apprentices Act, 1802. 42 Geo. 3, ch. 73 ["first Factory Act"].
Housing Act, 1936. 26 Geo. 5 & 1 Edw. 8, ch. 51.
Housing Act, 1957. 5 & 6 Eliz. 2, ch. 56.
Housing (Scotland) Act, 1925. 15 Geo. 5, ch. 15.
Housing (Scotland) Act, 1935. 25 & 26 Geo. 5, ch. 41.
Housing (Scotland) Act, 1950. 14 Geo. 6, ch. 34.
Industrial Training Act, 1964. 1963, ch. 16.
Local Government Act, 1948. 11 & 12 Geo. 6, ch. 26.
Local Government Act, 1958. 6 & 7 Eliz. 2, ch. 55.
Local Government (Scotland) Act, 1947. 10 & 11 Geo. 6, ch. 43.
London Government Act, 1963. 1963, ch. 33.
National Assistance Act, 1948. 11 & 12 Geo. 6, ch. 29.
Physical Training and Recreation Act, 1937. 1 Edw. 8 & 1 Geo. 6, ch. 46.
Physical Training and Recreation Act, 1958. 6 & 7 Eliz. 2, ch. 36.
Public Libraries and Museums Act, 1964. 1964, ch. 75.
Remuneration of Teachers Act, 1963. 1963, ch. 20.
Remuneration of Teachers Act, 1965. 1965, ch. 3.
Science and Technology Act, 1965. 1965, ch. 4.
Teaching Council (Scotland) Act, 1965. 1965, ch. 19.
Technical Instruction Act, 1889. 52 & 53 Vict., ch. 76.
Welsh Intermediate Act, 1889. 52 & 53 Vict., ch. 40.

Statutory instruments

(in chronological order)

England and Wales

Social and physical training grant regulations, 1939. Grant regulations, no. 13.
Social and physical training grant amending regulations no. 1, 1940.
Social and physical training grant amending regulations no. 2, 1944.
Regulations for scholarships and other benefits, 1945. SR & O 1945 no. 666.
Further education grant regulations, 1946. SR & O 1946 no. 352.
Educational services and research grant regulations, 1946. SR & O 1946 no. 424.
Further education grant amending regulations no. 1, 1946. SR & O 1946 no. 1067.

County colleges order, 1947. SR & O 1947 no. 527.

The regulations for technical state scholarships, 1947. SR & O no. 1471.

The state scholarships (mature students) regulations, 1947. SR & O 1947 no. 1472.

The scholarships and other benefits amending regulations no. 1, 1948. SI 1948 no. 688.

The further education grant amending regulations no. 2, 1948. SI 1948 no. 847.

The regulations for technical state scholarships, 1948. SI 1948 no. 1629.

The state scholarships (mature students) amending regulations no. 1, 1948. SI 1948 no. 1737.

The provision of clothing regulations, 1948. SI 1948 no. 2222.

The scholarships and other benefits amending regulations no. 2, 1948. SI 1948 no. 2223.

The technical state scholarships amending regulations no. 1, 1949. SI 1949 no. 1364.

The state scholarships (mature students) amending regulations no. 2, 1949. SI 1949 no. 1365.

The state scholarships (mature students) amending regulations no. 3, 1950. SI 1950, no. 625.

The technical state scholarships amending regulations no. 2, 1950. SI 1950 no. 626.

The local education authorities recoupment (further education) regulations, 1954. SI 1954 no. 815.

The local education authorities recoupment (further education) amending regulations, 1955. SI 1955 no. 222.

The local education authorities recoupment (further education) amending regulations, 1956. SI 1956 no. 1588.

The school health service regulations, 1959. SI 1959 no. 363.

The handicapped pupils and special schools regulations, 1959. SI 1959 no. 365.

The special schools and establishments (grant) regulations, 1959. SI 1959 no. 366.

The further education (local education authorities) regulations, 1959. SI 1959 no. 393.

The further education (grant) regulations, 1959. SI 1959 no. 394.

The milk and meals grant regulations, 1959. SI 1959 no. 410.

The general grants (pooling arrangements) regulations, 1959. SI 1959 no. 447.

The local education authorities recoupment (primary, secondary and further education) amending regulations, 1959. SI 1959 no. 448.

The further education (local education authorities) amending regulations, 1961. SI 1961 no. 1582.

The university and other awards regulations 1962. SI 1962 no. 1689.

The state awards regulations, 1963 SI 1963. no. 1223.

The university and other awards amending regulations 1963. SI 1963 no. 1396.

The Secretary of State for Education and Science order 1964. SI 1964 no. 490.

The special schools and establishments (grant) amending regulations 1964. SI 1964 no. 1083.

The university and other awards amending regulations 1964. SI 1964 no. 1128.

The further education (local education authorities) amending regulations 1964. SI 1964, no. 1309.

The further education (grant) amending regulations 1964. SI 1964 no. 1310.

The further education (grant) second amending regulations 1964. SI 1964 no. 1514.

The further education (local education authorities) second amending regulations 1964. SI 1964 no. 1515.

The university and other awards amending regulations no. 2 1964. SI 1964 no. 1980.

The further education (local education authorities) amending regulations 1965. SI 1965 no. 2.

The local education authorities recoupment (further education) amending regulations 1965. SI 1965 no. 512.

The university and other awards regulations 1965. SI 1965 no. 1404.

The remuneration of teachers (farm institutes) order 1965. SI 1965 no. 2029.

The remuneration of teachers (further education) order 1965. SI 1965 no. 2030.

The university and other awards amending regulations 1966. SI 1966 no. 985.

Scotland

Code of regulations for continuation classes. Cd. 562. With a *Memorandum*, Cd. 563. 1901.

The Scottish Certificate of Education Examination Board regulations 1963. SI 1963 no. 2131 (S.121).

Circulars and administrative memoranda

(in chronological order)

Circulars: England and Wales

BOARD OF EDUCATION. Organisation of art instruction. *Circular* 1432. 1933.

Ibid. The service of youth. *Circular* 1486. [With appendix.] HMSO, 1939.

Ibid. The challenge of youth. *Circular* 1516. HMSO, 1940.

MINISTRY OF EDUCATION. Reorganisation of the Ministry's art examinations. *Circular* 4. 1944.

Ibid. Local administration of education: schemes of divisional administration. *Circular* 5. [With appendix.] HMSO, 1944.

Ibid. Community centres. *Circular* 20. [With pamphlet *Community centres* attached.] 1944.

Ibid. Educational provision for civilian patients in hospitals and sanatoria. *Circular* 15. [With appendix.] 1945.

MINISTRY OF AGRICULTURE AND FISHERIES *and* **MINISTRY OF EDUCATION.** Agricultural education. Ministry of Agriculture and Fisheries *Circular* 1, Ministry of Education *Circular* 25. 1945.

MINISTRY OF EDUCATION. Education Act, 1944: draft regulations under Section 81: scholarships and other benefits. *Circular* 26. [With draft regulations attached.] HMSO, 1945.

Ibid. Teachers (Superannuation) Act, 1945, *Circular* 36. HMSO, 1945.

Ibid. Provision of facilities for recreation and social and physical training. *Circular* 51. [With memos. A.W.1 and A.W.2.] HMSO, 1945.

Ibid. Courses of training for those engaging in the youth service. *Circular* 53. 1945.

Ibid. Further education: some immediate problems. *Circular* 56. 1945.

Ibid. Demobilisation and adult education. *Circular* 57. 1945.

Ibid. Training of disabled persons. *Circular* 68. 1945.

Ibid. Russian studies. *Circular* 81. [With appendix.] HMSO, 1946.

Ibid. Regional organisation of further education. *Circular* 87. [With 2 appendices.] 1946.

Ibid. Research in technical colleges, *Circular* 94. HMSO, 1946.

Ibid. The status of technical, commercial and art colleges. *Circular* 98. 1946.

Ibid. Examinations in secondary schools. *Circular* 103. HMSO, 1946.

Ibid. Awards for university students. *Circular* 104. HMSO, 1946.

Ibid. Courses of training for those engaging in the youth service. *Circular* 116. [With appendix.] 1946.

Ibid. Further education: homecraft. *Circular* 117. HMSO, 1946.

MINISTRY OF AGRICULTURE AND FISHERIES *and* **MINISTRY OF EDUCATION.** The relations between local education authorities and the national agricultural advisory service. Ministry of Agriculture and Fisheries *Circular* 3, Ministry of Education *Circular* 123. HMSO, 1946.

MINISTRY OF EDUCATION. School sites and buildings procedure. *Circular* 130. [With "first Cleary Report" attached.] 1946.

Ibid. Schemes of further education and plans for county colleges. *Circular* 133. [With attached addendum, not to be confused with separate Addendum no. 1 (1947) and Addendum no. 2 (1947).] 1947.

Ibid. Schemes of further education and plans for county colleges. *Circular* 133 (Addendum no. 1). 1947.

Ibid. Schemes of further education and plans for county colleges. *Circular* 133. (Addendum no. 2). [With appendix.] 1947.

Ibid. State scholarships. *Circular* 137. HMSO, 1947.

Ibid. Plans for county colleges. *Circular* 139. 1947.

Ibid. School records of individual development. *Circular* 151. 1947.

Ibid. Village halls. *Circular* 51 (Addendum no. 1). HMSO, 1948.

MINISTRY OF AGRICULTURE AND FISHERIES *and* **MINISTRY OF EDUCATION.** Grants in aid of agricultural education provided by local education authorities in England and Wales. Ministry of Agriculture and Fisheries *Circular* 4, Ministry of Education *Circular* 161. 1948.

MINISTRY OF EDUCATION. Training institutions for the physically handicapped. *Circular* 164. 1948.

Ibid. Examinations in secondary schools: the report of the Secondary School Examinations Council. *Circular* 168. HMSO, 1948.

Ibid. Provision of clothing regulations. *Circular* 183. [With appendix.] 1948.

Ibid. Royal College of Art. *Circular* 199. 1949.

Ibid. Examinations in secondary schools: the report of the Secondary School Examinations Council. *Circular* 205. HMSO, 1949.

Ibid. Expenditure of local education authorities. *Circular* 210. HMSO, 1949.

Ibid. Rules governing the award of the Ministry's diplomas and certificates in art. *Circular* 220. 1950.

Ibid. Teachers' Superannuation Acts: full-time service. *Circular* 224. HMSO, 1950.

Ibid. Professional bodies' requirements in terms of the General Certificate of Education. *Circular* 227. [Revised 1952, 1955.] HMSO, 1950.

Ibid. Educational expenditure. *Circular* 242. HMSO, 1951.

Ibid. LEA awards under Section 81 of the Education Act, 1944. *Circular* 247. 1952.

Ibid. Examinations in secondary schools: 1952 report of the Secondary School Examinations Council. *Circular* 251. HMSO, 1952.

Ibid. Awards at universities and other institutions of higher education. *Circular* 252. 1952.

Ibid. Advanced technology. *Circular* 255. 1952.

Ibid. Examinations in secondary schools. *Circular* 256. HMSO, 1952.

Ibid. Selection for local education authority awards at universities. *Circular* 263. [With appendix.] 1953.

Ibid. Education (Miscellaneous Provisions) Act, 1953. *Circular* 268. [With Appendix.] 1953.

Ibid. Advanced short courses for scientists and technologists engaged in industry. *Circular* 270. [With 2 appendices.] 1953.

MINISTRY OF AGRICULTURE AND FISHERIES *and* **MINISTRY OF EDUCATION.** Working party on agricultural education. Ministry of Agriculture and Fisheries *Circular* 5, Ministry of Education *Circular* 275. [With "Carrington Report" attached.] HMSO, 1954.

MINISTRY OF EDUCATION. Secondment of teachers for overseas service. *Circular* 277. [With 3 appendices.] HMSO, 1954.

Ibid. Treatment for income tax and profits tax of gifts etc. by traders to technical colleges etc. for the purpose of vocational education or research. *Circular* 281. [With Appendix.] 1954.

Ibid. Educational building. *Circular* 283. [With appendix.] HMSO, 1954.

Ibid. Awards at universities and other institutions of further education. *Circular* 285. 1955.

Ibid. Examinations in secondary schools. *Circular* 289. HMSO, 1955.

Ibid. Technical education. *Circular* 299. 1956.

Ibid. Special educational treatment for physically handicapped children. *Circular* 300. 1956.

Ibid. Milk in schools scheme. *Circular* 302. 1956.

Ibid. The organisation of technical colleges. *Circular* 305. [With appendix.] HMSO, 1956.

Ibid. Fees for further education. *Circular* 307. 1956.

Ibid. The education of patients in hospital. *Circular* 312. [With appendix.] 1956.

Ibid. Awards for post-graduate study. *Circular* 315. 1956.

Ibid. Advanced short courses for scientists and technologists engaged in industry. *Circular* 270 (Amendment no. 1). 1957.

Ibid. Hostels at technical colleges. *Circular* 320. 1957.

Ibid. Libraries in technical colleges. *Circular* 322. 1957.

Ibid. Libraries in technical colleges. *Circular* 322 (Amendment no. 1). 1957.

Ibid. Liberal education in technical colleges. *Circular* 323. HMSO, 1957.

Ibid. Examinations in secondary schools. *Circular* 326. HMSO, 1957.

Ibid. Teaching service and the teaching of English overseas. *Circular* 330. 1957.

Ibid. Welfare of overseas students in technical colleges. *Circular* 332. [With 2 appendices.] 1958.

MINISTRY OF EDUCATION *and* **MINISTRY OF AGRICULTURE, FISHERIES AND FOOD.** Awards for post graduate study in agriculture and veterinary science. Ministry of Education *Circular* 335, Ministry of Agriculture, Fisheries and Food *Circular* EAS 58/1. 1958.

MINISTRY OF EDUCATION. Recruitment of teachers for technical colleges. *Circular* 336. [With annex.] 1958.

Ibid. Professional bodies' requirements in terms of the General Certificate of Education. *Circular* 338. HMSO, 1958.

Ibid. Art education: report of the National Advisory Committee on Art Examinations on proposed changes in the art examinations and in the length of the diploma course. *Circular* 340. [With appendix.] HMSO, 1958.

Ibid. Public relations in further education. *Circular* 343. [With *Britain's future and technical education* attached.] 1958.

Ibid. Divisional administration in excepted districts. *Circular* 344. 1958.

MINISTRY OF AGRICULTURE, FISHERIES AND FOOD *and* **MINISTRY OF EDUCATION.** Agricultural education. Ministry of Agriculture, Fisheries and Food *Circular* EAS 1959/1, Ministry of Education *Circular* 346. 1959.

MINISTRY OF EDUCATION. Local Government Act, 1958: changes in administrative procedure. *Circular* 350. 1959.

Ibid. The further education (local education authorities) regulations, 1959. *Circular* 351. 1959.

Ibid. School health service, medical examinations, handicapped pupils, handicapped pupils (boarding) and special schools and establishments (grant) regulations, 1959. *Circular* 352. 1959.

Ibid. The school meals service: finance. *Circular* 353. 1959.

Ibid. Technical education: the next step. *Circular* 1/59. [With appendix.] 1959.

Ibid. The schools and the Commonwealth. *Circular* 2/59. [With 2 appendices.] 1959.

Ibid. Further education for commerce. *Circular* 5/59. 1959.

Ibid. Governing bodies for major establishments of further education. *Circular* 7/59. 1959.

Ibid. Welfare of overseas students in technical colleges. *Circular* 332 (amended appendices). 1960.

Ibid. The future development of management education and of business studies. *Circular* 1/60. [With report of Joint (Examinations) Executive Committee for Management Studies ("Arnold Report") attached.] 1960.

Ibid. The youth service: building programe. *Circular* 3/60. 1960.

Ibid. *Your future in industry. Circular* 4/60. [With wall chart *Your future in industry* attached.] 1960.

Ibid. Further education for agriculture. *Circular* 7/60. [With "first Lampard-Vachell Report" attached.] 1960.

Ibid. The education services and training for industry. *Circular* 9/60. 1960.

Ibid. Teaching service in the Commonwealth and other countries overseas. *Circular* 10/60. [With 3 appendices.] HMSO, 1960.

Ibid. The youth service: progress report and further development. *Circular* 11/60. [With appendix.] HMSO, 1960.

Ibid. Children unsuitable for education at school and school leavers requiring care from health authorities: the Mental Health Act, 1959. *Circular* 12/60. 1960.

Ibid. First report of the National Advisory Council on Art Education. *Circular* 16/60. 1960.

MINISTRY OF AGRICULTURE, FISHERIES AND FOOD *and* **MINISTRY OF EDUCATION.** Local education authorities and the national agricultural advisory service. Ministry of Agriculture *Circular* 5 (Addendum no. 1), Ministry of Education *Circular* 275 (Addendum no. 1). 1961.

MINISTRY OF EDUCATION. Governing bodies of major establishments of further education: farm institutes. *Circular* 7/59 (Addendum no. 1). 1961.

Ibid. *Better opportunities in technical education. Circular* 1/61. 1961.

Ibid. Regional colleges. *Circular* 3/61. 1961.

Ibid. University and comparable awards. *Circular* 5/61. [With 4 appendices.] HMSO, 1961.

Ibid. Further education for agriculture. *Circular* 6/61. [With "second Lampard-Vachell Report" attached.] 1961.

Ibid. Changes in the General Certificate of Education advanced level examinations. *Circular* 9/61. [With appendix.] HMSO, 1961.

Ibid. Special educational treatment for educationally sub-normal pupils. *Circular* 11/61. 1961.

Ibid. State scholarships for mature students, 1962. *Circular* 12/61. 1961.

Ibid. Organisation of business studies in colleges of further education. *Circular* 15/61. 1961.

Ibid. *Youth service building: Building bulletin no. 20. Circular* 17/61. [With appendix.] 1961.

Ibid. The Education Act, 1962. *Circular* 4/62. 1962.

Ibid. Professional bodies' requirements in terms of the General Certificate of Education. *Circular* 5/62. HMSO, 1962.

Ibid. *The building code. Circular* 6/62. 1962.

Ibid. The building code. [An album of circulars and administrative memoranda.] 1962.

Ibid. Awards for first degree and comparable courses: the university and other awards regulations 1962. *Circular* 9/62. [With 3 appendices.] HMSO, 1962.

Ibid. Vocational courses in colleges, schools and departments of art. *Circular* 11/62. 1962.

Ibid. The training of part-time youth leaders and assistants. *Circular* 12/62. 1962.

Ibid. Awards for first degree and comparable courses: the university and other awards regulations 1962. *Circular* 9/62 (Addendum no 1). HMSO, 1963.

Ibid. Awards for first degree and comparable courses: the university and other awards regulations 1962. *Circular* 9/62 (Addendum no. 2). HMSO, 1963.

Ibid. Welfare of overseas students in technical colleges. *Circular* 2/63. [With 3 appendices.] 1963.

Ibid. Welfare of overseas students in technical colleges: list of student officers or cultural attaches in London specially concerned . . . . *Circular* 2/63 (revised Appendix no. 1). 1963.

Ibid. Training of teachers. *Circular* 7/62. [With 3 appendices.] HMSO, 1962.

Ibid. Organisation of further education courses. *Circular* 3/63. [With "Pilkington Report" of NACEIC attached.] 1963.

Ibid. The Certificate in Office Studies. *Circular* 4/63. [With *Rules 128* attached.] 1963.

Ibid. Sandwich courses. *Circular* 6/63. [With "Russell Report" of NACEIC attached.] 1963.

Ibid. Management education. *Circular* 7/63. [With "first Platt Report" of UKACEM attached.] 1963.

Ibid. Grants to students. *Circular* 8/63. 1963.

Ibid. The Certificate of Secondary Education. *Circular* 9/63. 1963.

Ibid. The training of part-time youth leaders and assistants: conference on training the trainers. *Circular* 10/63. [With appendix.] 1963.

Ibid. Grants for students attending post graduate courses in the teaching of English as a second language and in education in tropical areas. *Circular* 11/63. 1963.

MINISTRY OF AGRICULTURE, FISHERIES AND FOOD *and* **MINISTRY OF EDU-CATION.** Local education authorities and the national agricultural advisory service. Ministry of Agriculture, Fisheries and Food *Circular* 5 (Addendum no. 2), Ministry of Education *Circular* 275 (Addendum no. 2). HMSO, 1964.

MINISTRY OF EDUCATION. Teaching service in the Commonwealth and other countries overseas. *Circular* 10/60 (Addendum no. 1). [With appendix.] HMSO, 1964.

Ibid. Industrialised building and educational building consortia. *Circular* 1/64. HMSO, 1964.

Ibid. Provision of language and export courses for business firms. *Circular* 2/64. [With appendices.] 1964.

Ibid. A higher award in business studies. *Circular* 4/64. [With "Crick Report" attached.] 1964.

Ibid. Awards for postgraduate study. *Circular* 5/64. 1964.

Ibid. The Secretary of State for Education and Science order, 1964. *Circular* 6/64. 1964.

DEPARTMENT OF EDUCATION AND SCIENCE. Further education for blind school leavers. *Circular* 8/64. 1964.

Ibid. Council for National Academic Awards. Circular 10/64. 1964.

MINISTRY OF HOUSING AND LOCAL GOVERNMENT *and* **DEPARTMENT OF EDUCATION AND SCIENCE.** Provision of facilities for sport. Ministry of Housing and Local Government *Circular* 49/64, Department of Education and Science *Circular* 11/64. HMSO, 1964.

DEPARTMENT OF EDUCATION AND SCIENCE. The Henniker-Heaton Report on day release. *Circular* 14/64. [With 2 appendices; and "Henniker-Heaton Report" attached.] 1964.

312   BRITISH FURTHER EDUCATION

Ibid. Training of teachers. *Circular* 15/64. HMSO 1964.
Ibid. Awards for first degree and comparable courses . . . . *Circular* 16/64. HMSO, 1964.
Ibid. The public relations of further education. *Circular* 17/64. [With "Alexander Report" of NACEIC attached.] 1964.
Ibid. The university and other awards amending regulations no. 2 1964. *Circular* 18/64. 1964.
Ibid. National Council for the Supply of Teachers Overseas. *Circular* 10/60 (Addendum no. 2). 1965.
Ibid. Training of teachers. *Circular* 15/64 (Addendum no. 1). HMSO, 1965.
Ibid. Public Libraries and Museums Act, 1964. *Circular* 4/65. HMSO, 1965.
Ibid. Awards for postgraduate study. *Circular* 5/65.
Ibid. The education of immigrants. *Circular* 7/65. [With appendix.] 1965.
DEPARTMENT OF EDUCATION AND SCIENCE *and* **MINISTRY OF HOUSING AND LOCAL GOVERNMENT.** *A policy for the arts.* Department of Education and Science *Circular* 8/65, Ministry of Housing and Local Government *Circular* 53/65. 1965.
DEPARTMENT OF EDUCATION AND SCIENCE. Post-diploma studies in art and design. *Circular* 11/65. 1965.
Ibid. Deferment of capital expenditure. *Circular* 12/65. 1965.
Ibid. Management studies in technical colleges. *Circular* 2/66. [With "second Platt Report" attached.] 1966.
Ibid. Awards to students. *Circular* 4/66. [With 5 appendices.] HMSO, 1966.
Ibid. *A plan for polytechnics and other colleges. Circular* 8/66. 1966.
DEPARTMENT OF EDUCATION AND SCIENCE *and* **MINISTRY OF HEALTH.** Co-ordination of education, health and welfare service for handicapped children and young people. Department of Education and Science *Circular* 9/66, Ministry of Health *Circular* 7/66. HMSO, 1966.
DEPARTMENT OF EDUCATION AND SCIENCE. Technical college resources: size of classes and approval of further education courses. *Circular* 11/66. [With appendix; and "Pilkington Report" of NACEIC attached.] 1966.
Ibid. Pre-diploma courses in art and design. *Circular* 12/66. 1966.
Ibid. Awards for postgraduate study. *Circular* 14/66. 1966.
Ibid. The training of part-time youth leaders and assistants. *Circular* 16/66. [With "third Albemarle Report" attached.] 1966.

Administrative memoranda: England and Wales

MINISTRY OF EDUCATION. Choice of employment for handicapped children. *Administrative memorandum* 94. 1945.
Ibid. Release of teachers to industry and commerce. *Administrative memorandum* 134. 1946.
Ibid. Aid by local education authorities to responsible bodies for adult education. *Administrative memorandum* 248. 1947.
Ibid. Aid by local education authorities to responsible bodies for adult education. *Administrative memorandum* 248 (Addendum). 1948.
Ibid. Ministry of Education maintenance rates for students at universities. *Administrative memorandum* 425. HMSO, 1952.
Ibid. Education in prisons and Borstal institutions. *Administrative memorandum* 440. 1953.
Ibid. Agricultural apprenticeship scheme. *Administrative memorandum* 452. [With appendix.] 1953.
Ibid. Section 12 of the Education (Miscellaneous Provisions) Act, 1953. *Administrative memorandum* 455. [With appendix.] 1953.
Ibid. Ministry of Education maintenance rates for students at universities. *Administrative memorandum* 502. [With appendix.] HMSO, 1955.
Ibid. Courses and classes in establishments for further education. *Administrative memorandum* 510. 1955.
Ibid. Training of blind adolescents. *Administrative memorandum* 511. 1955.
Ibid. Education in prisons, Borstal institutions and detention centres. *Administrative memorandum* 440 (Addendum no. 1). 1956.

Ibid. Local education authorities and responsible bodies for adult education. *Administrative memorandum* 526. 1956.

Ibid. The Lord Mayor Treloar College, Frayle, near Alton, Hants. *Administrative memorandum* 527. 1956.

Ibid. Approval of courses in establishments of further education. *Administrative memorandum* 545. 1957.

Ibid. Sandwich courses 1957/58. *Administrative memorandum* 559. [With *List 182* attached.] 1957.

Ibid. Courses and classes in establishments for further education. *Administrative memorandum* 510 (Amendment no. 1). 1958.

Ibid. Awards for students on advanced sandwich courses. *Administrative memorandum* 567. 1958.

Ibid. Higher National Diplomas and Certificates and advanced technicians' courses in electrical engineering. *Administrative memorandum* 570. [With joint statement by Ministry of Education and Institution of Electrical Engineers.] 1958.

Ibid. Approval of courses in colleges of further education. *Administrative memorandum* 3/59. [With appendix.] 1959.

Ibid. Arrangements for pooling educational expenditure. *Administrative memorandum* 11/59. [With appendix.] 1959.

Ibid. National Certificates and Diplomas in Business Studies. *Administrative memorandum* 7/61. [With appendix.] 1961.

Ibid. General engineering courses. *Administrative memorandum* 10/61. [With 3 annexes.] 1961.

Ibid. Educational building: progress of work. *Administrative memorandum* 12/61. 1961.

Ibid. Educational building: progress of work. *Administrative memorandum* 12/61 (Addendum no. 1). 1961.

Ibid. Approval by the Ministry of Education of courses leading to the Diploma in Art and Design. *Administrative memorandum* 13/61. 1961.

Ibid. The youth service: status of qualified youth leader. *Administrative memorandum* 16/61. 1961.

Ibid. The youth service: training of part-time leaders and assistants. *Administrative memorandum* 17/61. [With appendix.] 1961.

Ibid. Measures to encourage the recruitment of teachers for service in the Commonwealth and other countries overseas. *Administrative memorandum* 18/61. [With 2 appendices.] 1961.

Ibid. Interchange of teachers with overseas countries. *Administrative memorandum* 19/61. 1961.

Ibid. Interchange of teachers with overseas countries. *Administrative memorandum* 19/61 (Amendment). 1961.

Ibid. National Certificates and Diplomas in Business Studies. *Administrative memorandum* 7/61 (Addendum no. 1). [With appendix.] 1962.

Ibid. Youth service: capital projects. *Administrative memorandum* 2/62. 1962.

Ibid. National Retail Distribution Certificates. *Administrative memorandum* 4/62. [With revised *Rules 121* attached.] 1962.

Ibid. *Forward from school*. *Administrative memorandum* 6/62. [With pamphlet *Forward from school* attached.] 1962.

Ibid. Interchange of teachers with overseas countries. *Administrative memorandum* 7/62. 1962.

Ibid. Education in prisons, Borstal institutions and detention centres. *Administrative memorandum* 440 (Addendum no. 2). 1963.

Ibid. Adult education (accommodation and staffing). *Administrative memorandum* 6/63. 1963.

Ibid. Awards for students on advanced sandwich courses. *Administrative memorandum* 7/63. 1963.

Ibid. Interchange of teachers and assistants with overseas countries. *Administrative memorandum* 8/63. 1963.

Ibid. Ordinary National Certificates and Diplomas in Sciences. *Administrative memorandum* 3/64. 1964.

DEPARTMENT OF EDUCATION AND SCIENCE. The Industrial Training Act, 1964. *Administrative memorandum* 4/64. [With Ministry of Labour booklet attached.] 1964.

Ibid. Interchange of teachers and assistants with overseas countries. *Administrative memorandum* 8/64. 1964.

Ibid. Council for National Academic Awards. *Administrative memorandum* 9/64. [With Charter of CNAA attached.] 1964.

Ibid. Approval of courses leading to the Diploma in Art and Design. *Administrative memorandum* 4/65. 1965.

Ibid. The Industrial Training Act, 1964: a progress report. *Administrative memorandum* 5/65. [With 2 appendices; and *Memorandum* no. 1 of CTC attached.] 1965.

Ibid. The role in higher education of regional and other technical colleges engaged in advanced work. *Administrative memorandum* 7/65. [With Secretary of State's Woolwich speech attached.] 1965.

Ibid. The Diploma in Management Studies. *Administrative memorandum* 8/65. [With memorandum by Committee for the Diploma in Management Studies attached.] 1965.

Ibid. Grants to students. *Administrative memorandum* 9/65. 1965.

Ibid. Interchange of teachers and assistants with overseas countries. *Administrative memorandum* 14/65. 1965.

Ibid. Salary scales for further education establishments and farm institutes maintained by local education authorities. *Administrative memorandum* 17/65. 1965.

Ibid. Information for applicants for full-time advanced courses in further education. *Administrative memorandum* 8/66. 1966.

Ibid. Revised agreement between the City and Guilds of London Institute and the regional examining bodies.*Administrative memorandum* 2/66 [With revised agreement attached.]1966.

Ibid. Interchange of teachers and assistants with overseas countries. *Administrative memorandum* 7/66. 1966.

Circulars: Wales

MINISTRY OF EDUCATION, WELSH DEPARTMENT. The organisation and responsibilities of the Welsh Department. *Circular* 22 (W). 1958.

Ibid. St. David's Day, 1961: the old order and the new. *Circular* 1/61 (W). 1961.

Ibid. St. David's Day, 1962: youth service in Wales. *Circular* 1/62 (W). 1962.

Circulars: Scotland

SCOTTISH EDUCATION DEPARTMENT. Scottish Certificate of Education: examination arrangements. *Circular* 30. [Revised annually.] HMSO.

Ibid. The provision of facilities for recreation and social and physical training. *Circular* 56 [With appendix.] Edinburgh, HMSO, 1946.

Ibid. Pre-vocational courses for the building industry. *Circular* 226. 1942.

Ibid. Pre-apprenticeship courses for the building industry. *Circular* 250. 1942.

Ibid. Secondment of teachers for overseas service. *Circular* 291. [With 3 appendices.] HMSO, 1954.

Ibid. Educational building. *Circular* 296. Edinburgh, HMSO, 1954.

Ibid. The education of handicapped pupils: the reports of the Advisory Council on Education in Scotland. *Circular* 300. HMSO, 1955.

Ibid. Teaching service and the teaching of English overseas. *Circular* 370. 1957.

Ibid. Further education. *Circular* 405. [With 2 appendices.] HMSO, 1959.

Ibid. Report of the Working Party on the Curriculum of the Senior Secondary School. *Circular* 412. HMSO, 1959.

Ibid. Schemes relating to the provision of further education. *Circular* 422. [With appendix.] 1959.

Ibid. Introduction of ordinary grade examination. *Circular* 424. [With 3 appendices.] HMSO, 1959.

Ibid. The future development of education for management in central institutions and further education centres. [With 2 appendices and "Arnold Report" attached.] *Circular* 429. 1960.

Ibid. Youth service. *Circular* 436. [With appendix.] HMSO, 1960.

Ibid. Teaching service in the Commonwealth and other countries overseas. *Circular* 443. [With 3 appendices.] HMSO, 1960. [Parallel with Ministry of Education *Circular* 10/60.]

Ibid. Training opportunities for young people leaving school. *Circular* 450. 1961.

Ibid. Scottish Certificate of Education: date of the examination and conditions for the award of the certificate. *Circular* 452. [With appendix.] HMSO, 1961.

Ibid. National Certificates and Diplomas. *Circular* 465. HMSO, 1961.
Ibid. Review of youth service. *Circular* 469. 1961.
Ibid. The training of part-time youth leaders. *Circular* 487. [With memorandum by SCCYSS attached.] 1961.
Ibid. Education (Scotland) Act, 1962. *Circular* 514. [With 2 appendices.] HMSO, 1962.
Ibid. Pre-apprenticeship courses. *Circular* 521. [With "Arrell Report" of STECC attached.] 1963.
Ibid. "From school to further education": report of the working party on the linkage of secondary and further education. *Circular* 530. [With annex; and "second Brunton Report" attached.] 1963.
Ibid. Management of further education colleges. *Circular* 549. [With appendix.] 1964.
Ibid. Facilities for sport and recreation. *Circular* 550. [With 2 appendices and addendum.] 1964.
Ibid. "From school to further education": report of the working party on the linkage of secondary and further education. *Circular* 558. 1964.
Ibid. National Certificates and Diplomas: revision of *Rules 1*. *Circular* 560. [With appendix; and *Rules 1* (1964 revision) attached.] HMSO, 1964.
Ibid. Provision of languages and export courses for business firms. *Circular* 563. 1964.
Ibid. Teaching service in the Commonwealth and other countries overseas: the National Council for the Supply of Teachers Overseas. *Circular* 443 (Addendum no. 2). [With constitution of NCSTO attached.] 1965.
Ibid. *A policy for the arts*. *Circular* 589. 1965.
Ibid. Links between youth and community services. *Circular* 598. [With interim report of SCCYCSS attached.] 1965.
Ibid. General Teaching Council for Scotland. *Circular* 601. 1965.

Memoranda: Scotland

SCOTTISH EDUCATION DEPARTMENT. Central Training Council memoranda. *Memorandum* 27/1966. [With *Memoranda* nos. 4 and 5 of CTC attached.] 1966.
Ibid. Industrial Training Act, 1966: charges for industrial training provided by further education colleges. *Memorandum* 35/1966. 1966.

Other central-government publications

Of education departments

Booklets and pamphlets

DEPARTMENT OF EDUCATION AND SCIENCE. The General Certificate of Education. HMSO, 1964.
Ibid. Careers guidance in schools. HMSO, 1965.
DEPARTMENT OF EDUCATION AND SCIENCE and **CENTRAL OFFICE OF INFORMATION.** Further education for school leavers. HMSO, 1966.
Ibid. Signposts to higher education: a guide to sources of information. HMSO, 1966.
MINISTRY OF EDUCATION. Community centres. [Pamphlet attached to *Circular* 20.] HMSO, 1944.
Ibid. The nation's schools, their plan and purpose. *Pamphlet* no. 1. [Afterwards withdrawn.] HMSO, 1945.
Ibid. A guide to the educational system of England and Wales. *Pamphlet* no. 2. HMSO, 1945.
Ibid. Youth's opportunity: further education in county colleges. *Pamphlet* no. 3. HMSO, 1945.
Ibid. Art education. *Pamphlet* no. 6. HMSO, 1946.
Ibid. Further education: the scope and content of its opportunities under the Education Act, 1944. *Pamphlet* no. 8. HMSO, 1947.

Ibid. Citizens growing up, at home, in school and after. *Pamphlet* no. 16. HMSO, 1949.
Ibid. Evening institutes. *Pamphlet* no. 28. HMSO, 1956.
Ibid. The story of post war school building. *Pamphlet* no. 33. HMSO, 1957.
Ibid. Schools and the Commonwealth. *Pamphlet* no. 40. HMSO, 1961.
Ibid. Forward from school: the links between school and further education. [Pamphlet attached to *Administrative memorandum* 6/62.] HMSO, 1962.
Ibid. Grants to students: first degree and comparable courses. N.d.
MINISTRY OF EDUCATION, WELSH DEPARTMENT. Education in rural Wales. Addysg Wledig yng Nghymru. *Pamphlet* no. 3. HMSO, 1949.
MINISTRY OF EDUCATION *and* **CENTRAL OFFICE OF INFORMATION.** Britain's future and technical education. [Booklet attached to *Circular* 343.] 1958.
Ibid. Why not teach for a time overseas? 1963.
SCOTTISH EDUCATION DEPARTMENT. Arrangements and conditions for the award of National Certificates and Diplomas. *Rules 1* (1964 revision). [Attached to *Circular* 560.] Edinburgh, HMSO, 1964.
Ibid. *Guide to student's allowances* . . . . annual.
SECRETARY OF STATE FOR SCOTLAND. Technical education in Scotland: an extract from *Education in Scotland in 1952* (Cmd. 8813). Edinburgh, HMSO, 1953.
Ibid. Pre-employment courses in Scotland: an extract from *Education in Scotland in 1959.* (Cmnd. 1018). Edinburgh, HMSO, 1960.
Ibid. Craft courses for building, engineering and allied industries: an extract from *Education in Scotland in 1962* (Cmnd. 1975). Edinburgh, HMSO, 1963.
Ibid. School and college libraries: an extract from *Education in Scotland in 1962* (Cmnd.1975). Edinburgh, HMSO, 1963.

Books

SCOTTISH EDUCATION DEPARTMENT. Public education in Scotland. Edinburgh, HMSO, 1963.
Ibid. *Further education in Scotland: a directory of day courses.* . . . Edinburgh, HMSO, annual.

Building bulletins

MINISTRY OF EDUCATION. New colleges of further education. *Building bulletin* no. 5. HMSO, 1951, 1955, 1959.
Ibid. The story of CLASP. *Building bulletin* no. 19. HMSO, 1961.
Ibid. Youth service buildings: general mixed clubs. *Building bulletin* no. 20. HMSO, 1961.
Ibid. Youth club Withywood Bristol. *Building bulletin* no. 22. HMSO, 1963.

Lists (in numerical order)

MINISTRY OF EDUCATION—DEPARTMENT OF EDUCATION AND SCIENCE *List 10*: *see* Bibliographies, etc.
MINISTRY OF EDUCATION. *List of special schools for handicapped pupils in England and Wales (including . . . establishments for further education and training of disabled persons).* *List 42*. HMSO, 1963.
MINISTRY OF EDUCATION—DEPARTMENT OF EDUCATION AND SCIENCE. *Selected statistics relating to local education authorities in England and Wales. List 71.* HMSO, annual.
MINISTRY OF EDUCATION. *List of sandwich courses and block release courses in further education establishments in England and Wales* . . . . *List 182.* HMSO, annual, 1957–61.
DEPARTMENT OF EDUCATION AND SCIENCE *and* **MINISTRY OF AGRICULTURE, FISHERIES AND FOOD.** *Full-time agricultural education in England and Wales. List 185 (1965–66).* HMSO, 1965.
SCOTTISH EDUCATION DEPARTMENT. Handicapped pupils in Scotland. *List G.* Edinburgh, SED. 1965.

Reports on education

MINISTRY OF EDUCATION—DEPARTMENT OF EDUCATION AND SCIENCE.
The technical colleges. *Reports on education*, no. 2, August 1963. HMSO.
Ibid. Paying for it. *Reports on education*, no. 3, September 1963. HMSO.
Ibid. Examinations and the curriculum. *Reports on education*, no. 4, October 1963. HMSO.
Ibid. The youth service. *Reports on education*, no. 5, November 1963. HMSO.
Ibid. Progress of the CATs. *Reports on education*, no. 10, April 1964. HMSO.
Ibid. How the money is spent. *Reports on education*, no. 13, July 1964. HMSO.
Ibid. Examinations and qualifications. *Reports on education*, no. 14, August 1964. HMSO.
Ibid. Education for commerce. *Reports on education*, no. 15, October 1964. HMSO.
Ibid. Advice and advance. *Reports on education*, no. 19, February 1965. HMSO.
Ibid. Grants and awards. *Reports on education*. no. 24, September 1965. HMSO.
Ibid. Education in the national plan. *Reports on education*, no. 25, October 1965. HMSO.
Ibid. National Certificates and Diplomas. *Reports on education*, no. 26, November 1965. HMSO.
Ibid. The Council for National Academic Awards. *Reports on education*, no. 30, June 1966. HMSO.

Statistical reports published separately

MINISTRY OF EDUCATION—DEPARTMENT OF EDUCATION AND SCIENCE.
Statistics of education, 1961, part 1. HMSO, 1962.
Ibid. *Statistics of education*, 1961, part 2. HMSO, 1962.
Ibid. *Statistics of education*, 1961, supplement to part 2. HMSO, 1962.
Ibid. *Statistics of education*, 1962, part 2. HMSO, 1963.
Ibid. *Statistics of education*, 1962, part 3. HMSO, 1964.
Ibid. *Statistics of education*, 1963, part 1. HMSO, 1964.
Ibid. *Statistics of education*, 1963, part 2. HMSO, 1964.
Ibid. *Statistics of education*, 1964, part 1. IIMSO, 1965.
Ibid. *Statistics of education*, 1964, part 2. HMSO, 1965.
Ibid. *Statistics of education*, 1965, part 1. HMSO, 1966.

Miscellaneous (leaflets, etc.)

DEPARTMENT OF EDUCATION AND SCIENCE. The educational system of England and Wales. HMSO, 1964.
Ibid. Report on the arts: partnership in patronage. HMSO, 1966.
Ibid. Report on civil science. HMSO, 1966.
MINISTRY OF EDUCATION. The General Certificate of Education. HMSO, 1953.
Ibid. Your future in industry. [Wall chart attached to *Circular* 4/60.] 1960.
MINISTRY OF EDUCATION *and* **CENTRAL OFFICE OF INFORMATION.** A call from overseas for technical staff: how you can help. N.d.

Of other departments

CENTRAL OFFICE OF INFORMATION. Vocational education and training in Britain. *Reference pamphlet* no. R.3087. [Duplicated for the use of overseas information services; available on loan.] 1955.
Ibid. Research and the United Kingdom Dependencies. *R.f.p.* 4035. 1958.
Ibid. Education in the United Kingdom Dependencies. *Reference pamphlet* no. 4. HMSO, 1959.
Ibid. Education in Britain. *Reference pamphlet* no. 7. HMSO, 1960.
Ibid. Technological education in Britain. *Reference pamphlet* no. 21. HMSO, 1960.
Ibid. Educational co-operation within the Commonwealth. *R.f.p.* 5067. HMSO, 1961.

Y

Ibid. Community development: the British contribution. *Reference pamphlet* no. 52. HMSO, 1962.
Ibid. Technical education in Britain. *Reference pamphlet* no. 21. HMSO, 1962.
Ibid. Youth services in Britain. *R.* 5506. HMSO, 1963.
Ibid. Britain and education in the Commonwealth. HMSO, 1964.
Ibid. Britain: an official handbook. HMSO, annual, 1954–.
CENTRAL OFFICE OF INFORMATION (CROW, D.). Commonwealth education: Britain's contribution. HMSO, 1961.
DEPARTMENT OF AGRICULTURE AND FISHERIES FOR SCOTLAND. Agricultural research advisory services and education in Scotland. Edinburgh, HMSO, 1965.
DEPARTMENT OF TECHNICAL CO-OPERATION *and* **CENTRAL OFFICE OF INFORMATION.** Teaching opportunities overseas. HMSO, 1963.
FORESTRY COMMISSION. Training as a forester. 1962.
GENERAL REGISTER OFFICE. Classification of occupations 1960. HMSO, 1960.
Ibid. Census 1961, England and Wales, preliminary report. HMSO, 1961.
GENERAL REGISTER OFFICE *and* **GENERAL REGISTRY OFFICE, SCOTLAND.** Census 1961, Great Britain: scientific and technological qualifications. HMSO, 1962.
HER MAJESTY'S STATIONERY OFFICE: *see* Bibliographies, etc.
MINISTRY OF LABOUR. Industrial Training Act, 1964: general guide: scope and objectives. HMSO, 1964.
MINISTRY OF OVERSEAS DEVELOPMENT. Study and serve overseas. [1965.]
MINISTRY OF OVERSEAS DEVELOPMENT *and* **CENTRAL OFFICE OF INFORMATION.** Opportunities overseas for teachers. HMSO, 1965.

Publications of local education authorities

COUNTY BOROUGH OF BOLTON EDUCATION DEPARTMENT. Reach for the top . . . . Bolton, annual.
HERTFORDSHIRE COUNTY COUNCIL. Building for education 1948–61. 1962.
SECOND CONSORTIUM OF LOCAL AUTHORITIES. SCOLA. N.d.
STAFFORDSHIRE EDUCATION COMMITTEE. Building for education in Staffordshire 1950 to 1963. 1964.
See also Reports of committees, etc.

Reports of committees, etc.

ADVISORY CENTRE FOR EDUCATION. List of CATs and technical colleges in the UK offering full-time courses leading to 1. Diplomas in Technology . . . and 2. external degrees of London University. [Duplicated; obtainable from 57 Russell Street, Cambridge.] N.d.
ADVISORY CENTRE FOR EDUCATION (HASTINGS, Merle). Grants for higher education. Cresset Press, 1964.
ADVISORY COUNCIL ON SCIENTIFIC POLICY: COMMITTEE ON SCIENTIFIC MANPOWER. Report on the recruitment of scientists and engineers by the engineering industry. HMSO, 1955.
Ibid. Scientific and engineering manpower in Great Britain 1959. Cmnd. 902. ["Zuckerman Report."] HMSO, 1959.
Ibid. The long-term demand for scientific manpower. Cmnd. 1490. ["Zuckerman Report."] HMSO, 1961.
Ibid. Scientific and technological manpower in Great Britain 1962. Cmnd. 2146. ["Zuckerman Report."] HMSO, 1963.
ADVISORY COUNCIL ON SCIENTIFIC POLICY: COMMITTEE ON SCIENTIFIC MANPOWER *and* **MINISTRY OF LABOUR AND NATIONAL SERVICE.** Scientific and engineering manpower in Great Britain. ["Zuckerman Report."] HMSO, 1956.

ANGLO-AMERICAN COUNCIL ON PRODUCTIVITY. Education for management. AACP, 1951.

Ibid. Training of operatives. AACP, 1951.

Ibid. Training of supervisors. AACP, 1951.

Ibid. Universities and industry. AACP, 1951.

Ibid. Final report of the Council. AACP, 1952.

ASSOCIATION OF ART INSTITUTIONS. Written evidence prepared for the Committee on Higher Education. AAI, 1961.

ASSOCIATION OF BRITISH CHAMBERS OF COMMERCE. Guide to commercial training. *Chamber of Commerce booklet* no. 8. ABCC, 1961.

Ibid. Pattern of business studies. ABCC, 1963.

ASSOCIATION OF SCIENTIFIC WORKERS. Science and education: a policy statement . . . . AScW, 1960.

Ibid. Science and adult education. AScW, 1963.

ASSOCIATION OF TEACHERS IN TECHNICAL INSTITUTIONS. The education of boys and girls between the ages of 15 and 18: being a memorandum prepared for the Central Advisory Council on Education (England). ATTI, 1958.

Ibid. Future of higher education: evidence submitted to the Robbins Committee . . . . ATTI, 1962.

Ibid. Development of day release: evidence submitted to the Henniker-Heaton Committee. ATTI, 1963.

Ibid. Industrial training: a policy statement . . . . ATTI, 1964.

Ibid. Is Robbins enough? A commentary on the Robbins Report. ATTI, 1964.

Ibid. Sandwich courses. ATTI, 1964.

Ibid. The Henniker-Heaton Report: a commentary. ATTI, 1964.

ASSOCIATION OF TEACHERS IN TECHNICAL INSTITUTIONS: HIGHER EDUCATION PANEL. The future of higher education within the further education system. ATTI, 1965.

ASSOCIATION OF TECHNICAL INSTITUTIONS and **ASSOCIATION OF PRINCIPALS OF TECHNICAL INSTITUTIONS.** Technical college buildings: interim report on non-teaching accommodation. ATI, 1962.

Ibid. Second interim report: the college library. ATI, 1962.

ASSOCIATION OF UNIVERSITY TEACHERS. Submissions to the Committee on Higher Education. AUT, 1961.

BOARD OF EDUCATION: CONSULTATIVE COMMITTEE. Report on attendance, compulsory or otherwise, at continuation schools. ["Acland Report."] Vol. 1: report and appendices. Cd. 4757. Vol. 2: summaries of evidence. Cd. 4758. HMSO, 1909.

Ibid. The education of the adolescent. ["Hadow Report."] HMSO, 1926.

Ibid. Secondary education with special reference to grammar schools and technical high schools. ["Spens Report."] HMSO, 1938.

BOARD OF EDUCATION: DEPARTMENTAL COMMITTEE ON JUVENILE EDUCATION IN RELATION TO EMPLOYMENT AFTER THE WAR. Final report. Cd. 8512. ["Lewis Report."] HMSO, 1917.

BOARD OF EDUCATION: SECONDARY SCHOOL EXAMINATIONS COUNCIL: SPECIAL COMMITTEE. Curriculum and examinations in secondary schools. ["Norwood Report."] HMSO, 1943.

BOARD OF EDUCATION: SPECIAL COMMITTEE. Report of the Departmental Committee on Examinations for Part-time Students. ["Atholl Report."] HMSO, 1928.

BOARD OF EDUCATION: SPECIAL COMMITTEE. Teachers and youth leaders . . . . ["McNair Report."] HMSO, 1944.

BOARD OF EDUCATION: YOUTH ADVISORY COUNCIL. The youth service after the war. ["Wolfenden Report."] HMSO, 1943.

BRITISH ASSOCIATION FOR COMMERCIAL AND INDUSTRIAL EDUCATION. Cmnd. 1892: BACIE memorandum to the Minister of Labour. *BACIE memoranda*, April 1963, pp. 9–12.

BRITISH COUNCIL: LONDON CONFERENCE ON OVERSEAS STUDENTS: STANDING COMMITTEE. Overseas students in Britain: a handbook for all who are interested in the welfare of overseas students. BC, 1964.

BRITISH COUNCIL and **ASSOCIATION OF COMMONWEALTH UNIVERSITIES.** Higher education in the United Kingdom: a handbook for students from overseas and their advisers. Longmans Green, biennial, 1952–. [First published 1936.]

BRITISH COUNCIL FOR REHABILITATION OF THE DISABLED: TWO WORKING PARTIES. The handicapped school-leaver. ["Thomas-Ferguson Report."] BCRD, 1963.

BRITISH COUNCIL OF CHURCHES. Over 15: a report on the further education of young people. BCC, 1961.

Ibid. The church and technological education. BCC, 1966.

BRITISH FEDERATION OF UNIVERSITY WOMEN: WORKING PARTY. Opportunities for girls and women in science and technology. BFUW, 1957.

Ibid. Working party on women in science and technology 1956–60: final report. BFUW, n.d.

BRITISH INSTITUTE OF MANAGEMENT. A conspectus of management courses. BIM, 1965.

BRITISH INSTITUTE OF MANAGEMENT: STUDY GROUP. The recruitment and training of men intended for management positions. ["Hooper Report."] BIM, 1955.

BRITISH INSTITUTE OF MANAGEMENT: STUDY GROUP. Management training in the building industry. . . . BIM, 1956.

BRITISH IRON AND STEEL FEDERATION. Report on the recruitment and training of technicians. BISF, 1961.

CENTRAL AFRICAN COUNCIL: SPECIAL COMMISSION. Report of the Commission on Higher Education for Africans in Central Africa. ["Carr-Saunders Report."] Salisbury, Rhodesia, 1953.

CENTRAL COUNCIL FOR THE CARE OF CRIPPLES. Disabled? Enquire within: a short guide to services for the physically handicapped in Great Britain. CCCC, 1960.

CENTRAL COUNCIL OF PHYSICAL RECREATION: SPECIAL COMMITTEE. Sport and the community. ["Wolfenden Report."] CCPR, 1960.

CHANCELLOR OF THE EXCHEQUER: SPECIAL COMMITTEE. Report of the Committee on the Training of Civil Servants. Cmd. 6525. ["Assheton Report."] HMSO, 1944.

CHESHIRE EDUCATION COMMITTEE. The service of youth. Chester, Griffith, 1961.

Ibid. Training for skill. [Report of five working parties.] Chester, 1961.

CITY AND GUILDS OF LONDON INSTITUTE. Further education for craftsmen. CGLI, 1964.

Ibid. Further education for technicians. CGLI, 1964.

CITY AND GUILDS OF LONDON INSTITUTE (WHEATLEY, D. E. and **TAYLOR, M. H.).** Further education for operatives. CGLI, 1964.

CITY AND GUILDS OF LONDON INSTITUTE: CONSULTATIVE COMMITTEE ON EDUCATION FOR THE PRINTING INDUSTRY. Education for the printing industry: a proposed plan for a revised structure of courses. . . . CGLI, 1964.

COLONIAL OFFICE: MISSION. Report of the Mission on Higher Technical Education in the British Caribbean. *Colonial* no. 336. ["Petter Report."] HMSO, 1957.

COMMITTEE OF CONSERVATIVE MEMBERS OF PARLIAMENT. The rising tide: youth in the 1960s. ["Smyth Report."] Conservative Political Centre, 1961.

COMMITTEE ON EDUCATION FOR SALESMANSHIP. Final report. ["Goodenough Report."] HMSO, 1931.

COMMITTEE ON MANPOWER RESOURCES FOR SCIENCE AND TECHNOLOGY. A review of the scope and problems of scientific and technological manpower policy. Cmnd. 2800. HMSO, 1965.

COMMUNIST PARTY. Higher education in the nuclear age. Communist Party, 1959.

Ibid. The development of higher education in Britain: evidence presented to the Robbins Committee. . . . Communist Party, 1961.

CONFERENCE OF ENGINEERING SOCIETIES OF WESTERN EUROPE AND THE UNITED STATES OF AMERICA. Report on education and training of professional engineers. Brussels, EUSEC, 1960.

COUNCIL FOR NATIONAL ACADEMIC AWARDS. Recognised degree courses. *List* no. 1. CNAA, 1965.

Ibid. *Statement* no. 1. CNAA, 1964.

Ibid. *Statement* no. 2. CNAA, 1965.
Ibid. *Statement* no. 3. CNAA, 1965.
Ibid. *Statement* no. 4. CNAA, 1966.
Ibid. Courses leading to the Council's degrees. CNAA, 1966.
DEPARTMENT OF EDUCATION AND SCIENCE. Scales of salaries and other provisions for determining the remuneration of teachers in primary and secondary schools in England and Wales. ["Burnham Main Report."] HMSO, 1965.
DEPARTMENT OF EDUCATION AND SCIENCE: CENTRAL ADVISORY COUNCIL FOR EDUCATION (WALES). Science in education in Wales today. ["Llewellyn-Jones Report."] HMSO, 1965.
DEPARTMENT OF EDUCATION AND SCIENCE: NATIONAL ADVISORY COUNCIL ON ART EDUCATION. Post-diploma studies in art and design: third report. . . . ["Third Coldstream Report."] HMSO, 1964.
Ibid. First report. . . . addendum: pre-diploma studies. HMSO, 1966.
DEPARTMENT OF EDUCATION AND SCIENCE: NATIONAL ADVISORY COUNCIL ON EDUCATION FOR INDUSTRY AND COMMERCE. The public relations of further education. ["Alexander Report"; attached to *Circular* 17/64.] HMSO, 1964.
Ibid. Committee on technical college resources: report on the size of classes and approval of further education courses. ["Pilkington Report"; attached to *Circular* 11/66.] HMSO, 1966.
Ibid. Report of the advisory committee on agricultural education 1966. ["Dadd Report" "Pilkington Report".] HMSO, 1966.
DEPARTMENT OF EDUCATION AND SCIENCE: SPECIAL COMMITTEE. Day release: the report of a committee set up by the Minister of Education. ["Henniker-Heaton Report"; attached to *Circular* 14/64.] HMSO, 1964.
DEPARTMENT OF EDUCATION AND SCIENCE: UNITED KINGDOM ADVISORY COUNCIL ON EDUCATION FOR MANAGEMENT. Management studies in technical colleges. ["Second Platt Report"; attached to *Circular* 2/66.] HMSO, 1965.
DEPARTMENT OF EDUCATION AND SCIENCE: YOUTH SERVICE DEVELOPMENT COUNCIL. Service by youth. ["Second Bessey Report."] HMSO, 1966.
Ibid. A second report on the training of part-time youth leaders and assistants. ["Third Albemarle Report"; attached to *Circular* 16/66.] HMSO, 1966.
DEPARTMENT OF EDUCATION AND SCIENCE *and* **MINISTRY OF EDUCATION, NORTHERN IRELAND: COMMITTEE FOR THE DIPLOMA IN MANAGEMENT STUDIES.** A memorandum on the Diploma in Management Studies. [Attached to *Administrative memorandum* 8/65.] HMSO, 1965.
DEPARTMENT OF HEALTH FOR SCOTLAND: SPECIAL COMMITTEE. The welfare needs of mentally handicapped persons: report by a committee of the Scottish Advisory Council on the Welfare of Handicapped Persons. ["Fraser Report."] Edinburgh, HMSO, 1957.
DEPARTMENT OF SCIENTIFIC AND INDUSTRIAL RESEARCH. Automation: a report on the technical trends and their impact on management and labour. HMSO, 1956.
DEPARTMENT OF TECHNICAL CO-OPERATION: SPECIAL COMMITTEE. Report on the development of a university in Northern Rhodesia. ["Lockwood Report."] Lusaka, Government Printer, 1963.
EDUCATIONAL INSTITUTE OF SCOTLAND. Observations to be submitted to the Committee on Higher Education. [Duplicated; obtainable from 46 Moray Place, Edinburgh 3.] 1961.
Ibid. Observations on the White Paper "Industrial training: government proposals" (Cmd. 1892). [Duplicated; obtainable from 46 Moray Place, Edinburgh 3.] 1963.
EUROPEAN PRODUCTIVITY AGENCY: *see* NATIONAL INSTITUTE OF INDUSTRIAL PSYCHOLOGY; ORGANISATION FOR ECONOMIC CO-OPERATION AND DEVELOPMENT.
FABIAN SOCIETY. The structure of higher education. *Fabian tract* 334. Fabian Society, 1961.
FEDERATION OF BRITISH INDUSTRIES. Public school and grammar school boys in industry. FBI, 1954.
Ibid. Overseas trainees in United Kingdom industry. FBI, 1960.

Ibid. The technical colleges and their government: an industrial appraisal. FBI, 1960.

Ibid. Further education for those in industry and commerce: an information booklet. FBI, 1961.

Ibid. Higher education: evidence to the government committee. FBI, 1961.

Ibid. Financing of sandwich course students: a policy statement. [First published 1958, revised 1963.] FBI, 1963.

Ibid. Education in transition: the implications for industry of the government reports on education and training, 1959 to 1964. FBI, 1965.

FEDERATION OF BRITISH INDUSTRIES: JOINT COMMITTEE. Industry and the technical colleges: a review of some current problems. FBI, 1956.

FEDERATION OF BRITISH INDUSTRIES: WORKING PARTY. Foreign languages in industry. FBI, 1962.

Ibid. Management education and training needs of industry. FBI, 1963.

Ibid. Foreign language needs of industry. FBI, 1964.

FIFE EDUCATION COMMITTEE. Report by working party on adult education. ["Connelly Report", "Fife Report".] *Scottish adult education*, no. 41, September 1964, pp. 11–18.

HOUSE OF COMMONS: SELECT COMMITTEE ON ESTIMATES. Technical education. Twelfth report. . . 1952–53. HMSO, 1953.

Ibid. Departmental replies, etc. . . . Technical education. Fifteenth report. . . 1952–53. HMSO, 1953.

Ibid. The youth employment service and youth service grants. Seventh report. . . 1956–57. HMSO, 1957.

Ibid. Observations of the Minister of Education and the Secretary of State for Scotland on the seventh report. . . 1956–57. . . , together with the remarks of the Committee thereupon. Third special report. . . 1957–58. HMSO, 1958.

INDUSTRIAL ASSOCIATION OF WALES AND MONMOUTHSHIRE. Memorandum on the Government proposals for industrial training (Cmnd. 1892). [Duplicated; obtainable from Aberdare House, Mount Stuart Square, Cardiff.] 1963.

INDUSTRIAL TRAINING COUNCIL. Co-operation between industry and education. ITC, 1960.

Ibid. Training boys in industry: the non-apprentice. ITC, 1960.

Ibid. Craft apprenticeship: training for a skilled craft or trade. ITC, 1962.

Ibid. Training girls in industry. ITC, 1962.

Ibid. Training advisory services available to companies. ITC, 1963.

Ibid. The training specialist in industry. ITC, 1964.

INDUSTRIAL TRAINING COUNCIL (GREIG, F. W.). Group training schemes. ITC, 1963.

INSTITUTE OF MUNICIPAL ENTERTAINMENT. A survey of municipal entertainment in England and Wales for the two years 1947–8 and 1961–2. IMEnt, 1964.

INSTITUTE OF THE MOTOR INDUSTRY (INC.): SPECIAL COMMITTEE. A report on education and training for the motor industry in Europe. ["Collins Report."] Hertford. [1964.]

INTER-DEPARTMENTAL COMMITTEE ON THE REHABILITATION AND RESETTLEMENT OF DISABLED PERSONS. Report. Cmd. 6415. ["Tomlinson Report."] HMSO, 1943.

JOINT COMMITTEE ON TRAINING IN THE BUILDING INDUSTRY. Report. ["Hall Report."] 1964.

JOINT NEGOTIATING COMMITTEE FOR YOUTH LEADERS. First report. Councils and Education Press, 1961.

Ibid. Second report. Councils and Education Press, 1962.

Ibid. Third report. Councils and Education Press, 1963.

Ibid. (JOINT NEGOTIATING COMMITTEE FOR YOUTH LEADERS AND COMMUNITY CENTRE WARDENS) Fourth report. Councils and Education Press, 1965.

KING GEORGE'S JUBILEE TRUST. Citizens of to-morrow: a study of the influences affecting the upbringing of young people. Odhams, 1955.

LABOUR PARTY. Signposts for the sixties: a statement of Labour's home policy accepted . . . at Blackpool, 2–6 October 1961. Labour Party, 1961.

Ibid. Let's go with Labour for the new Britain: the Labour Party's manifesto for the 1964 general election. Labour Party, 1964.

LABOUR PARTY'S STUDY GROUP ON HIGHER EDUCATION. The years of crisis. ["Taylor Report."] Labour Party, 1963.

LIBERAL PARTY: SPECIAL COMMITTEE. Education. ["Pattison Report."] Liberal Publications Department, 1962.

LIBRARY ASSOCIATION. Standards for library service in colleges of technology. LA, 1959.

Ibid. 1964. College libraries: recommended standards of library provision in colleges of technology and other establishments of further education. LA, 1965. [Summary published in advance, 1964.]

LIVERPOOL CITY POLICE. The police and children. Liverpool, City Police, 1957.

LONDON AND HOME COUNTIES REGIONAL ADVISORY COUNCIL FOR HIGHER TECHNOLOGICAL EDUCATION. Libraries in colleges of further education. LHCRACHTE, 1954.

Ibid. (LONDON AND HOME COUNTIES REGIONAL ADVISORY COUNCIL FOR TECHNOLOGICAL EDUCATION). Libraries in colleges of technology, commerce and art 1958-9. LHCRACTE, 1959.

LONDON AND HOME COUNTIES REGIONAL ADVISORY COUNCIL FOR TECHNOLOGICAL EDUCATION: ARCHITECTURE AND BUILDING ADVISORY COMMITTEE: WORKING PARTY. Creativity in technical education. ["Lisborg Report."] LHCRACTE, 1964.

LONDON COUNTY COUNCIL: SPECIAL COMMITTEE. On from school: educational provision for young people under the age of 18 who have left school. ["Briault Report."] LCC, 1962.

LORD PRESIDENT OF THE COUNCIL: SPECIAL COMMITTEE. Scientific manpower. Cmd. 6824. ["Barlow Report."] HMSO, 1946.

MINISTER OF AGRICULTURE AND FISHERIES: SPECIAL COMMITTEE. Report of the Committee on Post-War Agricultural Education in England and Wales. Cmd. 6433. ["Luxmoore Report."] HMSO, 1943.

MINISTER OF AGRICULTURE AND FISHERIES: SPECIAL COMMITTEE. Report of the Committee on Higher Agricultural Education in England and Wales. Cmd. 6728. ["Second Loveday Report."] HMSO, 1946.

MINISTER OF AGRICULTURE, FISHERIES AND FOOD and **MINISTER OF EDUCATION: SPECIAL COMMITTEE.** Report of the Committee on Further Education for Agriculture provided by Local Education Authorities. Cmnd. 614. ["De La Warr Report."] HMSO, 1958.

MINISTER OF EDUCATION: SPECIAL COMMITTEE. The youth service in England and Wales. Cmnd. 929. ["First Albemarle Report."] HMSO, 1960.

MINISTER OF EDUCATION and **SECRETARY OF STATE FOR SCOTLAND: SPECIAL COMMITTEE.** Grants to students. Cmnd. 1051. ["Anderson Report."] HMSO, 1960.

MINISTER OF LABOUR AND NATIONAL SERVICE: COMMITTEE OF INQUIRY. Report... on the rehabilitation, training and resettlement of disabled persons. Cmd. 9883. ("Piercy Report.") HMSO, 1956.

MINISTER OF WORKS AND PLANNING: COMMITTEE ON LAND UTILISATION IN RURAL AREAS. Report. Cmd. 6378. ["Scott Report."] HMSO, 1942.

MINISTER OF WORKS AND PLANNING: EXPERT COMMITTEE ON COMPENSATION AND BETTERMENT. Final report. Cmd. 6386. ["Uthwatt Report."] HMSO, 1942.

MINISTRY OF AGRICULTURE AND FISHERIES: WORKING PARTY. Report... on agricultural education. ["Carrington Report"; attached to Ministry of Education *Circular* 275.] HMSO, 1953.

MINISTRY OF AIRCRAFT PRODUCTION: INTERDEPARTMENTAL COMMITTEE. A college of aeronautics. ["Fedden Report."] HMSO, 1944.

MINISTRY OF EDUCATION: CENTRAL ADVISORY COUNCIL FOR EDUCATION (ENGLAND). School and life. ["Clarke Report."] HMSO, 1947.

Ibid. Early leaving. ["Gurney-Dixon Report."] HMSO, 1954.

Ibid. 15 to 18. 2 vol. ["Crowther Report."] HMSO, 1959.

Ibid. Half our future. ["Newsom Report."] HMSO, 1963.
MINISTRY OF EDUCATION: CENTRAL ADVISORY COUNCIL FOR EDUCATION (**WALES**). The county college in Wales. ["Aaron Report."] HMSO, 1951.
Ibid. Education in rural Wales. ["Second Oldfield-Davies Report."] HMSO, 1960.
Ibid. Technical education in Wales. ["Third Oldfield-Davies Report."] HMSO, 1961.
MINISTRY OF EDUCATION: COMMITTEE ON GENERAL STUDIES. General studies in technical colleges. HMSO, 1962.
MINISTRY OF EDUCATION: COMMITTEE ON RECRUITMENT, TRAINING AND CONDITIONS OF SERVICE OF YOUTH LEADERS AND COMMUNITY CENTRE WARDENS. Report. ["Jackson Report."] HMSO, 1949.
MINISTRY OF EDUCATION: NATIONAL ADVISORY COMMITTEE ON ART EXAMINATIONS. Report. ["First Freeman Report."] HMSO, 1952.
Ibid. Report on proposed changes in the art examinations and in the length of the diploma course. ["Second Freeman Report."] HMSO, 1957.
MINISTRY OF EDUCATION: NATIONAL ADVISORY COUNCIL ON ART EDUCATION. First Report. . . . ["First Coldstream Report."] HMSO, 1960.
Ibid. Vocational courses in colleges and schools of art. ["Second Coldstream Report."] HMSO, 1962.
MINISTRY OF EDUCATION: NATIONAL ADVISORY COUNCIL ON EDUCATION FOR INDUSTRY AND COMMERCE. The future development of higher technological education. ["Weeks Report".] HMSO, 1950.
Ibid. Report on sandwich training and education. Appendix B of "White Paper" *Technical education* (Cmd. 9703). HMSO, 1956.
Ibid. Report of the Advisory Committee on Further Education for Commerce. ["McMeeking Report."] HMSO, 1959.
Ibid. A report on the wastage of students from part-time technical and commercial courses. ["Watts Report."] 1959.
Ibid. Advisory Sub-Committee on Further Education for Agriculture: first report. ["First Lampard-Vachell Report"; attached to *Circular* 7/60.] 1960.
Ibid. Advisory Sub-Committee on Further Education for Agriculture: second report. ["Second Lampard-Vachell Report"; attached to *Circular* 6/61.] 1961.
Ibid. Report of the special committee on the Crowther Report. ["Pilkington Report"; attached to *Circular* 3/63.] 1963.
Ibid. Report of the Advisory Sub-Committee on Sandwich Courses. ["Russell Report"; attached to *Circular* 6/63.] 1963.
Ibid. A higher award for business studies: report of the Advisory Sub-Committee. . . . ["Crick Report"; attached to *Circular* 4/64.] HMSO, 1964.
MINISTRY OF EDUCATION: NATIONAL ADVISORY COUNCIL ON THE TRAINING AND SUPPLY OF TEACHERS. The recruitment and training of youth leaders and community centre wardens. ["Fletcher Report."] HMSO, 1951.
Ibid. Report of the Sub-Committee on Educational Research in Further Education. *Paper* no. 220. ["Oliver Report"; duplicated.] 1960.
MINISTRY OF EDUCATION: SECONDARY SCHOOL EXAMINATIONS COUNCIL. Examinations in secondary schools. [First report.] HMSO, 1947.
Ibid. Examinations in secondary schools: second report. HMSO, 1952.
Ibid. The General Certificate of Education and sixth form studies: third report. . . . ["Lockwood Report".] HMSO, 1960.
Ibid. The Certificate of Secondary Education: a proposal for a new school leaving certificate other than the GCE: fourth report. . . . ["Lockwood Report".] HMSO, 1961.
Ibid. The Certificate of Secondary Education: notes for the guidance of regional examining bodies: fifth report. . . . ["Lockwood Report."] HMSO, 1962.
Ibid. Sixth form studies and university entrance requirements: sixth report. . . . ["Lockwood Report."] HMSO, 1962.
Ibid. Scope and standards of the Certificate of Secondary Education: seventh report. . . . ["Lockwood Report."] HMSO, 1963.
MINISTRY OF EDUCATION: SECONDARY SCHOOL EXAMINATIONS COUNCIL: SPECIAL COMMITTEE. Secondary school examinations other than the GCE. ["Beloe Report".] HMSO, 1960.

MINISTRY OF EDUCATION: SPECIAL COMMITTEE. Higher technological education. ["Percy Report."] HMSO, 1945.

MINISTRY OF EDUCATION: SPECIAL COMMITTEE. Report of the Committee on School Sites and Buildings Procedure. ["First Cleary Report"; attached to *Circular* 130.] HMSO, 1946.

MINISTRY OF EDUCATION: SPECIAL COMMITTEE. Education for management: management subjects in technical and commercial colleges. ["Urwick Report."] HMSO, 1947.

MINISTRY OF EDUCATION: SPECIAL COMMITTEE. Report of the Committee on Art Examinations. ["Bray Report."] HMSO, 1948.

MINISTRY OF EDUCATION: SPECIAL COMMITTEE. Report. . . on education for commerce. ["Carr-Saunders Report."] HMSO, 1949.

MINISTRY OF EDUCATION: SPECIAL COMMITTEE. The organisation and finance of adult education in England and Wales. ["Ashby Report."] HMSO, 1954.

MINISTRY OF EDUCATION: SPECIAL COMMITTEE. The supply and training of teachers for technical colleges. ["Willis Jackson Report."] HMSO, 1957.

MINISTRY OF EDUCATION: UNITED KINGDOM ADVISORY COUNCIL ON EDUCATION FOR MANAGEMENT: First report. . . . ["First Platt Report"; attached to *Circular* 7/63.] HMSO, 1962.

MINISTRY OF EDUCATION: WORKING PARTY. National Advisory Council on Education for Industry and Commerce. ["Hardman Report."] HMSO, 1947.

MINISTRY OF EDUCATION: WORKING PARTY. Report of the Technical Working Party on School Construction. ["Second Cleary Report."] HMSO, 1948.

MINISTRY OF EDUCATION: WORKING PARTY. Report of the working party appointed to examine the scheme of management studies. ["Arnold Report"; attached to *Circular* 1/60 and Scottish *Circular* 429.] 1960.

MINISTRY OF EDUCATION: WORKING PARTY. The training of part-time youth leaders and assistants. ["First Bessey Report."] HMSO, 1962.

MINISTRY OF EDUCATION: YOUTH ADVISORY COUNCIL. The purposes and content of the youth service. ["Wolfenden Report."] HMSO, 1945.

MINISTRY OF EDUCATION, WELSH DEPARTMENT: ADVISORY PANEL. Report. . . on the provision of advanced technical education at the technical colleges at Wrexham, Denbighshire and Kelsterton, Flintshire. ["Chance Report."] HMSO, 1958.

MINISTRY OF EDUCATION, WELSH DEPARTMENT: WELSH YOUTH COMMITTEE. The post war youth service in Wales. ["Griffiths Report."] HMSO, 1945.

MINISTRY OF EDUCATION *and* **MINISTRY OF AGRICULTURE AND FISHERIES: JOINT ADVISORY COMMITTEE.** The provision in secondary schools of courses preparatory to agricultural employment. ["First Loveday Report".] HMSO, 1945.

Ibid. Interim report on agricultural and horticultural institutes. ["Third Loveday Report."] HMSO, 1947.

Ibid. Interim report on the provision of part-time instruction by local education authorities for agriculturists, horticulturists and domestic producers. ["Fourth Loveday Report."] HMSO, 1949.

MINISTRY OF EDUCATION *and* **SCOTTISH EDUCATION DEPARTMENT: SPECIAL COMMITTEE.** The teaching of Russian. . . . ["Annan Report".] HMSO, 1962.

MINISTRY OF HEALTH *and* **DEPARTMENT OF HEALTH FOR SCOTLAND: WORKING PARTY.** Report. . . on social workers in the local authority health and welfare services. ["Younghusband Report."] HMSO, 1959.

MINISTRY OF LABOUR: CENTRAL TRAINING COUNCIL. Industrial training and further education. *Memorandum* no. 1. [Attached to *Administrative memorandum* 5/65.] 1965.

Ibid. Industrial training and further education: a further statement. *Memorandum* no. 4. [Attached to Scottish Education Department *Memorandum* 27/1966.] Ministry of Labour, 1966.

Ibid. Approach to industrial training: an assessment of the main tasks facing industrial training boards. *Memorandum* no. 5. [Attached to Scottish Education Department *Memorandum* 27/1966.] Ministry of Labour, 1966.

MINISTRY OF LABOUR: CENTRAL YOUTH EMPLOYMENT EXECUTIVE. Careers guide: opportunities in the professions, industry and commerce. HMSO, 1962.

MINISTRY OF LABOUR: CENTRAL YOUTH EMPLOYMENT EXECUTIVE: NATIONAL YOUTH EMPLOYMENT COUNCIL: WORKING PARTY. The future development of the Youth Employment Service. ["Second Albemarle Report."] HMSO, 1965.

MINISTRY OF LABOUR: MANPOWER RESEARCH UNIT. The pattern of the future. *Manpower studies* no. 1. HMSO, 1964.

MINISTRY OF LABOUR: REPRESENTATIVE COMMITTEE. Selection and training of supervisors: progress report. ["Marre Report."] HMSO, 1964.

MINISTRY OF LABOUR: SPECIAL COMMITTEE. Report of the committee on the selection and training of supervisors. ["Barnes Report."] HMSO, 1962.

MINISTRY OF LABOUR: WORKING PARTY. Report. . . on workshops for the blind. ["Stewart Report."] HMSO, 1962.

MINISTRY OF LABOUR AND NATIONAL SERVICE: COMMITTEE OF INQUIRY. Report. . . on the training of supervisors. ["Wilson Report."] HMSO, 1954.

MINISTRY OF LABOUR AND NATIONAL SERVICE: NATIONAL JOINT ADVISORY COUNCIL: SUB-COMMITTEE. Training for skill: recruitment and training of young workers in industry. ["Carr Report."] HMSO, 1958.

MINISTRY OF LABOUR AND NATIONAL SERVICE: SPECIAL COMMITTEE. Report. . . on the juvenile employment service. ["Ince Report."] HMSO, 1945.

MINISTRY OF LABOUR AND NATIONAL SERVICE: STANDING COMMITTEE ON THE REHABILITATION AND RESETTLEMENT OF DISABLED PERSONS. Services for the disabled. . . by government departments, local authorities and voluntary organisations in the United Kingdom. HMSO, 1961.

MINISTRY OF LABOUR AND NATIONAL SERVICE: WORKING PARTY. Report on the employment of blind persons. ["Taylor Report."] HMSO, 1951.

MINISTRY OF RECONSTRUCTION: ADULT EDUCATION COMMITTEE. Final report. Cmd. 321. ["Smith Report", "1919 Report."] HMSO, 1919.

MINISTRY OF WORKS: SPECIAL COMMITTEE. Standard construction for schools. *Post-war building studies* no. 2. ["Wood Report."] HMSO, 1944.

NATIONAL AGRICULTURAL AND DAIRY EXAMINATION BOARDS. Agriculture as a career, with special reference to the National Diplomas in Agriculture and Dairying. 1964.

NATIONAL COUNCIL FOR DIPLOMAS IN ART AND DESIGN. The Diploma in Art and Design. *Memorandum* no. 1. ["Summerson Council" memorandum.] NCDAD, 1961.

Ibid. First report. . . . ["Summerson Council" report.] NCDAD, 1964.

NATIONAL COUNCIL FOR TECHNOLOGICAL AWARDS. Memorandum on the industrial training of students following courses recognised as leading to the Diploma in Technology. ["Hives Council" memorandum.] NCTA, 1960.

Ibid. The Diploma in Technology and Membership of the College of Technologists. ["Hives Council" memorandum.] NCTA, 1961.

NATIONAL COUNCIL OF SOCIAL SERVICE. The welfare of the disabled: selected papers. NCSS, 1957.

Ibid. Young people today. NCSS for SCNVYO, 1960.

NATIONAL ECONOMIC DEVELOPMENT COUNCIL. Conditions favourable to faster growth. HMSO, 1963.

NATIONAL FEDERATION OF COMMUNITY ASSOCIATIONS. Creative living: the work and purposes of a community association. *Community associations new series*, no. 1. NCSS, 1964.

NATIONAL FOUNDATION FOR EDUCATIONAL RESEARCH IN ENGLAND AND WALES. Notes on the work. . . for 1963–4. NFER, 1963.

NATIONAL INSTITUTE OF ADULT EDUCATION. Liberal education in a technical age: a survey of the relationship of vocational and non-vocational further education and training. Parrish, 1955.

Ibid. Accommodation and staffing for adult education. ["Tylecote Report."] *Adult education*, vol. 35, no. 5, January 1963, pp. 229-312.

NATIONAL INSTITUTE OF INDUSTRIAL PSYCHOLOGY. Training factory workers: a report on a survey. . . of the European Productivity Agency. Staples Press, 1956.

NATIONAL JOINT COUNCIL FOR THE BUILDING INDUSTRY. Full-time pre-apprenticeship courses in building. NJCBI, 1960.

NATIONAL SPASTICS SOCIETY: EMPLOYMENT COMMITTEE: After school what? NSS, 1959.

NATIONAL UNION OF STUDENTS. Memorandum to the Committee on Higher Education. NUS, 1961.

Ibid. Student support: the case against loans. [Duplicated; obtainable from 3 Endsleigh Street, London W.C.1.] [1965.]

Ibid. Interim report on adult students. [Duplicated; obtainable from 3 Endsleigh Street, London W.C.1.] N.d.

NIGERIA: FEDERAL MINISTRY OF EDUCATION: SPECIAL COMMISSION. Investment in education: the report of the Commission on Post-School Certificate and Higher Education in Nigeria. ["Ashby Report."] Lagos, Federal Government, 1960.

THE 1963 CAMPAIGN FOR EDUCATION. A manifesto. 1963 Campaign, 1963.

NORTHERN RHODESIA COPPERBELT TECHNICAL FOUNDATION, GOVERNMENT OF NORTHERN RHODESIA and **GOVERNMENT OF THE FEDERATION OF RHODESIA AND NYASALAND: SPECIAL COMMITTEE.** A survey of technical and commercial education in Northern Rhodesia. ["Keir Report."] Kitwe, 1960.

ORGANISATION FOR ECONOMIC CO-OPERATION AND DEVELOPMENT. Issues in management education. [Report of a survey by European Productivity Agency among member and associated countries.] Paris. OECD, 1963.

Ibid. Resources of scientific and technical personnel in the OECD area: statistical report of the third international survey of the demand for and supply of scientific and technical personnel. Paris, OECD, 1963.

Ibid. Science, economic growth and government policy. Paris, OECD, 1963.

Ibid. Economic aspects of higher education. Paris, OECD, 1964.

Ibid. Inventory of training possibilities in Europe. Paris, OECD. 1965.

ORGANISATION FOR EUROPEAN ECONOMIC CO-OPERATION. Forecasting manpower needs for the age of science. Paris, OEEC, 1960.

ORGANISATION FOR EUROPEAN ECONOMIC CO-OPERATION: MANPOWER COMMITTEE. Shortages and surpluses of highly qualified scientists and engineers in Western Europe. *Document* C (55) 160. Paris, OEEC, 1955.

OVERSEAS DEVELOPMENT INSTITUTE LTD. British aid 3: educational assistance: a factual survey of the government and private contribution to overseas development through education and training. ODI, 1963.

OXFORD UNIVERSITY: DEPARTMENT OF EDUCATION (HUTCHINGS, D. W. and **HEYWORTH, P.).** Technology and the sixth form boy. Oxford, OUDE, 1963.

PARLIAMENTARY AND SCIENTIFIC COMMITTEE. Universities and the increase of scientific manpower. PSC, 1946.

Ibid. Colleges of technology and technological manpower. PSC, 1947.

Ibid. Technical education and skilled man-power. PSC, 1950.

Ibid. Memorandum on higher technological education. PSC, 1954.

Ibid. Memorandum on educational research. [Duplicated; obtainable from 7 Buckingham Gate, London S.W.1.] 1961.

PLAID CYMRU. Plan for a new Wales. Cardiff, Plaid Cymru, n.d.

POLITICAL AND ECONOMIC PLANNING. Colonial students in Britain: a report by PEP. PEP, 1955.

Ibid. Advisory committees in British government, 1960. Allen & Unwin, 1960.

POLITICAL AND ECONOMIC PLANNING (ELPHICK, M, and **MANLEY, R.).** Teachers for the Commonwealth: the British contribution. *Planning*, vol. 30, no. 482, August 1964, pp. 245–280.

POLITICAL AND ECONOMIC PLANNING (CURRIE, Jean and **LEGGATT. T.).** New Commonwealth students in Britain, with special reference to students from east Africa. Allen & Unwin, 1965.

POSTMASTER GENERAL: COMMITTEE ON BROADCASTING, 1960. Report. ["Pilkington Report."] HMSO, 1962.

PRIME MINISTER: COMMITTEE ON HIGHER EDUCATION. Higher education. Cmnd. 2154. Report and appendices one, three and four, 1963. Appendices two (A), two (B) and five, and 7 vol. of evidence, 1964. ["Robbins Report."] HMSO.

PRIME MINISTER AND FIRST LORD OF THE TREASURY: COMMITTEE OF ENQUIRY. Committee of enquiry into the organisation of civil science. Cmnd. 2171. ["Trend Report."] HMSO, 1963.

REGIONAL ADVISORY COUNCILS IN ENGLAND AND WALES. Higher education: full-time and sandwich courses in colleges of advanced technology and colleges of technology, agriculture, art and commerce. 1964.

ROYAL AGRICULTURAL SOCIETY OF ENGLAND (CROWTHER, C.). The training of the young farmer. RASE, n.d.

ROYAL COMMISSION ON POPULATION. Report. Cmd. 7695. HMSO, 1949.

ROYAL INSTITUTE OF BRITISH ARCHITECTS. Schools of architecture recognized by the RIBA. RIBA, 1965.

SCOTTISH COUNCIL FOR COMMERCIAL EDUCATION. Foreign language and export courses. ["Workman Report."] Edinburgh, SCCE, 1964.

SCOTTISH COUNCIL FOR RESEARCH IN EDUCATION. Social implications of the 1947 Scottish mental survey. University of London Press, 1953.

SCOTTISH EDUCATION DEPARTMENT: SCOTTISH TECHNICAL EDUCATION CONSULTATIVE COUNCIL. A report by the committee on the government of local technical colleges. ["Dimwiddie Report."] Edinburgh, SED, 1962.

Ibid. Development of Day Release Committee: first report. ["Oakley Report." Parts I and II only.] Edinburgh, SED, 1962.

Ibid. Report of Pre-apprenticeship Courses Committee. ["Arrell Report"; attached to *Circular* 521.] Edinburgh, SED, 1962.

SCOTTISH EDUCATION DEPARTMENT: SCOTTISH YOUTH ADVISORY COMMITTEE. The needs of youth in these times. ["Keith Report."] Edinburgh, HMSO, 1945.

SCOTTISH EDUCATION DEPARTMENT: STANDING CONSULTATIVE COUNCIL ON YOUTH AND COMMUNITY SERVICE IN SCOTLAND. Interim report of linkage committee. [Attached to *Circular* 598.] Edinburgh, SED, 1965.

Ibid. Progressive joint training of part-time youth leaders. ["Inches Report."] Edinburgh, SED, 1966.

SCOTTISH EDUCATION DEPARTMENT: STANDING CONSULTATIVE COUNCIL ON YOUTH SERVICE IN SCOTLAND. The training of part-time leaders. [Attached to *Circular* 487.] 1961.

SCOTTISH EDUCATION DEPARTMENT: STANDING CONSULTATIVE COUNCIL ON YOUTH SERVICE IN SCOTLAND: TRAINING COMMITTEE. Recommendations on the long-term provision of professional training for youth leaders. ["Noble Report."] Edinburgh, SED, 1962.

SCOTTISH EDUCATION DEPARTMENT: WORKING PARTY. Report ... on the curriculum of the senior secondary school: introduction of the ordinary grade of the Scottish Leaving Certificate. ["First Brunton Report."] Edinburgh, HMSO, 1959.

SCOTTISH EDUCATION DEPARTMENT: WORKING PARTY. From school to further education. ["Second Brunton Report"; attached to *Circular* 530.] Edinburgh, HMSO, 1963.

SECRETARY OF STATE FOR EDUCATION AND SCIENCE: COUNCIL FOR SCIENTIFIC POLICY. Enquiry into the flow of candidates in science and technology into higher education: interim report. Cmnd. 2893. ["Dainton Report".] HMSO, 1966.

SECRETARY OF STATE FOR EDUCATION AND SCIENCE: SPECIAL COMMITTEE. Report of the Committee on Social Studies. Cmnd. 2660. ["Heyworth Report."] HMSO, 1965.

SECRETARY OF STATE FOR SCOTLAND: ADVISORY COUNCIL ON EDUCATION IN SCOTLAND. Compulsory day continuation classes: fourth report. [Also sometimes called "Fyfe Report."] Edinburgh, HMSO, 1943.

Ibid. Technical education. Cmd. 6786. [Called in this book "Fyfe Report."] Edinburgh, HMSO, 1946.

Ibid. Further education. Cmd. 8454. ["McClelland Report."] Edinburgh, HMSO, 1952.

SECRETARY OF STATE FOR THE COLONIES: SPECIAL COMMISSION. Report of the Commission on Higher Education in the Colonies. Cmd. 6647. ["Asquith Report."] HMSO, 1945.

SECRETARY OF STATE FOR THE HOME DEPARTMENT, SECRETARY OF STATE FOR SCOTLAND *and* **MINISTER OF AGRICULTURE, FISHERIES AND FOOD: INTERDEPARTMENTAL COMMITTEE.** The demand for agricultural graduates. . . . Cmnd. 2419. ["Bosanquet Report."] HMSO, 1964.

STANDING CONFERENCE OF NATIONAL VOLUNTARY YOUTH ORGANISATIONS OF ENGLAND AND WALES. Partnership in the service of youth 1945. SCNVYO, 1945.

Ibid. Young people today: an account of young people in voluntary youth organisations. NCSS, 1960.

Ibid. The work of a local standing conference. SCNVYO *and* NCSS, 1964.

STANDING CONFERENCE OF VOLUNTARY ORGANISATIONS CO-OPERATING IN OVERSEAS SOCIAL SERVICE. Overseas service and voluntary organisations: a directory. NCSS, 1963.

SURREY EDUCATIONAL RESEARCH ASSOCIATION. School leavers: attitudes and aspirations of Surrey school leavers towards youth service, further education and training. Kingston-upon-Thames, Surrey County Council, 1964.

TRADES UNION CONGRESS. Statement on higher education. Appendix A of *Report of proceedings at the 88th annual Trades Union Congress. . . Brighton . . . 1956.* TUC, 1956.

Ibid. Promotion and encouragement of the arts. *Report of proceedings at the 93rd annual Trades Union Congress. . . Portsmouth. . .1961.* TUC, 1961.

Ibid. Memorandum of evidence to Committee on Higher Education. *Report of 94th annual Trades Union Congress. . . Blackpool. . . 1962.* TUC, 1962.

UNITED NATIONS EDUCATIONAL, SCIENTIFIC AND CULTURAL ORGANIZATION. Adult education: current trends and practices. *Problems in education,* 2. *Publication* no. 636. Paris, UNESCO, 1949.

Ibid. Universities in adult education. *Problems in education,* 4. Paris, UNESCO, 1952.

Ibid. Education in a technological society: a preliminary international survey of the nature and efficiency of technical education. Paris, UNESCO, 1952.

Ibid. International directory of adult education. Paris, UNESCO, 1952.

Ibid. New trends in youth organizations: a comparative survey. *Educational studies and documents,* no. 35. Paris, UNESCO, 1960.

Ibid. Study abroad 16, 1966–68. Paris, UNESCO, 1965.

Ibid. Economic and social aspects of educational planning. Paris, UNESCO, 1964.

UNITED STATES OF AMERICA: THE PRESIDENT'S COMMISSION ON HIGHER EDUCATION. Higher education for American democracy. Washington, DC, 1947.

UNIVERSITIES COUNCIL FOR ADULT EDUCATION: WORKING PARTY. The universities and adult education. Bristol, UCAE, 1961.

UNIVERSITY GRANTS COMMITTEE: SPECIAL COMMITTEE. Report. . . on university teaching methods. ["Hale Report."] HMSO, 1964.

UNIVERSITY GRANTS COMMITTEE: SPECIAL COMMITTEE. Report. . . on Latin American studies. ["Parry Report."] HMSO, 1965.

UNIVERSITY GRANTS COMMITTEE: SPECIAL SUBCOMMITTEE. Report. . . on Oriental, Slavonic, east European and African studies. ["Hayter Report."] HMSO, 1961.

UNIVERSITY GRANTS COMMITTEE, DEPARTMENT OF EDUCATION AND SCIENCE *and* **SCOTTISH EDUCATION DEPARTMENT: SPECIAL COMMITTEE.** Audio-visual aids in higher scientific education. ["Brynmor Jones Report."] HMSO, 1965.

UNIVERSITY OF LONDON INSTITUTE OF EDUCATION *and* **LONDON AND HOME COUNTIES REGIONAL ADVISORY COUNCIL FOR TECHNOLOGICAL EDUCATION: WORKING PARTY.** Research into technical education. ["Judges Report."]LHCRACTE, 1963.

WORKERS' EDUCATIONAL ASSOCIATION. Memorandum of evidence to Committee on Higher Education. [Duplicated; obtainable from 27 Portman Square, London, W.1.] N.d.

WORKERS' EDUCATIONAL ASSOCIATION: WORKING PARTY. Trade union education. WEA, 1953.
WORKERS' EDUCATIONAL ASSOCIATION: WORKING PARTY. Aspects of adult education. WEA, 1960.
YORKSHIRE COUNCIL FOR FURTHER EDUCATION. The reconstruction of further education. Leeds, YCFE, 1943.
Ibid. The liberal aspect of technical education. *Pamphlet* no. 70. Leeds, YCFE, 1962.

Miscellaneous annual publications

Reports of central government departments and committees

ADVISORY COUNCIL ON SCIENTIFIC POLICY—COUNCIL FOR SCIENTIFIC POLICY. *Annual report.* Cmnd. HMSO.
CENTRAL OFFICE OF INFORMATION: *see* Other central-government publications.
COMMONWEALTH RELATIONS OFFICE *and* **COLONIAL OFFICE** . . . *Report of the Commonwealth Scholarship Commission in the United Kingdom for the year.* . . . HMSO.
DEPARTMENT OF SCIENTIFIC AND INDUSTRIAL RESEARCH—SCIENCE RESEARCH COUNCIL. *Studentships and fellowships.* . . . HMSO.
DEPARTMENT OF SCIENTIFIC AND INDUSTRIAL RESEARCH—SCIENCE RESEARCH COUNCIL *and* **BRITISH COUNCIL.** *Scientific research in British universities and colleges.* . . . HMSO.
HER MAJESTY'S STATIONERY OFFICE: *see* Bibliographies, etc.
LORD PRESIDENT OF THE COUNCIL *and* **SECRETARY OF STATE FOR EDUCATION AND SCIENCE: DEPARTMENT OF SCIENTIFIC AND INDUSTRIAL RESEARCH—SCIENCE RESEARCH COUNCIL.** *Annual report.* Cmnd. HMSO.
MINISTER OF EDUCATION—SECRETARY OF STATE FOR EDUCATION AND SCIENCE. *Education in.* . . . Cmnd. HMSO.
MINISTRY OF EDUCATION—DEPARTMENT OF EDUCATION AND SCIENCE: *see* Other central-government publications.
MINISTRY OF LABOUR: CENTRAL TRAINING COUNCIL. *Report to the Minister.* HMSO.
SCOTTISH EDUCATION DEPARTMENT: *see* Other central-government publications.
SCOTTISH EDUCATION DEPARTMENT: SCOTTISH TECHNICAL EDUCATION CONSULTATIVE COUNCIL. *Annual report.* Edinburgh, SED.
SECRETARY OF STATE FOR SCOTLAND. *Agriculture in Scotland: report for.* . . . Cmnd. Edinburgh, HMSO.
Ibid. *Education in Scotland in.* . . . Cmnd. Edinburgh, HMSO.

Reports of other bodies

ARTS COUNCIL OF GREAT BRITAIN. State of play: 19th *annual report*, 1963–4. Arts Council, 1964.
ASSOCIATION OF BRITISH CHAMBERS OF COMMERCE. *Annual report.* ABCC.
CITY AND GUILDS OF LONDON INSTITUTE. *Annual report.* [In 8 parts.] CGLI.
COUNCIL FOR NATIONAL ACADEMIC AWARDS. *Report.* CNAA.
NUFFIELD FOUNDATION. *Annual report.* Oxford, Oxford University Press.
STANDING CONFERENCE OF NATIONAL VOLUNTARY YOUTH ORGANISATIONS OF ENGLAND AND WALES. *Annual report and directory.* . . . SCNVYO.

See also Publications of local education authorities *and* Addresses at meetings.

Prospectuses, regulations, guides, etc.

CITY AND GUILDS OF LONDON INSTITUTE. *General regulations: form 1.* CGLI.
Ibid. *New and revised schemes for the session. . . : form 2.* CGLI.
Ibid. *Regulations and syllabuses.* [For separate subjects.] CGLI.
NATIONAL COUNCIL FOR TECHNOLOGICAL AWARDS. *List of. . . courses (at. . . colleges) which are now recognised by the Council as leading to the Diploma in Technology. List no.* 16 with Addendum. ["Hives Council" list.] NCTA, 1964.
NATIONAL UNION OF TEACHERS. *Annual guide to careers for young people.* NUT.
Ibid. *University and college entrance: the basic facts.* NUT.
SCOTTISH COUNCIL FOR COMMERCIAL EDUCATION. *Handbook.* Edinburgh, SCCE.

See also Other central-government publications *and* Reports of committees, etc.

Yearbooks

ASSOCIATION OF ART INSTITUTIONS. *Year book. . . .* AAI.
ASSOCIATION OF TECHNICAL INSTITUTIONS. *Year book.* ATI.
DENT, H. C. (*ed.*). *The year book of technical education and careers in industry.* Black.
The education authorities directory and annual. School Government Publishing Co.
The education committees year book. Councils and Education Press.
NATIONAL INSTITUTE OF ADULT EDUCATION. *Adult education in . . . : the year book of the . . . .* NIAE.

Addresses at meetings

BAKER, E. I. Recent developments in business studies. At ATI, Torquay, 1962. ATI, 1962.
BRAY, F., BOSWORTH, G. S. *and* **VENABLES, P. F. R.** Sandwich courses. At Ministry of Education/BACIE conference, London, 1956. *BACIE journal,* vol. 10, no. 2, April 1956, pp. 50–73.
BRITISH ASSOCIATION FOR COMMERCIAL AND INDUSTRIAL EDUCATION. The implications of the Crowther Report:. . . spring conference . . . London . . . 1960. BACIE, 1960.
Ibid. Policy in perspective: a critical survey of recent policy recommendations in the field of education and training. . . annual conference . . . Cambridge. . . 1960. BACIE, 1960.
Ibid. Education for survival:. . . ninth annual conference . . . East Midlands Group, Buxton . . . 1960. BACIE, 1960.
Ibid. New routes to further education:. . . spring conference . . . London . . . 1961. BACIE 1961.
Ibid. Continental comparisons:. . . annual conference . . . Nottingham . . . 1961. BACIE, 1961.
Ibid. The spectrum of higher education:. . . annual conference 1962 . . . Nottingham. BACIE, 1962.
Ibid. Cmnd. 1892: the next step:. . . conference, London . . . 1963. BACIE, 1963.
Ibid. Economic growth and manpower:. . . spring conference . . . London . . . 1963. BACIE, 1963.
Ibid. The Industrial Training Act:. . . spring conference, London . . . 1964. BACIE, 1964.
BRITISH COUNCIL FOR THE WELFARE OF SPASTICS. 1960. Spastic school leavers' employment? [Report of addresses by **H. B.** and **M. O. Davies,** December 1960.] BCWS, 1961.
BRITISH INSTITUTE OF MANAGEMENT. Management training techniques. BIM, 1962.
BUSSIÈRE. E.: *see* UNITED NATIONS EDUCATIONAL, SCIENTIFIC AND CULTURAL ORGANIZATION.

COUNCIL OF EUROPE: COUNCIL FOR CULTURAL CO-OPERATION. Engineering education. . .: an international discussion . . . . Strasbourg, Council of Europe, 1963.

COX, (Sir) **H. R.** The coming of the Council for National Academic Awards. At ATI, Brighton, 1964. ATI, 1964.

DICKINSON, G. The one year full-time, pre-senior, pre-apprenticeship course for building. Extract from an address at the annual conference of the Yorkshire Educational Association for the Building Industry, York, 1959.

EAST ANGLIAN REGIONAL ADVISORY COUNCIL FOR FURTHER EDUCATION. Links with industry: . . . annual conference, Clacton-on-Sea, 1961. Norwich, EARACFE, 1961.

EDMUNDSON, J. Physical education in the technical college. At ATI, London, 1961. ATI, 1961.

EDWARDS, E. G. The interaction of the work of colleges and industry. A symposium of higher scientific and technological education sponsored by WFSW and others, Moscow, 1962. Moscow, 1962.

ELVIN, H. L. Education and the end of empire: a lecture at University of London Institute of Education. *Studies in education*, no. 8. Evans, 1957.

ENGLISH, C. R. Commonwealth co-operation in technical education and vocational training. At ATI, London, 1965. ATI, 1965.

FEDERATION OF BRITISH INDUSTRIES. Report of the technical colleges and industry conference: . . . Ashorne Hill, Leamington Spa. FBI, 1954.

Ibid. Report of the conference on industry and technical education . . . Loughborough. [Organized by FBI and RACOFEEM.] FBI, 1955.

Ibid. 1955. Industry and the public and grammar schools: . . . conference at Ashorne Hill, 1955. FBI, 1956.

Ibid. Report of the second national conference between industry and the technical colleges . . . 1957, at FBI headquarters. FBI, 1957.

Ibid. 1957. Cambridge conference on industry and the technical colleges . . . 1957. [Organized by FBI and EARACFE.] FBI, 1958.

Ibid. 1957. Windsor conference on industry and the technical colleges . . . 1957. [Organized by FBI and SRCFE.] FBI, 1958.

Ibid. Chester conference on industry and technical education. FBI, 1959.

Ibid. 1960. Invest in the future: . . . a conference on recruitment and training policy in the small and medium-sized firm: Buxton, 1960. FBI, 1961.

Ibid. Stocktaking on management education: . . . conference . . . London. FBI, 1961.

Ibid. From sixth form to industry: . . . conference . . . Cambridge . . . 1963. FBI, 1963.

HEATON, R. N. The Commonwealth Education Conference. At ATI, London, 1960. ATI, 1960.

HENTHORNE, T. K., LEWIS, E. *and* **WHITEHOUSE, B. C.** The bridge between schools and further education. At ATI, London, 1961. ATI, 1961.

HOGAN, J. M. The future of the youth service. Leeds, University of Leeds Institute of Education, 1965.

HOLMES, B. *and* **DRYLAND, Ann.** Aspects of US and UK examination systems. At ATI, London, 1965. ATI, 1965.

INSTITUTION OF MECHANICAL ENGINEERS. Engineering education and career patterns. *Proceedings of the Institution of Mechanical Engineers*, vol. 178, part 3F, pp. vi + 95.

INSTITUTION OF PRODUCTION ENGINEERS. The automatic factory: what does it mean? Conference, London, 1955. I Prod E, 1955.

KING GEORGE'S JUBILEE TRUST. Youth service to-morrow: . . . a meeting at Ashridge. KGJT, 1951.

LEWIS, C. S. The abolition of man. Riddell Memorial Lectures at University of Durham. Iles, 1943.

LEWIS, L. J. Partnership in oversea education: a lecture at University of London Institute of Education. *Studies in education*, no. 9. Evans, 1959.

MINISTRY OF EDUCATION: UNITED KINGDOM NATIONAL COMMISSION FOR UNESCO. 1956. The universities and adult education: . . . regional European seminar . . . Bangor . . . 1956. HMSO, 1957.

MUMFORD, D. E. 16–19, school or college? At ATI, London, 1965. ATI, 1965.

NATIONAL FOUNDATION FOR EDUCATIONAL RESEARCH IN ENGLAND AND WALES. 1962. Technical education and training in the United Kingdom: research in progress 1962–64: report of the colloquium... Eltham... November 1962... with 82 summary accounts of research in progress, with supplement, 1963-64, of reported researches. Compiled **HEYWOOD, J.** *and* **ABEL, R. Ann.** *Occasional publication* no. 8. NFER, 1965.

NATIONAL INSTITUTE FOR THE DEAF. Report of the 1960 conference on the care of the deaf. NID, 1960.

THE 1963 CAMPAIGN FOR EDUCATION. The case for advance. [5 addresses at a mass meeting, Westminster.] The 1963 Campaign, 1963.

OXFORD UNIVERSITY: DEPARTMENT OF EDUCATION. 1948. The education of the young worker:... conference... Oxford... 1948. Oxford, Oxford University Press, for KGJT, 1949.

Ibid. 1949. The education of the young worker:... second conference... Oxford... 1949. Oxford, Oxford University Press, for KGJT, 1950.

Ibid. 1950. The education of the young worker:... third conference... Oxford... 1950. Oxford, Oxford University Press, for KGJT, 1951.

Ibid. 1951. The education of the young worker:... fourth conference... Oxford... 1951. Heinemann, for KGJT, 1952.

Ibid. 1954. The young worker: education for human relations:... fifth conference... Oxford... 1954. Heinemann, 1955.

Ibid. The young worker: training for the untrained:... sixth conference... Oxford... 1956. Heinemann, 1956.

ROYAL INSTITUTE OF BRITISH ARCHITECTS. Teaching laboratories:... a symposium on design... 1958. RIBA, 1958.

RUSSELL, *Sir* **Lionel.** The binary system of higher education. At ATI, London, 1966. ATI, 1966.

SELLEY, W. T. Developments in secondary education and their effects on further education. At ATI, Torquay, 1962. ATI, 1962.

SOCIETY OF FORESTERS OF GREAT BRITAIN (*ed.* **PALMER, R. W. V.**). Education in British forestry... report of the fifth discussion meeting, Cirencester... 1965. Oxford University Press, 1965.

THOMPSON, C. A. The impact on technical colleges of... the Newsom Report. At ATI, London, 1964. ATI, 1964.

UNITED NATIONS EDUCATIONAL, SCIENTIFIC AND CULTURAL ORGANIZATION. 1960. Second world conference on adult education... Montreal, 1960. *Educational studies and abstracts*, 46. Paris, UNESCO, 1963.

Ibid. 1962. The development of higher education in Africa: the conference... at Tananarive ... 1962. Paris, UNESCO, 1963.

UNITED NATIONS EDUCATIONAL, SCIENTIFIC AND CULTURAL ORGANIZATION (BUSSIÈRE, E.). Summary report of the international conference on adult education at Elsinore, Denmark... 1949. Paris, UNESCO, 1949.

UNITED NATIONS EDUCATIONAL, SCIENTIFIC AND CULTURAL ORGANIZATION *and* INTERNATIONAL BUREAU OF EDUCATION. Training of technical and scientific staff: measures to increase facilities: a comparative study. 22nd international conference on public education, Geneva. *Publication* no. 206. Paris, UNESCO, 1959.

UNITED STATES OF AMERICA: CONGRESS: Report on automation and technological change: hearings before the Sub-Committee on Economic Stabilization of the Joint Committee on the Economic Report. Washington, D.C., 1955.

WEST, A. C. Technical education in Scotland. At ATI, Aberdeen, 1959. ATI, 1959.

WORK, A. L. Industrial training. At ATI, Brighton, 1964. ATI, 1964.

Other books and pamphlets

ALLAWAY, A. J. The educational centres movement: a comprehensive survey. NIAE, 1961.

Anon. The story of Ruskin College. Oxford, Oxford University Press, 1955.

z

ARGLES, O. M. V. South Kensington to Robbins: an account of English technical and scientific education since 1851. Longmans, 1964.

ARGYLE, M. *and* **SMITH, T.** Training managers. Acton Society Trust, 1962.

BANKS, Frances. Teach them to live: a study of education in English prisons. Parrish, 1958.

BEVERIDGE, A. Apprenticeship now: notes on the training of young entrants to industry. Chapman & Hall, 1963.

BROOKS, C. An educational adventure: a history of the Woolwich Polytechnic. Woolwich Polytechnic, 1965.

BUTTON, L. (*ed.*). Youth service: the contribution of the local education authorities: a report of a national survey. [1953–4]. National Association of Local Education Authority Youth Service Officers, n.d.

CAREY, A. T. Colonial students: a study of the social adaption of colonial students in London. Secker and Warburg, 1956.

CARTER, C. F. *and* **WILLIAMS, B. R.** Science in industry: policy for progress. Oxford University Press, for Science and Industry Committee, 1959.

CARTER, M. P. Home, school and work: a study of the education and employment of young people in Britain. Oxford, Pergamon Press, 1962.

CLAY, Hilary M. How research can help training. *Problems of progress in industry*, no. 16. HMSO, for DSIR, 1964.

CLEUGH, M. F. Educating older people. Tavistock Publications, 1962.

COOKE, D. (*ed.*). Youth organizations of Great Britain 1963. Jordan, 1963.

COTGROVE, S. Technical education and social change. Allen & Unwin, 1958.

CROFT, Margaret. Apprenticeship and the 'bulge'. *Research series*, 216. Fabian Society, 1960.

CROW, D.: *see* CENTRAL OFFICE OF INFORMATION (Other central-government publications).

CROWTHER, C.: *see* ROYAL AGRICULTURAL SOCIETY OF ENGLAND (Reports of committees, etc.).

CURRIE, Jean: *see* POLITICAL AND ECONOMIC PLANNING (Reports of committees, etc.).

DAVIES, L. Liberal studies and higher technology. Cardiff, University of Wales Press, 1965.

DAWSON, J. Education Acts 1944, 1946 and 1948: a detailed index. School Government Publishing Co., n.d.

DICKERSON, R. W. V. Recruitment and training for the Institute of Municipal Treasurers and Accountants. IMTA, 1965.

DOUGLAS, J. W. B. The home and the school: a study of ability and attainment in the primary school. McGibbon & Kee, 1964.

DOWNES, D. *and* **FLOWER F.** Educating for uncertainty. *Fabian tract* 364. Fabian Society, 1965.

DOWNIE, J. H. The training of young people in industry: summary of an investigation by the study groups based on HRH the Duke of Edinburgh's Commonwealth study conferences. IWS, 1965.

DUTT, R. P. The crisis of Britain and the British Empire. Lawrence & Wishart, 1953.

EDWARDS, H. J. The evening institute. NIAE. 1961.

ELPHICK, M.: *see* POLITICAL AND ECONOMIC PLANNING (Reports of committees, etc.).

ELSDON, K. T. Centres for adult education. ECA *and* NIAE, 1962.

FERGUSON, A. An essay on the history of civil society. Edinburgh, Creech, Bell & Bradfute, 1783.

FERGUSON, R. W. *and* **ABBOTT, A.** Day continuation schools. Publication department, Bournville, *and* Pitman, 1935.

FLOUD, Jean, HALSEY, A. H. *and* **MARTIN, F. M.** Social class and educational opportunity. Heinemann, 1957.

FRANKS, *Lord*. British business schools. ["Franks Report".] BIM, 1963.

FURNEAUX, W. D. The chosen few: an examination of some aspects of university selection in Britain. Oxford University Press, for Nuffield Foundation, 1961.

GLADDEN, E. N. British public service administration. Staples Press, 1961.

GLASS, D. V. (*ed.*). Social mobility in Britain. Routledge & Kegan Paul, 1954.

GOLDSMITH, M. Careers in technology. Harmondsworth, Penguin Books, 1963.

GRAHAM, J. One hundred and twenty-five years: the evolution of commercial education in Glasgow. Glasgow, SCCE, 1964.

GREIG, F. W.: *see* INDUSTRIAL TRAINING COUNCIL (Reports of committees, etc.).

GUNZBURG, H. C. Senior training centres: an outline of the principles and practices of social education and training for older mentally subnormal people. NAMH, 1963.

HALSEY, A. H., FLOUD, Jean *and* **ANDERSON, C.A.** (*eds.*). Education, economy and society: a reader in the sociology of education. New York, Free Press of Glencoe, 1961.

HARBISON, F. *and* **MYERS, C. A.** Education, manpower and economic growth: strategies of human resource development. New York, McGraw-Hill, 1964.

HARGROVE, Aphra L. The social adaption of educationally subnormal school leavers. NAMH, 1954.

Ibid. Serving the mentally handicapped. NAMH, 1965.

HARMAN, H. Commercial apprenticeship. Pitman, 1958.

HARRISON, J. F. C. Learning and living 1790–1960: a study in the history of the English adult education movement. Routledge & Kegan Paul, 1961.

HASTINGS, Merle: *see* ADVISORY CENTRE FOR EDUCATION (Reports of committees, etc.).

HEATH, Kathryn. Ministries of Education: their functions and organization. Washington, D.C., Department of Health, Education and Welfare, 1962.

HEYWORTH, P.: *see* OXFORD UNIVERSITY, DEPARTMENT OF EDUCATION (Reports of committees, etc.).

HOGBEN, L. T. (*ed.*). Political arithmetic: a symposium of population studies. Allen & Unwin, 1938.

HOGG, J. C. ABC guides to the Education Acts 1944 and 1946. Philip & Tacey, n.d.

HUNTER, G. Residential colleges: some new developments in British adult education. *Occasional papers*, no. 1. New York, Fund for Adult Education, n.d.

HUTCHINGS, D. W.: *see* OXFORD UNIVERSITY, DEPARTMENT OF EDUCATION (Reports of committees, etc.).

HUTCHINSON, V. G. An examination of the role of the county colleges with special reference to the less able child. Unpublished dissertation for Diploma in Education, University of Liverpool. [In School of Education library.] 1965.

HUXLEY, A. Brave new world. Chatto & Windus, 1932.

JACKSON, B. *and* **MARSDEN, D.** Education and the working class. Routledge & Kegan Paul, 1962.

JAFFE, A. J. *and* **STEWART, C. D.** Manpower resources and utilization: principles of working force analysis. New York, Wiley; Chapman & Hall, 1951.

JAHODA, Marie. The education of technologists: an exploratory case study at Brunel College. Tavistock Press, 1963.

KÄHLER, A. *and* **HAMBURGER, E.** Education for an industrial age. Ithaca and New York, Cornell University Press; Cumberlege, 1948.

KELLY, T. A history of adult education in Great Britain from the middle ages to the twentieth century. Liverpool, Liverpool University Press, 1962.

KELSALL, R. K. Report on an inquiry into applications for admission to universities. AUBC, for Committee of Vice-Chancellors and Principals of the Universities of UK, 1957.

KITCHEN, P. I. From learning to earning: birth and growth of a young people's college. Faber & Faber, 1944.

KUENSTLER, P. H. K. Youth work in England: extracts from Ministry of Education and other publications relating to statutory and voluntary youth work in England. *University of Bristol Institute of Education publication* no. 6. University of London Press, 1954.

LABOVITCH, C. (*ed.*). Directory of opportunities for school leavers 1965. Watts, for Cornmarket Press, 1965.

LEGGATT, T.: *see* POLITICAL AND ECONOMIC PLANNING (Reports of committees, etc.).

LIEPMANN, Kate. Apprenticeship: an enquiry into its adequacy under modern conditions. Routledge & Kegan Paul, 1960.

LINDSAY, K. Social progress and educational waste. Routledge, 1926.

LIVINGSTONE, A. S. The overseas student in Britain, with special reference to training courses in social welfare. Manchester, Manchester University Press, 1960.

MACKINTOSH, M. Education in Scotland yesterday and today. Glasgow, Gibson, 1962.

MACLENNAN, A. Technical teaching and instruction. Oldbourne, 1963.

MANLEY, R.: *see* POLITICAL AND ECONOMIC PLANNING (Reports of committees, etc.).

MARKS, H. Community associations and adult education. *Community associations booklet* no. 3. NCSS, for NFCA, 1949.

MARSH, D. C. The changing social structure of England and Wales 1871–1951. Routledge & Kegan Paul, 1958.

MARX, K. 1887. Capital: a critical analysis of capitalist production. Allen & Unwin, 1938.

McCRENSKY, E. Scientific manpower in Europe. Pergamon Press, 1958.

MILLERSON, G. The qualifying associations: a study in professionalization. Routledge & Kegan Paul, 1964.

MILLS, H. R. Techniques of technical training. Cleaver-Hume Press, 1953.

MONTGOMERIE, J. F. The handicapped person: a report on the provision of welfare services for handicapped persons in Scotland. Edinburgh, SCSS, 1958.

MONTGOMERY, R. J. Examinations: an account of their evolution as administrative devices in England. Longmans, 1965.

MORSE, Mary. The unattached. Harmondsworth, Penguin Books, 1965.

MOSSON, T. M. Management education in five European countries: Belgium, France, Italy, Spain, United Kingdom. Business Publications, 1965.

MURRAY-BROWNE, Eva. Going to university and technical college: a guide to courses and careers. Batsford, 1963.

MUSGROVE, F. Youth and the social order. Routledge & Kegan Paul, 1964.

NEAL, K. W. Technical college libraries: a guide to problems and practice. Wolverhampton, the author, 1965.

NICHOLSON, J. H. Help for the handicapped: an enquiry into the opportunities of the voluntary services. *Ref.* no. 528. NCSS, 1958.

NOZHKO, K. G. Methods of estimating the demand for specialists and of planning specialized training within the USSR. Paris, UNESCO, 1964.

OAKLEY, C. A. (*ed.*). Commercial apprenticeships. (**TONKINSON, E., THOMAS, R. E.** *and* **MAGNUS-HANNAFORD, R. E.**) University of London Press, 1962.

PAYNE, G. L. Britain's scientific and technological manpower. Stanford, Stanford University Press; Oxford University Press, 1960.

PEDLEY, F. H. A parent's guide to examinations from primary school to university. Oxford, Pergamon Press, 1964.

Ibid. The educational system in England and Wales. Oxford, Pergamon Press, 1964.

PEERS, R. Adult education: a comparative study. Routledge & Kegan Paul, 1958.

Ibid. Fact and possibility in English education. Routledge & Kegan Paul, 1963.

PETERSON, A. D. C. Investment in people: a Liberal design for education. *New directions*, 62, no. 6. Liberal Publication Department, 1962.

PRANDY, K. Professional employees: a study of scientists and engineers. Faber & Faber, 1965.

PRICE, Barbara. Technical colleges and colleges of further education. Batsford, 1959.

PRITCHARD, D. G. Education and the handicapped 1760–1960. Routledge & Kegan Paul, 1963.

PROUDHON, P. J. 1846. Système des contradictions économiques ou philosophie de la misère. Paris, Rivière, 1923.

RAPHAEL, L. H. Full-time degree courses outside universities. Truman & Knightley, 1964.

RAYBOULD, S. G. University extramural education in England, 1945–62: a study in finance and policy. Joseph, 1964.

RAYBOULD, S. G. (*ed.*). Trends in English adult education. Heinemann, 1959.

RICHARDSON, W. A. The technical college; its organization and administration. Oxford University Press, 1939.

SADLER, *Sir* Michael (*ed.*). Continuation schools in England and elsewhere: their place in the educational system of an industrial and commercial state. *Publications of the University of Manchester, education series,* no. 1. Manchester, Manchester University Press, 1907.

SIKLOS, T. Partnership incorporated: an account of a joint effort to solve the problems of apprentice training. CGLI, 1963.

SILBERSTON, Dorothy. Youth in a technical age: a study of day release. Parrish, 1959.

Ibid. Residence and technical education: a report on residence as a liberal element.... Parrish, 1960.

SIMON, B. Intelligence testing and the comprehensive school. Lawrence & Wishart, 1953.

SMITH, D. L. *and* **BAXTER, E. A.** College library administration in colleges of technology, art, commerce, and further education. Oxford University Press, 1965.

SMITH, S. J. To Wigan—a college: a short history of the Wigan and District Mining and Technical College from its beginnings in 1857 to the present day. [Duplicated.] 1965.

STANLEY, B. The education of junior citizens: an essay on the principles of education for club-leaders and teachers in county colleges. University of London Press, 1945.

TAYLOR, G. *and* **SAUNDERS, J. B.** The new law of education. Sixth edition. Butterworths, 1965.

TAYLOR, M. H.: *see* CITY AND GUILDS OF LONDON INSTITUTE (Reports of committees, etc.).

TOURAINE, A. *and others.* Worker's attitudes to technical change. Paris, OECD, 1965.

TURNER, J. D. Language laboratories in Great Britain 1963–4. University of London Press, 1963.

TYLECOTE, Mabel. The future of adult education. *Research series*, 214. Fabian Society, 1960.

VAIZEY, J. The costs of education. Allen & Unwin, 1958.

Ibid. The economics of education. Faber & Faber, 1962.

VENABLES, P. F. R. British technical education. Longmans, for BC, 1959.

Ibid. Sandwich courses for training technologists and technicians. Parrish, 1959.

VENABLES, P. F. R. *and others.* Technical education: its aims, organisation and future development. Bell, 1955.

VENABLES, P. F. R. *and* **WILLIAMS, W. J.** The smaller firm and technical education. Parrish, 1961.

VENESS, Thelma. School leavers: their aspirations and expectations. Methuen, 1962.

WALLER, R. D. A design for democracy: an abridgement of . . . the 1919 Report with an introduction *The years between*. Parrish, 1956.

WATERFALL, Edith, A. The day continuation school in England. Allen & Unwin, 1923.

WATTS, A. G. (*ed.*). Which university? Cornmarket Press, 1964.

WELLENS, J. Education and training in industry. Manchester, Columbine Press, 1955.

Ibid. The training revolution from shop-floor to board-room. Evans, 1963.

WHEATLEY, D. E. (*ed.*). Industry and careers: a study of British industries and the opportunities they offer. Iliffe, 1961.

WHEATLEY, D. E.: *see* CITY AND GUILDS OF LONDON INSTITUTE (Reports of committees, etc.).

WILLIAMS, *Lady* **Gertrude.** Recruitment to skilled trades. Routledge & Kegan Paul, 1957.

Ibid. Apprenticeship in Europe: the lesson for Britain. Chapman & Hall, 1963.

WILSON, N. The British system of government. Oxford, Blackwell, 1963.

WOOD, Ethel M. A history of the Polytechnic, London. Macdonald, 1965.

WRAY, W. J. *and* **FERGUSON, R. W.** (*eds.*). A day continuation school at work: papers by twelve contributors. Longmans, 1920.

YOUNG, J. T. Technicians today and tomorrow. Pitman, 1966.

Articles

Anon. Survey of the employment of technicians in the chemical and engineering industries. *Ministry of Labour gazette*, December 1960, pp. 464–467.

BARKER, G. R. Specialist training in the USSR. *Times educational supplement*, 29 April 1955, pp. 408–409.

BRITISH ASSOCIATION FOR COMMERCIAL AND INDUSTRIAL EDUCATION. Symposium on liberal studies. [Articles from *BACIE journal*.] BACIE [1965.]

D'AETH, R. Proposal for an educational research council and some of its implications. *Nature*, 12 October 1962, pp. 116–118.

GURR, C. E. Reflections on county colleges: the next ten years. *Times educational supplement*, 29 July 1955, p. 811.

LAUWERYS, J. A. United Kingdom (England and Wales). The international study of university admissions: access to higher education: 2: national studies, pp. 489–589. Paris, UNESCO *and* IAU, 1965.

LEESE, J. Examinations in further education. *Technical education and industrial training*, vol. 7, no. 5, May 1965, pp. 206–207.

McVEY, P. J. The colleges of advanced technology. AUT, *British universities annual 1963*, 1963, pp. 33–42.

PETERS, A. J. The changing idea of technical education. *British journal of educational studies*, vol. 11, no. 2, May 1963, pp. 142–166.

TRADES UNION CONGRESS. A new look for job training? *Labour*, January 1963, p. 14.

WHEATLEY, D. E. City and guilds examinations: a complex and evolving pattern. *Vocational aspect*, vol. 11, spring 1959, pp. 31–59.

WILLIAMS, P. R. C. Impact of the Robbins Report on the developing countries. AUT, *British universities annual 1964*, 1964, pp. 102–121.

Subappendix. Committee reports known by chairman's name

Aaron: *see* MINISTRY OF EDUCATION: CENTRAL ADVISORY COUNCIL FOR EDUCATION (WALES).

Acland: *see* BOARD OF EDUCATION: CONSULTATIVE COMMITTEE.

Albemarle: *see* (1) MINISTER OF EDUCATION: SPECIAL COMMITTEE ("first"); (2) MINISTRY OF LABOUR: CENTRAL YOUTH EMPLOYMENT EXECUTIVE: NATIONAL YOUTH EMPLOYMENT COUNCIL: WORKING PARTY ("second"); (3) DEPARTMENT OF EDUCATION AND SCIENCE: YOUTH SERVICE DEVELOPMENT COUNCIL ("third").

Alexander: *see* DEPARTMENT OF EDUCATION AND SCIENCE: NATIONAL ADVISORY COUNCIL ON EDUCATION FOR INDUSTRY AND COMMERCE.

Anderson: *see* MINISTER OF EDUCATION *and* SECRETARY OF STATE FOR SCOTLAND: SPECIAL COMMITTEE.

Annan: *see* MINISTRY OF EDUCATION *and* SCOTTISH EDUCATION DEPARTMENT: SPECIAL COMMITTEE.

Arnold: *see* MINISTRY OF EDUCATION: WORKING PARTY.

Arrell: *see* SCOTTISH EDUCATION DEPARTMENT: SCOTTISH TECHNICAL EDUCATION CONSULTATIVE COUNCIL.

Ashby: *see* (1) MINISTRY OF EDUCATION: SPECIAL COMMITTEE; (2) NIGERIA: FEDERAL MINISTRY OF EDUCATION: SPECIAL COMMISSION.

Asquith: *see* SECRETARY OF STATE FOR THE COLONIES: SPECIAL COMMISSION.

Assheton: *see* CHANCELLOR OF THE EXCHEQUER: SPECIAL COMMITTEE.

Atholl: *see* BOARD OF EDUCATION: SPECIAL COMMITTEE.

Barlow: *see* LORD PRESIDENT OF THE COUNCIL: SPECIAL COMMITTEE.

Barnes: *see* MINISTRY OF LABOUR: SPECIAL COMMITTEE.

Beloe: *see* MINISTRY OF EDUCATION: SECONDARY SCHOOL EXAMINATIONS COUNCIL: SPECIAL COMMITTEE.

Bessey: *see* (1) MINISTRY OF EDUCATION: WORKING PARTY ("first"); (2) DEPARTMENT OF EDUCATION AND SCIENCE: YOUTH SERVICE DEVELOPMENT COUNCIL ("second").

Bosanquet: *see* SECRETARY OF STATE FOR THE HOME DEPARTMENT, SECRETARY OF STATE FOR SCOTLAND *and* MINISTER OF AGRICULTURE, FISHERIES AND FOOD: INTERDEPARTMENTAL COMMITTEE.

Bray: *see* MINISTRY OF EDUCATION: SPECIAL COMMITTEE.

Briault: *see* LONDON COUNTY COUNCIL: SPECIAL COMMITTEE.

Brunton: *see* (1) SCOTTISH EDUCATION DEPARTMENT: WORKING PARTY ("first", 1959); (2) SCOTTISH EDUCATION DEPARTMENT: WORKING PARTY, ("second", 1963).

Burnham Main: *see* DEPARTMENT OF EDUCATION AND SCIENCE.

Carr: *see* MINISTRY OF LABOUR AND NATIONAL SERVICE: NATIONAL JOINT ADVISORY COUNCIL: SUB-COMMITTEE.

Carrington: *see* MINISTRY OF AGRICULTURE AND FISHERIES: WORKING PARTY.

Carr-Saunders: *see* (1) MINISTRY OF EDUCATION: SPECIAL COMMITTEE; (2) CENTRAL AFRICAN COUNCIL: SPECIAL COMMISSION.

Chance: *see* MINISTRY OF EDUCATION, WELSH DEPARTMENT: ADVISORY PANEL.

Clarke: *see* MINISTRY OF EDUCATION: CENTRAL ADVISORY COUNCIL FOR EDUCATION (ENGLAND).

Cleary: *see* (1) MINISTRY OF EDUCATION: SPECIAL COMMITTEE ("first", 1946); (2) MINISTRY OF EDUCATION: WORKING PARTY ("second", 1948).

Coldstream: *see* MINISTRY OF EDUCATION: NATIONAL ADVISORY COUNCIL ON ART EDUCATION (1960 and 1962) and DEPARTMENT OF EDUCATION AND SCIENCE: NATIONAL ADVISORY COUNCIL ON ART EDUCATION (1964 and 1966).

Collins: *see* INSTITUTE OF THE MOTOR INDUSTRY (INC.): SPECIAL COMMITTEE.

Connelly: *see* FIFE EDUCATION COMMITTEE.

Crick: *see* MINISTRY OF EDUCATION: NATIONAL ADVISORY COUNCIL ON EDUCATION FOR INDUSTRY AND COMMERCE.

Crowther: *see* MINISTRY OF EDUCATION: CENTRAL ADVISORY COUNCIL FOR EDUCATION (ENGLAND).

Dadd: *see* DEPARTMENT OF EDUCATION AND SCIENCE: NATIONAL ADVISORY COUNCIL ON EDUCATION FOR INDUSTRY AND COMMERCE. (Also called "Pilkington").

Dainton: *see* SECRETARY OF STATE FOR EDUCATION AND SCIENCE: COUNCIL FOR SCIENTIFIC POLICY.

De La Warr: *see* MINISTER OF AGRICULTURE, FISHERIES AND FOOD *and* MINISTER OF EDUCATION: SPECIAL COMMITTEE.

Dinwiddie: *see* SCOTTISH EDUCATION DEPARTMENT: SCOTTISH TECHNICAL EDUCATION CONSULTATIVE COUNCIL.

Fedden: *see* MINISTRY OF AIRCRAFT PRODUCTION: INTERDEPARTMENTAL COMMITTEE.

Fife: *see* FIFE EDUCATION COMMITTEE.

Fletcher: *see* MINISTRY OF EDUCATION: NATIONAL ADVISORY COUNCIL ON THE TRAINING AND SUPPLY OF TEACHERS.

Franks: *see* FRANKS, Lord (Other books and pamphlets).

Fraser: *see* DEPARTMENT OF HEALTH FOR SCOTLAND: SPECIAL COMMITTEE.

Freeman: *see* MINISTRY OF EDUCATION: NATIONAL ADVISORY COMMITTEE ON ART EXAMINATIONS (1952 and 1957).

Fyfe: *see* SECRETARY OF STATE FOR SCOTLAND: ADVISORY COUNCIL ON EDUCATION IN SCOTLAND (a series of wartime and early post-war reports); in this book *Technical education* (1946) is the one meant, but *Compulsory day continuation classes* (1943) is also mentioned.

Goodenough: *see* COMMITTEE ON EDUCATION FOR SALESMANSHIP.

Griffiths: *see* MINISTRY OF EDUCATION, WELSH DEPARTMENT: WELSH YOUTH COMMITTEE.

Gurney-Dixon: *see* MINISTRY OF EDUCATION: CENTRAL ADVISORY COUNCIL FOR EDUCATION (ENGLAND).

Hadow: *see* BOARD OF EDUCATION: CONSULTATIVE COMMITTEE (1926); not to be confused with other Hadow Reports *Primary education* (1931) and *Infant and nursery schools* (1933).

Hale: *see* UNIVERSITY GRANTS COMMITTEE: SPECIAL COMMITTEE (1964). There was also an interim report on the use of vacations by students (1963).

Hall: *see* JOINT COMMITTEE ON TRAINING IN THE BUILDING INDUSTRY.

Hardman: *see* MINISTRY OF EDUCATION: WORKING PARTY.

Hayter: *see* UNIVERSITY GRANTS COMMITTEE: SPECIAL SUBCOMMITTEE.

Henniker-Heaton: *see* DEPARTMENT OF EDUCATION AND SCIENCE: SPECIAL COMMITTEE.

Heyworth: *see* SECRETARY OF STATE FOR EDUCATION AND SCIENCE: SPECIAL COMMITTEE.

Hooper: *see* BRITISH INSTITUTE OF MANAGEMENT: STUDY GROUP.

Ince: *see* MINISTRY OF LABOUR AND NATIONAL SERVICE: SPECIAL COMMITTEE.

Inches: *see* SCOTTISH EDUCATION DEPARTMENT: STANDING CONSULTATIVE COUNCIL ON YOUTH AND COMMUNITY SERVICE IN SCOTLAND.

Jackson: *see* MINISTRY OF EDUCATION: COMMITTEE ON RECRUITMENT, TRAINING AND CONDITIONS OF SERVICE OF YOUTH LEADERS AND COMMUNITY CENTRE WARDENS; not to be confused with the Willis Jackson Report.

Willis Jackson: *see* MINISTRY OF EDUCATION: SPECIAL COMMITTEE.

Brynmor Jones: *see* UNIVERSITY GRANTS COMMITTEE, DEPARTMENT OF EDUCATION AND SCIENCE *and* SCOTTISH EDUCATION DEPARTMENT: SPECIAL COMMITTEE.

Judges: *see* UNIVERSITY OF LONDON INSTITUTE OF EDUCATION *and* LONDON AND HOME COUNTIES REGIONAL ADVISORY COUNCIL FOR TECHNOLOGICAL EDUCATION: WORKING PARTY.

Keir: *see* NORTHERN RHODESIA COPPERBELT TECHNICAL FOUNDATION, GOVERNMENT OF NORTHERN RHODESIA *and* GOVERNMENT OF THE FEDERATION OF RHODESIA AND NYASALAND: SPECIAL COMMITTEE.

Keith: *see* SCOTTISH EDUCATION DEPARTMENT: SCOTTISH YOUTH ADVISORY COMMITTEE.

Lampard-Vachell: *see* MINISTRY OF EDUCATION: NATIONAL ADVISORY COUNCIL ON EDUCATION FOR INDUSTRY AND COMMERCE (1960 and 1961).

Lewis: *see* BOARD OF EDUCATION: DEPARTMENTAL COMMITTEE ON JUVENILE EDUCATION IN RELATION TO EMPLOYMENT AFTER THE WAR.

Lisborg: *see* LONDON AND HOME COUNTIES REGIONAL ADVISORY COUNCIL FOR TECHNOLOGICAL EDUCATION: ARCHITECTURE AND BUILDING ADVISORY COMMITTEE: WORKING PARTY.

Llewellyn-Jones: *see* DEPARTMENT OF EDUCATION AND SCIENCE: CENTRAL ADVISORY COUNCIL FOR EDUCATION (WALES).

Lockwood: (1) all reports of the MINISTRY OF EDUCATION: SECONDARY SCHOOL EXAMINATIONS COUNCIL from the third (1960) onwards are sometimes called "Lockwood Reports"; (2) *see also* DEPARTMENT OF TECHNICAL CO-OPERATION: SPECIAL COMMITTEE.

Loveday: *see* (1) MINISTER OF AGRICULTURE AND FISHERIES: SPECIAL COMMITTEE ("second", 1946); (2) MINISTRY OF EDUCATION *and* MINISTRY OF AGRICULTURE AND FISHERIES: JOINT ADVISORY COMMITTEE ("first", "third" and "fourth": 1945, 1947 and 1949 respectively).

Luxmoore: *see* MINISTER OF AGRICULTURE AND FISHERIES: SPECIAL COMMITTEE.

Marre: *see* MINISTRY OF LABOUR: REPRESENTATIVE COMMITTEE.

McClelland: *see* SECRETARY OF STATE FOR SCOTLAND: ADVISORY COUNCIL ON EDUCATION IN SCOTLAND.

McMeeking: *see* MINISTRY OF EDUCATION: NATIONAL ADVISORY COUNCIL ON EDUCATION FOR INDUSTRY AND COMMERCE.

McNair: *see* BOARD OF EDUCATION: SPECIAL COMMITTEE.

Newsom: *see* MINISTRY OF EDUCATION: CENTRAL ADVISORY COUNCIL FOR EDUCATION (ENGLAND).

Noble: *see* SCOTTISH EDUCATION DEPARTMENT: STANDING CONSULTATIVE COUNCIL ON YOUTH SERVICE IN SCOTLAND: TRAINING COMMITTEE.

Norwood: *see* BOARD OF EDUCATION: SECONDARY SCHOOL EXAMINATIONS COUNCIL: SPECIAL COMMITTEE.

Oakley: *see* SCOTTISH EDUCATION DEPARTMENT: SCOTTISH TECHNICAL EDUCATION CONSULTATIVE COUNCIL.

Oldfield-Davies: *see* (1) MINISTRY OF EDUCATION: CENTRAL ADVISORY COUNCIL FOR EDUCATION (WALES) (two reports: "second", 1960, and "third", 1961; the "first", *The arts in Wales*, was a trilogy of three smaller reports).

Oliver: *see* MINISTRY OF EDUCATION: NATIONAL ADVISORY COUNCIL ON THE TRAINING AND SUPPLY OF TEACHERS.

Parry: *see* UNIVERSITY GRANTS COMMITTEE: SPECIAL COMMITTEE.

Pattison: *see* LIBERAL PARTY: SPECIAL COMMITTEE.

Percy: *see* MINISTRY OF EDUCATION: SPECIAL COMMITTEE.

Petter: *see* COLONIAL OFFICE: MISSION.

Piercy: *see* MINISTER OF LABOUR AND NATIONAL SERVICE: COMMITTEE OF INQUIRY.

Pilkington: *see* (1) POSTMASTER GENERAL: COMMITTEE ON BROADCASTING, 1960; (2) MINISTRY OF EDUCATION: NATIONAL ADVISORY COUNCIL ON EDUCATION FOR INDUSTRY AND COMMERCE; (3) DEPARTMENT OF EDUCATION AND SCIENCE: NATIONAL ADVISORY COUNCIL ON EDUCATION FOR INDUSTRY AND COMMERCE.

Platt: *see* (1) MINISTRY OF EDUCATION: UNITED KINGDOM ADVISORY COUNCIL ON EDUCATION FOR MANAGEMENT ("first"); (2) DEPARTMENT OF EDUCATION AND SCIENCE: UNITED KINGDOM ADVISORY COUNCIL ON EDUCATION FOR MANAGEMENT ("second"); not to be confused with MINISTRY OF HEALTH: *The welfare of children in hospitals* (1959), nor with ROYAL COLLEGE OF NURSING *and* NATIONAL COLLEGE OF NURSES OF THE UK: SPECIAL COMMITTEE: *A reform of nursing education* (1964).

Robbins: *see* PRIME MINISTER: SPECIAL COMMITTEE.

Russell: *see* MINISTRY OF EDUCATION: NATIONAL ADVISORY COUNCIL ON EDUCATION FOR INDUSTRY AND COMMERCE; not to be confused with MINISTRY OF EDUCATION: NATIONAL ADVISORY COUNCIL ON THE TRAINING AND SUPPLY OF TEACHERS: *Teachers for further education* (1961).

Scott: *see* MINISTER OF WORKS AND PLANNING: COMMITTEE ON LAND UTILISATION IN RURAL AREAS; not to be confused with MINISTRY OF HEALTH: CENTRAL HEALTH SERVICES COUNCIL: STANDING MENTAL HEALTH ADVISORY COMMITTEE: *The training of staff of training centres for the mentally subnormal* (1962).

LIST OF PERIODICALS CONCERNED WITH BRITISH FURTHER EDUCATION IN 1966

(showing title, publisher, number of issues per year and price of each issue in UK at the time of writing)

X—issues appear irregularly.

Adult education	NIAE	6	5s.
Aspects of education (until 1963: *Studies in education*)	Hull, University of Hull Institute of Education	2	6s.
BACIE journal	BACIE (with monthly bibliographical supplement)	4	7s. 6d.
BACIE memoranda	BACIE	7	
British education index	LA, for librarians of British institutes of education	3, cumulated every two years	£5 p.a.
British journal of educational psychology	Methuen, for BPsS and ATCDE	3	£1 (or £2 p.a.)
British journal of educational studies	Faber & Faber, for Standing Conference on Studies in Education	3	12s. (or £1. 10s. p.a.)
Bulletin	Aberystwyth, Faculty of Education, University College of Wales, Aberystwyth	1	1s. 6d.
Bulletin	Cambridge, Cambridge Institute of Education	2	free
Bulletin	Nottingham, University of Nottingham Institute of Education	3	1s.
Bulletin	University of London Institute of Education	3	3s. 6d.
Commonwealth Institute journal	Oxford, Pergamon Press, for Commonwealth Institute	12	free
Comparative education	Oxford, Pergamon Press	3	£1
Durham research review	Universities of Durham and Newcastle upon Tyne Institutes of Education	1	5s.
Education	Councils and Education Press, for AEC	52	9d.
Education abstracts	Paris, UNESCO	4	3s.
Education in chemistry	RIC	4	£2 p.a.
Education index	New York, Wilson	10	$18.00 p.a.
Education in science	ASE	6	2s.

Education libraries bulletin	University of London Institute of Education	3	3s. 6d.
Education today	College of Preceptors	6	2s.
Educational research	Newnes, for NFER	3	7s. 8d. (or £1. 3s. p.a.)
Educational review	Birmingham, University of Birmingham Institute of Education	3	£1 p.a.
Forum	Leicester, PSW (Educational) Publications	3	3s. 6d. (or 10s. p.a.
Gazette	University of Manchester School of Education	X	free
Higher education journal	NUT	3	free
Industrial training international	Pergamon Press	12	5s.
International journal of adult and youth education (until 1961: *Fundamental and adult education*)	Paris, UNESCO	4	2s. 3d.
Journal (until 1963: *Durham University Institute of Education journal*)	Universities of Durham and Newcastle upon Tyne Institutes of Education	5	6d.
Journal of the Careers Research Advisory Centre	Cambridge, CRAC	4	£2. 5s. p.a.
Liberal education	Association for Liberal Education	2	Free to members
New education	New Education Ltd.	12	3s.
Occupational psychology	NIIP	4	5s.
On course	HMSO, for DES	4	
Oversea education	HMSO, for Colonial Office	4	2s.
Overseas challenge	HMSO, for NCSTO		
Papers (until 1963: *Researches and studies*)	Leeds, University of Leeds Institute of Education	1	5s.
Physics education	Institute of Physics and Physical Society	4	5s.
Scottish adult education	Alloa, SIAE	3	3s. 6d. p.a.
Scottish education journal	Edinburgh, Pergamon Press (Scotland), for EIS	52	6d.
Scottish youth news	Edinburgh, HMSO, for SED	4	6d.
Sociology of education abstracts	Liverpool, University of Liverpool Department of Adult Education and Extra-mural Studies	4	£1. 1s. p.a.
STECC newsletter	Edinburgh, SED, for STECC	4	free
Teacher, the (until 1960: *Schoolmaster and women teacher's chronicle*	Schoolmaster Publishing Co., for NUT	52	6d.
Technical education abstracts from British sources	NFER	X	10s. 6d.
Technical education and industrial training	Evans	12	3s. 6d.
Technical journal	ATTI	9	2s.
Technologist, the	Pitman	4	7s. 6d.
Times educational supplement, the	Times Publishing Co.	52	6d.
Times review of industry and technology, the (until 1963: *Technology*)	Times Publishing Co.	12	3s. 6d.
Training for progress in Europe and the world	Geneva, ILO: CIRF	4	$2.80 p.a.
Trends in education	HMSO, for DES	4	3s. 6d.

Vocational aspect of secondary and further education, the	Oxford, Pergamon Press, for the Principals of the four Colleges of Education (Technical)	3	7s. (or £1 p.a.)
WEA news	WEA	4	
Where?	ACE	4	2s. 6d.
World yearbook of education (until 1964: Yearbook of education)	Evans, for University of London Institute of Education and Teachers' College, Columbia University, New York	1	£3. 3s.
Youth employment	IYEO		2s.
Youth service	HMSO, for DES and COI	10	5s. p.a.

References

Toase, Mary (ed.): *Guide to current British periodicals* (1964);
UNESCO: *Educational periodicals* (1963).

INDEX

Only page numbers are given. Those of material in tables are in *italic* type. More important references are in **bold** type. For material in footnotes the page number is followed by "n" or "*n*". Notes on further study and Appendices are not covered.

AA